Early Intervention & Autism

REAL-LIFE QUESTIONS, REAL-LIFE ANSWERS

JAMES BALL, ED.D., BCBA

Future Horizons, Inc. • Arlington, Texas

Early Intervention & Autism

All marketing and publishing rights
guaranteed to and reserved by:

FUTURE HORIZONS INC.

721 W. Abram Street
Arlington, TX 76013
Toll-free: 800-489-0727
Phone: 817-277-0727
Fax: 817-277-2270
Website: *www.FHautism.com*
E-mail: *info@FHautism.com*

Printed in the United States of America

Cover and interior design © TLC Graphics, *www.TLCGraphics.com*
Cover: Monica Thomas; Interior: Erin Stark

ISBN 13: 978-1-932565-55-3

Dedication

. . . .

I dedicate this book to my beautiful wife, Nancy ...
Not only are you a strong woman,
a great mother and a wonderful wife,
you are also my rock; you believed in me when others did not ...
I thank you for your love, support and friendship.
I love you very much.

"we"

Acknowledgements

I HAVE BEEN BLESSED TO BE ON MANY GREAT TEAMS THROUGHOUT MY CAREER and I would like to thank all the people I have had the good fortune to work with and come in contact with during my twenty years in the field of autism. Each of you has taught me something that has made me a better practitioner.

Thanks to all the children and adults with autism I have worked with or been fortunate enough to know: CJ, Jack, Christopher, Laura, Robby, Michael, Tommy, Matt, Teddy Paul, Brandon, and Payam—you have been my teachers in ways you will never know: You have inspired me and, Michael, at times, made me feel a little crazy and question if I was doing the right thing. Yet you, and many others too numerous to list, were always there to guide me. Out of our experiences arose the strategies explored in my work and this book. You are the real catalyst behind everything I do.

How can I thank the kids without also thanking their parents? The struggles and joys you have shared with me have broadened my understanding of autism and of family structure. They have helped me be a better father to my kids and husband to my wife. Your strength and commitment to your children are unmatched. You make me proud to be in this field.

I also want to thank my family—especially my kids, Stephen, Amanda, and Zach. From each of you I have discovered something special that has enhanced the information in this book: from you, Stephen, your great sense of humor; from you, Amanda, your strong sense of loyalty; and from you, Zach, your infectious innocence.

Last and certainly not least, many thanks go to Veronica Zysk for all her assistance as the book's editor. Your contribution was invaluable and this project would not have become a reality without your friendship, support, and encouragement.

About the Author

DR. JAMES BALL, A BOARD CERTIFIED BEHAVIOR ANALYST, HAS BEEN IN THE autism field for twenty years providing educational, residential, and employment services to children and adults affected by autism. He is currently the Clinical Director of Caring Technologies, a web-based company that explores the way technology can enhance the lives of individuals on the autism spectrum. Also, he provides private consultation to organizations, schools, and families regarding staff training, parent training, and home/classroom support services.

Dr. Ball is the Director of Clinical Services for New York Families of Autistic Children, a private not-for-profit organization providing support and training for children and families in New York City. He is also a member of the New Jersey Center for Outreach and Services for the Autism Community (COSAC) Board of Trustees, and a member of the COSAC Professional Advisory Board. A past member of the Autism Society of America Board of Directors, he is currently co-chairperson of the ASA Panel of Professional Advisors and sits on the advisory board for the Autism Asperger's Digest magazine. Dr. Ball has lectured nationally and internationally on various topics related to autism, such as inclusion services, functional behavior assessment, social skills training, behavior management, direct instruction, sensory issues, and accountability.

Contents

Foreword

by Temple Grandin, Ph.D.

EARLY INTERVENTION CAN DRAMATICALLY CHANGE THE COURSE OF A CHILD'S life for the better. Not just the child's life, but the family's life, too. It's that powerful. A strong foundation of learning in the early years increases a child's chances for success as an adult. Yet, parents are often left in the dark when their child is diagnosed, not knowing where to begin. This book is the guiding light you need to illuminate those early, and often frightening times.

If you have a child with autism, *Early Intervention & Autism: Real-life Questions, Real-life Answers* will become an essential addition your library, the book that sits at your bedside table, the one you open again and again when questions loom large. It explains early intervention, but it offers so much more. In a simple to understand, question and answer format, readers follow two parents as they move from first diagnosis through the myriad questions all parents face when autism becomes part of the family. It describes services, qualities of a great team for your child, what early intervention is, and why it's so important. It also describes many of the best-known treatment approaches available to help parents find a good match for their child and their family culture. Even better, *Early Intervention & Autism* gives parents the hands-on tools and strategies to start working effectively with a child, even before EI services kick in. Autism is a continuum; each child with ASD is unique. As Dr. Jim makes clear, there is no one-size-fits-all intervention. His focus is always on the child, treating the child, not the symptoms.

When I was two, I had no speech and severe autistic symptoms, but through excellent therapy, my speech started and I learned new skills. There are some children who may never learn to speak, but individualized early therapy will greatly improve their communication abilities, which encompass far more than speech.

The strategies and interventions described in this book provide structure for the child with autism. I can't tell you how important this is. When I was growing up in the fifties, we had a lot more structure than kids have today. I was taught manners, etiquette rules, turn taking, and how to play with others. I played lots of structured games with neighborhood children. In school, there were rules I had to follow. I was expected to interact with other people and had to learn that certain things were allowed, and other things were not. This kept me connected to the world. If I behaved badly, there were consequences. Today there are fewer rules in society pertaining to children's behavior, but all kids with autism need structure and predictability. That's why early intervention is so crucial to development; it provides the structure a child needs, within which learning can occur. The brains of very young children are like a sponge—learning can occur at a rapid pace. At later ages, children can still be taught, but it is more difficult. Ineffective learning habits have had time to take hold. The good news is that the practical teaching strategies outlined in this book apply to all ages! It's never too late for the child with autism to learn.

Dr. Jim delves into the sensory problems many kids with ASD face, and reminds readers that these challenges will differ from child to child, and day to day. The world can literally be a painful place for these children, which is why it is so important to distinguish between normal "bad behavior" and behavior that stems from a child's sensory sensitivities. Some children will not be able to tolerate loud noises, for example, or fluorescent lights, certain smells, or scratchy clothes. My mother had to cut out all the tags from my clothing because they felt unbearably itchy to me. I still have to wash new clothes many times before they are soft enough for me to wear comfortably. Other children may refuse to eat certain foods, or will eat only certain foods. Yet these issues can be successfully dealt with; Dr. Jim tells you how.

At conferences, I often talk about the importance of using a child's perseverative interests to teach them academic subjects. If the child is interested in trains, he can write about trains in English class, calculate the speed of trains in math class, draw trains in art class, write about the history of trains in history class, and so on. Engaging children through their interests is also important because their interests can lead to fulfilling careers later in life. Dr. Jim echoes these words throughout this book. He describes how to use a child's interests to reach them and bring them into the wider world. When kids perseverate on a certain topic, it may be annoying to adults. But by ignoring or discouraging these interests, parents miss out on a wonderful chance to connect with the child.

The worst thing you can do with a young autistic child is nothing. If your child sits in front of the TV all day, or stims and rocks for hours, he will tune out the world and this may be detrimental to brain development. When I dribbled sand through my fingers, the rest of the world disappeared, as I studied each little pebble as it flowed through my hands. I was allowed to stim for one hour a day to calm down, but the rest of the day I had intensive one-to-one speech therapy and played turn-taking games with my nanny and sister. If you are in a situation where you have to wait many months for a diagnosis, or services are not available, you *must* start working with your child now. A very young child should have a minimum of twenty hours a week where he or she is kept actively engaged with a person who is a good teacher.

Grandmothers, parents, and students can all be effective teachers. My mother, my nanny, and a talented speech therapist created my program before formal programs for autism existed. You must start engaging your child NOW—do not wait until your name reaches the top of an agency's list. This book will help you do that; it gives you many good ideas that will work for your child.

Dr. Jim Ball's 20+ years of professional experience working with children and adults on the autism spectrum uniquely qualifies him to educate parents, doctors, and therapists about the importance of early intervention. Parents reading this book will be grateful for the knowledge and expertise he so freely shares. *Early Intervention & Autism* contains page after page of practical help, and is peppered with real-life wisdom and real-life stories from parents.

Dr. Jim's goal is to help parents understand their child better and learn to be an effective teacher in the child's life. He accomplishes that goal admirably, and in the process, sends a message to parents everywhere that their children's future is infused with hope and possibilities. Then he goes even one step further: he gives them the tools to make it happen.

Introduction

FROM THE TIME I WAS SEVEN YEARS OLD, I WANTED TO GO TO COLLEGE, GET a teaching degree and become a high school history teacher—not because I was a history buff, but because I deeply and passionately wanted to be a kids' football coach. The teaching degree was secondary. I pursued this goal with single-minded determination and got into a good teaching college, Trenton State College (now The College of New Jersey). I did well in college and played football most of my time there. My life was unfolding just as I had planned it … or so I thought.

In high school, one of the football coaches had asked me to volunteer at a field day for kids with special needs. I really didn't want to do it. My Saturday mornings were generally reserved for "sleeping in." But he convinced me that not only would it be a worthwhile thing to do, but that if I wanted to continue in his favor, I would make the field day. I went. And it was an unbelievable day.

I was assigned to help one student through the day: make sure he was at his events on time, ate lunch, and found his parents at the end of the day. I met Matt and he was a cool guy. He was about eighteen—older than I was—and he had Down Syndrome. Matt made me laugh the entire day and was great fun to be around. He won a few medals and I gained a greater appreciation for kids who were different from me. That day, Matt taught me it was "okay" to be different. He really liked himself and had a love of life that I have yet to see surpassed. I enjoyed myself so much, the following year I helped organize the field day, and worked with Matt again.

Life has a way of interrupting even our best-laid plans. Sometimes the individual events go unnoticed, but in hindsight we see how each one played a part in our journey. While the memory of Matt and that summer field day were still fresh in my mind, I was asked to help out at an indoor basketball event for kids with special needs. I eagerly said yes, and was assigned a kid to hang out with for the day. This activity was a little different; we were teaching the kids basketball. I met my guy, Rich. He was my age, a straight-A student (something I was not), and he had cerebral palsy. We got a basketball, went to one of the baskets and started our day. It was horrible. I had no clue how to help Rich. He became really frustrated when his body wouldn't do what he wanted it to do, and when he talked, he spit. After the first three or four times it hit me in the face, I quickly adjusted so when he spoke, he missed me. Rich kept apologizing and I kept telling him not to worry about it. We both were feeing inadequate.

As the morning wore on, we both became even more frustrated—with ourselves, not so much with each other. When lunch finally came around we sat down and had a great conversation. We discovered we had many similar interests. At one point Rich looked at me and said, "Why me, why did I have to get this? I know what I want to do and my body just can't do it." I didn't know what to say to him; it wasn't something I had ever faced or thought of. During the afternoon session I finally figured out a way to help Rich succeed: with hand-over-hand physical prompting. It felt uncomfortable at first, but seeing the joy on Rich's face when he made his first basket erased any apprehension I felt, and the rest of the afternoon was great. I felt sad for Rich, though, and thought I could never work with kids with special needs. My heart broke when he spoke of kids making fun of him, how he needed people to help him go to the bathroom, and even though he was an A-student, people still thought he was stupid. When I got home, I was so thankful for my own good fortune. After that, anytime I felt sorry for myself, I thought of what Rich had to endure. If he was making the best of his life, I could do the same. That experience reinforced my lifelong dream to be a history teacher and coach football. It was the right choice.

Several years later, my college football coach asked me to work at Friendship Day for kids with special needs, starting at 8:00 o'clock on a Sunday morning. Now, I still loved to sleep late on Sundays, but I had a chance of starting in the upcoming football season, and my coach had the ultimate power over me. I agreed to help out with the kids.

The set-up was similar: we were to play some games, go outside and throw the ball around, have lunch, and help our assigned kid with his homework. I met Phil, who came without a disability label. He did not talk, but he would use some signs (which I did not understand) to communicate. He loved the physical games we played, but not the board games. At one point he got very frustrated at me and began to hit himself in the head. I didn't know what to do, so I just grabbed his hands. When I did that he looked at me and stopped. I then asked him to show me what he wanted and he went to the water fountain. He wanted a drink. In hindsight, I'm sure Phil had autism, but back in 1982, I had no understanding of the disorder; not many people did. By the end of the day I was physically exhausted, yet I had really enjoyed myself. The thing that made the most lasting impression on me was Phil's attitude. Although one of the other kids made fun of him and the way he communicated, Phil did not even bother with him; he just went about his business. I looked at him and said "good for you." I realized that Phil really didn't care what other people thought. He was who he was and, obviously, he was proud of it. I thought to myself afterwards, *I could work with kids like Phil.* I volunteered at Friendship Day several more times, but never saw Phil again, and didn't do anything more involving kids with special needs during the rest of my undergraduate years.

When I started graduate school, I realized I was going to need a day job. I was looking in the paper and saw the word *Therapist.* I knew that when I was done with my Master's degree I would be called a therapist, so I read on. "Therapist working with students with autism." I wasn't familiar with autism but I was in desperate need of a job, so I decided to look into it. Keep in mind that, at the time, all I knew about autism I had learned from the TV show, *St. Elsewhere.* One of the doctors on the show had a son with autism, and I remembered an episode in which the son was having a "meltdown." No one could stop him from hitting himself in the head. All of a sudden a Native American entered the room, and the boy stopped. From that day on I thought only Native Americans could work with kids with autism. Talk about misinformed.

Nevertheless, I walked into the Eden Institute in Princeton, New Jersey and was hired as a teacher's assistant at $6,000 per year, working with two students with autism (Laura, eight years old and Kevin, six years old). I fell in love with the kids, their families, and the program. And, as the saying goes, "the rest is history."

That was twenty years ago. Since then, autism has been not only my profession, but also my passion. I was taught early in my career that if I really wanted to make a difference with this particular population, I needed to look at my job as a lifestyle rather than a 9:00 to 5:00 proposition, and that is what I have done. I've worked with thousands of individuals, from first diagnosis (18 months) through adulthood (70 years old), and over the years these wonderful, creative, one-of-a-kind individuals have taught me as much as I have taught them. There's never a dull moment in the world of autism. It is uniquely challenging, and it is also uniquely rewarding.

In my professional career, first as a teacher's assistant, then as a Behavioral Specialist, followed by many years as Vice President of the YCS: Sawtelle Learning Centers in New Jersey, overseeing seven programs from early intervention through elementary grades, and now as a national autism consultant, I have witnessed parents struggle to find answers to the many complex issues that are part and parcel of autism spectrum disorders (ASD). We have sat, face to face, through tears of joy and sorrow, discussing their questions about autism, their child's behaviors, which services are "best," and how to keep their family together in light of the tremendous strain autism places on their daily lives.

The diagnosis alone can be a devastating experience. Parents are suddenly thrust into a world of strange terminology, strange systems and even stranger reactions from those around them. Their grief is deep; their need to act—and quickly—a burden of immense proportions. They find themselves having either too little information or too much: a simple Google search on the keyword "autism" returns over 47 *million* results. How does a parent sift through—let alone read and understand—47 million results? Who helps them distinguish between genuinely helpful information and what might steer them in the wrong direction? Aside from that, where will the time possibly come from? There's "real life" to deal with: jobs, meals, housekeeping, family, other kids. I've watched many a parent simply shut down, paralyzed by the glut of information and terrified of making any decision at all, lest it be the "wrong" one.

It was witnessing this same experience in parents over and over that propelled me to write a book, *this* book. I'd written numerous articles, provided hundreds of training sessions, and given presentations at prestigious national conferences. Parents across the country and around the world all asked me the same few questions, in one version or another:

What do I need to *know* first?
What do I need to *do* first?
What program is *right* for my child?

In a nutshell, the purpose of this book is to answer those questions. In it you will learn about autism: what it is and what it is not. It will educate you on early intervention and examine the components of a "perfect" program for young children with ASD. You will be introduced to various proven techniques and given the tools to assess whether or not they "fit" your child and your family. The book concludes with a how-to guide for setting up an effective Individual Family Service Plan (IFSP) and transitioning your child into a public school program.

Together, we will make the journey through the unfamiliar and uncharted territory into which you have suddenly found yourself thrust. You are not alone in this experience. The knowledge you gain will help you better understand your child and formulate a game plan so you, your child, and your family will do more than just survive—you will thrive!

I tell my wife and friends that I have the best job in the world. Working with children with ASD has taught me to always be positive and never to settle for "less than." This may sound trite, but for me it stems from confidence that has come through experience: I truly do learn something new from the kids I work with every day. Every child is unique. Each child thinks differently and reacts to things differently. They have given me the opportunity to stretch my mental muscles, to widen my perceptions, to push my personal and professional boundaries into new frontiers. It has been both challenging and exciting. I have learned that to be successful with this population, I must be willing to suspend what I have been taught, and to "see" things differently.

When people discover what I do for a living they always say, "You must be so patient." I look at them and say "no, actually I am not patient." Being patient, I would miss opportunities to engage with a child who needs my help. Being patient, I might not find the way to teach so that a child learns what he needs to know in order to be successful. Being patient, I might just settle for what they can give me, and not push them to achieve their own potential. Yes, there is a time and place for being patient with this population, but not with myself. These children depend on me to find a way to connect with them. Each day I strive to help just one child, because change happens one child at a time, one family at a time, one school at a time, one community at a time.

Right now, I'm here to help one child and one family—yours. It's an adventure that will change us all, in ways yet hidden and perhaps unimagined, but they are ways that will enrich our lives beyond measure. Let's take the first step.

> *Think about looking up at a stage with accomplished actors,*
> *vibrant sets and skilled crew. Wonderful, engaging, profound and*
> *beautiful performances are produced on this stage. We "play out"*
> *the stories of our lives on this stage, for it is big and wide and deep*
> *enough to accommodate every one of us who can find our way to it.*
> *Those who can't make it onto the stage become observers; they miss*
> *the chance to play out their stories in a way that others appreciate.*

> *Early intervention for children with autism spectrum disorders is a*
> *child's access ramp to the stage of life where wonderful, engaging,*
> *profound and beautiful performances occur. As parents, it's our job*
> *to light the way for our children. Let your light be ever so bright.*

> — JUDY RUDEBUSCH, DIRECTOR OF SPECIAL PROGRAMS,
> IRVING INDEPENDENT SCHOOL DISTRICT, IRVING, TX

chapter one

A Real-life Look at the Autism Spectrum

I'M MEETING FOR THE FIRST TIME WITH PARENTS MAUREEN AND ROB. THEIR three-year-old son, Mark, has just been diagnosed with autism by the staff of their local Early Intervention Center staff, and they have many questions.

Dr. Jim: Hi, Maureen, hi, Rob. Thanks for coming in to meet with me. I know that the diagnosis was a bit of a shock, and that this is a difficult time for you both, emotionally. Parents in your situation feel all sorts of conflicting emotions. You may be blaming yourselves, and may even be blaming each other. You're unfamiliar with autism and you probably feel ill-equipped to make the decisions that face you. I want you to know that I'm here to help you. The one thing I ask is that you try to be open and honest with me, and with each other, as we work together over these next few months. Please ask questions—lots and lots of questions! That's the only way you'll learn about autism, how it manifests itself in your child, and how you can help him, yourselves, and your family.

1

Maureen: I just can't believe Mark has autism. Are you sure about the diagnosis? Could there have been a mistake? I went home and looked up autism on the internet. Mark has eye contact. He loves to be hugged. He doesn't hit or bite himself. Yes, I know his speech isn't developing as it should, and his play-skills are a little odd, and he has that vacant stare at times, but he's verbal. Aren't kids with autism nonverbal?

Dr. Jim: It's great you're so interested in learning about autism. You're learning first hand that not all the information you hear or read about this disorder is accurate. Some kids on the autism spectrum are very verbal. Many love hugs and many don't. My job will be to help you sift through the information you find and learn what to keep and what to disregard. In our session today we'll talk about the many faces of autism and the vast differences in the nature and degree of challenges we see in these kids. However, we're sure about Mark's diagnosis. I know it's hard to accept; give yourself some time to adjust. It'll be a while before you start feeling comfortable with the diagnosis. Go easy on yourself.

Rob: Go easy on myself? There's nothing easy about this and how I feel. I feel devastated, depleted, depressed and discouraged. I feel as though I've been run over by an 18-wheeler and then dropped into a bottomless well, falling and falling, just waiting to hit bottom, yet I never do. I've dealt with boot camp in the army, tough bosses, worked my way through multi-million dollar business deals, but I've never been so afraid in all my life as I feel right now.

Dr. Jim: I know how you're feeling. It's frightening and you wish someone would make it all go away. But I need you both to believe this: *it will get better!* Day by day, you'll learn more about autism, you'll start to understand Mark's actions and thinking better, and you'll see progress being made. It's today, right now, that's so difficult to get through. This is partly because your emotions are overriding everything else and partly because your mind is filled with questions and you have little concrete knowledge to balance out the uncertainty. Let's get started with today's session and I'll bet you'll feel better—even if only a little—by the time we're through.

◎　◎　◎

What basics do I need to know about autism?

Right from the start, I want you to always keep in mind that children with autism are children first. Their autism is part of their functioning, but autism is not all of who they are. It's easy for parents to be so overwhelmed with the diagnosis that they lose sight of the child and only see the autism. Don't let that happen. Every single person with autism is different, just as we neurotypicals (NTs) are all different. We all have our own personalities. We all like some things, tolerate some things, and hate others. We all play, laugh, cry, and love. Kids with autism just do these things a little differently than we do. Outwardly, they look like everyone else. What's different, however, is the way they think, process information, and learn. They see the world in a more literal way—they take information, events, and people, literally, at their face value. If something *seems* a certain way, then that's what it must *be*. One of the results of this way of thinking is that kids with autism miss subtle nuances. They do not understand the deception or ulterior motives that can hide behind a false smile. Sarcasm is lost on them. Metaphors and idioms make no sense to them. That makes total sense to me—does it to you, too?

Are the kids really all that different from one another?

Yes they are! Children with autism spectrum disorders (ASD) are very different from one another. They will present with a variety of strengths, weaknesses, and combinations of characteristics. Autism is a spectrum disorder, meaning that at one end of the spectrum, kids can be extremely challenged, have mental retardation present, be nonverbal, and self-injurious or aggressive. On the other end of the spectrum are kids who are academically gifted, have a stellar vocabulary, and manifest their biggest challenges in the area of social thinking and social skills. The spectrum is vast and complex, and kids can fall anywhere along it. We'll talk more about this as we go along.

But aren't there some common characteristics that all kids with ASD manifest?

ASDs severely affect a person's functioning in three specific areas:

- *Communication:* the ability to speak or, if the child can speak, being able to get their needs and wants met through language.

- *Behavior:* an inability to interact with their world can result in their manifesting inappropriate behaviors such as hand flapping, rocking, repeating the same phrase or language, tantrums, etc.

- *Social Skills:* being able to understand themselves in relation to others and interact effectively with other people, especially children their own age, in an appropriate way.

When does autism usually appear?

Children develop at different rates. While some of the characteristics mentioned above may be present and noticeable in children as young as 12-18 months of age, most children are not formally diagnosed until they are 2-3 years old. Because of some overlap with typical development, some individuals, especially those for whom language is not impaired, may not be diagnosed until much later. The average age for an Asperger's diagnosis is seven. Some parents even report their child hit all their developmental milestones, right on time. Autism is four times more prevalent in boys than in girls and is currently one of the top childhood disabilities in the world, and growing. According to the Centers for Disease Control, one of every 150 children born today will be diagnosed on the autism spectrum.

Is this a biological or a psychological disorder?

ASDs are a brain-based disorder, meaning autism impacts the normal development of the brain. This in turn affects the child's ability in the areas of social interaction, behavior and communication skills. Research suggests that the information pathways in the brain don't connect effectively with each other. The message goes in and sometimes makes the right connections, but most of the time it does not, or gets lost altogether. What's important to glean from this is that autism renders kids *unable* to process information and learn as do NT kids; it's not a case of being *unwilling* to understand and learn. It's an important distinction and one that many parents (and professionals) seem to forget to a greater or lesser degree as time passes.

Some individuals with ASD also have other disorders that affect the functioning of the brain, such as epilepsy or mental retardation, or genetic disorders such as Fragile X Syndrome, Down Syndrome, Landau-Kleffner Syndrome, William's Syndrome or Tourette's Syndrome. Approximately 25-30 percent may develop a seizure pattern at some period during life. When autism is diagnosed alongside one of these other conditions it is called a "co-morbid" disorder. It should be mentioned that even though autism may occur with a variety of other disabilities, treatment should be focused on the individual, not on the symptoms.

Many children diagnosed with autism will test in the range of mental retardation, although as our understanding of ASD grows, we are learning that our current way of testing may not be as reliable a marker of ability as we once thought, because of the differences in the thinking patterns of people on the spectrum. In some cases, these individuals test poorly, but have higher cognitive abilities than the test results indicate.

Why did my child get autism? Is it something we did?

We don't know why autism develops in some kids and not others, but we do know this: it's not something either of you did. You're not at fault. It's not the glass of wine you had before you knew you were pregnant, or anything else that you did.

Current research suggests there may be a genetic origin in some kids, not from one gene or two but perhaps as many as 10 genes together. Other researchers are looking at environmental insults in combination with an already weakened immune system. I know this is important to you—you want to know "why" autism happened to your child. Parents desperately want to be able to find a cause-and-effect relationship for their child's disability so it makes sense to them. This may be difficult to hear right now, but you may never understand why your child developed autism. The more you can let go of this need to understand "why," the better off you will be in the long run. Many parents get so caught up in this question that they embark on a crusade to "figure autism out" and find the one thing that caused the autism. Please, don't let that be you. Your efforts are better directed toward the future—getting to know your child and finding appropriate services.

Is autism present at birth, or does it develop later, as the child grows?

There isn't professional consensus about this, because we don't yet know what causes autism. Therefore, you may hear or read the terms "classic autism" and "regressive autism." Let me explain each further.

Classic autism describes the child whose development, from birth or a very early age, seems "off" somehow. I have spoken with countless parents who tell me they always knew there was a problem. As the child grew older it became more and more evident. The child's language never really developed or didn't progress beyond single words or basic labeling (e.g., cup, spoon). Parents mention that they never really felt as though they bonded with the child. He or she may not have been comfortable being held, or didn't respond to the parents' smiles or coos or attempts to engage in peek-a-boo games.

Regressive autism, on the other hand, sneaks up on parents. Generally this child seems to be developing just fine and hits a great many developmental milestones. These are children who walked on time, said their first words on time, played like typical kids, but at some point began to lose these skills. Little by little parents realized the child wasn't using as much language, didn't engage as much, didn't seek out playful exchanges as often.

It wasn't until camcorders and videotape became more commonplace that we, as professionals, really noticed regressive autism. Many of us used to think parents just didn't understand the disorder or typical child development, especially if this was their first child. I vividly remember the first time a family brought me a videotape of their son. The child who

6

sat in front of me that day had all the symptoms of classic autism: he was completely nonverbal, avoided eye contact and displayed no social skills. After I viewed the tape, I realized how wrong I was. I saw a child who at an earlier age had language, made eye contact, and who was very social, playing with his cousin in a kiddie pool. From that point forward, I had to accept that regressive autism did, indeed, exist.

So there may be several different sub-classifications of autism: autism that is present from birth and that may have a genetic basis, and autism that develops after the child is born, perhaps resulting from a combination of environmental and physiological factors.

Why are there so many names associated with autism? It's so confusing!

Unfortunately, professionals take quite a bit of liberty in characterizing ASDs, which doesn't help parents of a newly diagnosed child. In your journey, you will undoubtedly encounter a variety of different "labels" used: autistic-like, PDD, mild PDD, autistic tendencies, mild autism and many others. Even though a formal diagnosis is governed by the description that exists in the DSM-IV-R (the Diagnostic and Statistical Manual, fourth edition, revised), because the diagnosis is based on observation of behavior rather than medical tests, professional subjectivity exists in assigning the different labels.

DR. JIM Suggests:

Labels can be good.
They can drive services.

◎

But never let the label define the child.

◎

Know the child,
not the label.

The best way to understand and relate to a label is to think of it as establishing some level of common understanding from which discussion of the child can ensue. The downside to this is when professionals base services and therapies on the label, rather than on an understanding of the child who carries the label. Parents need to be ever vigilant in making sure the child gets the attention, and not the label.

Within the DSM-IV-R classification system, individuals who fall under the broad, umbrella category, Pervasive Developmental Disorder (PDD) exhibit commonalties in communication, behavior, and social deficits, but differ in terms of severity. Some of the major points that distinguish one label from another are as follows:

- *Autistic Disorder (autism):* impairments in social interaction, communication, and imaginative play prior to age three. Stereotyped behaviors, interests and activities.

- *Asperger's Disorder:* impairments in social interactions and the presence of restricted interests and activities, with no clinically significant general delay in language; testing in the range of average to above-average intelligence.

- *Pervasive Developmental Disorder-Not Otherwise Specified (PDD-NOS; commonly referred to as "atypical autism"):* a diagnosis made when a child does not meet the criteria for one of the other PDD categories, but the child exhibits a severe and pervasive impairment in specified behaviors.

- *Rhett's Disorder:* a progressive disorder which, to date, has occurred only in girls. Characterized by a period of normal development followed by a loss of previously acquired skills, loss of purposeful use of the hands replaced with repetitive hand movements, beginning at the age of 1-4 years.

- *Childhood Disintegrative Disorder:* normal development for at least the first two years, followed by significant loss of previously acquired skills.

(American Psychiatric Association 1994)

How inclusive a "spectrum" of autism is there?

We're still discovering that day by day. As mentioned earlier, the symptoms and characteristics of ASDs can present themselves in a wide variety of combinations, and in differing degrees of severity. Remember exponential equations in high school (e.g., 10^5) and how quickly a small number of differences could produce a huge number of possible combinations? That's the autism spectrum. It's a million characteristics to a millionth power of possibilities, and is what makes autism both fascinating and challenging. With so many combinations of abilities and such a huge spectrum of possibilities, finding the right intervention strategy can often seem like finding a minnow in the Pacific Ocean. That's how it feels to you now, but success can be achieved.

The enormous variability of the autism spectrum is also part of the reason for the diversity of thought and language used when referring to it. You will begin to hear all sorts of sometimes-confusing terminology associated with ASDs, such as high versus low functioning, more able versus less able, and mild versus severe. Although ASDs are defined by a certain set of behaviors, children and adults can exhibit any combination of the behaviors in any degree of severity. Two children, both with the same diagnosis, can act very differently from one another and have varying skills. And they can change from day to day!

But isn't it useful to label a child's functioning level as high or low?

Yes and no. It depends on how and why it is done. In my experience, it ends up being more of a detriment to the child to do so. Most people make the ability distinction based on the verbal level of the child, which can be a very dangerous road to follow, especially with younger kids. I have worked with many children who were completely nonverbal, very aggressive, and with little or no desire for personal contact, and they made remarkable progress, began to talk, control their behaviors, and seek out social interactions.

Parents and professionals alike would do well to curb their desire to classify children as high or low functioning. Looks can be deceiving, and often our own perceptions of ability can be the downfall for a child. It affects how we relate to that child and what actions we take or don't take. A more effective approach is to concentrate on the strengths and weaknesses in the child and work from this base of understanding. For instance: people look at a child who is affectionate, talks, and smiles at you and say, "he must be high functioning." They see a child who is nonverbal, has an odd behavior or two and does not make eye contact, and assume he is low functioning. It is very difficult to determine exactly what a child knows and does not know, especially with kids with limited verbal capabilities or who are in the early stages of development.

Sharon, for example, had a great vocabulary. She could carry on a conversation with anyone about anything, but if you ended up telling her where you lived in New Jersey, you would trigger one of her self-stimulatory behaviors and she would launch into a lengthy recitation about your county, its seat of government, and every other fact she knew—which was probably more than any adult. Sharon was indeed highly verbal, yet she could not get her needs and wants met effectively through her language. She could talk, but wasn't an effective communicator. Frank, on the other hand, was nonverbal and never made eye contact, but out of all the kids I ever worked with, he was the brightest. His receptive language was the best and it allowed him to connect with people on many different levels.

Slotting kids into groups of high or low functioning also leads parents and professionals into the deadly trap of under- or over-inflated expectations. This, in turn, can set up a vicious cycle of low self-esteem and failure in both adult and child when too-high expectations crash and burn, or when adults withhold opportunities from children to whom they have assigned low expectations. We need to stay focused on strengths and challenges, and never stray away from what is most important: capitalizing on the abilities the child brings to the interaction or experience.

Okay, so tell me more about how these differences manifest themselves along the spectrum. I need real-life examples, not textbook descriptions. What does autism look like in real life?

I'll answer that question, but only if you promise to keep in mind what we talked about earlier: the spectrum nature of the disorders. As I mentioned, children and adults with ASD typically have difficulties in verbal and nonverbal communication, social interactions, and leisure or play activities. When put with a group of other little kids, a child with autism will most likely play by himself. He may play next to another child (called "parallel play"), or he may not be able to tolerate someone else in his space and prefer to play alone. On the playground, he may appear to be interacting with other kids, but when you analyze the situation, you see he is just doing the same set of activities over and over again, sometimes coming upon a peer who is also playing that way, sometimes not.

Because autism is a different way of thinking and processing information, the disorder makes it hard for kids to communicate with others and relate to the outside world. They tend to be very concrete in their thinking, taking what a person says very literally. For example, if you were kidding around with a person with autism who had just said something shocking, you might say "get out of here"—and they would! They would stand up and leave, because they process language concretely. Our language is very imprecise and is constantly in a state of flux as each generation adopts its own "code." As an example of what I mean, just listen to a group of teenagers talk.

To further compound matters, kids on the spectrum don't pick up on all the nonverbal cues that are a part of communication: our tone of voice, facial expressions, body language—they miss all these clues that normally developing children learn to identify through their everyday interactions with others. It goes back to brain wiring—missing connections in their brain prevent them from understanding all the nonverbal nuances of social interaction. The good news is that these different types of social skills can be taught. What's important to "get" at this point is an appreciation of this deficit. It's an important one, because our world is highly social and built on nuance rather than clearly defined social rules.

Behavior will probably be one of your main areas of concern. It is for most parents and teachers. In some cases, aggressive and/or self-injurious behavior may be present. Persons with autism may exhibit repeated body movements (hand flapping, finger-flicking, body rocking), unusual responses to people (hugs everyone she sees or hates being hugged by anyone) or attachments to objects (his favorite item might be a scrap of fabric or a piece of wood from the backyard). Kids on the spectrum are often highly resistant to changes in routine; even very minor deviations can result in a tantrum. Individuals may also be "sensory sensitive" in one or more of the five senses: sight, hearing, touch, smell, and taste. (There are two more senses we'll talk about in a different session).

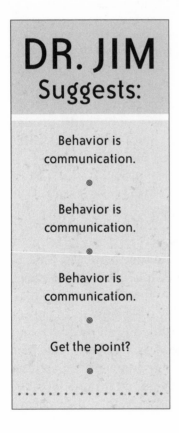

DR. JIM
Suggests:

Behavior is
communication.

◎

Behavior is
communication.

◎

Behavior is
communication.

◎

Get the point?

◎

It's important for parents to keep in mind that a child's behavior can also fluctuate on a moment-to-moment basis, for a variety of reasons. For example, if the child hears a loud noise while sitting in the doctor's office, he may not make a sound or even react to the noise. However, when the fire alarm in the school goes off, the child may begin to tantrum, put his hands over his ears and throw himself to the floor because the noise is causing him physical pain. Every child is different. With some kids on the spectrum, you could walk up behind them and clap cymbals together, and the child wouldn't budge. But begin to unwrap a piece of candy, and the child's head spins around immediately. The point is: don't generalize about a child unless you have first gotten to know his behaviors and what function they serve for him.

Some of the other ways the typical characteristics of ASD look in real life:

Characteristics	What you see in the child
Insistence on sameness; resistance to change	Takes all the cans out of the cabinets and lines them up; there's just one route you can drive to any destination; his toys must be always in the same place
Difficulty in expressing needs	Will take your hand and lead you to the object or food and place your hand on it
Acts as if they are deaf	Will continue to play with an object or continue to engage in an activity while you are calling them, with no acknowledgement. Then you open the cookie jar, and the child is right next to you
Shows distress that is not apparent to others	Will start to laugh uncontrollably while sitting alone, then will begin to cry.
No real fear of dangers	Will run out into the road or out of the house when they get a burst of energy; not hesitant around fire or with heights

If autism spectrum disorders are so variable, and people make assumptions about the kids and the disorder, how do I know what information to trust?

You're starting to understand that with this disorder, *knowledge is power*. The more you learn about ASD the better equipped you will be to assess what you read or hear. The more you learn about your child, the better equipped you will be to advocate for him, assess particular therapies or strategies in light of his strengths and weaknesses, and work effectively with therapists and teachers.

There are a variety of myths associated with autism. Being cognizant of some of the more common ones will give you the opportunity to educate people you meet and alleviate their fears. Fear—both your own and that of others—can render you ineffective when dealing with the child with ASD. It's hard to calmly assess what to do in the middle of a challenging situation if you don't know your child, and even worse if you're afraid to take action because you're uncertain of the outcome. Ignorance may be bliss, but not when it comes to ASD. Be curious about your child and learn why he does what he does.

Ten of the more common myths follow. Unfortunately, some are still actively circulated within and outside the autism community. As a result, the general public has a very narrow view of individuals on the autism spectrum. You will encounter these perceptions, sometimes in people who genuinely want to help, such as family members or close friends. Don't shy away from giving them accurate information about the disorder and your child. Remember: change happens one person at a time.

1. They can't learn, so why try teaching them?

Hundreds of research studies and thousands of parents and teachers say otherwise. Yet, believe it or not, this is still a common perception about kids with ASD, especially those who are more severely challenged by the disorder. This is blatant ignorance at its very worst.

2. Inadequate parenting causes autism.

Back in the 1950s, it was believed that autism was caused by mothers who gave their children too little love and attention. That hogwash of a theory was debunked in the early 1960s, yet still appears from time to time in various manifestations. The truth is that autism is a brain-based disorder; it's not the result of a parenting style.

This myth can arise when professionals who are unfamiliar with ASD attribute parental concern to some psychological disorder on the part of the parents. Considering the vast amount of information that is now readily available to virtually everyone, it is startling that medical or other professionals still harbor this kind of misinformation about autism. A family I had the honor of working with related the following story to me. When their son was two years old, his mother took him to the doctor's office and complained that he was not "right." This was her first child and the doctor chalked up her fears to her being an "uneducated" parent, and sent her home. A week later she showed up in the emergency room because her son was not eating and had become dehydrated. Her pediatrician was called and once again she was sent home, this time with medication and instructions on how to "properly" feed her child. Two weeks later she showed up again, because her son was having bowel problems. Rather than being praised for her love and concern for her son, she was questioned by Child Protective Services about her "issues" with the child. Soon after this experience, they moved to a different town—where the child was diagnosed with autism.

3. *"The doctor always knows best."*

If you think your child has a problem, pursue it even if the doctor says, "He will grow out of it" or "Let's wait and see." You know your child better than anyone, and if his development causes you concern, or the doctor doesn't take your concerns seriously, seek out professionals who have a more thorough knowledge of ASD. By accepting the "wait and see" approach, you lose valuable time in getting the appropriate therapy and services that could benefit your child.

Many parents have told me that their initial concerns about their child fell on deaf ears when voiced to their pediatrician. In some cases, not months but years go by before further action is taken and the diagnosis finally received. Be proactive and don't always accept that your doctor knows best. Especially doctors who are not well-trained in ASD.

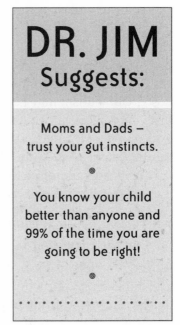

DR. JIM Suggests:

Moms and Dads – trust your gut instincts.

◎

You know your child better than anyone and 99% of the time you are going to be right!

◎

4. *People with autism don't have feelings, and do not care about others or their feelings.*

People with autism have feelings just as we all do, but they may not understand their feelings or be able to express them in conventional ways. And they care about other people, but may manifest their caring in different ways than do neurotypical people.

In many instances, their different emotional behaviors result from a lack of education and training, not a lack of feelings. I was asked to do a diagnostic evaluation on an eight-year-old student who was having difficulties at school. When he was on the playground with other students, he would go up to the other boys and kiss them, which would set off a chain of behavior issues between him and the other students. When I met with the boy I asked him, "Why do you kiss the other boys?" His response was, "Because I want to play with them." The boy had never been taught how to appropriately join others in play. This was the only skill he knew to get their attention, and boy, did it! The problem was solved easily by teaching the young man appropriate social skills.

5. People with autism all have a special or "savant" skill.

I call this the "Rain Man myth" because it arose from the 1988 movie, *Rain Man*, starring Dustin Hoffman as an adult with autism. In reality, only a very small percentage of individuals with autism have extraordinary talents in math, music, memory, calendar skills, or scientific calculations.

6. Children with autism don't talk.

Remember that ASDs are a spectrum of challenges. A child diagnosed with Asperger's Syndrome, by definition, has language. A child diagnosed with autism may have reduced verbal skills or be nonverbal. But that is not necessarily a long-term prognosis. Many nonverbal children learn functional language with appropriate intervention. Most children can be taught some form of functional communication skills, such as sign language, use of picture cards, communication boards, etc., even if language remains delayed.

7. There's a normal child locked inside your son or daughter; find the "key" and your normal child will emerge.

Autism is a lifelong disability that affects far more than the child's physical and chemical structure. This myth is unhealthy because it suggests that a neurotypical thinking pattern exists within the child and with the "right" intervention, a neurotypical child who understands the world around him will suddenly appear. The reality is that autism is a different way of thinking and processing information, and no "key" will change that. In other words, there is no On/Off switch for autism. Each child will progress based on their own strengths and weaknesses. Learning will occur, but as a process. Encourage your child to learn, capitalize on his strengths and help him overcome his challenges.

8. Kids with ASD only make progress during early intervention, while their brains are malleable. Once they reach elementary school, learning stops.

Now, isn't this just silly? Think about it. Does learning ever stop? No, it doesn't. It's true that when children are young, their brains are like sponges, absorbing new information and new experiences easily. The learning window is wide open. As children age, learning doesn't stop, but sometimes behavioral and emotional patterns start taking hold that slow the pace at which learning occurs. But that's more indicative of our teaching environment than of the learning ability of the child. Early intervention is important, yes. But learning doesn't stop once the child turns three or five. Learning is a lifelong process and all people with autism continue to learn, just like the rest of us, throughout life. Our goal is to never stop teaching!

I once worked with Stephen, a student who was nonverbal. Even though we explored a variety of verbal communication skills with him, he never uttered a sound. We used a variety of communication systems and one day, when he was seven, his mother and I decided to move away from verbal language and rely on other communication systems. The very next day, Stephen's teacher called me down to his room. When I walked in Stephen came up to me and said "Hi." I almost fell over. After that, he began to use verbal language. The moral of the story: don't give up. Even when learning is not obvious, it is still occurring.

9. There's a "magic bullet" that will take your child's autism away and make life right again for your family.

This myth is similar to #6, in that it teases parents with the idea that there is one product or therapy or program model that is so perfect for the child that once it's found, you won't need to deal with autism any-more. Some parents cling to this myth so desperately that they latch onto any and every new "fad" treatment that comes along, hoping it will reverse the autism and bring stability and restore a sense of normalcy to life. These parents live in a state of denial of their child's autism. They see autism as a war to be fought, a battle to be won, which sets up autism as something "outside" themselves and their child. The truth is that autism is not outside your child, you, or your family. Autism is part of your child, part of who he is, part of what makes him the unique, wonderful little person he is. You need to find a way to accept that, work with it, and love your child in spite of it. I'm not advocating that you abandon looking for treatments and therapies that can help your child to be a functioning member of society. But I am cautioning you to appreciate that autism is not your "enemy"— don't lose sight of your child as a *person* who has autism. And keep this in mind: if you view autism as your "enemy," what message are you sending your child about who he is? What example are you modeling for him—that part of who he is, is "bad," to be eradicated at any cost? Think about it.

10. Autism is the reason for every problem in the child's life.

We all inherit certain personality traits from our parents and grandparents. We're introverts or extroverts, like alone time or are gregarious and social, are stubborn or compliant—the list is endless. Your child with ASD is no different. He has a unique combination of traits that make up his personality. Some of the behaviors you see in your child will stem from his autism, from his different way of thinking and understanding the world around him. Others will occur simply because he is who he is! The more you know about your child, the better able you'll be to separate the source of behaviors, attitudes and perceptions. See the child, not just the autism.

A mother asked me to come to her home and observe her son, who had ASD. The boy was two-and-a-half years old and she was worried about his play skills. I watched him play with his brother. When he wanted a toy his brother had, he took it, which made his brother cry. Mom looked at me and said, "See, what did I tell you?" to which I replied, "That's how a typical child his age would get the toy if he wanted it. That's not his autism, that's his age!"

18

You keep mentioning that people with autism "think differently." What does that mean?

It is absolutely critical that anyone who comes into contact with people with ASD understands and accepts that they have a unique way of thinking. Because of the way their brains are wired, information processing occurs in ways that seem foreign to us. We keep trying to teach them from our neurotypical frame of reference, which doesn't make sense to them, and then become frustrated when they don't learn. It can be a catch-22 that seriously impacts how much and how quickly they learn.

Some of the ways their thinking is different:

Many kids "think in pictures" rather than words. If your "native language" is pictures, think of how confusing our language-based teaching style might be to them.

They think specific to general, rather than general to specific, as most NTs do. This affects concept formation and the ability to group objects or ideas into categories. It also affects their ability to notice similarities and differences. For example, no one specifically taught you the concept "dog," did they? You saw all different types of dogs and your brain grouped them into a broad classification based on common characteristics. Not so for most kids with ASD. A black dog is different from a white dog, and a Terrier is different from a Great Dane. Without categories, these observations sit in the child's brain as unrelated pieces that do not connect in logical ways to each other. It makes learning very difficult.

"Generalization" of skills is not innate. Neurotypical kids can learn a skill in one environment and they intuitively understand that it applies to other environments; in other words, they generalize. Teach a child to cross the street outside your home and he'll use that skill at all the streets he later encounters. Teach a child with ASD to cross at the intersection of South Wall and Park Streets, and that's the extent of the "lesson." His mind, which thinks "concretely," sees this experience as discrete—unconnected to crossing at Main and Copeland Street, because that's a *different* intersection. The sequence of skills he learned

19

at one intersection doesn't generalize to all future intersections. In the same way, learning to wait in line at the grocery store is different (in his mind) than waiting in line at the movie theatre, which is different than waiting in line at McDonald's. The skill "waiting in line" will need to be taught repeatedly in different environments. It's a significant difference in thinking that impacts all aspects of learning for the child with ASD.

Their thinking tends to be very rigid (like a lot of neurotypicals I know!). It's not being what we call "stubborn"; it's different than that. With these kids, it's more like an absolute necessity that things stay the same, that a precise order has to exist or their world falls apart. It's not a desire—something we want but can live without. For them, it's a basic need, like air or water. Many children and adults live in a state of all-encompassing anxiety and the only way they keep "intact" is through rigid routines and unswerving thought patterns. This, of course, plays out differently at two than it does at twelve, but the end result of deviating from these routines is pretty much the same: inappropriate behavior, ranging from increased anxiety to a full-blown meltdown. For example, I was driving some guys with ASD to their work placement, and we had to take a detour because of road construction. Bobby was not happy and began to get very upset. He kept pointing to the "right" way we should have gone. Once we got back on the main road he calmed down and stopped pointing, but he did not understand that it was okay to deviate from the route and that we would end up at the same location nonetheless. The interruption in the routine was troublesome. Parents will encounter this type of situation often with a young child on the spectrum; it almost always ends up in a behavior tantrum until the child can be systematically taught to accept everyday changes that are a part of life.

At an early age, typical kids learn through their play experiences with others, and by watching other kids, especially older kids. They understand that the experiences of others also apply to them. When two-year-old Margie watches another little girl take her sand pail, go into the sand box, sit down next to another child and start playing in the sand, Margie "gets it" that this sequence of actions is something she can do too, to join another child to play. This is an aspect of social

20

thinking called "perspective taking." We NTs understand that our minds work in similar ways, but that we each have unique thoughts and reactions. Children with ASD do not learn by watching others, and many have very weak perspective-taking skills. In most cases, young ASD children do not play effectively with others, or pay attention to what is going on around them unless it interferes with what they are doing. They don't appreciate that other people are sources of information for learning about the world around them. These children have to be specifically taught the social skills that typical children learn intuitively.

Children on the spectrum process visual information better than auditory information. Meaning: They do not always "hear," retain, or remember verbal instructions. Coupled with their concrete thinking, this style of learning lends itself best to being *shown* how to do something, rather than being *told* how to do it. Tangible objects are more meaningful to children on the spectrum than are photographs or line drawings of the same objects—especially when the children are very young. For example, an apple is tangible; it can be held, smelled, felt. A photo of an apple is less tangible, more abstract, and a line drawing of an apple is even more abstract. These kids respond better to what is tangible than what is abstract. They must be taught the relationship of concrete to abstract in ways that are meaningful to them.

Their thinking and information processing is uneven. People with autism process and respond to information in unique ways. They take in information and do not always readily respond. Hearing and responding is a complex mental task and for many children and adults on the spectrum, their processing speed is delayed. They may take a while to process the information and formulate a response. Because of their weak perspective-taking skills, some individuals do not feel an innate desire to "connect" on a purely social level with others. Given that much of our communication with others is socially driven, ASD individuals may take in information presented to them, but because it has little or no significance to them, they see no need to respond. Educators and other service providers must consider this unique pattern of thinking when assessing learning and behavior to ensure effective intervention. Furthermore, the abilities of an individual with autism may fluctuate from day to day due to difficulties in concentration, information processing, or anxiety. The child may show evidence of learning one day, but not the next. This is not something they can control, yet many people inaccurately assume they can, and regard the child as being "obstinate" or "defiant" or "not trying hard enough." It's important for adults to always keep in mind that learning is not a linear process for kids with ASD. The patterns of learning in typical kids are not present in spectrum kids, even those with average or above-average verbal, memory or spatial skills.

I've said it before and will say it again: ASDs are a brain disorder and we need to understand that the brains of these young people are "wired" differently; they think and learn differently. Temple Grandin, the most well-known high functioning individual with autism in the world, describes in candid detail the way she thinks and the information processing differences in people with ASD in several of her books (*Thinking in Pictures*; *The Unwritten Rules of Social Relationships*). She discusses rigid thinking patterns, the need for sameness and routine, and helps parents and teachers understand that spectrum children thrive in environments that are consistent and predictable. For example, kids with ASD respond well to visual schedules that guide them through an activity. It allows them to see the sequence of actions, know what comes next, and when they are finished.

Temple also talks at length about behavior, that inappropriate behaviors are usually a signal that something is amiss in the child's environment or his understanding. A great deal of the time, people unfamiliar with autism think these kids behave the way they do "on purpose." This, of course, is an inaccurate perception. The "crossed wires" in their brains and their different ways of thinking and processing information result in disruptive behavior because they simply do not understand what to say or do. An illustration: at a grocery store, a mother asks her son to put a toy he's playing with back on the shelf. The child just keeps playing with it. The mother goes over, takes it away and puts it back herself. The child begins to tantrum, hit and kick his mother and throws himself to the floor. Other people watch and think to themselves, "What a spoiled brat." In reality, there may be several things going on in this situation. 1) The child may have been so engrossed in what he was doing that he did not hear what his mother said. It would have been more effective if mom had gone to her son, put her hand on the toy, got his attention and then made her request. 2) The boy may not have understood why he could no longer play with the toy. Or, 3) he may not have been specifically taught how to protest effectively or appropriately ask mom to buy the toy. Social situations are never as simple as they seem. And behavior is a complex equation of variables. Remember what we said previously: behavior is communication. As adults, it's our responsibility to figure out how the different thinking and learning patterns in the ASD child are affecting the outcome, and make accommodations or teach needed skills accordingly.

How does this "different thinking" affect teaching and learning?

Great question! If every parent and teacher keeps this question in the forefront of their thinking and planning for a spectrum child, learning will happen! In essence, we're asking, "How can I teach in a way that is aligned with the ASD way of thinking?" By doing that, we are acknowledging and respecting the inherent differences in individuals with ASD. We are finding effective and appropriate teaching methods that are meaningful to the spectrum child, rather than asking them to "learn" from a system that is based on neurotypical thought and styles of learning. *We have to change the way we teach when we are teaching a child with ASD.* We have to capitalize on their strengths, help them work through their weaknesses, and understand that they do not learn the same way we do.

At times it appears they are learning the way we do, and this can easily lure us away from appreciating their different thinking patterns. We become less vigilant in our efforts to stay curious about what works and what doesn't. Yes, we'll see progress and they may appear to be learning "our way," but please don't assume it means they are. These kids are not going to understand language that is indirect, or contains subtle innuendos or hidden meanings. They are going to process your words exactly as you said them. For example, a teacher who wants immediate action from a child with ASD and says to him, "Hop to it now" should not be surprised—nor assume the child defiant—when he starts hopping across the room. He's only following the instruction as his very literal mind has processed it.

There's so much to learn. Will it always be this hard?

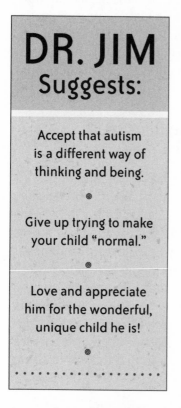

DR. JIM
Suggests:

Accept that autism is a different way of thinking and being.

◉

Give up trying to make your child "normal."

◉

Love and appreciate him for the wonderful, unique child he is!

◉

In time, it gets better. It feels so difficult and devastating right now because it's new, and you know so little about the disorder. In our next session we'll talk more about these feelings, but for right now, today, you'll go back to your child having a little better understanding of him, his different thinking and learning styles, and the reasons he does what he does, than you did when we started this session. You'll start noticing things we talked about and "seeing" him in a new light.

Every child is different and every child will learn and grow in his own way. It would be very unfair for me to predict how your child will be in the future. If you encounter people who do this, run away from them. They are seeing autism, but not appreciating the individual nature of your child. However, let me leave you with this: the future for your child is filled with promise, with better-educated teachers and professionals, and more research being done with this population than ever before. You are living in a time where we know so much more about ASD than we did ten, or even five years ago. Public awareness of the disorder is at an all-time high, and most people know someone who has a child on the spectrum now. Although myths and misperceptions still exist, little by little they are being replaced by a greater understanding of, and appreciation for, individuals with ASD and the positive contributions they make to our world. It's not all doom and gloom, as it used to be—partly because greater awareness has resulted in more effective teaching models and programs for these children and adults. And adults on the spectrum are coming forward and being vocal about their experiences and their lives. We're learning, first hand, from the people who are on the spectrum, what this disorder is really all about.

With appropriate services and guidance, all people with ASD can learn to be part of the world around them, and live a meaningful and productive life. The first step is early diagnosis, and individualized, early intervention services for the child, and training for the parents.

I know, I know. All this information is confusing; so much to learn, and at a time when you're already feeling pressured and emotionally distraught. *Too much! Too much!* you may be thinking, but I'm asking you to hang in there, and make a conscious choice to stay with me and keep going. It's true, there are no easy answers when it comes to autism. No neat "if this, then that" scenarios to remove the guesswork or the legwork you will need to do over the next few months to get a program set up for your child. Some of the truth about dealing with autism isn't pretty; some of it is downright difficult. I'm not here to sugarcoat what you need to know, because as I said earlier, knowledge is power.

But there's a silver lining to this dark cloud. As perplexing as autism can be, it's also fascinating. If you're willing to learn from your child and love him unconditionally, you will find your life enriched by the experience. It happens all the time. Parents and family members the world over become more compassionate, learn the power of love, and discover reserves of courage, determination, creativity, and fortitude they never knew they possessed. You will, too. Right now, autism is a minute-by-minute learning experience. Be gentle with yourself right now, but *don't give up!* See you next session!

◎　◎　◎

*"Autism is a lifelong diagnosis but not a death sentence.
We live, we grow, and we get stronger day by day.
We did; you will too."*

— ANDREW, PARENT OF ANTHONY

NORMAL DEVELOPMENTAL MILESTONES

In order to understand how autism affects your child, it's helpful to first understand typical child development. Many parents report their child later diagnosed with ASD "hit" a majority of the developmental milestones and they were unaware of any problems until they were mentioned by a preschool teacher or other caregiver. Following are developmental milestones consistent with typical developmental, as recognized by the Zero to Three Organization.

A great many of these skills can and will be achieved by a child with ASD, but knowing when they are "stuck" or do not progress past a particular skill allows us to investigate more fully what is wrong and make needed changes so progress continues.

BIRTH TO 8 MONTHS

Behaviors

- I suck anything I can get into my mouth.
- I know I have hands and feet.
- Crying gets me what I want and I am secure with my parents.
- I can comfort myself, for a little while.
- I can make things respond to me.

Emotions

- I have many feelings and I can show them in many different ways. I cry when I am scared or need attention. I smile when you are around because I like playing with you.

- I look for you and am happiest with you.

Relationships

- I can tell the difference between Mommy and Daddy and other people.

- I like to look around and see new things and play games with people I know.

Physical

- I hold my head up.
- I roll over.
- I may sit up.
- I can crawl and even walk with assistance.
- I develop a favorite position.

Communication

- Even as a newborn, I can communicate – I cry to get your attention to my needs and wants.

- I learn I can make different sounds that mean different things (pleasure, sleepy, hungry, wet, etc).

- I use gestures to get what I want, like outstretched arms to be picked up.

8 TO 18 MONTHS

Behaviors

- I can identify my body parts.
- I can say "no".
- I respond to my own name.

Emotions

- I can show extreme happiness (e.g., laughing out loud).
- I can show extreme displeasure (e.g., hitting, pushing, or biting).
- I will lean against you at times when I am unsure.

Relationships

- I have favorite foods, toys, and I like to choose what I wear.
- I like to be with other kids my age or older than I am.

Physical

- I can feed myself (e.g., with my hands, with a cup, or with a spoon or fork).
- I begin to imitate Mom and Dad in everything they do.
- I understand cause and effect. If the ball goes behind the chair, it will come out the other side and I will change my focus to see that.

Communication

- I make eye contact to get your attention.
- I point at what I want.
- I understand the tone of your voice.
- I can string two or more words together to make a sentence.
- I use gestures to get what I want, like outstretched arms to be picked up.

18 MONTHS TO 3 YEARS

Behaviors

- I need clear and consistent boundaries, even though I will test them all the time.
- Your tone of voice lets me know how I am doing.
- I am learning self-control.

Emotions

- I like what I make for you and when I perform, I look for and like your response.

- I may still tantrum because I am scared or frustrated.

- Through your good example, I am able to control what I do and how I react.

- I realize you have feelings too and I will recognize that (e.g., rub your back if you look sad).

Relationships

- I begin to become aware of other kids who are my age and sex.

- I can tell who is missing from a group.

- I begin to pretend play (e.g., going to work, cleaning the house).

- I can take turns and share even though at times it's very hard.

- I know when Mom and Dad are pleased with me or when they are upset at me.

Physical

- I can turn the pages of a book and even scribble with a crayon.

- I can walk stairs, stand on one foot and kick or throw a ball.

- I can pour, not always accurately. I can also eat with a fork and spoon.

Communication

- I know over 200 words and can use them in sentences.

- I can tell you about the past and the future.

- I like to be read to and love stories that are about things I know.

- I use imaginative play skills (e.g., use objects for things other than what they are meant for, a wooden spoon as a microphone).

Red Flags for Autism

The Centers for Disease Control and Prevention (CDC) in partnership with many organizations, such as the Autism Society of America (ASA), have developed resources for both parents and pediatricians that assist in identifying children at risk of having autism. These helpful materials focus on knowing the signs of typical development, so if your child is lagging behind, you can seek help. The First Signs Organization (www.firstsigns.org) has also developed red flag indicators to determine if your child is "at risk" for autism. They are:

- No big smiles or other warm, joyful expressions by 6 months or thereafter

- No back-and-forth sharing of sounds, smiles, or other facial expressions by 9 months or thereafter

- No babbling by 12 months

- No back-and-forth gestures, such as pointing, showing, reaching, or waving by 12 months

- No words by 16 months

- No two-word meaningful phrases (without imitating or repeating) by 24 months

- Any loss of speech or babbling or social skills at any age

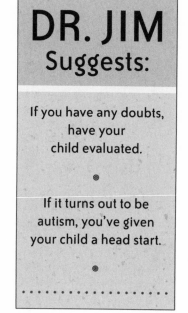

DR. JIM Suggests:

If you have any doubts, have your child evaluated.

If it turns out to be autism, you've given your child a head start.

If your child displays any of these indicators, it does not mean that he has an ASD, but you should have him evaluated to determine if there is any need for concern. Knowing the difference between what is "typical" and what is "part of the disability" will give you a better idea about how to approach the situation.

chapter two

Family Issues: The Personal Side of Autism

MAUREEN AND ROB ARE RETURNING TODAY FOR THEIR SECOND SESSION WITH me. These first few months of the diagnosis are often a haze for parents. Even for those who suspected autism in their child, the day they actually hear the diagnosis is one they will never forget. Within the span of mere moments, their world is forever changed.

My goal today is to talk with them about the feelings they may be experiencing and issues related to family matters. Autism impacts everyone involved: parents, siblings, grandparents and other close family members, often in ways that are incompatible with one another. I want them to know there are simple, concrete things they can do during this "transition" time to work through their emotions and build a strong family foundation that will help them all work together for Mark's benefit and their own.

Dr. Jim: Welcome back, Maureen and Rob. How have things been since you were here last?

Maureen: One day I feel positive and think I'm getting a handle on it all, the next I feel so filled with anger I scream at everyone: Rob, the kids, even little Mark. Other days are even worse. I disconnect from everyone— intentionally or not—and feel lifeless, like a robot, just going through the motions. It just hurts too much to deal with it. And I'm exhausted by it all. Depressed, exhausted and really, really angry.

Dr. Jim: Those feelings are common when your child is diagnosed with a disability, especially one like autism, with no clear-cut answers and solutions. You're grieving, just as you would if someone you loved had died. And, in a sense, someone has: the child you dreamed Mark would be.

Maureen: It feels like a death—as if our futures died when Mark was diagnosed—but here we are, and I know we have to go on. So on top of everything else, I feel guilty about spending time "processing" my feelings, feeling sad and sorry for myself when there's so much to think about and do for Mark. It's seems wrong for me to think about myself right now, like I'm cheating Mark in some way. He's what's important, not me.

Dr. Jim: I know life seems dismal and dark now, and all you can think about is Mark, but I'd like you to consider this: who is Mark depending on to love him and care for him, to become his advocate, his teacher, his guide? YOU! And, you're not going to be very effective over the long haul if you don't take care of yourself now and give yourself permission to have the feelings you do.

Maureen: I hear what you're saying, but my heart feels one thing—broken—and my mind keeps playing this single track over and over: "What am I doing? What do I do next? Is it enough? What am I doing? What do I do next? Is it enough?" It's like parts of me are at war with each other and every blow dealt takes more and more of the life out of me. Sometimes I just collapse in a heap and cry for hours!

Dr. Jim: Rob, you're being pretty quiet. What's going on with you?

Rob: No disrespect, doc, but aren't we just wasting time talking about our feelings? Mark has autism; there's no turning back now. Let's get on to talking about the important things, services and programs for him. We're just wasting our time talking about all this emotional stuff!

Maureen: That's typical of you, Rob. You never want to discuss Mark's autism and what's happened to us . . . all of us. You can't even use the "a" word in public when talking about Mark. I feel like I'm going through this by myself, like I've been suddenly widowed and had my son diagnosed with autism, both at the same time.

Rob: All you do is cry—that's not helping anything! I go to work and you're crying, I come home from work and you're crying! When are you going to get over this so our family can get back to normal?

Dr. Jim: Time out—time out. Rob, it's clear to me that your emotions are running high too; it's not just Maureen who's finding it hard to deal with the situation. Yet you're each reacting to the diagnosis differently. Maureen is crying, and you, Rob, what are you doing? You're reacting like most dads, by burying your feeling under a tough-guy shell.

Autism affects the whole family, not just the child who carries the label. True, Mark is the one who lives with the disorder and for him, the challenge will be the greatest. But as his parents, the individuals who love him, care for him, and want what's best for him, your lives are affected too—deeply and in ways you don't even realize yet. This is a perfect segue into what we'll be talking about in today's session— family dynamics—so let's get right into it.

◎   ◎   ◎

How does a diagnosis of autism impact the family?

Family issues are extremely complex and, even in the best of circumstances, can be very difficult to work though. When autism is added to the mix, the dynamic takes on a whole new dimension. Parents, grandparents and siblings are generally uneducated about and unfamiliar with the disability world. This brings an element of uncertainty to relationships that breeds fear and feelings of inadequacy. And everyone else picks up on it, even young siblings. Our natural reaction is to shy away from things that are unfamiliar to us, but this is the least effective way to handle autism. Honest, open communication among all family members, sharing both feelings and information, goes much farther in the long run.

You referred to autism feeling like a death of sorts?

In her book, *On Death and Dying*, Elizabeth Kubler-Ross describes five stages people go through when receiving news of a catastrophic illness. Over the years this has morphed into the five stages of grief and loss people experience when someone dies or another catastrophic event takes place in their life—such as learning your child has a disability. From grandparents to siblings, each family member of a newly diagnosed child with autism experiences similar stages of grief. The "loss" in this case is the image of who the child might have been, might have become, as defined by the person experiencing it (i.e., the child as a son, a grandson, a brother, etc). The five stages as defined by Kubler-Ross are:

Denial

People will attempt to explain away the situation and/or will lie to themselves that it isn't real. A parent or family member may disregard the autism diagnosis or under-rate the degree of impairment in the child.

- *"I don't care what that doctor says, he doesn't have autism. He's just a late bloomer. He'll come around in time."*

- *"So he has autism. It's just some medical label. We'll go on treating him like the rest of his brothers and sisters—no special treatment for this one."*

Anger

"Why me? "What did I do to deserve this hardship?" People get angry at the world for what has happened. It's natural to want to blame someone for the child's autism. Couples find themselves angry at each other, even unconsciously (or consciously) blaming each other for their child's condition. Or their anger is diffuse and pervasive, at anyone and everyone.

Bargaining

People think they can "fix" the situation if they make a bargain with doctors, spouses, or even God. "What do I have to do to make this go away?"

Depression

They feel so overwhelmed or so filled with unfamiliar emotions that they retreat from the experience. Because they can see no way "out," they feel sad or depressed, not only about the immediate situation, but also their life, their future and that of their family.

Acceptance

The loss is finally accepted (though not completely), and the person begins to move on with life.

As adults, we often assume these stages are one big cycle we have to work through, and once we get to "acceptance," we're done. However, even after a significant period of time has elapsed, events can occur that will reactivate the feelings of grief in major or minor ways. For example: a little girl wakes up and looks right at Mom and says in a sleepy voice, "good morning." Mom smiles and is touched by the connection with her daughter. As they make their way downstairs, the child runs her hands along the ridges of the wallpaper leading to the kitchen. Mom moves her hands away from the wall and the child begins to tantrum. Dad hears what's going on, comes into the room and in a loud voice reprimands the child. Mom looks at the child and walks away, dejected by the interaction. Feelings of hope that things can get better are squashed in mere minutes. These phases of hope and depression can cycle around and around when a child is first diagnosed. Seemingly little things can reopen tender wounds just beginning to heal.

Do we go through these stages in succession?

Not really. Some people go from denial to acceptance in a very short period of time, some get stuck in one stage or another, and some skip stages altogether. Grief is a very complicated personal experience, made up of multiple layers of feelings and thoughts. What's important for couples and families to keep in mind is that each person travels toward a place of acceptance differently. What often happens is that parents find themselves out of sync in the process and conflicts arise because of it. A dad won't even admit his son has autism and remains stuck in denial, mom is angry at the world and the child's grandparents are working through depression. These different dynamics will affect a family's ability to communicate, reach consensus on treatment, and demonstrate care for one another. It's very, very complicated.

Outside counseling can be extremely helpful at times like this to guide parents and families through their feelings of loss and grief. The acronym TEAR briefly sums up the help trained counselors can provide:

> **T** = To accept the reality of the loss
> **E** = Experience the pain of the loss
> **A** = Adjust to the new environment
> **R** = Reinvest in the new reality

Do people all experience these stages the same way?

No, they don't, which further complicates the experience.

We all have our own personal expectations of our kids: who they will grow up to be and how they are going to get there. While children are in the womb, parents fantasize and dream about what their son or daughter will be like, the color of their hair and eyes, their personality, what they will do for a living, when they will marry, etc. Once our children are born we transfer those thoughts to them through our interactions with them. And gender differences will affect how we interact with each other and, once a child is diagnosed, how we deal with the issue.

Are you saying that moms and dads handle the diagnosis differently?

That's exactly what I'm saying. Let's look at typical gender roles:

- Mom: Caregiver, keeper of the family, responsible for schooling, emotional support

- Dad: Disciplinarian, fixer, breadwinner

Moms and dads come into our office to discuss family issues, and more often than not, their issues arise from unspoken and unconscious assumptions both partners make about their role as a parent. We assume that mom is the one who cares for the children, is the nurturer and provides emotional support, while dad is the breadwinner, doles out discipline and is responsible for providing financial support for the children. Moms typically want everyone to be happy with a decision; dads will "lay down the law" as they see fit. Of course, these are generalizations and stereotypes, but they are powerful underlying perceptions still active in our culture.

Enter autism, and these gender differences play out in other ways. Mom becomes the information gatherer; she scours the internet late at night, downloads and prints out all sorts of articles and strategies, reads every book she can lay her hands on to come up with a "game plan" (a male gender term) to address the child's autism. She generally views it as a collaborative process, involving many different people who work together to achieve consensus. She's willing to see the specialists, gather the information, assemble all the necessary elements to put together the plan.

Dad, on the other hand, is a "fixer." He wants to "fix" the child's autism, not "deal with it," and the sooner the better. That's what dads do. They recognize a problem, grab the required tools and rectify whatever is wrong. For dads, any situation that can't be fixed is a personal reflection of inadequacy. The trouble is, autism can't be "fixed." There's no gadget that will eradicate it, no sledgehammer to destroy it. For many dads, seeing the child's autism, day in and day out, is a constant reminder they have somehow "failed" the family.

Moms and dads are heartfelt in their desire to help their child, but they approach the situation from different angles, ones that are often at odds with each other. Just recognizing these different gender roles and perceptions can be immensely helpful for parents and family members in accepting how each is working through the stages of grief. Unfortunately, many parents neither recognize nor accept these differences, and the result is that both parents feel alienated from one another. In most cases the child's education becomes delegated to mom. She becomes the partner who is responsible for finding solutions and deciding on treatment, while dad assumes the responsibility for financing them.

Couples can easily drift apart at this delicate juncture. Dad goes off to work each morning and Mom starts to resent his "freedom." He doesn't have to deal with the child's relentless tantrums, doesn't have to clean up yet another mess the child's gotten into, or deal with the stares or whispers of strangers in the grocery store when the child's favorite cereal is missing from the shelf. For her, autism is a never-ending job. She often feels alone and unappreciated. Dad, on the other hand, starts feeling alienated. Without regular, direct exposure to the child, he doesn't learn how to handle the autism. He feels inadequate when he tries. All Mom has time for is the child and autism. She spends every waking hour gathering information, talking on the phone with other parents. Dad no longer feels needed. Moms can inadvertently shut dads out of the information loop, setting up a pattern of learned helplessness.

Learned helplessness is what I call "fathers' syndrome." After my father retired from his job, I remember my mother saying, "Things are going to change around here. Your father is going to cook, clean, and do more, now that he has time." I looked at my mother and said, "Mom, you created that monster many years ago and he is not going to do anything more than he has been doing." Because years earlier, the first time she asked him to do the dishes, he did them, but did a sub-par job. When my mother came down and saw what he had done, instead of calling him back to redo the dishes, she just said to herself, "It's easier if I just do them myself." After that, she never asked him to do the dishes again. It's a perfect example of learned helplessness: if he's not made to do it, or taught to do it correctly, he will never learn to do it successfully. This also holds true in working with a child with autism, which we will discuss in a later session.

Every year for the past six years, I have had the great fortune of being involved with a presentation at the Autism Society of America's Annual Conference, called "For Fathers Only." Even though this presentation focuses on the thoughts, and yes, feelings of fathers, I want to share with you a list of things not only dads can do, but strategies that help the whole family stay involved. This list is excerpted from an article

that originally appeared in a very helpful resource for parents and professionals, the *Autism Asperger's Digest* magazine.

10 Things Every "ONE" Can Do

1. *Be involved at home!*

The responsibility for the care of your child with autism does not rest
solely on your spouse's shoulders, no matter how "busy" or "stressful"
is your professional life. Ask about ways you can help. Sometimes just
bringing home a bucket of chicken can make a world of difference.

2. *Accept that it's not your fault.*

Moms especially feel this, but dads go through it too. Was it my genes?
Something I did when I was younger?

3. *Share in the decisions and responsibilities for the child with ASD.*

In a family with multiple children, the mom often handles all the needs
of the child with autism, and the dad is involved solely with the typically developing kids. Our session stresses the need for husband and
wife to sit down and create a Partnership Plan that allows mom and
dad to both share in the challenges, the joys, the decisions and the
responsibilities. Yes, this can bring up significant issues that will need
to be resolved. Be willing to break from traditional husband-wife roles
and responsibilities in order to learn what works best for your relationship—it can really help.

4. *Make time for you and your partner to be together alone.*

Find the respite care; do whatever you need to do. You won't be able
to build a quality program for your child if you don't maintain a quality relationship with your spouse. You may both survive, but you
won't thrive.

5. *Create a Family Plan.*

Define each of your roles in relation to the child's care and your family's
physical, emotional and mental health. Involve siblings—they often

have great compassion and are eager to help. Strive for balance as much as is possible.

6. Communicate with your partner and family on a regular basis.

This is not the time for any family member to keep thoughts and feelings bottled up inside. It builds resentment, blame and distance within the family unit. Make the effort to talk about things, even when it's difficult.

7. "Network" with other parents of children with ASD.

Once a month get together and go bowling, attend a sports event or play pool. Sure, you'll end up talking about autism in one form or another. The fact that there are other men out there experiencing the same challenges you are is important for dads to learn, too.

8. Everyone attends IEP/team meetings!

Whether or not it's "fair," most educational professionals sit up and take notice when a dad attends the IEP meeting. Men have clout. Furthermore, dads tend to help moms stay on an even keel, emotionally, during the meeting, so often more productive work and cooperation happens. Go into each meeting with a plan. Know what you want for your child and have a strategy going in—will there be the need for "good cop-bad cop," or do the school officials and teachers work proactively with you to help formulate your plan? Once there, gauge the attitude of the administrators and educators as well, and adjust your strategy. Remember, you both need to keep emotions in check, but be passionate. Take a break and split away from the group if things start to get out of control. Reassemble your thoughts and come back into the meeting presenting a united front. If things are not going smoothly, pull back and say, "We really want to make sure we come up with an IEP that genuinely benefits our son, and gives him the best opportunities to succeed and grow." We know sometimes this is easier said than done.

9. Try to keep autism from dominating your lives.

This is a major problem for families. Often, the child with autism has sleeping, behavior, gastro or other issues and challenges that keep the family from doing typical activities. The bedtime issues can cause dramatic problems when parents go weeks and even months without a good night's sleep. Parents and families also tell us they often feel as though they were prisoners in their own homes: afraid to go to the mall, recreation center, restaurants, or other public places because of the potential for problems to occur. We encourage families to create a plan that slowly introduces the child with autism to activities out in the community. Accept that there can be and probably will be problems, but more importantly, recognize the need for the family to try to do these activities together. Good school programs incorporate functional plans that both the child and family can work on to create opportunities for fun.

10. Enjoy your child!

Autism is only a *part* of your child and often includes unique, humorous, and interesting insights that can and should be celebrated. Be optimistic—good times *are* ahead. See the positives rather than the negatives. All it takes is a shift in perception—yours!

All of this advice is great, but how do we make it work in real-world time?

If you remember only one thing from this session, let it be this: Communication is the indestructible Velcro that will keep your family together and moving forward. When communication breaks down, so will your relationships.

Autism can be a traumatic stressor on the family. With the strain of being thrown unexpectedly into the world of disability, the depression, exhaustion, and sleepless nights of worry, the uncertainty over the future, the guilt over unequal attention to other siblings, your life can easily descend

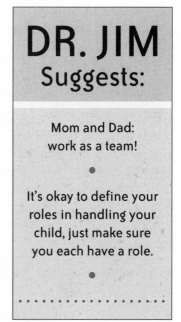

DR. JIM
Suggests:

Mom and Dad:
work as a team!

◉

It's okay to define your roles in handling your child, just make sure you each have a role.

◉

into what I call "survival mode." The family lives moment-to-moment, trying to be as normal a family as possible, reacting to whatever happens as it happens, but never pulling together proactively to consciously create a new future for themselves. The most important thing to do during these times is to communicate with your spouse, other children, relatives, and any other people close to you. I realize this is much easier said than done, and that it may sound like a cliché. But it works, and cannot be stressed enough.

Any "quick tips" for communicating you'd like to share? I'd love the luxury of spending a weekend at a seminar or an hour a week learning to be a more effective communicator, but I have a little child with autism, you know.

Sheri and Bob Stritof, authors of *The Everything Great Marriage Book* and popular workshop presenters on communication skills, family issues and relationships, tell us that conversation fills a variety of needs:

- To be connected to another.
- To have our feelings and thoughts heard and respected.
- To learn new things.
- To sort through issues and problems.
- To discuss and explore solutions.

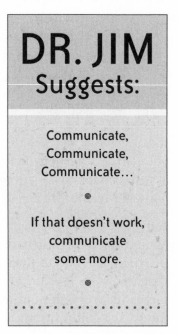

DR. JIM Suggests:

Communicate,
Communicate,
Communicate...

◉

If that doesn't work, communicate some more.

◉

Conversation helps each individual in a relationship feel of value and enables the couple to move forward and experience success. In *The New Father: A Dad's Guide to the Toddler Years,* Armin Brott suggests that once we understand the needs fulfilled by communication, we follow three simple rules:

- Open your mouth
- Close your mouth
- Speak the same language

This may seem almost too simplistic to be useful, however, it can be extremely effective. Brott also offers useful strategies for putting these rules into practice:

- Always have a schedule. Set up a time and place to meet to talk.

- Be honest about what you need to tell each other. Prioritize topics, talk about one topic at a time; do not take on too much at once.

- Have your partner reflect back what you said to prevent misunderstanding. It will help you better understand each other's thoughts and feelings.

- If the partner heard what you said accurately, thank him or her for listening. If anything is misunderstood, try saying it again until the partner hears it right.

- Start at number 2 again, so you each take turns talking.

- Try to reach agreement, if needed. Let go of what you can, compromise on what you can, and clearly convey those things you can't give up.

Honest, heartfelt communication is the key to preserving a strong relationship, whether between you and your spouse, you and your parents, you and your other children or you and your child's therapists. These simple rules and strategies can help you, but only if you make the effort to use them. Sometimes it will be easy; other times you'll need to really work at keeping lines of communication open and honest. Make it a priority; make it a value you never lose sight of and your family will make it through the difficult early times. Autism reaches far beyond you and your spouse. It affects the other children in the family (if any), your decision to have more children, your relationship with your parents, other relatives, and friends.

How "honest" should I be with others in our family?

The answer depends largely upon the existing relationship you have with your family members, how often you talk, how close you are, the level of personal conversations you have shared about other things.

Some people and families are very private; others talk about anything and everything. I do encourage you to be honest with your family, though, about what autism is and what autism isn't. As we discussed before, people generally fear what they do not understand. Because this is so new to you, you're bound to feel apprehensive about telling your parents, brothers and sisters or your spouse's family members about your child's condition. You do not know how they might handle it or if they will even try to understand. Realize that this can be done in stages, over time. It's not a "one-time" conversation. Provide them with as much initial information as you can, coupled with several other sources for finding information on their own. During the first few months, be as open and honest as you can about what is happening to you and to your child. Discuss new information you're learning about programs and therapies. Share progress with family members as often as possible.

How do I handle family members who offer their own "opinions" about everything?

Generally, the child's grandparents, aunts and uncles are genuinely interested in the welfare of the child, but often feel either helpless or uncomfortable with the situation because they don't know what to do. Out of that fear and ignorance, they may say things that hurt your feelings. Again, honest communication goes a long way. Let them know the decisions you've made with regard to the child's treatment, discuss goals you've developed for your child. Explain how people with autism think, and the importance of routine and consistency during the child's early stages of learning. If a tantrum occurs in their presence, explain why it happens as best you can, point out the factors that may have contributed to it, so they start understanding autism on an experiential basis, not just based on what they read in books. Remind them that it's not just the child who is learning; you are all learning how to deal with autism, and none of you will be successful at the first try.

During the early stages of your child's development you want family members to understand what is going on with your child and what you expect from them. Be clear about what they can do with the child and what they should not do. Explain the nuances involved in language and offer them examples of how to communicate with the child, verbally and nonverbally. Discuss behaviors, responses, assistance, etc. This consistency among adults will support your child's overall development, and also help family members realize that they can be an important part of your child's progress.

Grandparents often take an active interest in helping out, especially those who live nearby. Let Grandma and Grandpa know it's okay to be themselves, but also explain that spoiling the child is not going to be in the child's best interest. Train grandparents so they know when to reward the child and when to be firm, how to recognize signs of sensory overload, or what to do during a tantrum or meltdown. The AARP offers some practical suggestions for grandparents when interacting with a grandchild with special needs:

5 Ways to be an Effective Grandparent for a Child with Special Needs

- Show your grandchild every day that you love him
  for the special person he is.

- Listen when the child's parents need to talk.

- Support the decisions they are making, even if you don't
  agree with all of them.

- Demonstrate an interest in the special programs and therapies
  they have found for the child.

- Offer to help with household chores.

Have some concrete things in mind when Grandma and Grandpa (or other family members or close friends) offer to help. Most people shy away because they don't know what to do; by being specific in your request, everyone benefits. You may feel uncomfortable at first about accepting help, but most people are willing to do things like cook a casserole for dinner, drop off/pick up dry cleaning, shop for groceries, mail packages, run the vaccuum, fold laundry, or do countless other daily chores that have to be done. If other siblings are feeling neglected, ask close relatives to give them some extra special attention doing things you know they will enjoy.

Not every situation is the same, nor is every family. The point is, as best as you can, create and maintain a support network. If it's not Grandma and Grandpa, it may be Uncle Ted and Aunt Phyllis or cousin Ed, or the next door neighbors you've been friends with for years. The adage, "It takes a village to raise a child" holds true; you need people to lean on, people you trust and you can count on to come to your aid when you need it. A positive perspective and open lines of communication are the building blocks of your network. If you find yourself without family nearby, nor close friends you can rely upon, try joining an autism support group. I am not a big fan of support groups unless they are well moderated. Too many times these groups turn into "bitch" sessions and breed negitivity, rather than promoting positive interactions and fostering the growth of supportive relationships. If you do decide to join a group, find one whose operations and personality are wholesome, positive, and support your family's and your own values.

And, what about our other kids? Any advice regarding them?

It is very easy to neglect the rest of the family once a child is diagnosed. It never happens on purpose—it's just an overwhelming time for parents who are trying to simultaneously understand autism, the unfamiliar world of disabilities and services, and everything else that comes with the diagnosis. The most important thing to remember when dealing with your other children is to set aside "special" time for them, to let them know they matter to you. Makes dates together; give them your undivided attention. Offer information about autism in ways they can understand; let them ask questions about anything and everything they may be thinking and feeling. Include them in the decision-making process whenever possible. And don't forget to create that Family Plan we discussed earlier. Many siblings look far into the future and wonder if they will end up being responsible for their brother or sister once their parents are gone. This can create a huge amount of stress, even in children as young as pre-teens and young teenagers. A

Family Plan often helps them feel more comfortable both in the present and in looking toward the future.

5 Things to Do to Keep a Healthy Family

1. *Go out as a family once a week.* Pick places that are fun for everyone. In the beginning try to go out during "down times," when fewer people are around (especially a good idea if your child has sensory issues). Try activities such as roller-skating or bowling, fishing, a hike and/or a picnic. Do the same activities over and over, so your child with ASD gets familiar with the routine and the environment. Let the child experience success in family outings before venturing into other activities that might require greater patience or skill sets.

2. *Prioritize the needs of the family and schedule times to tackle them.* As the parent, you do not have to be "on" all the time. Pick out those things that most directly affect the family and handle them in order of their importance. For example: if your spectrum child is having issues during meal time, schedule a time when you can teach him needed social or behavior skills. Your older, typical child is having trouble with homework; schedule a "homework time" when you can give the child your complete attention and help. This also goes for your spouse; be sure you both attend to each other's needs for time alone, caring, and affection. Schedule a time for that too.

3. *Start a Family Game Night.* This is not only a great way to teach the child with ASD important social skills, but it gives everyone an opportunity to "hang out" together. It's also a great way to get siblings involved with their brother or sister with autism.

4. *Eat meals together.* As often as you can, try to eat meals together. This family gathering can be a time to learn about each others' day and share information about what's happening within the family. And it's another opportunity for the child to practice daily living/social skills!

5. *Parents: give yourself a break on a regular basis.* Go out together as a couple and/or alone and do something fun or relaxing. Feed your spirit and your own personality. It could be as simple as taking an

hour to go to the local book store and read a book (even on autism if you like), or take a class in yoga or painting. Or it could be as complex as attending a National Conference on autism every year, or taking a vacation with your friends. Consider yourself and your own needs important, so you can find ways to refresh yourself, and not feel "consumed" by autism or the situation you find yourself in at the time.

Autism seems like such an uphill battle right now. How can I not be "consumed" by it all?

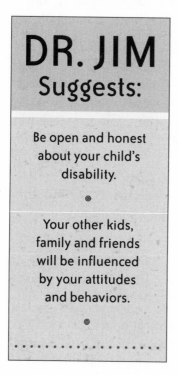

DR. JIM
Suggests:

Be open and honest about your child's disability.

◎

Your other kids, family and friends will be influenced by your attitudes and behaviors.

◎

It's good that you're asking questions like this one. It tells me you're able to step away from your situation, even briefly, and look at it with some measure of perspective. That's actually very positive.

One thing I tell every parent I meet and work with is this: how well you fare with autism, how quickly or slowly you work through the stages of grief and come to a place of true acceptance of autism in your child's and your life, rests very much in your attitude towards it. *It's all about attitude—YOURS!*

This plays out on so many levels. Your child hears everything you say, your tone of voice, and whether you're reacting positively or negatively. You may think he is oblivious to what's going on around him, but hear this: he senses you and your attitude. He senses it in others, too. Kids with ASD have an uncanny ability to know when you believe in them and when you don't, when you're loving them for who they are or finding "fault" with them. Your perception of autism will be a decisive factor in how your child develops. This may not be what you want to hear right now, on top of everything else you are feeling, but it is important, and it's important NOW. I want to be sure you understand how widespread your influence can be … because it's *already* a factor in your child's life. Right now. Today. How you act or react to your child and what is happening is vital to his overall success. Do you view autism as an "enemy" with whom you need to "do battle"? Think of the adversarial nature of that stance. Do you expect that your little child can separate himself from his autism and understand that it's not him you are battling, but his autism? Of course he can't. To him, your words, your tone of voice, your actions are about *him*.

How else do you view his autism? Do you see it as an insurmountable challenge, and feel defeated before you even try? Or can you view it in a more proactive light, that everyone is unique, everyone has challenges, and yours is a little bigger than others, but together we can work through this? Is your relationship with your child characterized by doom and gloom? What message does that convey to your child—that you are happy with who he is, or that he is somehow "less than"? Do your words and actions reflect a "can-do" approach or a "can't-do" attitude?

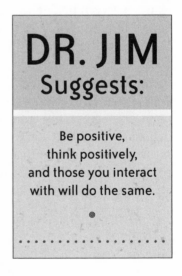

DR. JIM
Suggests:

Be positive,
think positively,
and those you interact
with will do the same.

I'll say it again (yes, I tend to repeat myself when it's something I want to be sure you understand). Attitude is a *huge* factor in how well the family adjusts to the diagnosis. Those who believe they can get through it, and want to do so together, generally do. Yes, it's difficult and yes, at times it may feel like an impossible challenge. There are times when you will need to separate your feelings from your need to take action. Your emotions don't need to rule your experience. If your attitude is positive (and I don't mean Pollyannish), you will succeed. Your family will not just survive, but thrive. Whatever the challenge that presents itself, you will know and believe you can work through it, in a way that benefits all the people who are involved.

That's a lot to take in right now, and to be honest, I'm not sure I like what you just said. Are you telling me I'm responsible for my child's future success or failure in life? That my attitude will "make" or "break" his progress? That's what it sounds like, and that's a heavy burden to lay on me!

In a sense that is what I'm saying, but not in the way you may be "hearing" it right now. Let me continue. Just like typical children, kids with ASD come into the world with their own personalities, their own capacities for learning, their own ways of relating to the world around them. There are parts of who he is as a person—aside from his autism—over which you will have little control. However, this child of yours also has autism. It's something he will live with his entire life. He will need to learn to accommodate it, work with it, navigate around it, and learn to accept himself if he is to reach his full potential. That's where your attitude affects him. Young children model what they see and experience. If you love him in spite of his autism, love him and his autism, you will instill feelings of confidence and acceptance, of self-worth and value in your son as he works through the challenges autism will present him. If you can't accept his autism, are constantly trying to "get rid of" the autism through this therapy or that, this program or another, you send a message to your child that he is somehow inadequate in your eyes, that something about him is deficient, less than, in need of fixing. This fosters low self-esteem in a child and promotes repeated cycles of failure.

Parents need to be cognizant of the unspoken messages they convey to their child. Over the years, working with hundreds if not thousands of parents, I've noticed that they fall into different groups regarding how they relate to the autism diagnosis. So today, I want you to ask yourself: *What kind of parent do I want to be from now on?* Read on.

The Angry Parent

These parents get stuck in the second stage of the grieving process. They are angry at the world, themselves, their spouse—someone, anyone—for their child's disability. They play the blame-game in every manner possible. Their anger prevents them from seeing any positive aspect to autism. They can miss micro-steps of progress that might otherwise bring them hope and open their hearts to unconditional love, and acceptance of their child's condition. For the angry parent, progress is never enough and always takes too long. Lack of progress is always the fault of others: the wrong program, the wrong teachers, the wrong strategies. Because they are stuck in anger, these parents become labeled in the system as "untouchables"—parents with whom no therapist will work on a long-term basis. The Angry Parent is not the same as a parent who uses anger, when appropriate, to voice dissension or objection to some aspect of the child's program or the way he's being treated. That parent has control over his or her anger and can choose when and how it is released. The Angry Parent, on the other hand, has no control. Such anger consumes energy that could be put to much better use.

The "Woe is Me" Parent

These parents usually see autism as a "death sentence"; they become mired in depression or, even worse, self-pity. Each challenging episode in their life is viewed as a personal attack against them. They feel powerless to bring about change, as though "luck" steers the rudder and is the wind in their sails as they journey through the autism experience. These parents are usually so focused on the challenges and struggles involved with ASD that they forget autism is happening to their child, not to them. No matter how difficult our lives as parents may be, we still operate in and understand the world of neurotypicals; we share their language, their thinking and their ways of learning. The Woe is Me Parent forgets that the struggle is so much more difficult for the child. It is critical that these parents understand that autism is not a personal attack on them, and that they refocus their attention on the child.

The Try Anything and Everything Parent

Parents stuck in the denial or bargaining stages of grief can easily become the "Try Anything" type of parent, always looking for the "magic bullet" to cure the child's autism. But trying every new therapy you hear about is not in the best interest of your child. New "cure alls" and "quick fixes" have been part of the autism landscape for a long time now. They come and they go, some offering a measure of help to a small segment of the population, while others involve sizeable amounts of real risk. It is good for parents to investigate new therapies, keep abreast of new developments in the field, and learn new techniques that can help a child reach his full potential. But these efforts need to be tempered by a realistic understanding of the lifelong nature of the disability. At present, there is no cure for ASD. The condition remains throughout the person's life. Yes, certain characteristics can diminish, and individuals can be taught functional skills that allow them to blend into our NT world more seamlessly. But autism is still present. The "Try Anything" parent has yet to fully accept autism as part of who the child is, and continually searches for something that will make it disappear. Valuable time, energy and financial resources are generally wasted as the child's life revolves around a constant stream of endeavors to discover the "one perfect thing" that will remove the autism.

The "Fix-Him" Parent

For these parents, there is nothing remotely positive about autism and how it affects their child. Autism is seen as a disease, a dis-ability, an unacceptable impairment. Just "fix" him is the message delivered in verbal and nonverbal communication with others—including the child. Fix-Him parents separate a child's autism into disparate segments, view each challenge as a separate condition, and lose sight of the interrelatedness of autism and the child. There's speech therapy to fix his language problems, and occupational therapy to fix his sensory issues and behavior therapy to fix his inappropriate ways of acting with others. These parents often view professionals as the "fixers," and rarely participate in the education of their child. They see the education system as the sole source of teaching and when things do not go well or the child's progress does not meet their (often unrealistic) expectations, they blame the system and the staff within it. The Fix-Him parent is usually looking for a quick cure. They want something done in a hurry and they want someone else to do it.

The Over-Educated but Stuck Parent

These parents immerse themselves in the world of autism via the library, internet, and any other source you can name. They read everything they can find, watch anything on autism on television or through online resources, in a most sincere desire to help their child. What happens? One of two things. They get overwhelmed by the amount of information and get stuck within it, afraid to try anything for fear of making the "wrong" choice. Or they learn a little about a lot of different therapies and get "stuck" in their expectations for progress. They set up treatments and therapies as if they were ordering Chinese food: one from column A, one from column B and one from column C. It can play out like this: I do a little Applied Behavior Analysis (ABA), with a smattering of Occupational Therapy (OT), with a pinch of Speech Therapy, and a dash of Floortime. An eclectic, individualized program is not always bad for a spectrum child. The difference is that the Stuck Parent doesn't stay with a plan long enough to find out if it really works. When results are not immediate or do not achieve the expected level of improvement, the parent moves on to another approach in hopes of obtaining better results elsewhere.

The Just-Right Parent

Obviously the most effective parent to be is the Just-Right Parent. Just-Right Parents have qualities of all the other parent types, with one noted distinction: they are the most balanced. They can be angry, given the right circumstances (e.g., not getting the services they feel their child needs); feel sorry for themselves for a time, but not let it overwhelm them; try a variety of different approaches, evaluating their effectiveness in an objective, systemized manner so they know which confer benefits and which don't; try to remedy some of the challenges autism brings to the child while appreciating that making the child "functional" is not the same as trying to make him "normal" again; and continue to educate themselves so they can make informed choices and participate in their child's overall program. Becoming a Just-Right Parent is a process; it takes time and training to come to that state of knowledge, awareness, understanding and acceptance. But once you become this type of parent, which I know you will, your attitude towards autism will take a quantum shift and you will view the journey you are on with your child in a new light, one that will make both of you stronger and more positive people.

DR. JIM
Suggests:

Don't separate the symptoms
of autism from the child.

◎

See the whole child.

◎

Be the Just-Right Parent who
loves unconditionally
and accepts autism.

◎

See the big picture.

◎

Cathy Pratt, Director of the Indiana Resource Center on Autism (*www.irca.org*) talks about this philosophy of acceptance using an analogy of going to the doctor. When you go to the doctor with a bad cough he will ask questions about your physical well-being. A good doctor understands that all parts of the body are connected and will search for the underlying cause of the problem, rather than just treating the cough. The cough is only a symptom. It's the same with individuals with ASD. Treating symptoms may help in the short term, but for long-term results, identifying the underlying cause of these symptoms guides us toward effective solutions that bring progress, and aid in the overall functioning of the individual.

I really want to be a Just-Right Parent, but everything is so new right now. I feel like I take one step forward, lose my footing and slide back down the hill. I'm so unsure of myself I live in a constant state of fear that I'm not making the right choices for my child or my family. Do you have any words of wisdom that might help me get through the insecurity and constant anxiety I feel right now?

Know this: inside you there are untapped pools of potential you don't even realize you have. You can handle this if you will just believe you can. And if you can't yet believe you can, then just tell yourself every day, every hour, every minute if you need to, that yes, you can handle this. I ask you to do this because your words, your thoughts, and your attitude are enormously powerful forces in your life and how it unfolds. Autism is challenging. Parents don't choose for their child to have it. You will be faced with all sorts of personal and family issues that will need to be discussed, debated, considered, and resolved. Each family creates a different way of doing so. However, if everyone in the family—together—accepts that autism is part of the family dynamics, just as gender differences, compulsions, habits, and personality quirks are, it can be dealt with in a positive, effective way.

If you view autism as a dis-ability, it will dis-able your family and your lives. See it rather as a different ability and find the positive aspects of autism. They are there; you just need to see them. When things get out of control and you lose direction, seek outside help. Support groups, a good friend, trained professionals (counseling) or a spiritual connection are all ways to navigate the often choppy seas of life in general, but can be life preservers for families of children with ASD. Find ways that help you stay afloat—as an individual, as a couple and as a family—when dark skies loom overhead. Always keep your focus on the child and his needs, but not by neglecting yourself or other members of your family. In order to truly help your child, you often need to first find ways to help yourself accept and love him, autism included.

Autism is a marathon, not a short race and then it's over. It is essential that parents do whatever they need to do to stay fit, conserve energy, and pace themselves so they can be positive, connected and effective over the long haul. Your child is counting on you to keep him in the race and teach him to run it to the best of his ability. One family comes to mind that truly epitomizes the "can do" attitude so important to a child's future. This family realized early on that they needed to set the bar high for their child, high enough so he and others were continually working at making progress and improvements. Yet they also knew that when he fell—for they realized that at times he would—they would always be there to pick him up, supporting him and each other as they learned and grew together. They were very realistic about their child, his strengths, his challenges, and his learning abilities. The thing they did that was the most impressive, however, is that they treated their child just as they did their other two kids. He was held accountable for his actions, expected to succeed to the best of his ability, applauded for his successes and loved in spite of his failures. They saw their son, not his autism. It's been years since I worked with that family, but I still remember the dad telling me: "Society is not going to change to accommodate my son's autism. But you know, our son can learn to "fit in" when he needs to, and to be himself where he can." They never, not even for a moment, thought their son "couldn't" or saw their son as anything other than capable. That attitude was the "magic" that allowed them to thrive as a family.

If you believe you can do it, you will. If you believe your child can do it, he will. If you believe your family can do it, you all will. Just believe.

HELPFUL BOOKS FOR PARENTS OF NEWLY DIAGNOSED CHILDREN WITH ASD

- *Children with Autism: A Parent's Guide* by Michael D. Powers

- *Asperger's Syndrome and Your Child: a Parent's Guide* by Michael D. Powers

- *Facing Autism: Giving Parents Reasons for Hope and Guidance for Help* by Lynn M. Hamilton

- *1001 Great Ideas for Teaching and Raising Children with Autism Spectrum Disorders* by Veronica Zysk and Ellen Notbohm

- *Ten Things Every Child With Autism Wishes You Knew* by Ellen Notbohm

- *Autism Spectrum Disorders from A to Z - Assessment, Diagnosis & More!* by Barbara T. Doyle M.S. and Emily Doyle Iland B.A.

- *Sometimes My Brother* by Angie Healy

- *The Effects of Autism on the Family* (Current Issues in Autism) by Eric Schopler (Editor), and Gary B. Mesibov (Editor)

- *Siblings of Children with Autism: A Guide for Families*, 2nd Edition by Sandra L. Harris

- *Supporting the Families of Children with Autism* by Peter Randall & Jonathan Parker

HELPFUL WEBSITES FOR PARENTS OF NEWLY DIAGNOSED CHILDREN WITH ASD

Autism Society of America
(news, information & referral, U.S. chapter network)
www.autism-society.org

**New Jersey Center for Outreach
and Services for the Autism Community**
(news, information & referral, services)
www.njcosac.org

Talk Autism
(news, information & inspiration)
www.talkautism.org

Future Horizons
(books & resources on ASD)
www.FHautism.com

Indiana Resource Center on Autism
(information, services, great articles)
www.irca.org

*"Parenting a child with autism is not a 'natural' occurrence.
If anything, you must 'unlearn' every bit of information you thought you
knew about parenting. I believe that once the diagnosis of autism has been
made, parent training should be a mandate. If I were told I could choose only
one 'treatment,' or given the opportunity to make one condition a mandate,
hands down, no contest, no questions asked, parent training would be the
only choice I'd make. Without a doubt, the parent training we continue to
actively obtain was (and still is) the greatest factor in our son's success."*

-DEB, PARENT OF CJ

chapter three

What is Early Intervention?

Dr. Jim: Hi Maureen. Hi Rob. You both look happy today! What's been going on?

Rob: I thought long and hard about the information you shared in our last session, especially about the assumptions I hold regarding the roles of "man" and "woman" when it comes to dealing with Mark's autism. I didn't like to admit it, but I saw myself in everything you described. Maureen and I have been having some heart-to-heart talks. This isn't easy sometimes, but we're slowly working our way through it. And, you know what? It's helping.

Maureen: It sure is! Rob and I may not have everything worked out—far from it—but I no longer feel we're at odds with each other, or that I'm going through this alone. Just talking about things—anything and everything we're feeling—is making such a difference. At first, we really got defensive with each other, which led to some unproductive arguments. But we made an effort to use some of the strategies you gave us, and it got better. We started listening to each other, rather than talking at each other. Adjusting to autism is hard enough by itself, but these conversations are somehow helping. I'm glad you were straight with us,

Dr. Jim. We may not have *wanted* to hear some of the things you said, but we *needed* to hear them, I guess. We both appreciate your candor.

Dr. Jim: At some time in the future, I'm going to remind both of you that you said that! I'm really glad you both are making an effort to face the reality of what's happening to Mark, yourselves, your marriage, and the family unit. The autism isn't going to go away, as much as you wish it would. This wish isn't going to disappear overnight—but it will fade a little every day, and one day you'll wake up and notice that it's gone. Many of the feelings you're experiencing right now may change over time. You might want to start keeping a journal. It can be very therapeutic to get your thoughts and feelings "out" in this way. And months and years from now, you'll be surprised to find how far you've come. There will be days or weeks when it doesn't seem as though any progress is occurring ... but when you read back through the journal, you will realize how far you and Mark have actually come.

Maureen: Hmm, that sounds like a good idea. Sometimes I need to vent my feelings—they're so overwhelming at times, it feels as though they are choking me, and I can't breathe. I used to cry to alleviate some of the pressure, but it's not the same anymore. It's like the feelings that made me cry have mutated into different feelings. They're more like unanswered questions running a million miles an hour in my brain than feelings of anger or loss or denial. And to be honest, while before my heart hurt, now I'm scared. Really scared down to my core about whether or not I can do this ... be the mom of a child with autism. Be tough enough, smart enough, loving and accepting enough. There are just so many questions about Mark's future, our future, how to help him, how to teach him ... they leave me spinning—almost disoriented.

Dr. Jim: Maureen, I know you feel overwhelmed, but it's actually a good sign that your feelings are changing as they are. It means you're starting to be able to separate *what you feel* from *what you need to do* to help your child. It's an important distinction, and one I'll probably remind you of often. You have a right to your feelings, whatever they are, good, bad, ugly, or indifferent. Rob does too. However, if you, as Mark's parents, want to be a strong, effective force in Mark's life, and help him as best you can, you'll need to be able to act in spite of your feelings. This is one of those "stand up and take notice" pieces of advice: *you can have your feelings, yet learn how to make good decisions and be effective in spite of them.*

Rob: I see where you're going with this, Dr. Jim, and being the "guy" I am, I like it! It's time for action, right? It sounds like you're telling us we're ready to start learning the nitty-gritty about how to deal with this autism, right? Stop talking and start doing?

Dr. Jim: Yes, Rob, that's where we're headed. In this session, I'm going to introduce you to early intervention programs and services. Then in the remaining sessions together, we'll talk about putting together a great team, we'll review existing autism programs that might be appropriate, and discuss how to put together the best possible program for Mark and your family. Let's go!

◎   ◎   ◎

What is Early Intervention?

"Early," as defined in *Webster's Dictionary* is: "near the beginning of a period of time." "Intervention" is defined as "to involve oneself in a situation so as to alter or hinder an action or development." This definition highlights the emphasis early intervention has had on the autism field in the past ten years. The overall goal of early intervention (EI) is to give very young children (birth to 36 months) a head start in closing developmental gaps that may have arisen because of a diagnosed disability or "at-risk" condition in their lives. EI enhances their overall development by teaching them skills that other kids their age acquire naturally. It was also created to teach the family effective ways to interact with the child and each other, and to provide targeted services that support this learning. With autism, in particular, it is vital that the family understand how to effectively deal with the child's inappropriate behaviors and encourage the child to use his or her communication systems.

Is early intervention a federal or a state program?

Actually, it's both. EI is a program mandated by the federal law called the Individuals with Disabilities Education Act (IDEA), reauthorized most recently in 2004. Early intervention services are described in Part C, The Program for Infants and Toddlers with Disabilities. IDEA contains other parts that govern the provision of special education services to school age children (Part B).

IDEA provides for a free and appropriate public education (FAPE), which is an important special education term for parents to know. At the heart of FAPE is the idea that the child's needs must drive the services provided, that they are free, and that educational progress is not just promised, but occurs. IDEA provides, at public expense, five specific functions that work together to assure this:

1. *Child Find:* identifying, locating, and evaluating all children with disabilities.

2. *Evaluation and Assessment:* tools used to determine the range and extent of specialized services the child needs in order for learning to occur.

3. *Service Coordination:* creation of a team that will plan out the programs and services based on the needs of the child, monitor progress, and make changes as required.

4. *Development and Review of the Individualized Family Service Plan (IFSP):* decision making based on individualized and appropriate goals and objectives that reflect the strengths and weaknesses of the child, including plans for transition to Part B services when the child turns three.

5. *Procedural Safeguards:* ensuring that decisions are data based and consistent with the IFSP.

The overarching purpose of Part C is to identify and treat young children who have a diagnosed disability or are at risk of developing one. Services address five developmental areas: physical, cognitive, communication, social or emotional, and adaptive.

Part C of IDEA operates as a federal grant program that provides funding to states to set up and administer EI programs and services. While the mandate for EI services originates at the federal level, states provide these programs, and as a result, definitions of eligibility and services offered can vary from state to state. However, two requirements govern all states offering EI programs: services are free of charge, no matter what the parents' income, and services are to be provided in "natural environments."

What are "natural environments"?

Since 1991, Congress has promoted the idea that early intervention should be family-centered—meaning services are to be provided to the child and the family within settings that capitalize on natural learning opportunities.

"To the maximum extent appropriate to the needs of the child, early intervention services must be provided in natural environments, including the home and community settings in which children without disabilities participate." (34 CFR §303.12 (b)).

Part C defines natural environments as "settings that are natural or normal for the child's age peers who have no disabilities." (34 CFR §303.18). What this means to you is that as much as possible, EI services are provided in settings that allow learning to occur within the family's daily routines and activities. At the heart of early intervention is helping you learn to work with your child within the common, everyday happenings of your life, as opposed to you taking the child to artificial "therapy" type settings for teaching to occur.

Does this mean EI services have to be provided in the home?

No. EI programs and services may occur in a variety of different settings where kids without disabilities participate, but are most often provided in the child's home. However, many states provide specialized programs and/or inclusive preschools that focus on developing play skills, social skills, and communication skills.

Federal law includes an exception for children who need services provided in more structured, formal settings: "the provision of early intervention services for any infant or toddler with a disability occurs in a setting other than a natural environment that is most appropriate, as determined by the parent and the individualized family service plan team, only when early intervention cannot be achieved satisfactorily for the infant or toddler in a natural environment." (20 USC § 1435 (a)(16)(B))

What's important for parents to glean here is this: 1) the exception must be agreed to by the parent and not forced upon parents by the child's EI team as the way they will provide EI services; and 2) settings that are not considered "natural environments" should be considered only when services have failed to be effectively provided in natural environments.

How does a child become eligible for EI services?

Typically, a child who is suspected of a disability is referred for EI services by either the child's doctor, a caregiver (e.g., a preschool teacher), or even by the parent. Every state's procedure is a little different and there's no consistency in what agency or agencies provide EI services. (See Appendix E – a list of each state, the Lead Agencies providing EI services, and their Program Coordinators.)

Professionals trained in early development evaluate the child to determine if he or she meets the state's definition of developmental delay (or a particular disability). Once the child is found eligible for EI services, an individualized assessment of the child is done to get a more accurate idea of the type and number of services the child requires. This assessment "intake" usually is done in the home. So first they determine eligibility for services. Then they assess what services are needed and how intensive they should be.

Once this information is gathered, the agency coordinating your "case" will create a formal, written plan, called the Individualized Family Service Plan (IFSP) under which services will be provided to the child and the family. Think of it as the contract for services. And usually a service coordinator is appointed who acts as your point person throughout the EI process.

Tell us more about the IFSP.

The IFSP is the vehicle through which EI services are provided. Parents are an integral part of creating this plan, and their ideas and goals, along with their family structure, family personality, and any cultural factors, should be taken into consideration when the IFSP is written. It documents and describes the extent of services to be provided to the child and the family, and the goals written into the IFSP will guide the team in determining how well existing services are resulting in learning and benefitting the child and family.

Once assessments of the child are completed, the individual services to be provided are discussed, agreed upon, and written into the IFSP. However, there are critical components that should be part of any intervention program included on the IFSP:

- intensity of engagement
- individualization of services for children and families
- family involvement
- systematic, planned teaching
- specialized curriculum
- objective measurements of progress
- opportunities for inclusion with typically developing peers in natural settings
- earliest possible start to intervention.

How important is parental participation in the EI process and the IFSP?

More than you probably imagine at this moment! One of the most important elements of IDEA, Part C, is parent participation. Parents are equal partners in formulating a plan to help the child. Congress was very clear in the legislation that parents are valued and integral in the special education process. This is especially true within Part C, which provides for services not just for the child, but for the family as well.

Early intervention is not just for the child; it focuses equally on parent and family education. *This is the only time during the child's life in which this is the case.* Once the child turns three, services become strictly child-focused. It can be a rude awakening to some parents who have been less involved during the EI process, thinking they have time "later." It's also an option not available to parents when children are diagnosed at a later age, after they turn three. Therefore, parents should grab every opportunity available during the EI process to learn strategies and procedures that can help the entire family adjust, learn and grow. It's a window of opportunity for the family that closes quickly.

Parents are vital decision makers in every aspect of their child's program. Under IDEA provisions parents can advocate effectively for their child, be part of the IFSP team and be made aware of everything being done for the child. While the legislation provides the mechanism for parents to be partners, the responsibility to do this falls squarely on your own shoulders. No one is going to come to your house and force you to learn about your child. The more effort you put into it, the more you'll get out of it and the more effective you'll be in the long run. Be proactive about asking for education, information, and training to help you learn how best to help your child. When you don't understand something, say so! Don't let opportunities to learn slide by because you're afraid of looking stupid. Autism is new territory for you both. Go into it with a high degree of curiosity and learn all you can. This will lay the foundation for advocating for appropriate services once the child moves into the public school setting.

What types of services can be provided through an EI program?

Services that address specific learning and developmental needs in the child can be provided, as well as services to help the family adjust to the diagnosis, learn about the child's autism and learn how to become effective parent-teachers. Various "coordination" services can also be provided. The list below outlines services specified in federal law; states can provide more services than these, but cannot provide less.

- Assistive technology devices and services
- Audiological services
- Speech and language services
- Occupational therapy
- Physical therapy, including sensorimotor work
- Vision and mobility services
- Psychological services, including parent and family counseling
- Nutrition services
- Special instruction
- Social work services, which includes social skills development in the child
- Family training, counseling, and home visits
- Health services necessary to benefit from other early intervention services
- Nursing services
- Medical services for Birth to Three diagnostic or evaluation purposes only
- Transportation or mileage reimbursement when necessary to receive other early intervention services
- Service coordination

Parents should keep in mind that while these services are decided at intake, they can be changed and adjusted as the child and family learn and grow. Service provision is not static; it should be flexible enough to accommodate the changing needs of the child and the family.

Furthermore, it is critical that all services the child requires be outlined in the IFSP in a very concrete way. For example, if the child requires Speech and Language Services, the document should address it with a statement something like this: Johnny will receive two 30-minute (equaling one hour) Speech and Language individual sessions per week. Note: Johnny is eligible for Speech and Language Services, services to be determined.

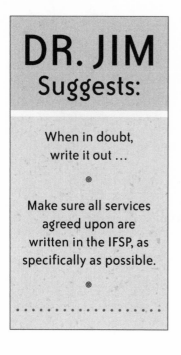

DR. JIM
Suggests:

When in doubt,
write it out ...

◎

Make sure all services
agreed upon are
written in the IFSP, as
specifically as possible.

◎

Since each state varies in the provision of services under IDEA, Part C, it is in parents' best interest to become familiar with this legislation and know their rights under the law. This is true for early intervention and even more so as children transition at three into public school programs. I don't want to sound alarming, but parents often find excellent early intervention programs in their area, only to encounter bitter disappointment when their child moves into public school programs, especially kindergarten and beyond. Be prepared. The best way to do this is to learn the law, know what services are available to the child and be a strong advocate for the child. That way you'll be prepared to handle a school with less-than-ideally trained teachers and/or inefficient programs for spectrum children.

Many states have departments with names like Division of Developmental Disabilities, Early Intervention Services, Division of Mental Health, or Division of Health and Human Services. These departments should have information that outlines the state's interpretation of early intervention services and, more importantly, who provides such services. The better informed you are, the better off your child will be.

You keep referring to age three. I thought early intervention continued through age five, or until the child enters kindergarten.

I'm glad you asked this question, because it is one of the most misunderstood aspects of early intervention. People generally think early intervention spans first diagnosis to age five. This age range makes sense when talking about early intervention from a developmental perspective. During these years children learn quickly, a great deal of development takes place, new skills are acquired and a great deal of intellectual growth happens. The child's mind is like a sponge, absorbing learning on a continual basis. However, from a "systems" perspective, Early Intervention is defined as first diagnosis to age three. Services and provisions available under Part C of IDEA cease at the time the child turns three. While the child continues to be eligible for services, they now fall under the provisions of Part B of IDEA, and are provided generally by the local school district. These services can vary tremendously within a state, from city to city, school district to school district and even from school to school within the same district. Again, it reinforces why parent education and knowledge of the law are so important.

Why is so much emphasis placed on Early Intervention if services are only available for these few short years?

It seems common sense, doesn't it, that we should help kids with special needs as early in their development as we can? Of course it does. But beyond this common sense approach, there are several practical reasons for the emphasis on early intervention.

1. The younger the child, the better able we are to close developmental gaps. Individuals with ASD or any other developmental disability don't "stop" learning once they turn three, but research suggests there exists a "window of opportunity" at the early ages where neurological brain paths are still growing and can be repaired, or new ones can be formed. It's called neuroplasticity. By enlarging the learning capacity of the child in this way, it provides greater opportunities over the entire life of the child.

2. The younger the child, the less ingrained are habits that detract from, rather than enhance learning. Young children are naturally curious about their environments. It's a perfect time to work with them before patterns of negative behavior set in too deeply.

3. Younger children do a majority of their learning through the medium of play and the years of diagnosis through three are natural times for them to acquire new skills while engaged in play in their natural

environments, i.e., at home with mom, dad or siblings, on the playground, in playgroups, in the community, etc.

4. The child can be the focal part of the intervention. EI services are meant to shine a spotlight on the child and be highly responsive to the child's needs. This is a time when the emphasis is on individualized instruction, one-on-one learning, rather than trying to help the child within the structure of a group lesson. This individual attention allows both parent and teacher to hone in on the needs of the child. Changes can be made quickly and easily. Furthermore, it helps the child better understand and respond to new expectations put upon him. For instance, prior to early intervention, everyone in the child's environment probably reacted to the child's behavior in a different way. That's understandable; no one knew about his autism or what to do in order to best help him. But stop and think how confusing this might have been to the child, and how this inconsistency would exacerbate his learning difficulties. With a consistent intervention plan, administered by knowledgeable professionals, coupled with training for the parents, the child has a much better chance of learning new skills in a shorter amount of time. Concentrated, focused teaching and learning opportunities are the hallmark of early intervention programs.

5. Very young children have few daily obligations. There is time for such concentrated learning to take place.

6. Children learn better in familiar, comfortable environments. What better setting for learning to occur than in the most natural environment of all—the home! And, by teaching a child within these natural learning settings, we have a leg up on teaching generalization of skills, right from the start. Consider this: up until the time a child is diagnosed, in all likelihood he had learned to manipulate his home environment to get his needs and wants met. No he didn't, you're saying? How about this example for those of you who think I must be kidding. What does your child do when he's hungry? Take your hand, lead you to the refrigerator or the cupboard, place your hand on the desired item and look up at you? Sound familiar? You may wish your son or daughter would make a request. But he's set up a

behavior action plan and you go along with it, right? Think about all the other times in the day when you find yourself going through the guessing game, trying to decipher what it is your child wants when there's no words or way for him to tell you. During intervention, the child will be required to communicate (verbally or nonverbally) what he or she wants prior to getting it. This will be very different—and uncomfortable at first—for the child. But the goal is to teach him to communicate, interact and become functional and independent. In the home setting, it's much easier. The child becomes more familiar with the new approach, more comfortable in learning new skills and begins to use these new skills more effectively. This sets up a positive cycle of learning and growing, which will give him the motivation to carry over his new skills to other environments.

Are there any documented research studies that support Early Intervention?

Yes and no. McEachin, Smith, & Lovaas conducted research in 1993 that concluded that 40 hours of intense applied behavioral analysis (ABA) therapy assists in the recovery from autism. Their study further qualified that the process needs to start early, and that direct instruction services be delivered by trained staff in a discrete trial format. This finding was later supported by the National Research Council in 2001. However, there are many critics of this individual approach, and there have been no studies conducted since that support the same claims.

Other research studies done on young children with ASD have focused on different program variables and how they play out in early intervention. One important variable is the intensity of engagement. Some studies suggest 40 hours per week of engagement, while others suggest that children may do just as well with fewer hours (as many as possible), provided a well-balanced approach is in place. All, however, point to the importance of direct engagement with the child as a condition for learning and success. Keep in mind though: What is important is how and how often you interact with your child with ASD, not the number of professionals who stream in and out of your house. They can help, but *you*, the child's parents, who interact with him or her 24/7, it is *you* who make the real difference for the child.

Another variable that has been addressed in research is the teacher-to-child ratio. Indications are that a small instructor/family member to child ratio is more effective, either 1:1 or a very small group. This actually dovetails with intensity of engagement. One-on-one instruction means the child gets individual attention, which permits highly responsive teaching and instruction. Children with ASD typically require lots and lots of practice to learn a new skill—much more than do their NT peers. The structure of the early intervention program allows for that naturally.

While research suggests this 1:1 approach works well, parents and EI specialists need to always keep in mind the need for generalization of skills, and find ways for the child to practice a new skill in different settings and with different people. Parents who are active partners in early intervention can easily provide for skill generalization by being involved in whatever activity is being taught. For example, if during an EIP session the professional introduces colors, either by identifying them or matching them, whenever possible during the day you should teach colors, too. When the child goes up to the couch, you can say, "What color is that?" Or pull out two color cards and say "match". Later in the day involve an older sibling in playtime to do color matching, like a game of "Ono," but change the rules to only match colors. Parents can teach all kinds of skills (waiting your turn, matching, colors, basic social interactions, simple one-step directions, etc.) in these naturalistic learning situations. Capitalize on these research findings about effective program strategies, but make them fit within your own family lifestyle and structure.

Aside from the common sense of providing early intervention, are there any other reasons that support the "earlier is better" approach to services?

Sure are—and they all have to do with money! It has been my experience that the earlier kids get involved in an effective program, the better the chance they will be able to transition into their regular neighborhood schools in an appropriate program once they are school age (five years old).

Money spent on early intervention services is money well spent. It reduces the overall cost of services for a child in later years. It's like the old Midas Muffler commercial, "Pay Me Now or Pay Me Later." The later services start, the wider is the gap between the child with ASD and his typical peers.

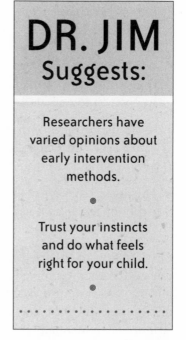

DR. JIM
Suggests:

Researchers have varied opinions about early intervention methods.

◎

Trust your instincts and do what feels right for your child.

◎

Because of budget concerns, kids in public school programs do not always receive the services that are considered most effective. They end up with the bare minimum required by law, and in many cases, even less than that. And because these kids receive less than what they need, it perpetuates their need for services and hence, compounds the cost of services over the child's lifetime. It's a vicious cycle and the child ends up on the short stack.

Most families initially do not know what services to ask for, or what their child really needs. They trust that the professionals involved with the child are there to make sure the child receives everything he needs. Sadly, that's not always true. In some states, the picture is really dismal. Parents who can advocate for services and explain the benefit of spending money on early intervention are often effective in obtaining needed services. So, play the money card!

Kid Source On-Line™ performed a literature search on the related costs of EI. Some of their findings follow.

- The Perry Preschool Project concluded that if they spent $3,000.00 for one year of preschool education for a child, they immediately began to recover that spending because the child did not require as intense special education services thereafter. They projected a lifetime savings of $10,798.

- Wood (1981) looked at the costs of special education services starting at birth, age 2, age 6, for students who required special education services the remainder of their school years. She concluded that the total education cost was less for students who received services earlier, rather than later, because again, they required fewer specialized services in later years. She calculated that the per-pupil cost of education was $37, 273 when services started at birth, as opposed to a per-pupil cost ranging from $46,816 to $53,340 when services were delayed to age 6. (And, this is in 1981 dollars; imagine the difference in costs in today's dollars!)

- In Tennessee, every dollar spent on EI services equated to a $7.00 return, primarily based on less need for residential treatment for severe behavioral students.

- During a three-year evaluation period, Colorado concluded they experienced a cost savings of $4.00 for every $1.00 spent on EI services.

On January 14, 2005, the Government Accountability Office (GAO) released a study on the costs of educating individuals with some type of autism spectrum disorder. The findings were interesting, to say the least, and suggest the vast financial resources that are being spent now, and will only exponentially grow as more children enter the school system.

> "Educating a student with ASD costs the Federal Government $18,800 per student. This exceeds the amount spent for the average special education student by $12,500. The Federal Government spends about $6,556 on educating regular education students."

NOTE: this figure does not take into account the amount states pay per student, meaning the costs are even higher. This is a clear case for putting an emphasis on early intervention programs, which significantly reduce the long-term costs of educating a student with ASD.

So, it seems the "theme" of this entire discussion is "family centeredness"—parents being indispensably involved in their child's early education and early programs. Is that right?

Absolutely! Family involvement is the glue and mortar of the EI program. And your choice of the word "indispensable" is spot on. You truly are indispensable in this part of the child's development. Parents need to be involved in every aspect of the program, be willing to work with the child so he gets the intensive engagement he needs, and take advantage of every service available so the child AND the family learn and grow together during these first years of intervention.

Each family will work this out a little differently, but it's of utmost importance to your child's success that you do so. It may mean one parent quits a job or works only part-time. It might mean changing the way you do things while the child learns basic social-cognitive and communication skills, or it might mean hiring some outside help to free up time to give the child the intensity of engagement he needs in order to learn basic skills. As parents, you need to make this happen. Sometimes outside counseling is helpful at this juncture to deal with the "negotiation" of wants versus needs that can be difficult to work through. There has to be balance—for the child, for mom, for dad, for the family unit, and for the marriage—if the program is to succeed. It's not always easy to do that alone. Emotions can stain perceptions a murky color, preventing parents from seeing the reality of the situation clearly. Get help if you need it.

The role of the family is by far the most important one in the whole EI process. As parents, you have a vested interest in the success of the child and, long term, have the most to gain from the child's success. You will be the most active participants. If you think it's the therapists who will be doing all the work, teaching the child skills needed for social and academic proficiency in later life, stop right now, and let's do a reality check. It's *YOU* who will be the primary teacher, the primary learning force in the child's life, the mover and shaker of the EI process. That's why it's so vital that the family stay connected, working in concert with each other. View the EI program as a "work in progress," an evolution of learning, flexible and responsive to the changing needs of the child and the family. Don't ever view it as a static, "because we made this choice we have to stick with it" operation. Consistency is good, but a consistently bad program is poison.

The Indiana Resource Center for Autism (IRCA) did a survey in their state on early intervention services. According to the parents who responded, the #1 "most effective practice" was Parent Training. Interestingly, only 21% of these same parents actually received such training. Make sure you receive the training you need. Make time for it; be emphatic about getting it. Don't let this be something you're "too busy" to get to. Knowledge is power, and you, your child, and your family will reap the benefits of this training for years to come.

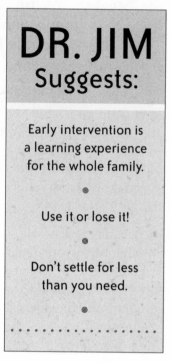

DR. JIM Suggests:

Early intervention is a learning experience for the whole family.

Use it or lose it!

Don't settle for less than you need.

Does EI provide all the services my child will need, or should I supplement the EI program with private services?

In an ideal world, all the services the child needs, or those that can benefit the family, would be provided through the EI program. But that's often not the reality. Some states are better purveyors of services than others, using their grant funding in more efficient and effective ways. In some cases, lack of in-depth knowledge of ASD on the part of professionals conducting the child's initial evaluations may mean that services your child needs are not being recommended or provided. There may be times when parent and IFSP team members disagree on what level of services are sufficient for the child, and the disagreement can't be resolved through negotiation. And some parents end up on waiting lists for services so long the child ages out of early intervention before they're even provided!

There are many reasons parents consider finding and funding private services. Just realize that if the team feels the child is receiving the services he needs through the EI program, these "extra" therapies will be your own financial responsibility. A great many families have the financial resources to provide these additional services. A great many families do not. There is no guarantee that "more is better," and parents need to try to maintain a balance between intervention services and letting the child just be a child. If you do decide to supplement the EI program with additional therapies, they should meet all the same criteria as do your existing services: they should be data-driven, have concrete goals and objectives, and be periodically evaluated to determine if they are working or not.

DR. JIM
Suggests:

Parent training is an indispensable component of your EI program. Grab all you can!

Many families who do not have the financial resources for extra services feel they are "bad parents" because they're not doing as much as are other parents. Don't fall into this negative rut. Remember, it's the "intensity of engagement" that results in success, not the therapy itself. And you can give that focused and meaningful engagement to your child. In the long run, an extra hour or two of attention by a trained therapist one day a week is not enough to dramatically change your child's life. It's the other 22 hours of the day, when you're spending time with your child, that's really the seat of learning. Don't lose sight of that.

What about time spent outside the home? Can EI services help us learn to be in the community with our spectrum child?

You raise a good point. It would be pretty dismal to contemplate being locked away by autism, spending all day, every day, for the next several years, at home with your child— doesn't it? No matter how much you love your son or daughter, they and you need to be out among other people, too. EI services can prepare you to handle the behaviors that may erupt in community settings, to recognize the warning signs of sensory overload, for instance, or know when you need to initiate Plan B (and know what that plan B will look like) rather than struggle with an existing situation. You're going to need to develop a bit of a thick skin, because handling some of these public situations will at first be difficult. The yelling and screaming tantrum in the middle of the grocery store on a busy morning or the out-of-nowhere shedding of your tot's t-shirt and shorts at the park (and absolute refusal to put the clothes back on) can be devastating for some parents. Have a few quips ready that you can rattle off to bystanders when this happens, and above all, don't let it get the best of you. Ask your behavior specialist to help you during your next session together. Little by little you'll learn to handle unexpected "surprises" and take them in stride.

What EI services will not do, however, is miraculously turn a child with ASD for whom the world is a strange and upsetting and perhaps even painful place to be, into a "normal" child again within a few months. I have witnessed parents who insist that the family maintain certain rituals and routines, and that the child with autism be included, well before early intervention has prepared any of them for the experience. He must go to church with the family every Sunday and sit quietly through the entire service. He must go to Aunt Julia's daughter's wedding and behave the entire time. Oh, the unrealistic expectations some parents place on their spectrum child! So listen up. If you have a child with sensory sensitivities and you insist on the family going together to a sensory-laden event like the circus "because you go every year," you're asking for trouble. Ditto for expecting the child to sit quietly during a 90-minute dinner out at a nice restaurant, to "behave" while you do your grocery shopping, despite his missed nap that afternoon, or to be able to control his own behaviors when you insert him into situations unsuited to his current level of functioning. Does this mean you'll never be able to go out as a family to your favorite restaurant ever again? Certainly not! But it might mean that for now, while your child learns functional behavior and communication skills, and you get better at spotting signs of impending disaster, you modify your routines. Be okay with leaving an event early. Have an exit strategy worked out before you even get to a new setting. Anticipate problems and plan around them. It's possible. Your EI therapists can teach you how to do it.

It's also important that you create structured opportunities for your child to be in situations where he or she can interact with typically developing children. The child's social skills aren't going to develop within the four walls of his room. Yes, you can teach him some of the foundation skills there, but "kid play" is highly spontaneous, filled with twists and change-ups. It's part of the learning process, and you want him to have ample opportunities to practice, practice, practice the social skills he's learning. There are many ways you can make this happen.

Play Dates
Set up times for your child and one or two other children to get together to engage in age-appropriate activities, with adult supervision. These "play dates" are more than just plopping kids down together while parents talk or head to the kitchen for coffee together. They need planning and definition to be successful. With a spectrum child, view play dates as a very structured time to teach, shape, and reinforce behaviors.

Sibling/Cousins Dates
If play dates with neighborhood kids are not possible, try the same idea with siblings or cousins instead.

Involvement in Community Activities
Try to get the child involved in as many community activities as tolerable (for both of you!). This might include gym activities, sports activities that are in keeping with his capabilities, "mommy/daddy and me" classes, etc. These are great opportunities for the child to participate in a structured activity not run by mom or dad. These are also appropriate times to introduce new skills to the child, such as requesting help from another adult, following directions from another adult,

and joint attention. Community activities also encourage generalization of skills learned in the home environment.

Community Outings

Plan regular community outings with the child: going to the park or the community pool, playing at the playground, visiting the zoo or the children's museum, or just going for a walk in the neighborhood. Practice skills the child is learning in the EI program. Be encouraging and offer a lot of praise. It is essential to give children with ASD multiple opportunities to practice emerging skills so they receive the associated "naturally occurring" reinforcement. Reinforcement is a topic we'll talk a lot more about in future sessions. It's not solely a "behavior modification," term as some people view it. It's a "life" response we all use (and want!).

I hate to say this, but it all sounds like so much WORK! I'm exhausted just thinking about everything you're suggesting I'm going to have to do. I don't think I can do it!

You're experiencing the fear and anxiety that every parent new to autism feels at this early juncture. Much of it is because you're unfamiliar with the strategies and techniques that will help you work with your child—you don't yet know what to do. You're unsure of yourself because of this lack of concrete information.

And I'll be honest with you. It DOES take a lot of time and energy on your part to put together and execute a good EI program for your child. The intensity and urgency that surrounds the EI process is often overwhelming. Do remember that at age three your child will be going into the local school system program, so there is light at the end of the tunnel. Do remember there are people who are here to help you, and you're not going through this alone. Do remember that the more you learn about ASD, the easier all this will be for you to handle. And do remember to take time for yourself. You'd be surprised how much a regular exercise program can help your energy level. How much better you can feel if you eat right and find ways to alleviate stress, like meditation, prayer, even sex! And, the biggest "do remember" of all for every mom and dad: your child is counting on you to do whatever is needed, and for you to be there for him. So is the rest of your family.

Let's close this session with some suggestions to think about until next time.

1. *Despite our emphasis on EI services, keep in mind that your child is a "child" first and that autism is only part of his make-up.*

(I know; you've heard this before, but it's *important*.) Autism doesn't account for everything that happens. A great deal of how the child develops may be due to maturity issues. Some of their behaviors may be just that—typical behaviors related to their age, not their autism. Child development during these early years shifts and changes quickly. Try to keep your child's unique personality in perspective and don't let his autism overshadow your ability to see him as your child, first and foremost.

2. *Autism is like a marathon; the course is a long one and you're going to need to learn to pace yourself.*

Attend to your own needs, be they physical, emotional, or spiritual. By doing so, you will be better able to concentrate on your child's needs. Take care of your family too. Without a solid family structure, the autism will pick away at each of you, and little by little erode your happiness and ability to remain focused and effective.

3. *Develop a plan and stick to it.*

Consistency is important for everyone, the child with autism and you, too. But don't let the plan become an albatross. When it's not working, find ways to get back on track.

4. *Keep the EI program family-centered and family-driven.*

That means you and the child's therapists should consider the child's needs as they play out within the day-to-day routines and patterns of your family. A program that asks you to dramatically change your normal style of living will be difficult to assimilate and feel good about. A therapist who insists that dad spend an hour each day in direct interaction with the child, while dad works two jobs back to back, is not creating a program that is sensitive to the family and its routines. Keep it real; keep it manageable.

5. Challenge yourself and your child.

Keep expectations high, yet reasonable. Remember, this will be the only time in your child's education that services will be this individualized, or where direct family involvement will be this integral to success. For some parents that's something of a relief: buckle down and provide as intensive a program as possible for a limited number of years. For others, especially those with larger families, it can be intimidating. Now is not the time to let your fears control you!. Push yourself; you can do it!

6. Take advantage of all the services you can from EI programs.

If your family is having difficulty accepting the diagnosis, take advantage of counseling or therapy services. If you need some basic education on effective behavior modification techniques, ask for it! If the child seems to have diet/nutrition deficiencies, or challenges with other physical issues like motor coordination or handwork (using scissors or holding crayons, for instance), seek those services in addition to what's being provided.

7. Watch and learn!

It may be tempting to run errands or do other things, like laundry or housecleaning, while the therapist is "in session" with your child, but don't. Be present, watch carefully how the therapist is working with your child and communicating with your child. An hour or two a week with the therapist is not nearly enough instruction for learning to occur in the child with ASD. Parents need to support this therapy with lots of further instruction between sessions. Learn from the experts helping you. That's why they're there!

8. Be curious and be creative when needed!

For instance, there may be times when you may not be able to stay in the room for therapy. Maybe the child tantrums when you are around or wants to be with you rather than do what the therapist is asking him to do. In those cases, the most effective way to stay connected is via a baby monitor. Set one up in the room when the therapy is taking place and listen in. You can also set up "distance learning" opportunities by video taping the session, using a web cam, etc.

9. Ask questions.

Lots of questions. About anything and everything—no matter how minor or silly it may seem. Your therapists are not mind-readers. Ask!

10. Involve siblings in the learning process.

Early intervention services can help NT brothers and sisters learn how to interact with the child with autism in effective ways. Kids are often glad to know more about autism and why their sibling acts the way he does. And they can be very effective teachers, not only in the home, but in social and community settings as well. Resist the urge to shelter your other kids from the autism experience. EI services can also provide much needed counseling to help siblings work through any difficult feelings they may be experiencing. Take advantage of these services.

Try with every ounce of your being to keep a life-giving, life-supporting and life-sustaining "can do" attitude alive. Be a can-do family. I can't offer this bit of advice often enough. Your own attitude and that of your other family members will affect whether you view autism as an adventure or a battle, something you can embrace or an experience that involves winners and losers.

Your attitude may not seem all that important at this point in your journey through autism, but it is. It's the #1 deciding factor for future success. It's the "magic bullet" you want so desperately to find. Families spend years looking outside themselves for the "one thing"—the one professional, the one program, the one intervention method that will make autism go away or at least become somehow "acceptable." You'll never find it outside yourself. It's inside; it's your attitude towards autism. And when your child is of a certain age, it'll be his or her attitude towards autism also. Attitude is the master key that will unlock doors for your child and your family today, tomorrow, next month, next year, a decade from now.

Human beings, by changing the inner attitudes of their minds,
can change the outer aspects of their lives.

—WILLIAM JAMES

"Early intervention gives a child the best chance for a positive outcome,
and has a positive impact on the family system. A child with a disability
places enormous stress on a family. This increased stress comes at a time
when strong coping strategies are needed to deal with the challenges the
disability presents. Early intervention programs can provide families with
the information, skills and support they need to successfully balance the
needs of their disabled child with those of the family."

—BARBARA MARKELL,
VP, CHIEF SCHOOL ADMINISTRATOR, YCS, NEWARK, NJ

chapter four

Building Your Dream Team

ROB AND MAUREEN ATTENDED THEIR FIRST EARLY INTERVENTION TEAM MEETING earlier today. Like most parents, they arrived at the meeting filled with fear and trepidation, not knowing any of the professionals in the room, or what would transpire during the meeting. I noticed how tightly Maureen clutched Rob's hand while we talked. They were great listeners, but their silence told me that everything was just too new to take in. Lots of head nodding, not very many questions. I'm sure their regular session with me should be interesting! Here they are.

Rob: Dr. Jim, I've been in hundreds of business meetings negotiating all sorts of business deals, but I have to tell you, this two-hour early intervention meeting has left me feeling dumber than a stump.

Maureen: Everything is so new. I didn't understand half the terms people were using, let alone follow the treatment recommendations everyone so easily seemed to agree on for Mark. It all felt so clinical, like Mark was a case study rather than a living, breathing child.

Rob: I've got this document now—what am I supposed to do with it? Is it a contract? I signed it—what if I don't like it once I've had a chance to absorb everything it says?

Maureen: They proposed all these therapy sessions, and I think we've got people—not people, strangers—coming into our house next week and I don't have any idea what they're going to do, or what we should be doing to prepare ourselves.

Rob: Am I supposed to be there? What about my work? Do they think I can just rearrange my clients to make room for this therapy?

Maureen: The house is such a mess. When will I find time to clean? There's a pile of laundry in the bedroom. Do they expect lunch?

Dr. Jim: WHOA! Slow down you two! The first IFSP meeting is overwhelming, I know. You're eager and anxious, and scared down to your bones. It's your first look at the people who will be working with your child. All the professionals in one room, across the table; it's intimidating. I'm sure at least half of what was discussed is a blur right now—that's not because you're dumb, it's a natural reaction when so much of what you're hearing is new. Confusing terms, services you've never encountered before, "program talk"—it'll get easier as time goes by. Trust that. You'll learn as you go along.

Maureen: I know it's all so new, and that right now, what I'm feeling is a reaction to being in unfamiliar territory, so to speak. But ... but ... I'm not sure I liked some of what was being said and how people were acting. I'm not sure I want some of those people in my home.

Dr. Jim: Your early intervention team is just that—a team. It's a group of people brought together with one common goal: to work with Mark, you, and Rob, to form a foundation of teaching and learning that includes basic functional skills for him, and autism education for you both. The team is your ally, and you both are important parts of the team. Team members each bring different skills to the lineup. We've assembled this unit based on our professional expertise in ASD and what we think is best for Mark at this point. Right now, you need to trust what we're doing and see how it goes. Give it a chance to work. Let's talk more about your "dream team" in today's session and the role they play in early intervention. Perhaps once you have more concrete information about who's involved and how you all fit together, you'll feel a little better.

◎　　　◎　　　◎

Where does the early intervention team come from— what agency handles this?

Each state has a State Interagency Coordinating Council (SICC) that bears the overall responsibility for early intervention services. The federal law, IDEA, describes the function of the ICC: to "advise and assist the lead agency in the performance of the responsibilities set forth in Section 635(a)(10) of the Individuals with Disabilities Education Act, particularly the identification of the sources of fiscal and other support for services for early intervention programs, assignment of financial responsibility to the appropriate agency, and the promotion of the interagency agreements...." Different agencies scattered across the state provide the pool of individual professionals and services, with the SICC handling all the financial and programmatic coordination.

Who chooses and assembles the early intervention team?

Once you qualify for EI services, you are assigned one person, often referred to as your family services program coordinator, who acts as "manager" of your program. This person works with the state coordinator to assemble the team. Selection of team members should be based on the strengths and weaknesses of the child and the scope of services needed by the child and the family.

How often does/should a team meet?

In the beginning, the team should meet weekly. Once the program is up and running, the team can decide on the frequency of further meetings. There's no set rule about this. It should be based on the needs of the child and the family.

Does this team generate the IFSP?

Yes, the team will develop the IFSP with input from a variety of sources (e.g., evaluations, assessments, and other documentation). Some of the professionals on the team are the same people who conducted the many assessments done on your child to determine his level of impairment and level of need.

Once the team is selected, is it a "fixed" entity?

No. The IFSP team should be an evolving, responsive group that changes as your child's needs change. Professionals who offer very specific services may leave if their participation is no longer needed, and new professionals may join the team.

Can a parent reject a team member?

Within the confines of the group, the parent is considered an equal partner and will have every opportunity to shape the team. But only the team as a whole can accept or reject a member. Everyone can offer opinions and bring information to the table for consideration, but major decisions like this are group-based.

Do all team members attend every meeting?

The team does not always have to meet as a whole. There can be mini-meetings, certain professionals who come together to discuss a particular aspect of the program. For example, if a language issue needs discussing, the child's speech therapist should be present but the occupational therapist (OT) may not be needed. However, it is critical that there be a reliable flow of information among all team members, so everyone on the team is aware of the goings-on of other team participants. Subsequent meetings can get bogged down with information updates without this communication flow. This compromises the team's effectiveness.

What types of professionals comprise the IFSP team?

The team should be comprised of individuals knowledgeable about autism spectrum disorders, and skilled in areas relevant to your child's needs. Your dream team can include:

- Early Intervention Specialist (from the SICC)
- Your IFSP coordinator
- Education specialist

- Behavior specialist
- Occupational Therapist
- Physical Therapist
- Speech and Language Therapist
- Social Worker
- Medical Professional (e.g., a Developmental Pediatrician, Neurologist, Vision specialist, Nutritionist or Biomedical expert)
- Psychologist
- Parents or Guardians

The team doesn't have to include all of these people, and there may be people not listed above who join the team from time to time. For instance, if the team decides on a particular method of intervention, a specialist in that method may become part of the team.

So, more is better? The more people on my child's team, the better his opportunity to grow and learn? The more services he gets?

Not necessarily. It's a slippery slope to navigate when you lock yourself into that type of thinking, and I'd caution against it. Some parents live in larger metropolitan areas where many autism professionals are available to provide EI services. Other parents live in states or areas within a state with few qualified professionals. Your dream team can consist of just three people, if those three people are the right people.

Over the years, I've noticed that the most effective teams were comprised of members who possessed certain personality traits. Look for team members who have the following qualities:

Knowledgeable about Autism

This is a "must have" for the EI team. Autism is such a unique disability, the professionals responsible for program development must have a solid, working understanding of the disability in order to develop any kind of effective program.

Very Reliable

Ability to carry through on assignments, be at scheduled sessions and be consistent in the application of expected instruction and services.

An Effective Communicator

Willing and able to say what needs to be said in a concise manner, while respecting the opinions of others.

An Active Listener

Ability to absorb others' thoughts and ideas without becoming defensive or argumentative.

An Engaged Participant

Stays the course through times when teaching is easy and especially during times when teaching is difficult; maintains a "can-do" attitude; is an active participant at meetings, with the family and the child.

Shares Information Freely

Keeps everyone informed about how the child is doing in their area of expertise, especially when team members are absent from meetings, or after a mini-meeting; freely shares new knowledge gained through experience or training opportunities.

Open-Door Attitude

Is available when needed to help the family; knows when to step in with advice and/or constructive criticism and when to take a "wait and see" approach.

Very Flexible

Ability to compromise with little or no stress when needed; does not get stuck in their own point of view; can evaluate both pros and cons of a situation; resists "this is the way we always do it" thinking patterns; can think "outside the box" when something isn't working.

A Problem-Solver

Ability to openly discuss problems and offer action-oriented ideas to overcome any obstacle; focused on solutions rather than blame or fault-finding.

Respectful and Supportive

Ability to maintain a professional attitude in all situations; understands the value of a sense of humor.

Committed to the Team

Ability to stay focused on the reason the team was created: the success of the child with ASD.

Do you mean, literally, that the EI team can be only three people?

Sure do, and sure don't. It all depends on the child's needs, which should *always* be the driving force in the selection of the team and the services provided. In most cases, the EI team will not consist of all the people mentioned above. Sometimes the team is small, just a core group of people: the child's parents/guardians, the Early Intervention Specialist and one or two providers. Most children need help with language/communication, behavior, sensory issues and social skills, at least part of the time. These professionals are typically part of the team, though not always. It might be just the SLP, or the SLP and the OT.

Who makes decisions about how the program is going—or not going?

The IFSP team, as a whole, is responsible for determining the effectiveness of a program. Input from all members of the team is important in evaluating whether or not a program or particular strategy is working. Since therapists may spend only a few hours a week with a child, it is vitally important for parents to bring concerns, observations and questions to the meeting. These should be presented in as objective a manner as possible. For instance, a parent who insists, "This program just isn't working!" is not providing the team with information that can help them assess the program. A parent who comes to the meeting with specific, documented descriptions will be giving the team better information on which to base a decision. "When I use the XYZ technique you suggested, Mark reacts with a temper tantrum four out of five times."

What do I do if a therapist isn't doing her job the way I think she should? I've heard some horror stories from other parents about therapists calling to reschedule again and again, arriving late for sessions or cutting them short, or not showing up at all!

Communication is key. If you are unsure why a therapist is working with your child in a certain way, speak up and ask questions. If the therapist is demonstrating unreliable behavior, talk with him or her about it early on and see if there's some reason. Don't wait until you're so angry you can't think straight. If a problem persists, or if at any time a therapist is not treating you or your child with respect and professionalism, contact your IFSP coordinator and discuss your concerns.

The team recommends a certain expert (e.g., biomedical, behavior specialists, etc.) but there's not one available in our area who is knowledgeable about ASD or can meet my child's needs. What options do I have?

Your first option is to go with the person you feel understands your child the most, even though they may not have a great deal of experience with children with autism. Their intimate understanding of your child will offer valuable information to the team. Your second option is to be present to share critical information about your child and autism during the evaluation process. Detailed information you provide may influence the team's response. For instance, they may decide they need to find an out-of-state professional to consult, if the need is greater than the team suspected. Or, upon hearing information you share, the team may have new recommendations that can address the same issue. A third option, one always present, is that the family seek out the expert privately, using their own financial resources. This option may not be realistic for all families, depending on their financial situation.

Our state is in dire need of autism professionals; the shortage has created long waiting lists for EI services. My coordinator told me the money is available, but not the professionals. What do I do now? Can I find team members on my own?

The best in-home program assistants I have encountered are college or high school students. Visit your local schools and meet with their special education department (college) or the guidance counselor's office and describe what you are looking for and what the timeline is for your program. You'll often find eager and willing participants. These individuals can be trained by the EIP professionals or by you, if you have been trained (which you should be—immediately—if you haven't). Keep in mind that these individuals usually have pretty full schedules already. Make sure you set up a schedule and stick to it and have "subs" if need be, so if something comes up with a certain worker, you have a standby.

Are there any general "guidelines" that turn a team into a "dream team"?

Parents often come to the EI process expecting to find a perfect team gathered together, that works in harmony and collectively creates a perfect program for the child. That isn't reality; it's fantasy. In real life, the team is a group of people with different personalities, different work ethics, different levels of professional and personal expertise, and different ways of communicating. Parents sometimes look at EI service providers as the "saviors" of their family and child. But to the professionals, this is a job. I bring this up because often team members fail to establish "common ground" among themselves so they can function as a unit and be productive for the child. Without common ground, the team often feels disjointed, and this can curtail progress in the group and the family.

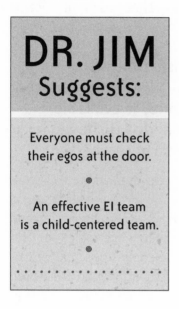

DR. JIM
Suggests:

Everyone must check
their egos at the door.

◎

An effective EI team
is a child-centered team.

◎

There are several essential characteristics that contribute to a productive team, but I think first and foremost it's this: *everyone must check their egos at the door.* An effective EI team is a child-centered team, no question about it. The group must do what is in that child's best interest. A few years ago I attended a meeting where Mom brought up some very valid questions about what type of curriculum/teaching method was most appropriate for her child, who didn't seem to be making the progress he should. The team leader, a professional, dismissed Mom's questions by saying, "This is the type of curriculum/teaching method we provide and if you don't like it, then perhaps you need to look for another service provider." She went on to say, "And by the way, we think he is progressing, you just don't because he's your child." Mom was noticeably taken aback by the response to her questions and it was evident from her face she felt stuck. This was the only program available to her child and if no one at that meeting had said anything, I'm sure she would have just accepted the answer.

I spoke up and asked the team leader if there was a way to explore some new options, take data on them and if they didn't work, then continue with the existing program. I didn't suggest we change the entire program, just take a couple of the objectives and teach them differently. The team leader said, "I guess we can take two and look at them." We developed a timeline to reassess the two objectives and decide whether to continue the new way and add in additional objectives or go back to the old way. By staying child-focused and discussing concerns in language such as "this child needs" rather than "I want" or "this is what we do," discussions can often be guided in a positive direction. When egos rear their ugly heads—meaning that you start hearing "I want" or "I think" or "you don't" type of language—work hard to bring the focus back to the child, his strengths and challenges, and reemphasize the need to stay flexible and child-centered.

This attitude adjustment applies to parents as well as to professionals. I have also been in meetings where Mom is unreasonable in her criticism of the service the child was receiving and not willing to budge on what she wanted. Everyone must be flexible and able to cooperate in order to work in the best interests of the child. Notice I did not say compromise. I don't feel anyone should have to compromise—meaning give up something that is valuable and meaningful—especially when it comes to sound judgments. Early intervention programs have a short time-frame. For many children, home-based EI services last a year or less. Therefore, professionals and parents must learn ways to cooperate without compromising. Otherwise, the child and family lose out.

There also needs to be a healthy level of respect for what each member brings to the team. There will be discussions and, while the group must reach consensus, that doesn't mean it will be without some disagreements beforehand. It's critical that everyone be able to keep personal emotions in check, especially Mom and Dad. Disagreements should never be taken personally. This only leads to a breakdown of trust, which results in a very dysfunctional team.

Professionals need to keep in mind the emotional toll that autism can take on a family, especially one with a child newly diagnosed. Outbursts or unrealistic demands often arise from a parent's unresolved feelings. I had a meeting with a family who brought with them a legal pad full of changes that "must" take place for their child to be successful. I listened to the first five, one being that the temperature of the room had to be a constant 72 degrees or the child would be distracted. My experience told me that a majority of their program issues were masking a deeper, unresolved emotional issue, so I asked them to leave the list so I could go through it and consider how best to adapt the program. And then, we began to just talk. What came out over the next hour was the anger they were feeling over their child's diagnosis and wondering "Why us?" Their list of demands arose out of that anger, not because they believed every change was needed in order for the child to learn and grow. As team members we need to listen to what is being said, and sometime "hear" past the emotions and probe deeper. Oftentimes the problem has nothing to do with the child's program.

As a whole, an effective team is a fluid entity. It must always have the opportunity to evolve and change over time, mirroring the changes in the child. The early intervention years are times when learning occurs in leaps and bounds. If the group gets static, the child will suffer. And because learning is often so rapid, ongoing reassessment is critical and should be discussed every time the team meets. Does the program meet this child's needs today, and if not, what changes need to be made so it will? As the child masters skills, the team will naturally make changes in goals and objectives. This same flexible mentality applies to the team: is the makeup of the team sufficient? Do we need to add new members, or is it time for other members to leave? As a team, are we moving in the right direction?

Your perfect EI program consists of a great many things. The IFSP is the roadmap to the child's learning and the IFSP team is the driving force behind it. Neither can exist without the other. Everyone involved in the program, parents and professionals equally, must have a vested interest in the success of the child. *It must be child-focused.* The program must also teach and expand the skill-set of the child's parents and significant others (family, siblings) to maximize the child's "level of engagement." *It must be family-focused.* Your team makes this happen.

Early intervention consists of a community of people who work collectively to provide opportunities for the child to learn, grow, and reach his or her potential. It all starts with the team.

> *"Nothing could have prepared me for the journey I would embark on after receiving a diagnosis of PDD-NOS and then later autism for my son Brandon at age two. As overwhelming and confusing as the diagnosis was in those early days and continues to be at times, one message was clear— early intervention was critical.*
>
> *The early weeks were emotionally draining for Brandon and our family. He was very resistant to the intrusion into his world. At times, two therapists would work with him to gain his attention and compliance— one prompting verbally while the other would model*

the prompt hand over hand. It took upwards of ten sessions to get Brandon to imitate "tap the table." But when he did, smiles emerged through his tears while responding to the praise. Soon thereafter, I witnessed Brandon imitating a friend pretend sleeping. The work was getting through, increasing Brandon's attention span and teaching Brandon how to learn through watching others and imitation. Brandon's brain didn't come hardwired with an infrastructure conducive for learning, but the strategies we were using were providing the building blocks of learning on a cognitive level.

Today, Brandon attends the local elementary school where he receives both special and regular education with supports. He just participated in the fifth grade play singing three ensemble numbers and handling the backstage curtain assignment.

It's during moments like these that I reflect on the many loving, dedicated professionals as well as family members and friends who have made all the difference in Brandon's life. When tackling the complexity of autism, families cannot do it alone. For me, the journey started with embracing the diagnosis, however difficult that was, taking the opportunity to educate myself and those around Brandon and then putting a plan into action.

I feel blessed that Brandon's early intervention experience has been so positive and effective, but more blessed with the child I have been given. He is a superstar and continues to shine every day of his life. I bask in his afterglow, not taking one minute of the miracle that is his daily achievements for granted."

-LEIGH, PARENT OF BRANDON

chapter five

Assessment:
A Picture of Your Child's
Strengths and Challenges

Rob: Before we wrap up this session today, I have some questions about the clinical reports discussed during our IFSP meeting. The team referred to them often and seemed to base many of their decisions about Mark's service needs on these reports.

Maureen: You know, Rob, we received a copy of all those reports in the mail before the meeting and I showed them to you—remember? Honestly though, it's a whole lot of unfamiliar "doctor speak" for us to wade through, and very intimidating. Every page reads like Greek to us. I'm sure they're important and all, but it would have been nice if someone had explained what they are, and why they are so important, and told us what they said in plain English. Maybe you can give us an overview so at least we have some general idea of what's going on?

Dr. Jim: You two are absolutely right! Sometimes we professionals who attend EI meetings on a daily basis drop the ball in giving parents the concrete information they need to understand the workings of the first

IFSP meeting. These assessment reports are very important tools, too, and we were remiss in not taking the time to explain them to you. I'm very glad you asked about it! Let's dive right into talking about assessment and the evaluations we use.

◎ ◎ ◎

What is "assessment"?

Assessment and diagnosis are two distinct terms used pretty loosely within the disability community. This often creates confusion for parents, especially once children move out of early intervention and into public school programs.

The process of "diagnosis" generally occurs when a child is suspected of having a disability or a medical condition. A trained professional observes the child, conducts tests, etc., in order to determine if the child's characteristics meet the symptoms associated with a particular condition. The end result is the label, for instance, autism or Asperger's Syndrome or the flu or chronic dermatitis. I usually associate the word diagnosis with "medical." The diagnosis of an ASD is the broad arena in which the stage is set to pursue the most appropriate services.

"Assessment" on the other hand, sets the ground rules for what needs to be done. I associate the word "services" with assessment. Assessment is the process of evaluating a child's strengths and weaknesses, usually to determine if they meet the criteria for services, but also for diagnosis. It provides a picture of the child's level of functioning at a particular point in time. Assessment results give us a baseline of the child's skill-sets in a variety of areas. This information is useful in deciding what services the child needs and how intensive those services should be.

It's important for parents to understand this: a child can be diagnosed with a disability, yet not meet eligibility criteria for services. This happens more often with children who are on the higher-functioning end of the spectrum, and this distinction will be more relevant when the child moves into public school programs than it is with early intervention.

Why are assessments so important?

Quality assessments should be the driving force behind services agreed upon for a child. As we've mentioned, autism is a spectrum disorder and no two children manifest the same set of symptoms in the same combination of severity. Therefore, there's no "one size fits all" approach to setting up a treatment plan. Professionals and parents need a starting point—tools they can use to measure areas in which the child excels and areas in which his skills are impaired. Assessments are those measurement tools. Beware of any group of professionals who want to recommend a plan of action for your child that is not based on assessment data. Comments such as "This is what we do for all kids with autism" or "This is our autism program, take it or leave it" are red flags to parents that professionals are not properly evaluating the needs of a child and creating child-centered programs based on individual needs.

Are there good and bad assessments?

Yes and no. Formal assessment tools—tests—are available for professionals to use. Some are autism specific; many are not, and not all should be used with spectrum children. They each have their pros and cons, especially those tools not designed specifically for use with children with ASD. Furthermore, some assessment instruments require quite a bit of training before they can be administered properly. What this all means is that the outcome of an assessment is partly driven by two things: 1) the level of autism expertise of the professional conducting the assessment and 2) whether or not the assessment tool is well matched to the child. For instance, some non-language assessment instruments rely heavily on verbal questions and verbal responses. Or the language level of the test may be too high for the child. A child who is challenged in this area may "test" poorly and the results won't truly reflect the child's abilities.

Well-trained professionals with a solid knowledge of ASD are better equipped to assess a spectrum child than is someone unfamiliar with the disorder and how its characteristics manifest in children. An autism professional will understand how to adapt assessment questions or

101

activities as needed, use language the child understands, or meaning-ful reinforcers, and be able to gauge which tests are appropriate or not for use with a particular child. The goal of a good assessment is not just to identify areas of weakness, but to also identify areas of strength. We want as complete a picture of the child as possible.

Initial assessments, like those done in preparation for creating the IFSP, should also collect data and information from a variety of different sources, not just formalized tests, to get a true picture of the child. This includes child observation and parental interviews. It's especially important to take into account information and insight the family can bring to the table. Parents offer a wealth of "real-life" information about the young child, information that may not be gained from a formalized test. "Good" assessments will gather information about the child from several different sources.

How often are assessments conducted?

Great question! A common misconception is that assessment is done once to set up the program. Actually, assessment is an ongoing process. It is not one or two events, but an ongoing information-gathering tool. Initial assessments are done so professionals have baseline data on the child. These assessments should be conducted in all areas of suspect-ed need, as appropriate to the child. As the child begins to learn and skills change, assessments can be redone, or new assessment tools used when problems of a different nature pop up.

What kind of information is provided by an assessment?

A professional conducting an assessment in a particular area of need—for instance, communication—will generally write up his findings in a report. The report will include test scores combined with narrative inter-pretations of the data. A good assessment will offer highly useful information about the child, describing areas of need in specific detail. Ideally, parents and service providers look for the assessment to also include treatment recommendations. Some assessment reports are better

DR. JIM Suggests:

Assessment is not one or two events.

◉

It is an ongoing information-gathering tool that should drive program decisions.

◉

than others when it comes to offering information about the types of services that will help the child, and the extent of services needed. Again, the more autism-savvy the professional conducting the assessment, the better the data interpretation will be.

Assessments used in formulating the IFSP often include a wide array of information that must be reviewed and evaluated by the team to determine service needs for the child. Again, this is why specific knowledge of ASD is invaluable. Without such knowledge the team may misinterpret assessment findings or not recognize important aspects of testing that are pivotal to learning and then plan accordingly. Team members who take attitudes such as "from my years of experience" or "I don't think any child needs that service" or those who disregard assessment data in favor of personal opinions are not going to be helpful in determining the best program or placement. While it is important to make sure the assessment is relevant and appropriate for the child, it is equally important to keep some level of objectivity in reviewing assessment results. Egos and personal bias do not belong in program planning meetings. The best assessment reports start out with interpreting the test results and providing a global picture of the child, and conclude with specific, concrete recommendations that can be easily turned into objectives in the IFSP.

Are some areas more important to assess at first than others?

Most children with ASD exhibit greater or lesser challenges in the area of communication. I always recommend communication be tackled first because it affects all other areas of functioning (e.g., behavior, social skills, etc.) where the child may also have difficulty. Many "behavior" issues stem from an inability to communicate. Notice I didn't say language. Communication involves far more than the spoken word. It is a vast system of nonverbal and verbal means of sharing our wants, needs, thoughts and feelings with others, which may include verbal language, verbal approximations, picture cards, sign language, gestures, and/or other vocalizations. A child without a functional communication system will exhibit problems in many other areas of functioning.

Are there specific assessment tools that are widely used with children with ASD?

In my years of assessing young children with ASD, I have found that two formal instruments consistently return relevant and meaningful information about the child. These tools assess developmental levels, identify areas of strengths and weaknesses and specific deficit areas, as well as provide concrete information to develop goals and objectives on the IFSP. I therefore consider these two assessments critical for a child with a diagnosis of autism.

The Psychoeducational Profile Revised (PEP-R)

The PEP-R is an excellent assessment tool for preschoolers with autism in that it assists in developing a clearer picture of the functioning level of the child. The PEP-R separates out the "splinter skills" that sometimes accompany children with autism. Children with autism tend to score very high in some areas and very low in other areas. For example, a child may score above age level in fine motor skills and cognitive skills, but score very low in gross motor skills and social skills. Tests that result in a "composite score" can be misleading. With the PEP-R, because the profile results look scattered, it shows a more accurate picture of the child's different areas of strength and weakness. Also, a majority of the answers are nonverbal, which renders a more accurate score. Based on the inability of a great many children with autism to verbally articulate their thoughts and feelings, the PEP-R makes use of a primary area of strength for a spectrum child: receptive language skills.

The specific areas assessed by the PEP-R are: Imitation, Perception, Fine Motor, Gross Motor, Eye-Hand Integration, Cognitive Performance, and

Cognitive Verbal areas. The PEP-R also identifies degrees of behavioral abnormality in Relating and Affect (cooperation and human interest), Play and Interest in Materials, Sensory Responses, and Language. The PEP-R scores the child based on typical development and takes into account the atypical behaviors children with autism often display. It is a good "road map" assessment to generate appropriate goals and objectives for the learner with autism.

The Assessment of Basic Language and Learning Skills (ABLLS)

The ABLLS is an excellent assessment instrument for several reasons. Not only is it an assessment tool, it is also a curriculum guide and a skills tracking system to monitor progress in the child. Furthermore, it focuses on various aspects of communication aside from spoken language, it is comprehensive in the areas it covers, and once the evaluation is completed, it interprets the data in a way that aids in developing an appropriate curriculum for the child. The ABLLS assesses the following areas:

- Cooperation and Reinforcer Effectiveness
- Visual Performance
- Receptive Language
- Imitation
- Vocal Imitation
- Requests
- Labeling
- Intraverbals
- Spontaneous Vocalizations
- Syntax and Grammar
- Play and Leisure
- Social Interaction
- Group Instruction
- Following Classroom Routines
- Generalized Responding

- Reading Skills
- Math Skills
- Writing Skills
- Spelling
- Dressing Skills
- Eating Skills
- Grooming
- Toileting Skills
- Gross Motor Skills
- Fine Motor Skills

The ABLLS is based on B.F. Skinner's work in the area of verbal behavior. The instrument enables professionals to track, through data collection, the progress of the child over time. It concentrates on everyday skills needed in order to communicate successfully with others, and therefore allows the child to learn from everyday activities. From the assessment results, professionals and parents together can develop effective goals and objectives, establish a baseline (the child's skill starting point), and evaluate the selected therapy strategies.

Are there other "informal" assessment tools helpful in designing an appropriate EI program for a child?

In addition to standardized assessments, the *Parent Interview* is another extremely important part of the overall assessment process. As previously mentioned, most children with autism do not test well. This makes it very difficult to truly assess their overall functioning level, especially when they're young and placed in unfamiliar situations, like the testing environment. A parent interview helps fill in the gaps that the assessments sometimes miss or do not report accurately.

Parent interviews can be designed in a variety of ways, can be written or verbal, occur in the home or a provider's office, and be short or long. No matter how they are created, they should provide opportunity for parents to share information about the child and his behaviors, interests, challenges and joys. The following questions would be helpful to ask parents in relation to their child and the child's actions in the most comfortable environment, the home.

- What are your child's strengths?
- What would you like to see your child do more of?
- How does she/he communicate?
- How does your child display displeasure?
- How does she/he interact with others in the family?
- What type of behaviors does she/he display?
- What activities seem most enjoyable to the child?
- How engaged is the child during social times with family?
- Describe the child's play skills.
- Is there anything unusual about the child that really stands out?
- How does your child react to changes in routine?

These questions are not an exhaustive list, merely a starting point to begin a dialogue with the family about their child.

The data gleaned from the parent interview is the most important information when it comes to creating a child-focused, family-focused EI program. Since most EI services occur in "natural environments," and most often that's the home, a parent interview conducted in the home gives the professional the best possible opportunity to gather essential program information. It's a first-hand look, an opportunity to learn about the parents' perspectives toward the child and autism and their expectations of treatment outcomes, evaluate the amount and type of parent training that might be needed, and gather information about daily routines and family life within which services will be provided. Parents have a "gut" reaction to their children and have a sixth sense about what their kids know and don't know. Even though this type of information is not "clinical," it is, nonetheless, equally valid in designing a treatment program and should not be discounted or disregarded in evaluating assessment findings.

Child Observation

Equally important in the overall assessment is direct observation of the child. Every assessment must have a segment that involves observations of the child. In most cases, this observation takes place in the child's home; however, it can also take place in other settings, as appropriate. These observations usually take several hours to complete; they need to be more than a cursory look at the child to observe his or her most obvious behaviors. You want to put the child in a variety of situations (e.g., respond to a demand, asking a question, playing alone and in a social situation, interacting within his environment with his parents and/or siblings, etc) to witness actions and reactions. Keep in mind: if the observation takes place in a clinical setting, you are probably not getting a true picture of the child. I am often asked about assessing a child when he's having a "bad day." I recommend continuing with the observation anyway. As a professional, I want to see the child in situations that evoke frustration or anxiety. This enables me to assess deficit areas and design programs that will assist the child in being successful in these situations, thus eliminating frustration and increasing self-esteem and self-reliance.

But don't these assessment tools paint an "unnatural" picture of the child?

Not if they are done correctly. Practitioners who insist on using only formal standardized tools to assess a child will undoubtedly create a picture of a child that is missing large segments of who he is and how he interacts with the world around him. That's why the parent interview and direct child observation are so important. A good assessment returns a comprehensive picture of how the child interacts with his environment and the people he encounters in it. Autism is a communication, social and behavioral disorder; it is essential that these three functioning areas be observed in as natural an environment as possible. And, since federal law specifies that services be delivered in natural environments, it's just common sense that observations of the child occur in the same environments in which treatment will be provided. This helps in developing goals and objectives that will be meaningful and appropriate for the child and the family.

How can standardized assessment tests, designed for the multitude, return goals and objectives that are meaningful to us, to our child, and our family?

That's where the IFSP team comes in, and where parents play an important role as part of that team. Assessment tools provide data, but it is in the interpretation of the data in light of parental input and direct child observation, that the actual goals and objectives for the child are written. It is the team that "personalizes" the data and makes the services child-centered and family-focused.

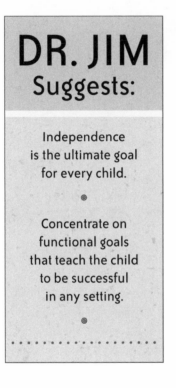

DR. JIM
Suggests:

Independence
is the ultimate goal
for every child.

◉

Concentrate on
functional goals
that teach the child
to be successful
in any setting.

◉

While goals and objectives will vary dramatically from child to child, they should all be functional in nature. I define functional to mean that which allows the child to be as independent as possible in any environment. For example, teaching the child to use his communication system to get a need or want met is more functional than teaching him to merely differentiate between a pear and an apple. This is not to say that being able to understand the difference between a pear and an apple is unimportant. However, asking for an apple when hungry is much more appropriate a skill to teach and moves the child further along the path to independence.

As parents, and as professionals entrusted with the education of these little children, we must always keep our eyes focused on the future and make programming decisions that foster continued independence in the child. After all, isn't this why we gather data in the first place? Assessment provides the information we need to help us nourish children so they will grow to be happy, independent, functioning adults.

*"At the start of our autism journey, the unknown was
the most frightening. As I began to understand the terminology
and challenges, I realized that my child was unique.
Autism can wear many hats. Focus on the needs of your child,
advocate for necessary services, and reach out for support."*

-BARBARA, PARENT OF IAN

chapter six

Blueprint for a Perfect Program

Dr. Jim: Rob, Maureen—this is an unexpected visit. What's wrong?

Rob: Thanks for seeing us on such short notice, Dr. Jim. We attended our first parent support group meeting a couple of nights ago and since then, our heads are spinning and we're feeling absolutely frantic and unsure of everything that's going on.

Maureen: I was looking forward to meeting other parents of kids like Mark, parents who were already living with autism, who could give us some advice ... someone to talk to who knew—really knew—what we're going through. I did find one mom who was very nice and offered to talk to me another time, but the others ....

Rob: Everyone was so willing to tell us what we're doing wrong, what we should be doing that we're not, what interventions or vitamins or therapists we absolutely have to try with Mark or else he'll be lost to us forever ... the trouble is, everyone was saying something different!

Maureen: One parent told us we had to find therapists to come into our home to do forty hours of "ABA" a week with our son. Another told us we didn't need forty hours and that the strict ABA format will turn Mark into a little robot, dependent on M&Ms in order to do anything.

Rob: A dad there said biomedical is the only way to go and we need to call immediately to get Mark tested by this famous doctor who lives halfway across the country. He said it would cost us $8,000 but it was worth every penny, that the tests and the supplements transformed his little boy from being completely nonverbal to talking up a storm within just two months. That's impressive isn't it? He told me not to waste my time on speech therapy or ABA or anything else—that biomedical can cure Mark of his autism.

Maureen: Everyone told us something different, Dr. Jim. We were reeling by the time we left that meeting. I thought I'd feel better after going to a "support" group—I felt a hundred times worse! There were about fifteen different families at that meeting, some couples, lots of moms by themselves ... some of the parents were almost ... zealous ... about their program being the "best of the best" and the only thing we should pursue. Others just sat there, looking so devastated, either saying nothing or complaining about how bad their lives are, how deficient the services and programs are in our state. A few were very bitter and angry, telling us we'll lose our positive attitude really fast once we get "into the system" and find out how badly it works. I know these parents mean well. But how can they know what's right for Mark? They've never even met him!

Dr. Jim: Now I understand why you didn't want to wait until our regular meeting next week! You got a taste of the diversity and decisiveness that exists within the autism community. It can feel like being hit by a tsunami of opinions and you find yourself drowning in options labeled "good" or "bad" by someone who's known you ten minutes. I will warn you right now: I'm not a big fan of support groups. Some are great, without question. But many morph into little more than parents sitting around complaining about everything that is wrong. It's easy to get sucked into feeling sorry for yourself and your child and lose the resolve to keep working at it.

You're going to hear all sorts of opinions about everything related to autism. Some parents will willingly share their ideas about the "best programs" or what's worked for their child to help you enlarge your knowledge base. Others will gladly pick apart your child's program and tell you what you're doing wrong, or not doing that you absolutely must do. "You must do ABA"; "Floortime is the only program to consider"; "You're not using biomedical? Don't you want your child to recover?" Resist the urge to immediately qualify options as good/bad or better/worse. Especially during these early intervention years when everything is so new and frightening, let these voices become part of your background. Concentrate on learning how autism affects your child, his skills, his needs.

Rob: Are you saying we should disregard everything we hear from other parents? That doesn't sound right either!

Dr. Jim: No, I'm not saying that. What I'm saying is that you need to listen critically and not take everything you hear as "fact"—no matter how people present it to you. You can easily become overwhelmed and full of apprehension—just as you are right now—if you believe everything you hear. You'll start doubting your inner wisdom and second-guessing your decisions. Are we doing what's right for our child? Is there something more we should be doing? Am I failing my child?

The information you hear from others or read in books or on the internet can be invigorating and energizing or discouraging and depressing—all in the same day! Learn to keep an open mind. Investigate and evaluate things that interest you. Just remember: parents are telling you *their* truth, not THE truth. They may want you to adopt it as your truth too—that would certainly validate in their own minds what they're doing with their own child. And, keep in mind it's not just parents who share strong opinions. Professionals can feed you good information, biased information and bad, outdated information. Consider no one exempt from careful scrutiny—including me! Dub no person your "guru" or "savior" in reference to your child or your family's functioning. You are learning to make informed decisions for your child, and this skill takes practice. These mental muscles are only honed through exercise, so follow Nike's lead and just do it … get involved, search for information, but take it all in with a healthy degree of caution and skepticism. The journey you're on is filled with twists and turns. Be patient with yourselves and keep your eyes focused on the goal: your child becoming a happy, functional, contributing adult.

Rob: *But if that's truly the case, how do we know if a program is good or bad, or right or appropriate—whatever adjective you want to use? If there's so much conflicting information and no "one" answer for all kids, how do we make those informed decisions you're talking about?*

Dr. Jim: That's the million-dollar question in the autism community, Rob. Let's talk a little today about quality program indicators—important elements any EI program should have in order to bring about progress and be meaningful to the child with ASD. Then in our next session I'll give you an overview of the different types of autism programs and describe some of the more popular ones currently available.

◎　◎　◎

Is there a perfect program for children with ASD?

I use the word "perfect," yet some of my colleagues abhor the word. A lot depends on what you think the word means, and that's quite subjective from parent to parent and professional to professional. If you think of perfect meaning "well matched, well suited," then yes, you can find—or create—a perfect program for your child. If you think of perfect as meaning "one and only one" or "that which continually meets every need of the child with 100% effectiveness" then no, there's not a perfect program for your child. Autism is a spectrum disability; the needs of these kids can fluctuate dramatically from year to year, month to month, even day to day. When looking at any form of therapy or organized program, consider how well it matches your child's strengths and weaknesses and whether it has the flexibility to evolve with your child. Evaluating programs from that standpoint will help you more in the long run than qualifying options as "right" or "wrong."

Remember our last discussion about assessment? A thorough assessment of the child by professionals who are well-trained in ASD is needed in order for the IFSP team members to have the information and data they need to design a program matched to the child's needs. Your child's program may—or may not—look like the program for another child with ASD you meet at your parent support group, or an autism workshop, or the grocery store. *Let this be okay.* Listen and learn, ask questions, explore the services other children are receiving, but do so as an information-gathering exercise, rather than out of some emotionally driven sense of "finding the one, perfect thing." That attitude will drag you down, deplete your energy, and cause you to question yourself. Be curious, yes. Just don't let your emotions get the best of you.

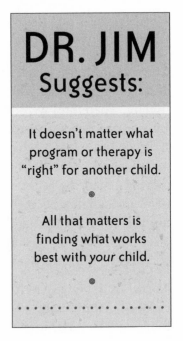

DR. JIM
Suggests:

It doesn't matter what program or therapy is "right" for another child.

All that matters is finding what works best with *your* child.

If there's no one right program, then how do I, as a parent, evaluate different programs and options?

Of course, there will be similarities in EI programs—it's natural, given that autism affects all children in the core areas of communication, behavior and social skills. You want to find programs that address these core components. What will differ from child to child are the goals and objectives developed within the program components, the amount of time devoted to each area, the types of teaching methods used with the child, etc.

So, there are certain core features that should make up the EI program?

That's right. You want your early intervention program to address the following seven program areas:

1. Communication
2. Sensory integration
3. Behavior

4. Play skills

5. Reinforcement

6. Social skills

7. Biomedical

Communication

Communication is absolutely the most critical skill a child with ASD needs in order to function in the world. It affects all other areas of functioning. Therefore, we advocate that communication training start as early as possible, rather than waiting to see if verbal language develops. If Bruce can tell us what he wants or can communicate "no" with regard to what he *doesn't* want, or if Margie can convey that she hurts or that something is causing her pleasure or pain, we can better assist them in understanding the world they live in. One of our most basic needs is to be "heard," and even very little kids manifest this, albeit on a simple level, through their behavior. Therefore, it is critical that the child's program emphasize functional communication training.

Notice I didn't say speech therapy. Speech is only a subset of communication—an important one, for sure, but don't make the mistake of thinking it's everything. Your goal is a *communication system* for your child, and that system should be taught whether your child is currently verbal or nonverbal. Verbal language is the ultimate goal, but for kids with impaired auditory and visual processing abilities, gross and fine motor coordination problems, and echolalia (words or phrases spoken by others and repeated by the child in place of originally generated language), a functional communication system gives them multiple ways to appropriately express their needs and wants. A communication system might include some combination of sign language, pictures, objects, gestures, voice output systems and verbal language. There will undoubtedly be times in your child's day or week when his verbal language is not going to be readily available and nonverbal communication is all he can manage (e.g., in moments of high stress). With a communication system, we give the child alternatives, so his communication can still be appropriate, while always encouraging the use of verbal language.

For example, by keeping the emphasis on communication rather than strictly on language, a familiar scenario might look like this. Your child takes your hand, leads you to the kitchen and puts your hand on the refrigerator. He obviously wants something (in this case it's juice). The adult takes the child's hand and "shapes" a functional point, has the child point at the refrigerator and the adult then says, "That's wonderful—you're telling me you want something." The adult then opens the refrigerator and helps the child point at what he wants—the carton of juice. As the next step in the communication system the adult may introduce a picture of the child's favorite juice carton. When the child goes to the refrigerator the adult can show the child the picture of the juice, hand the child the picture card and have him hand it back, and then say, "That's great, you want juice."

As time goes on, the child may begin to point to what he wants, like juice. The adult can start attaching verbal labels to objects, saying "juice" each time the child points to it, followed by "Now you say it: 'juice.'" We always want to encourage the child to use verbal language within the broader scope of the communication system. When language is the only option children have, frustration can easily take its place. If the child attempts to use language, heavily reinforce the child. If the child does not use his language initially, the adult can use a picture of the juice, pour the juice in the cup and then say, "Say juice," before handing it to the child. This provides him multiple opportunities to use verbal language.

Sensory Integration

Sensory challenges are very common in children with ASD. Any of the five senses—sight, hearing, smell, taste and touch—along with two other senses—vestibular (balance) and proprioceptive (feedback from joints and muscles)—can be affected in any combination. Children can be hyper-sensitive (over-sensitive) or hypo-sensitive (under-sensitive) in any of the senses and this can vary from day to day.

Sensory issues greatly affect a child's ability to attend, learn and be part of any experience. It is eminently important for parents to understand that these sensory challenges are neurologically based—they have a

117

physical basis—and can't be controlled at will by the child. Many sensory insults are painful—for instance the sound of a dishwasher, or even a table fan, can be painful to some kids. Grocery stores or malls with all their sights, sounds and smells—super-duper sensory stimulators—can be absolutely intolerable for many children on the spectrum. The result? When overloaded, children let us know, with their behavior, they can no longer tolerate the sensory insults. A tantrum or meltdown occurs.

People without sensory issues do not appreciate the enormous anxiety and stress children experience because of sensory challenges. We are able to "tune out" some of the sensory input around us so as not to be overwhelmed. The good news is that sensory integration training can be very effective in alleviating some of the child's sensory challenges. This happens over time, and is not a quick fix. But progress can be made.

Your EI program must be cognizant of the many different types of sensory challenges in children with ASD and attend to them. Sensory activities to arouse sluggish sensory systems or calm easily excitable systems should be part of the overall programming. Much of sensory programming is fun for the child, often combining music and movement. Parents can be trained to become "sensory smart" about their child, and notice the signs of impending overload before the child experiences a meltdown.

It is important for parents to understand that an inappropriate behavior is often the *end result* of a sensory issue. A child may tantrum in the grocery store because he's on sensory overload. The squeaky wheels on the shopping cart, the smells from the fish counter or the bakery, people chatting, cell phones ringing, shiny surfaces reflecting the fluorescent lights—they can easily become too much to handle. By looking only at the behavior, and not its cause, efforts to change that behavior can be ineffective. Unless the underlying sensory issue is handled, in most cases the child will exhibit a new, equally inappropriate behavior to communicate that he is no longer able to exist within the environment.

Another example: while watching a favorite video (Barney) Josh gets so excited he starts flapping his hands uncontrollably and jumping up and down. This type of behavior occurs every time Josh gets excited.

This might be "cute" in a two-year-old, but we're looking down the road. How cute will it be when Josh is seven, and he's still flapping his hands and jumping up and down every time he gets excited? The EI team has its Occupational Therapist assess Josh's behavior, and the OT suggests that Josh's parents have him jump on a mini trampoline or bounce on a therapy ball. These activities are offered to Josh on a schedule (e.g., every thirty minutes or five times a day at specific times). By giving Josh regular opportunities to receive the type of sensory input he needs and/or release his pent up energy, he can be taught more appropriate ways of expressing his excitement. Children with sensory challenges often crave "therapy" time and can learn to self-regulate their sensory systems. Many children are aware that they're approaching overload or running low on energy, and will request their sensory time.

Behavior

As alluded to in the previous paragraph, behavior is usually the end result of some interaction between the child and his environment. *All behavior happens for a reason.* Let this become one of your mantras when working with your child. To understand why a child exhibits inappropriate behavior, we must first figure out what's causing it, and the function the behavior serves for the child. *It is only when we understand the cause and function of a behavior that we can design an effective behavior strategy that replaces the inappropriate behavior with an appropriate one that meets the same need.*

Positive and supportive behavior management should be a core element in any EI program. Service providers should be well trained in positive behavior support strategies and should never take a punitive approach to behavior management. Parent training is usually an integral part of this behavior management component, as what we say and do affects the child's behavior. Effective behavior training will be predicated on the following ideas:

Functional Assessment
The first step in behavior management is finding out why the child is engaging in the behavior. Behavior is a means of communicating something the child cannot tell us in words. Our goal is to help the child do

that in a more socially appropriate, effective way. A technique called Functional Behavior Analysis (FBA) is a systematic way of analyzing behavior to discover the reasons behind it. It removes the "guessing game" adults sometimes use in figuring out a child's behavior. Good programs use FBA as a regular working tool to gather information they need before making recommendations about how to change behavior.

Without first understanding the reason for the behavior, it is virtually impossible to create effective behavior strategies that will help the child use appropriate behaviors. There are many reasons for behaviors; the five most common ones are communication, attention seeking, escape/avoidance, not getting what they want when they want it, and self-stimulation (i.e., because it physically feels good to the child, like hand flapping). The function of the behavior dictates the intervention to be selected.

Positive Approach
Behavior strategies should be positive in nature. No one likes being punished and kids with ASD are no different. Look for a program that offers the child lots and lots of praise and reinforcement and frequently catches the child "being good." We all too often notice when children are not doing what they should, and we less frequently call attention to when they are doing what we want them to do.

The use of punishment by parents or service providers within a behavior program is not recommended. In most cases, children with ASD "misbehave" because they "can't" comply, rather than "won't" comply. It goes back to their neurological impairments, their inability to communicate, their lack of social skills and a host of other reasons. A positive behavior plan recognizes the difference between *can't* and *won't* and offers the education children need rather than punishing them for what they honestly don't know how to do.

Parents and adults must also watch their own behaviors when working with this population. It's easy to inadvertently reinforce the very behaviors we are trying to change in a child. Negative attention is as powerful, if not more powerful, than positive attention. And parents often give the child-in-the-middle-of-a-tantrum heaps of negative attention. This is where parent training in positive behavior strategies is important and vital to the continued progress of the child. It also helps parents feel more self-confident in their ability to handle their child's behavior in different environments.

Behavior Management Principles

A well-designed behavior management program is more than just a piecemeal assembly of things to do. It is a coordinated set of strategies carried out within a set of principles that govern the way the adult will act and react with the child in order for him to learn new skills and new ways of behaving. Two very important principles that contribute to effective behavior management are these: 1) consistency and 2) predictability. For parents unfamiliar with handling problem behaviors, these principles may not be "intuitive" but will need to be learned over time. Inconsistent adult behaviors are one of the top reasons kids don't learn the replacement behaviors adults want them to. Keep an eye on yourself when working on your child's behaviors!

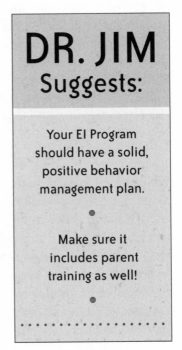

DR. JIM Suggests:

Your EI Program should have a solid, positive behavior management plan.

◎

Make sure it includes parent training as well!

◎

If you say something, you have to mean it. Not 20% or 50% or 80% of the time, but 100% now, an hour from now, tomorrow, next week. If you are going to ask the child to do something, let him know what will happen if he does it, and the consequence if he doesn't. Then you need to follow through on his choice right away, not in a little while, or later, but now. Young children need routine, structure and boundaries. The child with ASD is no different. Their concrete-thinking mind craves consistency and predictability. Yet, just like any other child, they will test how far they can push a parent. As we mentioned before, autism is not the reason behind everything the child does. He's still going to go through the terrible twos and she will still act out during the troublesome threes; autism doesn't erase that part of their normal development. It will, however, confuse their ability to understand the rules and boundaries parents apply. Be doubly consistent and doubly predictable.

Play Skills

Young children learn about their world through play. Kids learn pivotal social skills such as imitation, turn taking, cooperation, negotiation, following rules, etc., through their playful interactions with other children. It's also a ripe environment for learning cause and effect, and learning about the world around them through the eyes—and experiences—of others like themselves (perspective taking). Kids on the autism spectrum have challenges in all of these areas and more. Their rigid thinking patterns and sometimes-odd ways of expressing their emotions can result in their being excluded from play. Therefore, play skills must be an essential component of the EI program. Play skills are foundation skills every child with ASD needs to be successful. Build the following core play skills into your EI program.

Imitation

Imitation is a building-block skill. It affects all future learning for the child. An inability to imitate will result in later difficulty learning social skills and communication. Imitation is the #1 skill a child with autism must learn in order to be successful. The good news is that imitation can easily be taught through play skills. It usually begins with having the child imitate a gross motor action: clap hands, stomp feet, or raise hands. Lots of early songs teach simple imitation skills. As the child becomes more proficient, the skill is generalized to other areas, like playing with toys, learning self-help skills, and eventually becomes a part of imaginary play, like "play fighting" with a fake light saber.

Observation & Modeling

Little kids are innately interested in other kids. They watch what other kids do as a means of learning what they should do themselves. This behavior develops naturally in NT kids but is one of the black holes in the social-cognitive learning patterns of kids with ASD. ASD kids don't learn by watching. They don't understand that others—mom, dad, siblings, peers—are sources of information about the world around them. So they don't watch other kids and model what other kids do.

We need to concretely teach the child with autism to watch other kids. Existing therapies do an excellent job getting kids with autism to interact with adults or other kids, but a poor job of having them attend to other kids. It's a skill that needs more emphasis within our EI programs. (More on this a bit later.)

Fine/Gross Motor Skills

Gross motor skills refers to our ability to use our large muscles to do things like walk, hop, run, push/pull, sit and stand. It also describes our ability to keep our balance and change our body position.

Fine motor skills, on the other hand, refers to our ability to use the smaller muscles in our fingers and hands to do things, such as draw, color, write, string beads, put sand in a bucket, zip a zipper and engage in a variety of other activities.

Play and regular daily life activities involve both gross and fine motor skills. Many children with ASD have difficulty with such skills, which can cause them to shy away from playful interactions with others and not be able to learn basic self-help skills. Specific exercises and activities can be done with the child (through the medium of play, of course, using imitation and modeling!) to strengthen these skills. These are usually developed by the team's OT and woven into the daily routine.

In general, play activities should always be fun, interactive, motivating and engaging for the child. They don't need to be verbal; they should depend on the functioning level of the child and the goals being worked on at the time. Care must be taken so that play is not overwhelming on a sensory level for the child. Keep in mind this can fluctuate from day to day, and with some kids, from hour to hour. Watch for your child's warning signs of impending sensory overload and adjust the activity accordingly.

"Play" is a much more complex activity than most parents appreciate. It involves a host of skills that typical children learn on a seemingly intuitive basis (like watching other kids). It's easy to assume spectrum kids—especially those less impaired—"know" how to play, yet this is not the case. A good EI program will teach parents the rudimentary elements of play, how play skills develop, and how to foster play skills in the child.

Initially, play skills may have to be prompted through the "watch and do" process described above. Lots of kids with ASD have "odd" ways of playing with toys. For instance, the fascination with a truck may be spinning its wheels, rather than the more typical "zoom, zoom" way of moving it on and around the furniture. Spectrum kids also tend to perseverate (do the same thing with the toy over and over again, in exactly the same way). Parents can encourage early play skills by introducing a variety of toys and showing the child how to play with them. This may have to start by simply putting a truck on the floor and pushing it back and forth, saying to the child "do this". Then hand the child the truck and have him model what you did. Or, if the child just pushes a train back and forth on the tracks, the adult can interrupt that perseverative behavior and introduce a new action by taking another train and going around the entire track.

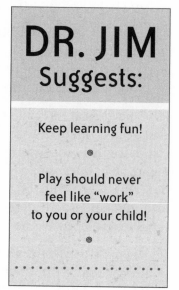

DR. JIM Suggests:

Keep learning fun!

◉

Play should never feel like "work" to you or your child!

◉

If the child models you, then reinforce him. If not, prompt him to do it (not verbally) and reinforce him. Keep introducing new ways to play with more favorite toys first; that keeps the child motivated and engaged. Widen the play world for the child one step at a time. Introduce other toys as the child becomes more flexible with the toys he likes. Once the child is playing successfully alone, encourage him to play next to other kids with their toys (parallel play). Then support the child in simple playful interactions with other children.

A well-designed play program will seamlessly incorporate appropriate social skills into the interactions between the child and his play partner(s), whether that is an adult or a peer. Parents will be taught how to facilitate and support the development of these social skills throughout the child's day. Remember: children with ASD need lots and lots of practice in order to acquire peer-level play and social skills.

Reinforcement

What's not to like about play and exploring the wide, wide world? Plenty, for some children with ASD. Contrary to what seems natural to us typical folk, spectrum children do not find learning inherently reinforcing, even learning disguised in the form of play. For most NT kids, involvement with others (i.e., a social connection) is intrinsically appealing. Not so for many kids on the spectrum. Notice I said "many" and not "all." Some kids love being cuddled and hugged and touched and involved with others. They are intrigued by the people and situations around them and naturally gravitate towards social connection. Others run away from physical touch, mainly because of sensory issues. Or they are the "loners"—always playing by themselves, content in their own little world, sometimes oblivious to what is happening around them. Others want involvement but have learned—the hard way—to avoid it, because their inappropriate ways of interacting result in time-out or punishment. To some extent children with ASD are introverts or extroverts because of their innate personality; to some extent it is because of their autism.

A good EI program will recognize the different levels of motivation in a child and use "reinforcement" as a tool to encourage participation and learning. Simply put, reinforcement is giving a person something he desires in exchange for something else, such as a word, an action, or a behavior. Reinforcement can take a variety of forms in an EI program: a favorite toy or object, time spent engaged in a preferred activity, like watching a favorite DVD, a food item, or it can be less concrete—such as verbal praise or some specific sign to indicate "good job!"

The idea behind reinforcement is easy for most adults to understand. What most fail to appreciate is that kids on the spectrum often have an odd taste in reinforcers, and a reinforcer is only as powerful as the interest it holds for the child. Don't assume because "all kids" enjoy a particular toy that your child will too. Test it out, make sure it's appealing. The more the child likes it, the more likely he will do what we ask, again and again, in order to get access to the reinforcer. Also keep in mind that the value of a reinforcer can fade over time. Regularly reassess the "strength" of the reinforcer being used. (This topic will be addressed in more detail later in the book.)

Social Skills

Ours is a social world, and social skills are essential for the spectrum child to survive in the neurotypical world. People are defined by their social graces and how they interact with one another. Individuals are welcomed into a group or dubbed "outsiders" based on how well their behavior meshes with others and reflects society's definition of "acceptable."

My favorite part of every preschool "report card" used to be: *Does the child play well with others?* I know, for a fact, I used to get an "unsatisfactory" in that area (and penmanship too) when I was young. I just didn't like to share. Children with ASD, however, have these social difficulties because of the way their brains are wired. They don't make social connections because they *can't*. That is, until they're taught how, and then they can. This is extremely important for parents to understand, and often very difficult for them to do. *Social skills need to be taught to children with ASD, in a very concrete manner,* starting when they are young. Please do not assume your child is just going to "get it" at some point and be able to interact in socially appropriate ways. Even some of the most simple tasks, like saying "no" (appropriately!) or asking for help, need to be explicitly taught to the child. Young children's actions are largely a product of their previous interaction with their environment, created through reinforcement, whether it's positive, negative, or absent. It is critical that social skills teaching begin as early as possible. By doing so, we provide the child the best possible chance for developing social relatedness.

Social skills and emotional relatedness are not quite the same thing. Every child needs to learn certain basic skills that enable him to interact with others according to the "rules" of society. That's social skills. Emotional relatedness is a more nebulous part of social functioning, having more to do with the feeling of connectedness than the outward display of appropriate behavior. Emotional relatedness is the "why" of acting in socially appropriate ways, and is one of the most difficult things to foster in a spectrum child. However, it is not impossible.

Just as behavior modification needs practice, practice, practice, social skills too need repeated practice for the child to learn them. Lots more practice than many parents assume when new to the autism experience. It's important for children with ASD to be put in social situations as often as possible and given good models to imitate (after they are taught to imitate, of course. Doing so before then will only cause frustration and perhaps a meltdown or two, or twenty). Through repeated opportunities to practice their emerging skills, they slowly get used to being in social situations and learn the correct way to interact. This, in turn, raises self-esteem, which positively affects motivation, which increases learning and *voilà*, the child is on the road towards independence, our ultimate goal for each child. (More on social skills later in the book.)

While practice is paramount to achieving mastery of social skills, parents and the EI team need to keep in mind that the child is still a child and needs time to play and be a kid. As much as possible, though, adults and therapists must engage the child to build a solid social-emotional bond and establish trust between the parent and child or therapist and child. We are asking the child to step into the realm of uncertainty many times every day in order to teach him the needed skills. Trust is needed so the child will venture into this uncomfortable territory and take these risks.

DR. JIM Suggests:

To foster social skills, keep the child engaged in the here and now as much as possible, while making the here and now a nice place to be.

Biomedical

Autism is a "whole person" disorder, meaning it affects children's entire beings.

It is much more than just the behaviors the child manifests and, therefore, a comprehensive EI program should address more than just behavior. The research being done on this population suggests strongly that a great many medical issues exist alongside autism. Whether the physical issues cause the autism, are part of the autism, or are the result of the autism is a question that will not soon be answered. However, this should not preclude the EI program including a biomedical component.

The Biomedical Approach, as it's often referred to, focuses on the physical or medical issues that impair the child's ability to function at optimal capacity. Think of any sick child; how well does any child attend and learn when his body is functioning at compromised levels? That's the Biomedical Approach in a nutshell. Biomedical treatments may include special diets, vitamins/supplements, allergy testing, yeast or heavy metal testing/removal, and other therapies that help the child's body regain healthier functioning levels. They are generally used in addition to, not as a substitute for, behavioral and educational strategies.

However, the biomedical approach is a relative newcomer on the autism block. Many options available lack rigorous testing or empirically validated research to support their use with this population. Members of the EI team may have conflicting opinions about the need to consider biomedical as part of the overall EI plan. A great deal of untried, unproven, and sometimes dangerous therapies have been introduced, often spreading by word of mouth or the internet, touting near miraculous results or promising to "cure" the child's autism. Caution is advised, yes. But enough children are being helped—and some are being helped in significant ways—that biomedical therapies should not be dismissed outright from the EI program.

Parents interested in pursing biomedical options need to be very careful and not be lured into trying an intervention without first thoroughly investigating the option and considering the risks as well as the benefits. They should never be started without first consulting with a physician familiar with ASD and with the various biomedical therapies available. Some of these options are quite expensive, also. Some parents have been successful in getting insurance to cover certain treatments by obtaining a separate diagnosis of a related disorder (e.g., gastro-intestinal issues or allergies).

If every "good" EI program is supposed to have these seven components, what makes the program individualized for my child? Wouldn't they all be the same cookie-cutter programs, all pretty much alike?

This is a great question and it goes back to the information on autism and assessments that we previously discussed. Each child on the spectrum is different. A good EI program recognizes this and plans for it. A good program is a flexible program and isn't one that takes a cookie-cutter approach to a child's EI plan.

Good programs incorporate these seven core elements but *how* they do it will differ from child to child. One child needs a lot of attention to fine motor work, social skills and sensory issues, but his behavior is pretty good. Another child's behavior is off the wall yet he has few sensory issues. The individual tests completed as part of the assessment pinpoint the various areas of strength and weakness in the child. The assessment report (hopefully) offers suggested goals and objectives that should be implemented for the child in each specific area. The EI team assembles this data, considers it in light of the child observations and the family interviews conducted, and meshes all this together into a plan of action for the child and the family.

What kind of goals and objectives belong on my child's IFSP?

Goals and objectives are "action statements" written into the IFSP that guide therapists in the provision of services to the child and the family.

Goals: These are broad statements relating to the overall area of functioning to be targeted, or the skill to be learned. For example, a targeted goal might be "expressive language" or "playground social skills."

Objectives: More detailed statements that describe the specific action or behavior to be learned by the child. For example, in the area of "expressive language," we might have several objectives to teach the child ways to use/develop his expressive language in a particular setting. Goals are generally unspecific; however, objectives should be anything but. Well-written objectives are like expert guides who know every inch of the forest; you know where you are at all times, how you're doing, and when you've arrived at your destination. Effective objectives are:

• concrete and specific enough that anyone reading them will understand what is to be done with the child
• measurable
• reflect the strengths and weaknesses of the child
• functional and meaningful
• described in behavioral terms (actual observation of a behavior)
• contain criteria for mastery of the skill.

Some well-written and not-so-well written goals and objectives are listed below. Note the types of words and descriptors that each contains.

Poorly written Goals & Objectives statements

Area: Social Skills.

Goal: The child will learn social skills. [What kind of social skills?]

Goal: The child will play well with other children. ["Well" is highly subjective and not clearly defined.]

Objectives:
• The child will participate during circle time with other children. [What does "participate" mean? How often will he participate?]
• The child will join group games offered by the teacher. [Which group games—all, even right from the start of the program? Indoors, outdoors, both? How often? When is this skill mastered?]
• The child will not grab toys from other children. [This objective is worded in the negative: What is the child supposed to do instead?]

Well-written Goals & Objectives statements

Area: Social Skills.

Goal: The child will increase his social interaction skills.

Goal: The child will be able to play with other children during play-dates.

Objectives:
- In three out of four occurrences, the child will be able to sit at a table for five minutes without leaving his seat.

- In three out of four occurrences, the child will be able to tolerate other children in his/her space within two feet, while playing with a toy.

- In three out of four occurrences, the child will be able to take turns in a ten-minute group game with another child.

As illustrated in the previous example, effective objectives are related to each other and listed in order of learning. They often build upon a prior skill the child masters. They are written in concrete language that contains both frequency of occurrence and describes the setting, as applicable.

Goals and objectives are tools that make up a working plan for the child and family and, as such, should be viewed as flexible, reviewed periodically and adjusted as needed. As the child learns, or as new situations arise, new goals and objectives can be added to the IFSP. Parents should always keep this in mind: any service that's to be provided to the child or family should be explicitly written into the IFSP. It doesn't "exist" if it's not part of the written plan.

Are there goals and objectives every EI program should contain—or at least consider for the child?

Yes. Some of the specific areas that should be addressed on the IFSP are listed below. Appendix B offers an example of the goals and objectives written for one specific child's EI plan, in various areas of need. This document gives parents an idea of how goals and objectives should be written and the types of skills that should be worked on through the EI plan.

A great many of the goals addressed below and in the Appendix over-lap into different categories. This is not a mistake; this is a good thing. It promotes generalization of skills in the child. Children with autism are notorious for their "one way" thinking process. Teach a child to say hello to Aunt Marge when she comes over to visit and he's learned just that, to say hello to Aunt Marge. When she comes over to visit. It does not mean he'll intuitively understand he can use this same skill to say hello to Aunt Marge when you run into her at the grocery store. Or that he'll know to use the skill to say hello to anyone else, like Cousin Freddy or the kid in the swing next to him on the playground. To the spectrum child, new conditions or variables call for a different response. This can be very perplexing and frustrating to the parents of spectrum kids who work so hard to help them acquire new skills. It just needs to be accepted as part of the different workings of the autism brain. Details are easy; generalization is not.

Therefore, generalization of skills needs to be built into the structure of the intervention methods we use with these kids. We always blame the kids for "not getting" generalization, when the problem is often due to the way we are (or are not) teaching the skill. "Old school" thought is that generalization is a separate skill to be learned "later" by the child. Teach the skills in different environments separately and then teach the child to "link" all these individual units into one by teaching generalization. However, generalization is not a "skill" *per se*—it's an information processing, information organizing mechanism. Unfortunately, that old school of thought is still widely used in programs across the country. A more effective way to teach spectrum kids is to program for generalization right from the very beginning. Build it into the structure. The best way to do this is to make sure all the goals address similar objectives (the actual skill) being performed in a variety of environments, with a variety of materials, and with different people.

Now, on to specific goals and objectives you should look for in an EI program.

Teach Communication Skills

When most people think of communication skills, they first think verbal language. As we've discussed previously, communication skills are a package or a menu of ways a child can communicate his needs and wants. It does not rely on verbal skills alone; it may incorporate pictures, symbols, or even a computer voice-output device, if the severity of the child's impairment warrants one. A functional communication system is a key factor in the child's future learning and success. The IFSP must reflect the team's intention to create one by describing the various communication methods to be used with the child and the communication goals the child will achieve.

The communication system must be very functional, as well as offer the child a variety of communication options. If equipment or devices are needed for working with the child, such as a touch or type communication machine or a communication board, this should be written into the IFSP. The system must also be universal and meaningful to the child and the family. For instance, a program that only uses English for a child who lives in a family where everyone speaks Spanish 90% of the time would not be the most universal option to pursue.

Individual communication objectives will look something like this:

- Can use a functional point to request a desired item
- Can utilize a communication system to request a desired item
- Can utilize a communication system to interact with an adult/peer for more than one communicative exchange
- Can utilize a communication system to express displeasure or show frustration
- Will use verbal imitation
- Will verbally label objects

Of course, these objectives would be further qualified based on the child's ability, the setting the skill will take place within, etc. For instance, the first objective may end up looking something more like this:

- Sarah will use a functional point to request a desired item during mealtime four out of five times.

It's true that we want the child to have verbal language, and as discussed earlier, we should encourage the use of language. However, teaching the child multiple ways to communicate means he can express his wants and needs under all levels of stress, not just on his "best" days, when all the mental and physical pieces come together to get his words out. An interesting side-note: encouraging nonverbal communication does NOT retard the development of verbal communication. Actually, research shows it helps it emerge. Make sure the child's IFSP teaches a variety of communication options.

Teach Joint Attention

Joint attention is the ability to use eye contact and gesturing to make a connection with another person during a social exchange. Here's a simple example: a mom and her son are having a picnic at the park. Mom notices a balloon drifting by, points to it and exclaims, "Look Ben, a red balloon!" Ben looks up from eating his chicken, looks at mom, follows her pointing finger and sees the balloon too. Joint attention. Typical children develop a functional point around nine months of age, and begin to use joint attention with adults around eighteen months of age, then a little later, with their peers. However, in most (perhaps all) children with autism this skill does not develop and must therefore be taught explicitly.

A functional point is one of the ways children engage others. Joint attention is also part of the early expression of perspective taking: understanding that other people may share your interests or feelings about something in the environment. I see an airplane in the sky and you might like to see it too, so let me point it out to you. Joint attention demonstrates and encourages social connections between people. It says to others that you think about them and desire to include them in your everyday actions. It is a pivotal skill to teach young children with ASD.

One of the more important parts of joint attention is looking at other children while they do things, like play or interact with others. This is one skill professionals do not yet teach effectively. We have done a great job teaching kids with ASD to interact with adults, but have been lax in teaching them to interact with their peers. There is a vast difference between how a child plays or interacts with an adult and how he plays or interacts with a peer. An entirely different set of skills is needed. Adults make split-decision allowances for the child on a continual basis, and structure interactions in favor of the child. Peers do no such thing, and the interaction unfolds in real-time, spontaneously. Our kids often end up lost and frustrated. That's partly why children with ASD will often seek out the company of adults for interaction, while avoiding their peers.

What to do? While children are in early intervention services, they should be exposed to some type of interaction with other kids. This will give them the time to be taught how to jointly attend to peers. Objectives for this goal area might be as follows:

- Establishes eye contact in response to hearing his name, independently, four out of five times

- Uses a functional point, independently, four out of five times

- Turns and looks at another child, when that other child is speaking, independently, four out of five times

There are many venues in which you can teach joint attention. Obviously, other children must be present, so teaching can occur during a play date, on the playground, with the child's siblings or cousins, etc. There are all sorts of opportunities to give a child plenty of practice with pointing and joint attention. Be creative!

Teach Appropriate Play Skills

Children explore the world and develop their social sense through toy play. They use toys as "tools" to navigate and interact with others in their environment. In children with ASD play skills are not always present, or if they are present, rather than being a means of connecting to their environment, they allow the child to escape it. Previously we mentioned perseveration, a spectrum child's tendency to play with the same toy in exactly the same way over and over again. Or a child may play out a "script" from a video or television show with a toy, never expecting any-

135

one else to be part of the play experience. Play skills, from the most basic to the more complex, need to be taught to the child with ASD.

Furthermore, there are two types of play that should be outlined in the IFSP and taught spectrum kids: Cognitive Play and Social Play. Some of the skills we want the child to learn within each of these types of play might be:

Cognitive Play

- *Functional Play:* plays with toys in an appropriate manner
- *Constructive Play:* is able to build things
- *Dramatic Play:* creates or replicates characters; pretend play
- *Rule-bound Play:* can follow game rules and participate in a group game

Social Play

Social play has many forms, ranging from solo play to structured and unstructured play with others. As skills develop and the child can tolerate having multiple play partners, we want to guide the child through increasingly more interactive forms of social play.

- *Solitary:* plays by himself
- *Onlooker:* watches others play
- *Parallel:* plays next to others without direct interaction
- *Associative:* responds or interacts with others
- *Coordinated:* is able to predict others' behaviors and stay in the interaction

Social play goals and objectives will start with very simple activities and build the child's skills slowly over time and as his related skills develop. Children with early, emerging play skills may have objectives something like these (again, depending on the child's strengths):

- Plays appropriately with toys
- Can build a tower with four blocks
- Can play next to another child, within two feet, for five minutes

Progressing to goals like this:

• Engages with another child in a pretend game, staying on topic for two social exchanges

• Plays a board game with another child, using waiting and turn taking skills

Depending on the child's strengths and weaknesses, it may be appropriate to teach some of these skills in isolation or work on several at the same time. The skills necessary to be successful at play overlap in a variety of ways with other skills, such as behavior, communication and joint attention. The sequence of skills to be taught is usually decided by the EI team. Parents should understand that these skills work in a progression, and build upon one another. Therefore, certain prerequisite skills need to be mastered before moving on to new skills. For example, if the child cannot play with a toy, she would need to be taught how to play with a toy appropriately before being placed in a parallel play situation.

And don't forget that spectrum kids need lots of practice to master skills well enough so they can use them again in various settings. We tend to rush kids into play scenarios that involve other children, sometimes before they are ready, or before we've given them the time to master those prerequisite play skills that will make them successful in the presence of other children. Be patient and go slowly. Rushing children into dyads (two-child interactions) or triads (three-child interactions) without foundation skills will only frustrate everyone involved. It can easily turn off potential play partners from wanting future involvement with the child, too. Make sure the child has appropriate skills at one level of play before introducing a new level.

Teach Social Skills

Social skills are difficult to teach to children on the autism spectrum. Many of these kids are rule-bound in their thinking patterns, hanging onto predictability and routine as though they were life preservers in the constantly shifting ocean of social interactions. Think about it: social skills are anything *but* rule driven. For every "rule" we teach the child, there are exceptions, and probably many of them. Let's consider one of the early social "rules" we teach young kids: *Always tell the truth.* Do we really mean always? Well, no we don't. Not really. Not in all situations. Not when the truth might make someone feel bad. What about simple greetings? That should be pretty easy to teach, right? After all, it's just "Hi," right? Yes, but it's "Hi" with a certain tone of voice, accompanied by eye contact or a wave of the hand, and it has to be timed right, and while you say it once when you first see a person, you don't repeat it every time you encounter the same person for the rest of the time together. Simple, eh?

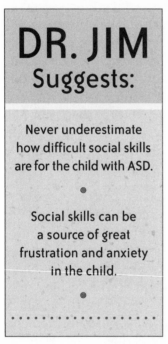

DR. JIM
Suggests:

Never underestimate how difficult social skills are for the child with ASD.

◎

Social skills can be a source of great frustration and anxiety in the child.

◎

Social skills are anything but simple. There are literally hundreds upon hundreds of different skills and even more variations of specific skills given the circumstances. Gender, age, culture, geographic location, and relationship all play a role in social interactions and partly dictate how we tailor a particular social skill to fit the situation. A well-tuned "social sense" is difficult enough for typical people, folks who function without the neurological impairments to the social-thinking parts of their brain. Imagine trying to navigate our world when the actions of those around us simply make no sense!

All that said, learning social skills is not an optional part of the life experience. Children with ASD must learn what constitutes "appropriate" social behavior and how to interact with other people in their environment, from the pastor at church on Sunday, to the neighbor across the street, to his or her siblings, to play-partners and teachers.

As with some of the other areas mentioned above, there are some fundamental, building-block social skills that should be worked on first. They are the keys to success in simple social interactions and open doors to further interactions of a more complex nature.

Can maintain attention to another person

In order to have any meaningful interaction, you must be able to attend to the other person. We show our desire to interact in many different ways. Most of us think attention means eye contact, but that's not necessarily so. We connect with another through our body position (turned toward the other person), a silent touch, or gestures that indicate attention (nodding our heads, even when we're not looking at the other person).

Has a communication system

We've said it before, but we'll say it again: This does not mean the child has to be verbal. However, the child does need a "universal" way to communicate with another person. Watch a couple of toddlers playing together; actually, there's very little language passing back and forth. It's more nonverbal looks, imitative play and sounds between them.

Has a concept of spatial issues

Kids with ASD will often get "up close and personal" with little regard for what we NTs call our "personal space." However, there are unspoken rules that govern spatial issues within social interactions. Too close and you're offensive; too far away and you're standoffish. This is one of the more nebulous parts of social interaction—how close is too close to stand next to someone—and again, it is dependent on a host of cultural and situational variables. The good news is that spatial issues lend themselves more easily to concrete definitions than do other social skills.

Spatial issues also refer to the child acknowledging the presence of another when there is some distance yet between them, or when direct one-on-one interaction has not yet been established.

A couple of example of objectives relating to spatial issues might include:

- Can maintain attention, standing within an arm's length of another child for five seconds
- Waves to say "Hi" when another child he knows enters the room

A verbal child can be encouraged to say "Hi" in addition to waving to the other child. However, initially, the wave should be taught for its universal communication and for those times when accessing language is difficult.

Aside from the seven components and these goals and objectives, are there any other factors that make up a perfect EI program?

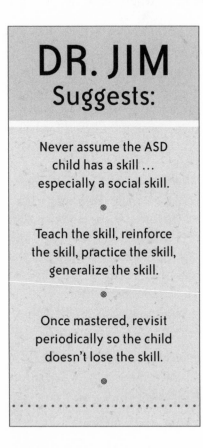

DR. JIM Suggests:

Never assume the ASD child has a skill ... especially a social skill.

❋

Teach the skill, reinforce the skill, practice the skill, generalize the skill.

❋

Once mastered, revisit periodically so the child doesn't lose the skill.

❋

There's just a few; some mentioned previously. The program must be child-focused and family-focused. That needs to be more than lip service, and be at the forefront of every topic discussed, every decision made, even during times when the team is in disagreement on a particular issue. The goals and objectives must be based on the individual assessments of the child, not on what might be good because "autism" or "PDD-NOS" is the child's diagnosis. Many programs fall apart in this area, including goals and objectives, because someone selects a program because it is applicable to "autism," not because it's applicable to this one particular child. The level of autism-specific training in the IFSP team will affect this area greatly. Professionals less trained in ASD are more apt to have "stock goals" on hand that they use over and over.

The program must be flexible and responsive to the child, the family, and their changing needs over time. Some kids learn skills quickly and others don't. Some families find their need for individual or family counseling or respite services actually grows over time, especially families who bury their emotions initially in favor of diving right into education and intervention. A good program will accommodate these shifting needs. Finally, the program must contain periodic reviews in order to know if strategies are bringing about growth and change in the child. EI services are short lived; program reviews should take place often, so time is not wasted.

The program components and goal areas outlined above, then, are like a menu of options that should be made available to my child? From these we select the ones most needed and just disregard the rest?

Actually, no. This is a common misunderstanding about EI program design and program development for children with ASD. It is critical to understand that this is not a menu of options, it is a program in and of itself. Based on years of experience working with this population, and years of getting to know children and adults all over the spectrum, this grouping of program components and goal areas brought about the greatest opportunities for positive growth and change in the young children with whom we worked. We found it was this combination, as a whole, that worked best.

When we view autism as a set of disconnected areas of impairment, rather than a different functioning *system*, we tend to take the "menu of options" approach to treatment. We'll take a little speech, combine it with a lot of behavior training, we'll omit sensory work altogether and throw in some respite care for the parents. That's your program.

Our kids deserve better. Early intervention is a time when little children's bodies and minds are malleable as in no other period in their development. We have to keep in mind that their parts are all connected and teach the child, not attend to the deficits. Communication affects behavior. Sensory issues affect communication. Social skills affect play skills and play skills affect social relationships. It's all circular and connected. What we do in one area affects all the others. Therefore, our approach should be programmatic, not piecemeal. When we create programs tailored to their needs, we offer each child a world of possibility. We lay out the map to guide their journey and set them on the road to independence.

Now, that's a perfect early intervention program!

> *"A strong partnership between home and school can accelerate a child's progress. This means brainstorming with family members to make sure progress continues, listening to strategies parents have found effective, and communicating successes more than failures or frustrations. The rapport established between home and an early intervention program, and between the child and professionals can be the most important strategy of all in achieving a perfect program."*
>
> — CATHY PRATT, PhD.
> DIRECTOR, INDIANA RESOURCE CENTER ON AUTISM

chapter seven

Options, Options, Options!

Choosing the Right Intervention Model for the ASD Child

Dr. Jim: Hi, Rob and Maureen. You're early today.

Rob: I know; we're just so excited about this session. We've been waiting for weeks now to hear what you have to say about all the different types of program models available to help Mark and spectrum kids like him. I want to know which one is the best for Mark.

Maureen: Me too. Since we attended the parent support group and heard so many different, and conflicting, opinions, I've run into a few other mothers who only gave me more of the same advice: "Only ABA has science behind it." "Only Floortime addresses the whole child." "We had great success with The Miller Method." "RDI saved my child and our family!" We need you to steer us in the right direction, because all these parents seem to have their own ideas about treatment!

Dr. Jim: That's what today's session is all about—helping you understand the different types of intervention models available and how to go about selecting the best match for your child. When we're done with the session, you'll still have plenty to think about, but you'll have a better understanding of each major program type and a game plan for finding or creating the program that will work best for your child.

◎   ◎   ◎

Where do I start in selecting a program model?

First understand this: Your child is a child with a unique *learning profile*. Your goal is to find a program most suited to him. His profile may be markedly different than that of the child of a parent you met at the support group meeting. The program right for that child might be disastrous for your child, or your family. You and your team will uncover your child's particular learning profile by considering the results of the various assessments done on the child, your observations and parent interviews. You'll then combine that information with your collective familiarity with existing program options to see which are a good match. As the parent, you have a right to ask questions and expect intelligent answers from these professionals about available programs. You also can inquire about program models not mentioned by the team, or bring information to share with team members to spur discussion about a model that seems to you to be possibly appropriate for your child.

Is there one "best" program for my child?

There are a variety of different therapeutic programs that could be effective for a child with autism. No single model is "the answer" for your child, which makes selecting program options frightfully perplexing for parents of spectrum children. Parents new to ASD naturally want clear, concise answers, and some search feverishly for that magic key that will alleviate everyone's problems. They want the one program that will be perfect in every way. In reality, children respond differently to treatment because of their unique learning profiles. Parents who adopt an attitude of looking for a "good match" will fare better in the long run than parents looking for "the cure" for their child's disorder.

Many programs claim they are the best for all spectrum children; some go as far as promising a "cure." Be careful in believing all you hear or read; I've said that before and I repeat it now for good reason. Parents can easily be misled by professionals and by programs that sound too good to be true. You want to believe that all professionals in the field have your and your child's very best interests at heart. Unfortunately, that's not always true. If a program sounds too good to be true, it probably is.

To date, there is no known cure for autism. It is a lifelong disorder. Yes, children can make great progress and grow up, live "typical" lives as best they can, given the amount of independent skill they have achieved, but that is not being "cured." That is becoming "functional" (a very good thing in and of itself!). And some children do so well they no longer meet the criteria for an autism diagnosis. These children—often referred to as "recovered"—still retain characteristics of autism. True, their autism may only slightly impair their ability to function in the neurotypical world, but the traces of autism still remain. Don't be fooled into believing it will all go away because of one treatment or another.

Who makes the decision about the program model to use with my child?

That decision ultimately resides with the child's parents. However, it's not a decision to be made in isolation, but in consultation with the IFSP team members and/or a trusted professional(s) who knows the child and the family. Your program choice should take into consideration several things:

- your child's learning profile and skill needs
- the family's values and perceptions of treatment methods
- time and financial resources
- the family's support system
- the program's credibility

Should I consider only research-based methods?

That depends on what you mean by "research." Whether or not a program is "research-based" is not necessarily the most effective way of making program decisions. And I'll tell you why.

I define research as carefully controlled studies conducted by qualified professionals not associated with the program, according to generally accepted principles of data collection, measurement and analysis. To me, research means clinical settings, large enough groups of well-matched participants, an equally homogeneous group of control subjects, benchmarks for measuring success and use of standard evaluation methods.

And therein lies the problem. Aside from one form of treatment, Applied Behavior Analysis, there are few, if any, other treatment models for children with ASD that meet this definition of being "research" based.

This is certainly not because people don't want proof their program works. It's more a factor of the variability among this population and the nature of the program models that exist. As you know by now (because I've said it so often!), autism manifests differently in each child. It's just about impossible to put together a group of "highly similar" kids to measure something as subjective or variable as "social skills" or "improved relationship skills." Some kids have sensory issues; some don't. Some have gastrointestinal problems; some don't. Some are highly verbal but their speech is low on social meaning. Some gravitate towards people; others prefer being alone. Research yields accurate results in direct proportion to how well defined and controlled the study variables are. There's not much that is "well-defined" and consistent in kids with ASD.

Confounding this issue is the fact that many treatment methods are relative newcomers in the autism community and have been developed by an individual person, maybe a clinical psychologist, an M.D., a speech therapist or an OT. The model arises out of their own years of experience working with this population. That's certainly wonderful and many excellent program models have been developed this way, ones that have helped thousands upon thousands of kids. But there are few researchers in the world who are willing to use their own hard-won grant dollars to independently study someone else's program to ascertain if it can be scientifically proven to work. In most cases where there is research associated with a program model, people directly associated with the program have conducted the studies—its founder or other program practitioners. Which, of course, can lend itself to program bias, and can't be really considered "independent" research.

Applied Behavioral Analysis (ABA) is viewed as the "gold standard" of treatments for children with ASD. It is the oldest and by far the most widely researched treatment method. Parents will encounter many professionals—and other parents—who only advocate the use of research-based methods, and therefore, only recommend ABA. Others take a more eclectic approach.

Of course, you're wondering: But what about all those program models currently being used, touted by parents across the country for the success they've produced in their children? These indeed are something to consider. But do understand that these parent testimonials are not the same as a method that is supported by impartial, controlled research. These results are considered "anecdotal," meaning they're based on subjective measures of success (i.e., parent testimony). Whether or not parents will consider a treatment method based on anecdotal research is a personal decision they must make as they evaluate various program options.

If a program can't be evaluated based on independent research, then how do I judge it's merit?

My professional opinion is that parents should first explore programs that are *evidence-based* and that lend themselves to objective measures of effectiveness, meaning the program methodology incorporates regular data-taking and advocates that all decisions made be based on that data. Not all programs have this component. Some determine a program's effectiveness through personal observation and subjective interpretations of success. A parent's idea of success may be entirely different than what the service provider considers to be success.

Furthermore, sometimes we see what we want to see, rather than the actual facts in a situation. Objective data gathering is an important part of effective program management. You want to know when a program is working or not working, and you want evaluation to be based on more than guesswork or vague statements like "I think so."

Choosing a program model feels like such a "finite" decision. Is that actually how it is?

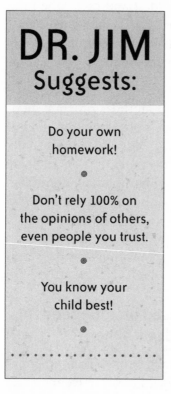

DR. JIM
Suggests:

Do your own homework!

◉

Don't rely 100% on the opinions of others, even people you trust.

◉

You know your child best!

◉

Yes and no. Once the program is selected, both parents and IFSP team members should remain objective, watch for progress or no progress, and set some interim time limits and goals right from the onset. IFSP teams who meet on a regular weekly basis are able to keep on track of the effectiveness of program choices and make adjustments when needed. Your choice is not "forever"—you are not married to it, and you can change it. However, stay conscious of the fact that this is a major decision for your child and your entire family, and one that should not be made in haste. Don't become a program "hopper," moving from one program to another. This will only stifle your child's overall progress and discourage you. Do your homework before you choose, make sure the overall program is aligned with your family's personality, and more importantly, fits your family's lifestyle. A family that cannot survive on one paycheck would be ill-advised to select a program that requires one parent at home full-time in order to carry out the program goals and objectives, and can only do so once they attend lengthy parent-training sessions that cost thousands of dollars. Be realistic and honest about what you can/cannot handle when making program choices.

Is every program really that different, or are there broad classifications of program models for children with ASD?

There are program models that address just one area of functioning (like speech or communication, or sensory issues) and program models that address the overall functioning of the child across many domains (behavior, social skills, language/communication, etc). There are literally dozens upon dozens of options currently available, yet most sift down into one of the following three categories:

- Skill-based programs (sometimes referred to as behavior-based therapies)

- Relationship-based programs (sometimes referred to as developmental therapies)

- Physical-based programs (which include, but are not limited to biomedical therapies)

Skill-based programs advocate that all children can learn appropriate behaviors through a system of rewards and reinforcement and that you must first build appropriate skills in various areas of functioning in order to establish a relationship with the child. These programs work on remedying the child's inappropriate behavior by substituting more socially appropriate and functional skills.

Relationship-based programs work from the premise that learning grows through the teacher-child relationship, which involves establishing a rapport with the child based on his unique interests and abilities, building a sense of trust and engaging the child within everyday, natural learning environments. You'll hear phrases like "enter the world of the child with autism" as part of the treatment philosophy.

The *physical-based programs* believe that ASD impairs the child's body to the point that learning is compromised and that by dealing with these internal issues the child has the best possible opportunity to learn skills taught through other methods. Each category of programs has unique qualities, pros and cons, yet similar strategies are often shared among them.

Are some programs more "accepted" than others within the ASD community?

The treatment methods that follow are among those best known, best researched, and thought to have the best chance of bringing about positive results in a child on the autism spectrum. This is not a comprehensive list of all available programs. The initial four programs are those that, in my professional opinion, are most likely to result in positive growth and development in a child. Programs currently known and used within the autism community, but that I do not personally endorse, follow them. The last section describes programs that can be helpful in addressing individual functioning domains in this population. I have included the following programs because you will hear about them, encounter them in your own searching, and I want you to understand something about them.

Again, I repeat: not all the programs that follow have independent research to support their claims. Some do not even have their own program research. Carefully evaluate a program model before making a decision to try it with your child, or adopt it as the program model upon which the EI program is based.

The Four Mainstay Programs for Children with ASD

Applied Behavioral Analysis (ABA)

Many programs that can help spectrum children have been misunderstood and misrepresented by parents and professionals in the autism community. It's like the gossip game you used to play as a child: one person begins with a statement and by the time it makes its way down to the tenth child, it's no longer the same. This is nowhere more true than in most people's understanding of ABA. Let's see if we can upright this apple cart.

First, ABA is NOT a program. It is a *systematic process* that examines behavior, using principles grounded in science: observation, reproduction, testing, objectivity. ABA is a framework within which children are taught appropriate behaviors, using positive reinforcement and manipulation of the child's environments. Within ABA methodology, behavior is viewed from a functional perspective, using what is commonly referred to as the "ABC" analysis of behavior, meaning for each behavior we look at the Antecedent (what comes right before the behavior), the Behavior itself (what the child does) and the Consequence (what happens as a result of the behavior). By understanding these three components of behavior, we can use strategies to teach an appropriate replacement behavior or teach new skills a child needs in order to interact with the world.

Baer, Wolf, and Risley (1968) outlined essential elements of an ABA-based program:

- It addresses socially important behaviors, i.e., those that allow the child to function in the world around him.

- Behavior is operationally defined, in clear and precise terms, and is reliably measured.

- The program provides convincing evidence, via data collection, that the strategies employed are responsible for a meaningful change in behavior.

- The program provides for the generalization of behaviors.

- Employs procedures based on the principles of behavior science.

There exist today a variety of program models that are ABA-based, and they range from very intensive, 40-hour per week, highly structured programs to less-intensive and much more naturalistic programs. All are "ABA."

ABA is based on the work in the field of behaviorism by B.F. Skinner, and is widely used to bring about behavior change. It grew in popularity as a model for children with autism through the work of O. Ivar Lovaas. Lovaas achieved success in teaching a small group of very young children with autism using a highly structured, intensive behavior modification program based on discrete trial teaching (DTT)—one method of behavior modification that falls within the larger framework of ABA. Parents in today's autism community often mistakenly say they are "doing ABA" when what they really mean is they are using a Lovaas-based program, i.e., using a structured, intensive (30-40 hours per week) behavior modification program centered on discrete trial teaching.

DTT is just one part of the ABA methodology and programs that rely exclusively on DTT are not state-of-the-art ABA programs. In fact, research suggests that these programs, especially those that take a "cookbook" approach to teaching skills, result in skills that do not generalize from training to other settings. Effective ABA-based programs use a variety of teaching strategies, blending DTT with other ABA-based techniques such as shaping and chaining, positive reinforcement, child-initiated instructional sequences, and imbedded generalization opportunities. Well-done ABA programs are far different than the archaic but still circulated image of the child sitting at a table in a sterile environment, responding on cue to a therapist's initiation, and rewarded with an M&M. A good ABA-based program makes learning fun and enjoyable for the child, while still incorporating the basic principles of behaviorism outlined above.

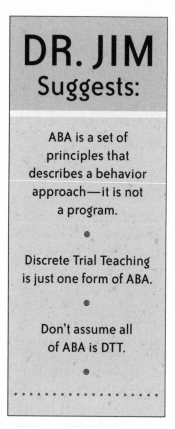

DR. JIM Suggests:

ABA is a set of principles that describes a behavior approach—it is not a program.

◎

Discrete Trial Teaching is just one form of ABA.

◎

Don't assume all of ABA is DTT.

◎

Critics of ABA are often people misinformed or misled about the broad nature of the methodology. Many make comments about "ABA" when they are really commenting on more regimented DTT-based programs. They claim this type of teaching does not allow children to establish relationships with others, that skills are not generalized and also that these children appear to be very robotic in their responses to others. That criticism may be true, but as pointed out above, that is an archaic view of ABA and refers to programs that are not state-of-the-art in design or methodology. Unfortunately, as with many strategies, a great many people practice these teaching techniques without proper training and without fully understanding the entire ABA philosophy. ABA methodology promotes generalization; when performed correctly skills are taught in a great many environments, with a variety of language, and with many different materials—from the very beginning of therapy. Yet, this is not what many parents hear about or encounter. This is a misunderstanding promulgated on inappropriate application of ABA techniques, rather than an inherent fault of the program methodology itself.

A variety of program models are based on ABA principles. Some of the names and/or terminology parents may encounter include Discrete-Trial Training, Lovaas program, UCLA model, Modified Lovaas Program, Intensive Behavior Intervention, Pivotal Response Training, Applied Verbal Behavior, Incidental Teaching, and Natural Environment Training. Again, while all these programs encompass ABA principles, they can and do function very differently one from another. To follow is additional information on some of these different ABA-based models.

Discrete Trial Teaching
A Discrete Trial Teaching-based program is a systematic way of teaching children with autism specific targeted skills, anything ranging from paying attention to making eye contact to more complex language and social skills. It involves breaking down a behavior into its basic, functional units and teaching each of these units in a progression. Each DTT has three components: a cue (e.g., touch your nose), a response (the child touches his nose, tries or does not touch his nose) and a reinforcer (a reward, either tangible or verbal). DTT also uses prompts, consequences, and measurement as part of its methodology. The skill is repeated over and over again until the child achieves a level of mastery (i.e., able to respond to the cue 80% or better over two days). "At the table" teaching is generally synonymous with DTT, but DTT can be taught in other locations as well. Behavior data is taken as the child learns and this data is used to make decisions on what to teach next. Generalization of skills occurs through practice sessions in different environments and with different variables (people, time, place, etc).

Incidental Teaching

Incidental Teaching is usually thought of as a more "natural" way to teach students while still adhering to ABA principles. It is similar to DTT and the same sequence is used to teach the skill; however, it is child-initiated rather than therapist-initiated instruction, with the "teaching moment" rising up naturally within the child's activity. The child works on the skill within its "need it now" environment, which promotes generalization and provides an added layer of motivation and reinforcement for mastering the skill. It also helps the child understand the functional component of the skill. For instance, instead of teaching a child to take turns while sitting at a table with the therapist, the teacher has the child work on the skill while playing a game with a peer.

Applied Verbal Behavior (AVB)

Applied Verbal Behavior is firmly grounded in the work of BF Skinner and is really a part of an overall ABA program, rather than a separate program model in itself. Just as Skinner analyzed physical behavior, he also applied this same analysis to verbal behavior. Essentially AVB is the functional assessment of language and refers to an ABA-based program that has an emphasis on verbal behavior. It breaks down language into verbal "operants" such as mands (a request), tacts (labeling an item), echoics (repeating a word), and interverbals (conversating). AVB is often viewed as a bridge builder, and is used in conjunction with behavior modification techniques to increase motivation in a child and provide him with a better understanding of words and their meanings. Jack Michael, Mark Sundberg, Jim Partington, and Vince Carbone have conducted and published research on verbal behavior and are at the forefront of teaching parents and professionals to use AVB techniques as part of their program for children with ASD.

Pivotal Response Training

Like DTT, Pivotal Response Training (PRT) is a behavioral intervention technique based on ABA principles. Developed by Robert L. Koegel and Laura Schreibman, PRT suggests that two behaviors are "pivotal" in the acquisition of other behaviors: motivation (reinforcement) and the ability to respond to multiple cues. This program model involves teaching children in naturalistic settings and includes components such as child choice, turn-taking and reinforcing all attempts. PRT has been used to target language skills, play skills and social behaviors in children with autism; however, newer research suggests certain profiles of students may be better candidates for PRT than others. It differs from DTT in that it is child-directed and uses reinforcement directly related to the task, rather than using food or toys as reinforcements, as is often the case with DTT.

DIR/Floortime

Dr. Stanley Greenspan, a child psychiatrist, and Serena Wieder, Ph.D., developed an interactive, relationship-based intervention model in the 1980s called the DIR (Developmental, Individual-Difference, Relationship-based) program. At the heart of DIR is the basic premise that all children pass through six developmental milestones that are critical to all learning and future development: 1) self-regulation and interest in the world; 2) intimacy; 3) two-way communication; 4) complex communication; 5) emotional ideas; and 6) emotional thinking. Typical children pass through these stages relatively easily but because of biological challenges, children with ASD do not. Through the individualized DIR program strategies developed, as the child participates in appropriate emotional experiences during each developmental phase, critical cognitive, social, emotional, language and motor skills develop, alongside a sense of self and place in the world.

When it is done in its entirety, DIR is an intensive and comprehensive program involving family members, educators and therapists. Parents take on the role of "team captain" and are integral to making the program successful for the child, the family and the therapists involved. Parents often refer to it as a "lifestyle" choice, since it is heavily dependent upon parent and family participation in implementing the philosophy of the program throughout all aspects of daily life. However, implementing the program to this degree is not a necessity and elements of the DIR approach can be incorporated into any child's program. A centerpiece of DIR strategy is Floortime: getting down on the floor in 20-30 minute sessions to engage the child and establish a relationship bond. Floortime attempts to establish reinforcement around relationships, not the skill level of the child.

One of the more important and meaningful strategies of the DIR approach is "communication circles." These are communicative inter-actions that happen between the child and the adult, where the behavior and ideas of one person are connected (verbally and/or non-verbally) to those of the other person. Circles of communication can be either adult- or child-directed and can involve gestures, eye contact, language or a combination of all. They start out simple and, as the child moves through the six stages of development, become more com-plex and address increasingly complicated ideas.

DIR/Floortime is a very natural way of teaching and the environment is based on play and social interaction, typically difficult yet highly impor-tant areas of mastery for the child with ASD. Critics of DIR contend there is not a great deal of empirically validated research in support of this approach in particular (as opposed to relationship-based method-ology in general) with children with autism. In 2005, Greenspan and Wieder released a follow-up study tracking the positive progress of six-teen individuals using DIR over a 10-15 year time period.

I include DIR/Floortime in the top four because I believe it is a method that can be used successfully with children with ASD. However, I feel the need to qualify my endorsement by saying that, in most cases, the child will need to start off in a behaviorally-based program. Then as the child progresses and acquires basic functioning skills that facilitate learning (imitation, attention, etc.), their development reaches a level where they can benefit from this type of program, and a change is made to DIR or a relationship-based program model, or some combi-nation of both strategies.

TEACCH

The Treatment and Education of Autistic and related Communication-handicapped CHildren program was established in the early 1970's at the University of North Carolina at Chapel Hill by its founder, Dr. Eric Schopler. It grew out of a five-year research project funded by the National Institutes of Mental Health that changed much of what was known about the nature of autism and how to treat it, and has evolved into the state-wide system in NC for educating both children and adults with autism.

The TEACCH model places emphasis on individualized assessment of the person with autism, creating a program around each person's skills, interests, and needs, adopting appropriate adaptations that promote maximum independence, and respecting "the culture of autism"—recognizing that people with autism have ways of thinking and functioning that are different, but not inferior to, the neurotypical world.

The cornerstone of the TEACCH philosophy is "structured teaching," which espouses organizing the physical environment, using schedules and work systems, and communicating clear and explicit instructions and expectations to the child.

Visual strategies, independent scheduling, individual work stations, and clearly labeled work boxes are a mainstay of the everyday routine of the child with autism to promote maximum independence at home or in school. Independent scheduling allows the child to work without adult interference, by following a written or picture schedule to complete tasks. This is coupled with attention to a structured, organized environment, which includes the use of specified areas for instruction, eating, playing and work.

The TEACCH approach is broad-based, addressing not just work skills, but communication, social skills, leisure skills, etc. The model can be used from first diagnosis through the child's school years and into adult life. It has a strong parent component and TEACCH strategies can be successfully used at home and within the school environment. Like ABA, many myths surround the TEACCH program, largely circulated by people who have not taken the time to thoroughly investigate and understand the whole program methodology.

The critics, although they generally like the theory behind the approach, are not sure of exactly how individual program strategies are taught. This may, again, be premised on inadequate knowledge of the entire program. The work boxes are excellent for teaching independence; however, in order to be effective, the student must have been taught to use them prior to their introduction. According to the TEACCH website, the approach is most effective when it is implemented on a systems level. While this may work well in a state like NC, where the program has been adopted statewide, the effectiveness of the model when it is used piecemeal remains unstudied. Finally, while Division TEACCH has produced prolific teaching and training materials, including assessment tools, videos and an 11-volume *Current Issues in Autism* set of books, and the model has certainly stood the test of time, the TEACCH method does not have a great deal of empirical data that supports its effectiveness in comparison to other autism program models.

Sensory Integration

At first glance, sensory integration (SI) might not seem to "fit" in this section addressing program models for children with ASD. However, consider this: the brain takes in all information about the world through our senses. The five basic senses (hearing, sight, smell, touch, taste) along with the two lesser-recognized senses (vestibular and proprioception) are the conduits by which we absorb data from the environment and feed it to our brains in order to figure out what's going on and respond. When our senses are compromised or unable to function properly because of neurological problems—as they are in many children with ASD—the result is too little or too much information being sent to the brain. This affects all areas of functioning: communication and language, social skills, play skills, daily living skills, and most importantly, "behavior." It really doesn't matter how effective the program model being used with a child is if the child can't regulate the information being taken in through the senses. A world that is too bright, too loud, too intense to the child will severely impair his ability to learn. It would be like holding class in the middle of a crowded airport. How much real progress would a child make in that type of environment? Conversely, a child who experiences hypo-sensitivity is not getting enough information to the brain for learning to take place. In this light, sensory integration is really a "whole child" form of therapy and affects all areas of a child's development.

Children with autism display a wide range of sensory issues that manifest themselves as a host of different behaviors. Show me a child with

ASD who is "acting up or out" and, in the majority of cases, I'll see a child who is experiencing some form of sensory overload or sensory disregulation. The most common behaviors people associate with autism are children's self-stimulatory behaviors or "stims." These include hand flapping, jumping up and down, mouthing objects, making noises, or tensing. However, the aloof "behavior-less" child who would rather pick at carpet fibers for two hours than play with his sister, or seems disengaged most of the time, can also be experiencing a sensory issue.

Sensory Integration therapy attempts to help children become aware of different sensory input, when they need "more" or "less" in order to stay in optimal learning mode, and give them appropriate ways to acquire the input they may be seeking. While SI itself works on the physical, biological body systems, the effect of this approach extends into all other domains. Think of it as priming the pump so that other therapy models can be effective with the child.

Sensory integration will be discussed in greater detail in a later chapter. As an intervention model, it has some of the same critics as DIR/Floortime. There is substantial anecdotal evidence that the technique is effective for individuals with ASD, but there is little empirical evidence to support this. However, SI is perhaps the only intervention strategy that has been described by adults on the spectrum as being critical to improved functioning in children. Hundreds of written accounts by adults with ASD document sensory challenges they experienced as a child, and that continue into adulthood. Anecdotal evidence generally arises from parents. This is one case where the "evidence"—while not scientific in nature—is coming from a source we cannot, and should not, overlook: the people who live with ASD on a day-to-day basis and understand it better than anyone.

Other Program Models

SCERTS™: (Social Communication Emotional Regulation Transactional Support)
SCERTS combines developmental, relationship-based and skill-based approaches into a framework for improving communication and

social-emotional skills in a child. The model arose out of the research and clinical practice since the mid-1970's of its authors, Barry Prizant, Ph.D., Amy Wetherby, Ph.D., Emily Rubin, CCC-SLP, Amy Laurent, Ed.M., and Patrick Rydell, Ed.D. The SCERTS model incorporates an assessment tool as well as practical guidance and strategies for helping children improve in three domains: Social Communication (spontaneous communication, relationship building), Emotional Regulation (controlling emotions and emotional responses to allow learning to occur), and Transactional Support (interpersonal learning and family supports). This model is said to be easy to use and can be combined with other intervention approaches.

RDI (Relationship Development Intervention)
RDI was developed by Dr. Steven Gutstein and is a developmental, systematic, parent-based treatment approach that is meant to co-exist alongside other therapeutic programs such as ABA, speech therapy, OT, etc. It is based on the idea that children with ASD need to learn more than language and social skills in order to be effective participants in the world around them. They need to grasp the "why" behind social interactions and feel what is called "experience sharing"—the joy of connecting with others. Dr. Gutstein's program is centered on the child learning six abilities that together constitute "dynamic intelligence": emotional referencing, social coordination, declarative language, flexible thinking, relational information processing, foresight and hindsight.

Parents can read Dr. Gutstein's books and use RDI strategies alongside other program models, or they can attend comprehensive parent training sessions to learn how to implement the model on a wider, more intensive basis. Like the other relationship-based programs, there is little empirical research that compares the efficacy of RDI to other programs or independently substantiates the success touted by program founders.

The Son-Rise Program®
Son-Rise is a one-on-one, home-based treatment and educational program designed to help children with autism in all areas of learning. This is another of the whole-child "lifestyle" programs that, like DIR,

calls upon parents to be captains of their child's program and take an active, integral role in affecting positive change in the child. At the heart of the Son-Rise Program is taking a nonjudgmental attitude towards the child's actions, and "joining" the child in whatever he is doing to establish a bond of trust, caring, and respect that leads to shared rapport from which learning can then blossom. The family becomes the "ultimate therapist" in their own home. Once the child is comfortable and rapport is established, a variety of teaching techniques can be used for skill acquisition, by the family and through other therapists working with the child.

The Son-Rise Program® was created by Barry Neil Kaufman and his wife, Samahria Lyte Kaufman, when their son Raun was diagnosed with severe autism in the early 1980s. In an attempt to reach their mute, withdrawn little boy, they spent endless hours in a simple, nondistracting environment with Raun, often mimicking whatever the little boy was doing in order to "enter his world" and make a connection from which they could lead him towards new ways of learning and interacting. After achieving remarkable success with Raun (he grew up to be a highly verbal, socially competent, educated and successful man), the Kaufmans established The Option Institute and the Autism Treatment Center of America™ to train parents in using The Son-Rise Program® with their own children. The Kaufmans—and their program—adhere to the idea that autism is not a behavioral disorder, but rather is a relational, interactional disorder. Therefore, successful treatment requires a focus on relating and connecting more than on teaching or changing behavior.

Critics of the program cite the lack of empirical research, the costs associated with the various levels of parent training (which can range from a few thousand to more than $10,000 for their one-week intensive training program) and the time commitment expected of parents for these training sessions, which all take place at the Center in Massachusetts. Furthermore, since The Son-Rise Program® is an intensive one-on-one parent-driven program, questions remain about how effective the program is when carried out in a less-intensive manner (40 hours per week are recommended, with no fewer than 20 hours per week advised) and how the child fares when faced with teachers who do not "live" by the nonjudgmental attitudes that play a central role in the program's basic philosophy.

DAN! Protocol

DAN or Defeat Autism Now! started in 1995 when Dr. Bernard Rimland, a pioneer in the field of autism, gathered together a group of thirty physicians and scientists from the U.S. and Europe to discuss possible biomedical underpinnings to autism spectrum disorders. As their mission statement says, DAN "is dedicated to educating parents and clinicians regarding biomedically-based research, appropriate testing and safe and effective interventions for autism." Out of that first meeting a protocol and treatment manual was established that could be used by physicians anywhere for the clinical assessment and treatment of individuals with ASD. DAN! is part of a larger group of treatments that fall under the category of Biomedical Therapies, which can also include special diets and the use of medications to alleviate associated symptoms of ASD. However, most frequently "biomedical approach" and the DAN! Protocol are interchangeable terms.

DAN! practitioners believe that the bodies of many children with autism have various metabolic errors and retain toxins because of impaired biomedical functioning in three main areas: mercury and other heavy metals (the children don't excrete these heavy metals as do typical children); food intolerances (an inability to synthesize gluten, casein, soy and corn) that lead to chemical imbalances and nutritional deficiencies; and yeast overgrowth (which results in toxins released in the body).

Physicians trained in the DAN! Protocol usually prescribe special diets (gluten and/or casein free), vitamins and/or supplements, and alternative treatment methods. The basic premise behind incorporating a biomedical approach is simple: when a child's body is balanced, from a biochemical standpoint, all other therapies have a much better chance of being successful. Those involved in the DAN! movement believe that adding the biomedical component of functioning greatly enhances the effectiveness of other educational interventions, behavioral approaches and individual therapies used with a spectrum child.

Programs that address specific functioning areas

In addition to comprehensive intervention models that address the core deficits of ASD, there exist a variety of therapy programs that focus on one particular aspect of functioning. Some of the more well-known and popular interventions are described below.

PECS (Picture Exchange Communication System)
The Picture Exchange Communication System is an augmentative communication system designed to assist nonverbal individuals with ASD to communicate in a functional and effective way. The system can be used with verbal children and has proved to be effective in facilitating language development in preschool children too. Many people (erroneously) think PECS is only picture cards, but it is important to note that PECS is a communication *system*, and is far more than simply using visual cards with children to stimulate communication.

PECS was developed in 1985 by Andrew S. Bondy, Ph.D. and Lori Frost, M.S., CCC-SLP as a training package to teach children and adults with ASD to initiate communication. It begins with teaching a child to exchange a picture of a desired item, for instance an apple, with an adult who honors the request with the object. The same procedure is used to convey a request (needing to use the restroom) or an emotion ("I am happy today!"). The advantages of using PECS are many. It is very easily understood and implemented; it is child-initiated; it requires a social contact; materials come pre-ready or can be "teacher made" and tailored so they are functional to the child; and the system can be implemented anywhere because it is nonverbal and therefore has universal appeal.

Auditory Integration Training (AIT)
Auditory Integration Training or AIT is considered to be a non-intrusive, alternative therapy designed to lessen and/or eliminate pain or discomfort and hypersensitivity in hearing. Developed more than thirty years ago in France by Dr. Guy Berard to rehabilitate disorders of the auditory system, such as hearing loss or hearing distortion, this intervention model has been used successfully to normalize hearing and the ways in which the brain of autistic individuals processes information. In a typical AIT session, an individual listens to specially designed

music through headphones. The music contains high and low sound frequencies that essentially "retrain" the ear to tolerate sound levels that are normally painful or cannot be heard and retrain a disorganized auditory system to function properly. Training occurs in two 30-minute sessions each day over a ten-day time period. It has been reported that individuals who go through AIT increase their expressive/receptive language skills and also experience an increase in their attention span. For some individuals the process produces remarkable results; others see little or no improvement, while some require a second "session" before improvements are seen. There are no independent, empirically validated studies to support these claims, although the founder and his colleagues offer several studies that suggest tangible improvements in many individuals.

Social Stories™
Social Stories are a way of teaching pro-social behaviors to individuals with ASD. Developed by Carol Gray in 1991, these stories describe a situation, a skill or a concept using a prescribed sentence formula to help the individual identify important social cues, and understand expected behavior and the reactions of others. Social Stories offer concrete ways to handle specific social situations, and are customized to the individual and the social situation. Social Stories can address simple social situations, and be used in helping individuals with ASD better understand the thoughts and perspectives of others, an area that can be particularly difficult for the ASD mind to comprehend. These stories can assist in developing a sense that others have their own ideas by describing concepts in a structured and concrete way, making them more understandable for an individual with ASD. The goal of a Social Story is not to change behavior, but rather to improve an individual's understanding of the events and expectations that make up the social situation, thereby facilitating the opportunity to learn more effective responses.

Music Therapy
Music Therapy is an intervention used to develop social/emotional, cognitive, and communication skills in individuals with a wide variety of special needs, including autism. It is viewed as an effective therapy

because it is universally fun and self-reinforcing (everyone loves music) and does not require verbal language from the participants. Children whose brains have difficulty processing verbal language (a complex action) can often sing along with music, be socially engaged and feel positively reinforced by their participation. For example, when teaching social skills, the music therapist could play a tune and request each of the participants to engage in a social activity as part of the sound that is being sung, fostering a social interaction between two or more people in the group. Some children with ASD will sing before they learn how to speak. In these instances, music therapy has helped in getting children to express themselves verbally, while modeling appropriate speech and bridging the gap between song and conversational speech. Music therapy also works on rhythm, coordination, and gross and fine motor control, all skills that are preparatory to the development of speech and language.

Hippo Therapy
Hippo Therapy has nothing to do with the hippopotamus. Its name comes from the Greek word "hippos" which means horse, and refers to horseback riding, an intervention that has been used successfully with individuals with ASD to improve neurological and sensory functioning. Hippo Therapy is conducted by trained professionals working one-on-one with a child in a controlled environment. It can begin with simply getting a child used to a horse and different sensory sensations, then incorporating individual goals into each session.

Therapeutic Horseback Riding is similar to Hippo Therapy, but differs in that the child is taught riding skills as part of the intervention method. This may start with the child being introduced to the animal, petting it, then sitting on the horse, followed by riding the horse while it is walking, then progressing to the child performing different movements atop the horse.

Both forms of horse therapy are often used to improve balance, coordination, range of motion, and gross motor skills. Other benefits include increased attention, concentration and verbal skills, bonding with the animal, improved social skills, self-confidence and self-esteem. As with most other intervention methods, few research studies

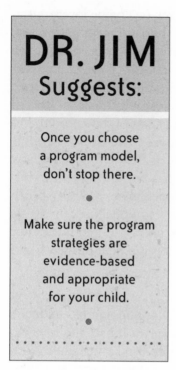

DR. JIM
Suggests:

Once you choose
a program model,
don't stop there.

⊙

Make sure the program
strategies are
evidence-based
and appropriate
for your child.

⊙

exist that document effectiveness with individuals with ASD.

You mentioned that many program models share program strategies. What does that mean?

It is equally important when designing an EI program that attention be given to using sound, evidence-based program strategies, no matter what intervention method is selected. Think of the method as the broad philosophical framework for treating children with ASD. Program strategies, on the other hand, are effective ways of working with kids that can be used within any framework. Strategies are the "how to" component of teaching the goals and objectives outlined in the IFSP.

Dr. Jim's Seven Effective Strategies for the Perfect EI Program

1. *Repetition*

Kids with autism learn through repetition, and needs lots of it, so any program should use repetition as a cornerstone of its teaching methods. Any and all skills need repetitive trials—even those we neurotypicals think are "simple." Parents new to the autism scene often don't realize how many repetitions are necessary in order for learning to occur. Some skills may literally require *hundreds* of repetitions over time, so don't give up too soon and think your child is incapable of learning a skill. *He* may just need more repetitions than *you* think he does. Plus, the more practice the child has at mastering a skill, the more opportunities you have to reinforce his work and his efforts. That goes a long way toward building self-esteem and keeping motivation high. Also, have the child perform the task in as many environments and with as wide a variety of materials as possible. For example, the child sees a yellow cup and the adult says, "What color is that? The child says, "yellow," and the adult reinforces the child, then hands him a banana and asks, "What color is that?" and the child says, "yellow," and the adult reinforces the child. The adult then asks the child to look outside at the daffodils growing in the yard and says, "What color are those flowers?" and so on. The take-home point here is to remember that the greater the number of opportunities to practice the skill, the greater the chance the child will learn and, much more critical, *use* the skill spontaneously.

2. Shaping

Shaping is accepting the approximation of a targeted behavior and reinforcing it while helping the child perform the skill correctly. For example, when the adult shows the child the yellow cup and the child says, "ye," the adult would heavily reinforce the attempt and say, "you're right, it's yellow," followed by more opportunities to practice as in the above example. Once the child repeats the approximation consistently, it's time to up the ante and require an even closer response—like "yell" in order for the child to receive the reinforcer. Again, the adult models the correct behavior being worked on, saying, "that's right, it's yellow." Shaping is just common sense—how long would you work toward a goal if the only reinforcement for your efforts came at 100% mastery? You want to encourage the child to do better each time, while realizing that in some instances, even simple tasks can be difficult for some spectrum children to learn and will require repeated practice and effort in achieving mastery.

3. Chaining

Shaping and chaining are often referred to in tandem, but they are very different techniques. Whereas shaping is usually used in teaching one specific skill or aspect of a skill, chaining is a teaching strategy that encompasses an entire sequence of behaviors or actions that, when put together, make up a complex skill. For example, chaining is used to teach skills such as self help, personal care and domestic chores that might include tooth brushing, hand washing, face washing, toileting, bathing, showering, setting the table, loading/unloading the dishwasher, bed making, and sweeping the floor.

Chaining involves breaking down a skill into its components parts and teaching each step in the chain until the child can perform the entire task. There are two types of chaining, forward and backward. In forward chaining, we start with the first step in the process and build from there. In backward chaining, we start with the finished skill (e.g., a child fully dressed) and proceed from there. When we teach a child with autism to brush her teeth, we use a forward chain. The child performs the first step, getting the toothbrush and toothpaste, until she can do it independently two times in a row, then the adult adds the next step, which might be teaching the child to remove the cap off the toothpaste. Each step is added in the same way. During teaching, the adult verbalizes the skill in simple language, saying something like "brush teeth" at the beginning of the learning session. Once the child has performed the desired step(s), the adult reinforces the child and prompts the child through the remainder of the steps, being careful not to use verbal prompts. Language is a complicated information-processing task for many children with ASD. Parents mistakenly surround the child with words, words, words, thinking this will facilitate language development. "Let's brush our teeth now." "It's tooth brushing time!" "Time to brush our teeth." We NTs naturally understand these three statements are all saying the same thing; to the child with ASD, they are like three different commands, each independent from the rest. Actually, this type of inconsistent language can delay skill acquisition more than spur it on, especially in the early stages of learning. Keep your language short, concrete and use the same words or phrase consistently. Let the child watch what you do without requiring her to also "process" data coming in through the auditory channel. It's an added layer of complexity and furthermore, verbal prompts do not allow the child to truly become independent in the skill. By always being given verbal prompts, the child becomes dependent upon these prompts as catalysts for the learning to "kick in" in their heads, and they will need an adult providing the prompt to be successful. The eventual goal is to have the child perform the entire task independently, and it's better for the child if we set up the learning environment to do this right from the start.

Backward chaining, on the other hand, is used to teach certain skills that may not make "sense" to the child when started from the first step. Let's use the skill of getting dressed to illustrate. To the child with ASD, putting on underwear may be so far away from being fully dressed that it just isn't meaningful. Using backward chaining, the adult goes through the motions of helping the child dress, by putting on his underwear, his socks, his shirt, and then stopping right before the last action, in this case, pulling his pants up. The parent teaches the child to pull up his pants as the first step in the chain, reinforcing the action, of course! Once the child can pull up his pants consistently, the adult adds the next to the last step, which might be pulling down his shirt over his head, (followed by the child pulling up his pants) and uses this backward progression until the child has mastered getting dressed.

4. Reinforcement

The most critical aspect of any program is motivation—keeping children engaged and wanting to learn. How do we entice children to build a relationship, complete a task, or learn a skill—especially during those times when all they want to do is what they want to do? We keep motivation and engagement active through the regular use of meaningful reinforcement. Note the word *meaningful*. It's meaningful! Reinforcement that has no appeal to the child will accomplish nothing more than stir up behavior issues.

Reinforcement is created on many different levels. If I want a child to play with me or do what I ask, I must first make the *environment* inviting, so the child wants to be there. This might mean making sure the space is conducive to learning, doesn't have all sorts of distracting elements and doesn't challenge any sensory issues in the child. We also want the environment to contain something—a *tangible motivator* the child finds highly pleasurable or favorable, such as some favorite toys (a motivator) to play with or a favorite stuffed animal (a motivator). Once I engage the child in this environment, I want him to stay engaged and come back for more learning opportunities (now and later). In addition to access to a favorite toy (tangible motivator) or a favorite snack (tangible motivator) like Cheerios, I may also use verbal praise (*intangible motivator*) or give a "high five" to motivate the child to continue with the lesson or another repetition of the skill. I want the child to feel positive about the actions we are engaged in and learn that performing requested actions yield rewards.

It's important for parents to know that not all children with ASD will work for verbal praise or for the intangible feeling of "togetherness," as do NT children. Concrete, tangible rewards are often the only thing that will keep them motivated. It's not good or bad; it just how it goes with some kids at some points in their learning process. Let that be okay and build from there.

Teachers and parents can use this relatively simple procedure to engage the child and teach new skills. As time goes on, if the child enjoys the activities, the quantity and quality of the reinforcement can be faded so the child is being reinforced at a rate consistent with any other child in the same environment, doing the same things.

5. Play

Children learn through play, and your EI program should teach through the medium of play. Keep in mind, though, that children with autism need to be taught how to play appropriately with their peers, and what better way to do this than to start at the ground level—literally! Teach lessons while on the floor with the child. It's the natural spot for preschool learning to take place. Arranging times to teach specific activities in a structured way, for instance, while seated in a chair or at a table, may be appropriate depending on the child's needs, but it should be the exception, not the norm on a daily basis.

Center all of the child's learning experiences around play activities. Incorporate all teaching within a play activity, giving the child as many opportunities as possible (repetition) to practice previously learned and emerging skills. Preschoolers are successful when they start school because they have learned to follow directions and have good play skills. These are easily taught during play activities. Again, there will be appropriate times to use a more structured teaching setting, but concentrate on play as the primary learning environment.

6. Extinction

Simply put, extinction means ignoring a child's inappropriate behavior. There will be times when the child displays inappropriate behaviors and we need a way to get the child back to the task at hand. Extinction is the preferred way to do this. We ignore the inappropriate behavior, *but we do not ignore the child.* It's a subtle but powerful distinction. An example: a child begins to tantrum during an activity. The adult ignores the tantrum behavior and calmly continues with the activity, using prompting techniques to get the child to follow through on the direction(s), and when he does, reinforcing him for completion. If the tantrum continues, you would use the same approach until the activity was over. Do NOT stop the activity for the tantrum. In doing so you would be teaching the child that the tantrum is going to get him what he wants (in this situation, termination of the activity). When you stop the activity, you are reinforcing the child's negative behaviors. This sets up a vicious cycle. The next time the child does not like the activity, the tantrum will begin earlier and last longer because the child does not know when you may stop the activity, but he does know you will stop it, because you did the time before.

Once you have used extinction to get the child through the tantrum and to completion of the activity or lesson, have the child use his communication system to terminate the activity appropriately (e.g., signing "stop," handing you a "stop" or "finished" card, or saying the appropriate word). This behavior modification strategy teaches the child that communication gets him what he needs, not the tantrum behavior. This is the most effective behavior management technique for preschoolers and should always be used first. Do remember: consistency in your adult behavior is paramount. Using this technique on a spotty basis will only confuse the child.

7. Rapport Building/Behavioral Momentum

One of the keys to success in teaching any skill is having a positive connection and foundation of trust between the child and the adult, be that adult the parent, a therapist or other in-home teacher. During initial sessions with the child, choice of activities should be based solely on what the child wants to do, with preferred objects and within situations that are enjoyable to the child. You want the bond of trust to be created and fostered early on in the teaching-learning process. We ask children with ASD to work very hard in acquiring the basic skills that come easily to NT kids. Without a solid bond between teacher and child, learning is that much more difficult. A positive rapport also makes the parent or teacher feel good about the interaction and feel reinforced for the time and effort expended in teaching the child. If the child is uncomfortable with an adult he may begin to tantrum when that person enters the room. Again, this is not conducive to the learning process.

Coupled with rapport building is a concept called behavior momentum. Each learning session should begin with practicing skills the child already knows, creating a successful, positive and nurturing feel to the session right from the very beginning. Then slowly move to introducing new or more challenging tasks for the child. You want the child to feel successful as much as possible. Intersperse difficult tasks with doing things you know the child can handle and do with ease. This alleviates some of the anxiety most spectrum children feel when working on new skills or unfamiliar tasks. Make sure your EI program works within this philosophy and the child is never caused to feel he is bad or incapable of learning.

It's a maze of options and strategies. How can I feel confident about making such serious decisions as these for my child?

First, remember you're not doing this alone or within a vacuum. Your IFSP team is ready, willing and able to guide you through this process. Take advantage of their expertise; pick their brains, ask questions, listen to their recommendations and trust your gut instincts. Furthermore, today there are literally hundreds of books and resources available to help you learn more about ASD, existing program models and teaching strategies. Learning takes time, not just for the child, but also for parents. Over time, as you work with the professionals involved in your EI services, your confidence will grow.

However, hear this: there is no "quick fix" or "one right answer" that will change your world overnight and solve all your problems. You're not going to find an easy solution in this community, or anywhere else in life, for that matter. You may not want to hear this, but it's the reality of the autism experience. Teaching a child with autism requires perseverance, patience and a lot of practice. You love your child and want what's best for him. In truth, this journey will be hard sometimes. Acknowledge that it's hard, get some outside counseling when you need it to get through particularly difficult periods—just don't give up. Your love for your child will sustain you. And never forget: as difficult as life may seem for you, your child is the one with autism. It's even more difficult for him. Don't lose sight of that.

Can these different methods really help my child?

In most cases, yes. Begin this journey with an unfailing belief that your child can learn. *He can learn.* He may require many more repetitions and repeated opportunities to practice emerging skills than do typical children, but he has the capacity to learn over time. Believe that he can do it. Believe in your child, even during times when learning seems stagnant or it feels like he's backsliding. Your belief is the inspiration he needs to be able to rise above his challenges and soar toward ever-wider horizons. Be the strength he needs.

Your child is a unique individual, a living, breathing entity who is much more than his diagnosis. You want an EI program that teaches the child, not his symptoms. (Sound familiar? That's strategy #1 in action!) Look for program models matched to his needs, to your family values, and that fit within the other parameters of your life. You're not looking for "the answer"—you're looking for a "good fit." Your child's needs will undoubtedly change over time. Resist the mindset that once you make a program decision, you can relax and not have to think about it again. Be curious about learning and ever mindful about assessing how a program is working, or not working, based not on your hunches, but on program evidence.

Are there any established guidelines for choosing the right program for my child?

The National Institute of Mental Health suggests the following list of questions parents can ask when planning a treatment program for their child:

- How successful has the program been for other children?
- How many children have gone on to placement in a regular school and how have they performed?
- Do staff members have training and experience in working with children with autism?
- How are activities planned and organized?
- Are there predictable daily schedules and routines?
- How much individual attention will my child receive?
- How is progress measured? Will my child's behavior be closely observed and recorded?
- Will my child be given tasks and rewards that are personally motivating?
- Is the environment designed to minimize distractions?
- Will the program prepare me to continue the therapy at home?
- What is the cost, time commitment, and location of the program?

Two other well-respected organizations in the autism community have valuable information related to appropriate treatment options. In 1997 the Autism Society of America adopted *Guidelines for Theory & Practice* that has helped thousands of parents make informed treatment choices. COSAC (The New Jersey Center for Outreach and Services for the Autism Community) offers their *Position Statement on Treatment Recommendations*, most recently updated in 2004. Both documents are included in Appendix D.

*"Only a few weeks after my son's second birthday, a diagnosis
of PDD sent both of our lives spiraling out of control. And after going
through all of the initial emotions that come with hearing the news,
I prepared myself for the most important few years of our lives.*

*I would not like to imagine where my son would be today had
he not received Early Intervention services. There is no doubt
in my mind that the amount of diverse therapy he received every day
at an early age was the most significant factor in his improved
development. He now spends his afternoons in a typical preschool
classroom, and is preparing for full-time typical kindergarten in the fall.
Still to this day, I refer to his Early Intervention therapists as his angels,
because they played such a huge role in where he is today. Their impact
was so great it is extremely difficult to express and quantify in words.*

*But take one look at my son today, the smile on his face when he interacts
with his friends on the playground, and suddenly words are not necessary."*

-DAVE, PARENT OF DAVID

Real-life Parents, Real-life Stories

Cynthia's Story

AS MY FIRST-BORN, MY SON KARL, GREW FROM 19 MONTHS TO TWO AND a half years, I went from happily checking milestones he had mastered to mulling over how to manage his increasingly bizarre, difficult and sometimes dangerous behavior. The strangest things would produce hours-long, teeth shattering tantrums that left me emotionally and physically drained. Most of the activities in a toddler book I had purchased—especially the ones prefaced with the assurance "every toddler loves this"—didn't even warrant a look from my son. Yes, he was making sounds that seemed to indicate words, but no one but I could understand them. As months rolled by, Karl's behaviors made it almost impossible to take him into any public place—restaurant, grocery store, etc.

Finally, in response to my worries, a family friend suggested I look up "Asperger's" on the internet. I did, and I was relieved but devastated at the same time. Relieved that my observations about my son were validated: I saw him reflected in the descriptions of kids with Asperger's Syndrome and autism. However, seeing words like "life-long disability," "no hope," and "institutionalization" devastated me. I cried for three hours in despair. I no longer knew what to hope for my precious boy.

When I was able to get myself together, the first person I called was a client who had mentioned she had a child with autism. She shared so much wisdom with me during that first phone call; her calm advice was a soothing balm on my wounded heart. I was astonished to hear that her training as a special education teacher had done nothing to prepare her to teach her own child and her caution to not expect very much from the public schools. She also introduced me to something called applied behavior analysis (ABA). This was 2001, and most pediatricians didn't know much about autism, nor provide any concrete advice in the way of treatment of these kids. Behavior analysts, however, did offer a way to deal with the bizarre and troublesome behaviors so that teaching and learning could begin, and they had been publishing research on how to do this for thirty years. ABA is a science that uses principles of behavior to redirect undesirable behavior into something more appropriate and functional. My client invited me to a play-group her behavior analyst would be facilitating. I decided to go and check it out.

I came away from that first play-group very impressed with the responses the behavior analyst was able to elicit from my son in such a short period of time. Eager to learn more, I started reading the book, *Behavioral Interventions for Young Children With Autism* edited by Catherine Maurice. I thought perhaps I could use some of these behavior techniques with him. It was more difficult than it seemed, and my first attempts to use it didn't go very well. I was already overwhelmed by nursing my five-month-old baby, keeping up with the laundry and the cooking and trying to keep up with a child who was in constant motion from the second he got up at 6:00 a.m. until the second his head hit the pillow at 7:00 p.m.. Where would I find the time, the energy, to take on this new program? I asked the behavior analyst to come out to the house and work with my son. It was during that session I noticed she saw and responded to a much slighter response from my son than I even knew to look for.

Right then I realized I needed more professional help. When a spot in her clinic opened up, I signed up Karl for as many hours of therapy we could afford—fifteen hours a week. At that time, it was recommended that children with autism receive somewhere near 40 hours a week of treatment. That weekly fifteen hours in the clinic cost us $1,800 a month—more than our house mortgage!!! I was really skeptical as to whether or not the therapy was going to be worth it. Proof arrived, however, soon enough. I had been unsuccessfully trying to get my son to answer a "yes" or "no" question for almost four months. I asked the behavior clinicians if they could work on this, and just two days later he was answering every yes or no question I asked him! This method really did work! I became an ABA convert that instant, and started attending any ABA-related training I could find. I committed to working with Karl myself to make up the remaining 25 hours of ABA we couldn't afford in the clinic. ABA quickly became part of our life.

When we first started at the clinic, the behavior analyst presented us with her resume and an explanation of behavior analysis. She made some statements I found odd at the time, being a complete newbie to the world of behavior analysis. She stated she "didn't do Lovaas" because the needs and learning style of the child should dictate which of the various methods derived from the science of behavior analysis were most appropriate. She explained that the choice of method would depend on what Karl was learning—a new skill, maintenance of a new skill, generalizing that skill in a variety of settings or with a peer. Some of the methods include DTT (discrete trial teaching), NET (natural environment teaching), pivotal response training, peer modeling, video modeling, discrimination, errorless learning, fluency training, and more. Some of Karl's sessions were very basic, involving the principles of behavior that are often used, such as extinction, shaping, prompting and fading. I learned that ABA is not just sitting at a table going through flash cards. It's so much more.

As I began learning how to prompt and reinforce my son, I became even more excited about the power and effectiveness of ABA. I learned to see the slight responses my son gave me and gradually "shaped" them into the more overt responses one sees in typical children. I learned to look at tasks from my son's perspective and began to realize how truly complicated and difficult some tasks, that a typical child picks up effortlessly, were for him. I had to break the task down into smaller steps for him. I learned how to track any behavior that was puzzling me to determine the antecedent causing it. As we all learned to work together, Karl began to fly quickly through his programs. His behavior change was positive and noticeable—sometimes dramatically so.

The entire community became my son's classroom. We worked on his programs at the grocery story, at the post office, in the car, on the playground, at home—anywhere an opportunity presented itself to work on a goal. I learned how to functionally keep track of data and keep these data sheets organized in a large three-ring binder. Decisions within an ABA program are based not on subjective assumptions about a child's behavior, but on reviewing concrete data to see exactly what's happening—or not—with a child.

I became a mom on a mission, focused on learning as much about autism as I could. I discovered Yahoo chat groups and rejoiced to finally connect with other moms on a similar journey. This road was a lonely one before there was the general awareness about autism there is now. Often family members didn't, or wouldn't, take the time to understand our situation. Although I was convinced that ABA was effective, the steep costs significantly impacted our budget and our social life. My husband worked long days to pay for Karl's ABA clinic time. He had recently landed a job that allowed us to afford the ABA, but as September 11, 2001 came and went, he was laid off in the mass of companies affected by the national disaster. I tried for months, unsuccessfully, to get our insurance company to pay for ABA. It was one more long, tough battle that I simply had neither the time nor energy to fight. We slowly began to use the funds from the sale of our house, our inheritance from my husband's grandmother, and finally our retirement, to continue Karl's program.

As timing would have it, my son started on the gluten-free portion of the GFCF (gluten-free, casein-free) diet his first day at the clinic. I had removed all milk products from his diet a few months previously. The improvements were immediate and dramatic. A week after I had removed milk from his diet, my father asked me if I had put him on a tranquilizer. With such a noticeable change, I decided that removing gluten would be worth the effort. As is common with many kids on this diet, we found ourselves working through a period where the GFCF diet revealed the true extent of my son's gastrointestinal problems and his diarrhea got increasingly worse. Again, having a network of moms to talk with brought me the help and information I needed. We added some enzymes to Karl's daily schedule, and he began having the first formed stools that I had seen in over six months. Since enzymes had helped him that much, I wondered if there was something else missing from his diet.

I learned about a conference on biomedical therapies for kids on the autism spectrum and decided to check it out. I'd been taking vitamins since I was a girl, so learning which supplements could improve my son's very limited diet seemed a very practical idea to me. At the conference in Dallas, Drs. Jeff Bradstreet and Jerry Kartzinel spoke about numerous supplements they used in children with autism they treated. I found a local nutritionist to monitor my son's nutritional program as we tried out various supplements I had learned about. The nutritionist had additional suggestions that worked as well. She also did NAET, a type of complementary allergy treatment. Using NAET, we slowly began treating the many, many foods to which my son reacted. About a year later, we added cranio-sacral therapy when my son began to have some inexplicable tantrums. It turned out to be a tremendous help too.

Karl is now nine and our journey continues. He is in public school in third grade for the first time; I home-schooled him through first and second grade. He'll be taking the grade-level academic testing along with the other third graders. His progress over a few short years has been amazing. He loves playing imaginative games with his younger sister, and I find him delightful most of the time. Just like any other kid, he has his moments that test my patience and parenting skills. We have a typical family life mostly—going out in the community and having a good time together.

Today Karl tests out of the autism spectrum with one assessment and barely in the spectrum with another. He does still have some issues, but continues to improve every day. I have many days when I forget that my son has a diagnosis of autism. It's a blessing that makes up for those days when the autism does show up and throws us for a loop. Just like any other child, Karl keeps learning and exploring his world. In 2007, he attended his first sleep-over camp for 6 days, 5 nights. It was an inclusion camp, and he was one of three campers with an aide. It was a big step for him, and he loved it. This summer he also began asking me about my special interest in children with autism. This has led to some very interesting conversations about his autism, what it means, how it affects him and when he's going to recover. He loves to call his grandparents who live out of state and has wonderful conversations with them. He continues to assure me that the real SuperKarl can do anything, and I believe him.

To the parents reading my story, you who are still reeling from the news of the diagnosis, anxious, scared and wondering where to start, I leave you with this one bit of advice: have more faith in your gut instinct about what is right for your child than any advice from any "expert." You know your child, and your feeling about the "rightness of something" is usually more important than anything you will hear or read. There are simply more questions about autism than there are answers right now. By the Grace of God, my son started out with the intervention method that had solid, peer-reviewed scientific research to back it up. ABA is still where I encourage people to begin. However, do your homework before choosing a program and professional. There is a tremendous lack of well-trained, well-rounded ABA practitioners who have sufficient experience with children with autism. There are a lot of people in the community with minimal training and experience, happy to make a buck doing something they claim is ABA. Start with a practitioner who considers parents an integral part of the team and who bases decisions on your child's individual needs and learning style instead of making your child fit their program. Ask lots of questions, and make sure you are comfortable with the answers you receive. If not, keep looking.

Despite how much we may wish for a crystal ball to give us answers and assurances that we're making the right choices, there simply isn't one. One thing I do know for sure: there is tremendous hope for our amazing children with autism. Each day we learn more about how to help them. It's a fascinating journey, filled with many joys and challenges. Run, don't walk, from anyone who would tell you otherwise.

Cynthia Singleton is a fifth-generation Texan and native Houstonian. She spends time enjoying the miracle of her son's emergence from autism, studying yoga and advocating on autism issues. In 2007 she led a grassroots effort to pass legislation in Texas that mandates insurance coverage for children three to five with the diagnosis of autism. Her mantra continues to be: what is my next step for today?

◎ ◎ ◎

Ashley's Story

OUR SON, LEO, WAS DIAGNOSED AT TWO WITH PDD-NOS. HE RECEIVED early intervention services through our local Zero to Three program. About a year after the diagnosis, we realized preschool age was quickly approaching. Our exposure to other special-needs children, particularly those with autism, was very limited, yet I knew, as Leo's mom, I needed to take a look at where he might go next, since once he turned three his early intervention services would be provided through our public school system. I began my search for a school, thinking Leo would be placed in a special education program that would address his needs. To my surprise, the programs I looked at seemed grossly wrong for my son. I may not have had a whole lot of experience with autism at that point, but I knew this like I know my own name. I realized then and there choosing a school and program were not going to be easy.

What was I going to do? The public school's special ed program had no other children like Leo in it. He could handle himself in a regular environment, and had mastered basic skills. His behaviors were manageable and he was ahead academically. At three, Leo had progressed to the point that he had some language, but the social skills gap between him and his peers was widening at an alarming rate. I knew it was only time until his social deficits were noticeable to everyone. But where did he belong?

Time was running out; I had to make a decision. Should I place him in the special ed school where he clearly didn't belong? Or should I keep my spot at the local regular preschool? I had signed him up when he was just one year old, before his diagnosis. I finally went with my gut, which told me the regular preschool, although challenging, was a far better fit, than the special ed program where he'd probably get away with murder and stim all day.

My big lesson? Even though my son was "high functioning," he still needed a formal, intensive program. No matter where your child falls on the spectrum, all ASD children need and deserve this.

I continued to research programs and therapies, trying to find a good match for Leo. To my surprise, I eventually found myself back right where I began, with ABA. Early on during this journey into early intervention and autism, my Zero to Three team told me ABA was a very bad approach, totally wrong for Leo. They scared me with horrible stories and, after hearing what they said, I trusted their judgment. I now realize that what they were describing was just bad ABA. Crappy ABA seems to dominate many environments, I'm sorry to say! And, parents need to be aware of this. As the saying goes, "There's more bad ABA than good ABA, and everyone is busy."

I believed my team advisors and, to their credit, they were partially correct. DTT (discrete trial teaching) wasn't the correct intervention method to address the goals and objectives exquisitely laid out by my Yale evaluation professionals. But that didn't mean ABA in general was wrong for Leo. I investigated further and through conversations with other ASD parents, finally found the right ABA delivery method for Leo, one that was built on two important premises: 1) detailed, individualized and intensive goals and objectives, and 2) the right therapy for each one. For Leo, the right intervention turned out to be ABA-NET. ABA-NET is a form of ABA where intervention is delivered in the natural environment—our family room, at school and day care. It also efficiently addresses higher-level social skills like perspective taking, Theory Of Mind, and Executive Functioning—the missing piece we were looking for in a program for Leo.

At home, Leo's one-to-one ABA therapy sessions were not at a table, but held mostly in our family room, living room, and sometimes outside. Leo "led" the play sessions with his "grown-up friend" (his therapist). Just like DTT, a Clinical Supervisor designed individualized ABA goals and objectives for him. The difference was how it was implemented (NET).

At the beginning of each session, the therapist reviewed Leo's list of programs and any previous session notes, and began the session by asking Leo what he'd like to do. After discussing various options, the therapist would incorporate a goal into play.

For example, Leo asked to play the board game Chutes and Ladders. While setting up the game, the therapist asked Leo to guess which player piece she'd choose. She and Leo would have a discussion about how Leo could figure out which token she might pick. They'd played the game many times, so the therapist used that prior knowledge to demonstrate how history can be helpful. Does the therapist choose the same piece each time? Why or why not? Leo was also asked to recall her favorite color, as every therapist has tastes and preferences just like Leo does. This conversation worked on the program goal Prediction.

It was common that, during the game, other spontaneous opportunities for learning something that applied to one of Leo's goals could arise. For instance, during the game, Leo's baby sister woke up from her nap, crying. Leo and the therapist heard her on the monitor. Taking advantage of the opportunity, the therapist asked Leo how he knew she was awake. He had no idea. They discussed ways Leo could know this information. Could he see her? No. Could he feel her? No. Oh, he could hear her. That was it! This conversation worked on the program goal Sensory Perspective Taking.

After a game is over, they might play again or move onto another activity. With goals and objectives in mind, the ABA-NET therapist continues to weave learning into natural activities and experiences. Throughout the session, the therapist redirected Leo away from stims and kept him on task, utilizing positive reinforcement. Leo worked hard, but he had a lot of fun during his sessions too. ABA is all about positive reinforcement! Snacks, sensory input, and a change of scenery may be considered. Depending on the day and duration of the session, Leo practiced some or all of his objectives. At the end of a session, the therapist filled out data sheets in paragraph-like form, describing what they did rather than reporting raw data, although some raw data was taken for stims, redirections, etc.

ABA-NET has the advantage of allowing the child some control (reinforcing in and of itself), and activities/materials chosen by the child tend to be more motivating. NET also makes it easier to utilize and/or introduce naturally occurring reinforcers (for instance, to play a game just because it's fun), which allows behaviors to generalize and persevere.

When not doing ABA-NET at home, one of Leo's ABA therapists took the role of a "shadow" at school and day care. She facilitated only when needed, remaining in the background as much as possible. The therapist facilitated social interactions, provided Leo with additional information, and gave feedback and prompting when necessary, all with Leo's goals and objectives in mind.

Taking the example of the program goal Prediction again, the shadow may ask Leo what a classmate might do first when they go out for recess. Will his friend Jack run straight for the swings as he did the last three days?

Leo had the ability to function in a normal setting, so this is where therapy resided, integrated into his and our lives at school and within regular home life (although we modified it quite a bit to reduce stimming and increase regular play and interests). Working in the real world, at school, at home with real games and teaching within the fluid structure of daily life events that come up unexpectedly made sense to all of us, since this is where Leo struggled. Working on the front lines with him streamlined his learning. There was no transition from "therapy" to "life." It all meshed together. Leo flew through his programs because of this delivery style.

A typical therapy day for Leo might look something like this:

8:30 – 9:00 a.m.: OT at elementary school

9:30 – 12:00 p.m.: Preschool with shadow the entire time (2.5 hours)

Lunch

1:00–4:00 p.m.: Day care setting with shadow (3 hours)

4:15 – 6:15 p.m.: 2 hours one-to-one ABA-NET at home (carryover issues from school/day care, work on current programs to games and play chosen by Leo)

Dinner and evening routine. Programs incorporated when possible.

We continued with Speech, OT, and PT. Some of the speech goals were moved within the ABA program. The ABA program drove all other interventions; it was the glue that pulled all components together. They even worked on OT and PT goals during their sessions.

ABA-NET would be difficult for a therapist or parent who is used to ABA table sessions. It's quite different. DTT is a very structured, data-driven teaching format, and it can be challenging for adults to adopt the mindset and alter their teaching style to manipulate the environment in order for the child to think he's in control. The child may be given several choices of what to do or play, all imbedded with skills to practice! I think ABA-NET is much easier to learn than DTT, RDI, and other approaches, but everyone is different.

For this reason I was always nervous about integrating a new therapist into the mix. With DTT any new therapist can just look at the data and notes, and get to work. With ABA-NET it takes a while to break in a new therapist. They have to spend time with the child, learn his patterns, his strengths and weaknesses. Only time reveals a child's subtle tricks to wiggle out of doing something he doesn't like or want to do, or to notice how stims impact learning. My Leo can be a great manipulator and new therapists don't recognize his patterns right away!

A therapist has to be very seasoned in working in general with children the age of their client. Therapists with experience in regular education settings often have an advantage, since regular education interaction is the goal, if not the place where a child will eventually be acquiring skills. It can be very hard to find good therapists who have these qualifications.

Parents who integrate almost any reliable therapy into their regular life have more success than those who remain "just the parent" and leave therapy up to the therapists. Just being the parent didn't work for me. I had an internal alarm bell that rang inside my head for about four years, continually pushing me to read anything I could get my hands on and observe most of Leo's sessions so I could copy their teaching strategies and work them into regular life. Taking the example of the Prediction program, while waiting in line at the drive-thru for lunch, I may ask "So Leo, what do you think Mommy will order for herself? What kinds of foods have you seen Mommy eat in the past? What did Mommy order the last time we came here?" Right before feeding the cat, I may ask "So Leo, what will happen when I shake the cat food container? What will Sydney do when I show her the hairbrush? Will she frown and start to cry? Or will she smile?" I believe this is the key to getting the most out of any intervention, giving success the biggest chance of settling in, and keeping the family involved and motivated.

It wasn't easy getting on board with the number of hours any intensive therapy requires of parents and the entire family. Leo's ABA program began at 10 hours per week; at most it topped off around 30 hours per week. Generally it was at least 20 hours each week, and lasted over several years. Once he entered the public school system, shadow time at the preschool and day care took up the majority of the hours of Leo's therapy. When he wasn't in that setting, however, we spent all of our time integrating learning into regular life. We knew his programs inside and out. If I didn't, we'd research it until we did. It didn't make sense to allow him to stim or play inappropriately when he wasn't in therapy. We wanted him to learn new, appropriate skills and behaviors; we thought it would be too confusing for him, two sets of behavior rules: one while in therapy and another for all the other times. I spent all of my extra time learning how to teach Leo the skills he was working on, and planning for the next set of programs. Our goal was to not waste any moment of waking time. After all, learning happens every-where! And the therapy was a big financial burden for us. But so were other therapies we had in place. I have come to believe that what you do for your child, within your own family circumstances, is a personal decision. Some families are willing to sacrifice more than others. There's no right or wrong, just parents doing their best with what they have.

Some parents have family support systems who jump on board when a child is diagnosed and early intensive intervention begins. With our family, no one was involved except myself, my husband and Leo's younger sister. Unbeknownst to her, she was instrumen-tal to Leo understanding others' perspectives, a concept that is so challenging for our children. Our dog even played a role too. Today as I write this, I still marvel at Leo's comments. He is telling me our dog is watching the neighbor's new dog. "His tail is straight up and he isn't moving at all, looking down the hill at the neighbor's dog, mom." Funny how Theory of Mind takes hold in our kids. He now even notices it in the dog.

Even though intensive ABA therapy can be challenging at times, ABA-NET gave me new insights into myself and my relationships with my family and friends; I understand human behavior on a whole different level now. It was a good match with our personalities as parents overall. This therapy was nothing but a positive influence on the quality of all our lives.

After years of living the life of a square peg, we adapted to NET pretty quickly. Looking back, I now realize that in the early years, when we were trying to make other styles fit our family, were actually the harder part. Everything we were supposed to do for Leo seemed opposite to my parental instinct. I coined the phrase, "Counter-Intuitive Parenting" to describe to new parents the feeling they get during those first few months post-diagnosis. Watching your child's first several therapy sessions can break your heart. It's all so foreign, so opposite to the way we feel learning should naturally occur. If you find yourself in that situation, take some time and learn about ABA-NET. Rethinking "therapy" as life-integrated learning does wonders to smooth this transition for everyone, especially the child.

I am happy to report we eventually stopped therapy because Leo had mastered all the concepts he needed in order to learn from his environment. We continue to monitor him, and if he requires assistance in the future, we'll step in and find instruction to address his needs. If I could do it all over again, the only thing I'd change would be to begin ABA-NET earlier, at two of course!

My Leo today is not the same boy as the child who existed before we began ABA-NET. Then, Leo didn't know how to play with other children or with other adults. He had chronic anxiety and wasn't a happy child. If left to his own devices, he would stim about 80% of his day. His language was limited to pointing and making simple requests. About three years later, Leo no longer met the diagnostic criteria for PDD-NOS, and today, he no longer requires any therapy. He leads the life of a typical third grader, with no label, no modifications or help of any kind. He doesn't have an IEP, and his current teacher hasn't even an inkling of what he's been through. He is today judged as an individual, not a label. His third grade teacher describes him as a confident child that other children seek as a friend. He is always willing to contribute, even when the topic may be challenging. He gives it his best shot. Although he is not the best test-taker, he is a solid B student at the top of his class on all subjects. Best of all, he is an active, involved part of our family and the special relationships that bind us together. He makes us all crack up regularly at home, his sister thinks he is the sweetest big brother ever, and to us, he's our beloved son. I wouldn't change a thing. Life is good.

Ashley Morgan is a full-time mom working part-time as a teacher. She also maintains an autism website focused on social skills and mainstreaming. Ashley's goal is to "pay it forward" by supporting newly diagnosed parents, or parents at a crossroads. She welcomes comments from readers, and can be reached at www.hiddenrecovery.com.

◉ ◉ ◉

Elizabeth's Story

I HAVE THREE CHILDREN—TWO BOYS AND ONE GIRL. WHEN MY OLDEST boy, John, was three, he received a diagnosis of PDD-NOS. We needed help as much as did our son. We had just missed the cut-off age for Early Intervention services, but received help through the local school district. They offered him a place in their public preschool program, and provided ABA therapists for John at our house. Having structured services was a real turning point for us all. We had other hurdles to jump later on, but for now we had some support.

After a short while I knew in my heart that the regimented type of ABA therapy being used with John was not going to be the long-term answer for him. I started looking for other alternatives.

Meanwhile, my second son, James, was showing some speech delay, and was, in my opinion, too unresponsive to the world around him. This time I was banging on Early Intervention's door when he was 18 months old. Early Intervention professionals assessed our little boy, and from the onset, this experience was different. The professional conducting the assessment was a DIR/Floortime specialist, and her emphasis was far more on the child and his comfort levels as a starting point for intervention. She suggested James would be a good candidate for this therapy, and having earlier experienced an ABA program I realized that Floortime would be far more appropriate for James. He was shy and uncommunicative, and needed a more subtle therapy centered on his play. We already knew he would shut down when things became too much for him. We had to work at his pace and comfort levels.

We started Floortime therapy through a local foundation here in Massachusetts, working alongside our Early Intervention agency. DIR/Floortime requires committed parental involvement, and our agency made it clear from the beginning that both my husband and I needed to attend the Floortime training program, where we were taught simple Floortime principles and strategies. We were encouraged to actively play with our son and use these play sessions as the vehicle for intervention—how enlightening and wonderful is that? I was encouraged by the simplicity of the DIR/Floortime model, with its six primary levels (measured goals children attain as their play becomes more sophisticated). It made sense to me, resonated with my own personal ideas of what therapy should be. Plus, it was a therapy I could do myself in my own home. James also received support from other Early Intervention specialists, such as occupational therapy, speech and language therapy, and a weekly Floortime-based playgroup to round out his program.

We were advised to try and do Floortime sessions with James several hours a day. But, with two small boys and a house to run, I found myself increasingly working in Floortime sessions during our normal daily routines: at the playground or the grocery store, on an international flight to Europe, and even in the doctor's waiting room. Some onlookers must have wondered at times! The DIR/Floortime principles seemed intuitive to me. When we were away from home without familiar toys, I found myself using wood chips and stones—anything to connect and inspire both my children to play. Practically anything could magically transform into cars, trains, trucks and ice cream shops to encourage that "gleam" in their eyes, and the willingness to communicate with me and others. This is at the heart of the DIR/Floortime model. After just a few months I was seeing results—so much quicker than I had hoped! This spurred me on.

I learned that Floortime is a subtle art, and reading children's body language is everything! Not all our ideas are winners and parents need to be able to work flexibly with a child and make adjustments on the spot. With my third child, Sophie, some Floortime techniques just didn't work at first. One technique is to very gently tease the child (playful obstruction) to encourage a response and widen the "circle" of communication. Some children, like my Sophie, hate to be teased or pushed too much. Therapists and caregivers must constantly modify their actions; otherwise, they risk losing the child's engagement or trust. We must back off and start again slowly. To be too overbearing or vocally loud can also throw off the child. Each session is different. For me this was very hard, and I still check myself on a regular basis to make sure I'm following my child's lead, and not trying to lead my child!

It's also important for parents to understand that DIR/Floortime is more of a "lifestyle" model than an intervention program that starts and stops according to some time schedule. Theoretically, from the moment I hug Sophie first thing in the morning, therapy begins. "What shall we wear today, Sophie—an elephant?" So begins the constant application of Floortime principles in everyday life— throwing her little world topsy turvy, and making her grin or laugh —just a little bit! At lunch I may say "Mom's going to the fridge, and I'm getting a giant…", pausing in anticipation while I wait for her reply, constantly looking at her. At times I may wait for a long while for a response, and finally, maybe Sophie replies "A giant ice cream with strawberries, Mom!" We then play ice cream shop, and pretend sandwich making, and I experience unbelievable little conversations with my two year old. After lunch we may play ice cream shops again, developing the ideas she has, and then airports, then tools and machines that make cup cakes and frosting, then doctors. Who knows what we will play, but she leads with her ideas, and it is fun, exciting, and of great benefit to Sophie. Those are the great days – not a typical day where interactions are less frequent or less creative or Sophie is less responsive. But I am happy with even a few great days here and there. They show me what is possible and motivate me to do the work that is involved with using DIR/Floortime.

Although parents are the center of the Floortime model, we also work with other Early Intervention therapists who have all been trained in DIR/Floortime, although their personal specializations may be in other areas. In my experience so far this has been of great benefit to Sophie, whose Early Intervention care has been all-encompassing. We work with a wonderful Floortime specialist once a week, who guides my own at-home Floortime therapy. I would not recommend "going it alone"—using DIR/Floortime without having some level of professional guidance. No child makes consistent improvement, and every once in a while will regress. To have the experience and guidance of a Floortime specialist on a weekly basis is invaluable, especially in those early years.

I would also recommend that at a later stage, after the initial training, parents or caregivers find time to go on a refresher course. Personally, I was amazed at how much information I had retained, and how much I had forgotten! A good rapport with a trained Floortime professional is everything, and I regard our therapists as mentors. Experience is everything, both in work and, it seems, in play, too.

James was the main beneficiary of using the DIR/Floortime model, but it was soon clear to me that John, my eldest, needed this therapy also. He had had a steady diet of ABA therapy since the age of three, but that therapy seemed so inflexible and formal for our little children, in contrast to Floortime, which offered them a chance to play and be imaginative. My husband and I often discussed the fact that we had two very different boys, with different personalities and learning styles. At times we were able to do Floortime with them both, but we admit it was not easy. One son was very outgoing and verbose, and the other shy and retiring. John dominated play at every opportunity, not allowing space for James to try out his ideas. With their younger sister, they occasionally join in the Floortime fun. It is a wonderful but rare moment when all three siblings do Floortime themselves. The children collectively eye the living room sofa, throw the cushions on the floor, and build a magic castle, unprompted by an adult. Our only stipulation at this point is that they clean up the mess afterwards!

DIR/Floortime therapy is creative in nature, and this suits my own personality. I am relatively relaxed about most things and have a background in music and the arts. I'm comfortable with not knowing what I'll do next with one of my children during a Floortime session. I have known other parents who struggle with Floortime, wanting more "structure" and "tick boxes" to guide their actions and assess progress in a more concrete manner. Everyone's different, and Floortime will be comfortable for some and be stress inducing and too "loose" for others. In its defense, however, I would say DIR/Floortime is quantative and has a core structure. That it doesn't is one of the biggest misconceptions about the model. However, that structure sits in the background, rather than the forefront in how it unfolds.

The specific levels of attainment must be constantly referenced (mentally) during interactions. Floortime parents and therapists have to be playful and flexible while children navigate through their play sessions, while constantly measuring children's levels of success and engagement. We adapt our own responses to our child's cues and body language. My husband is an engineer, and although he made the commitment to do Floortime therapy with his children, he naturally leans towards more traditional structure and data collecting within treatment. But even he admits to the success of Floortime, and I am pleased to report we are still happily married. I think he recognizes the strength and simplicity of Floortime therapy, which focuses on the child and play, and understands that, for our children, this model is the best "fit."

There is a financial investment in using DIR/Floortime. The initial parent training program, plus travel and accommodations costs several thousand dollars when everything is factored in. Having regular consultations and guidance from a trained Floortime practitioner may become an out-of-pocket expense once the child ages out of Early Intervention. However, for those parents for whom this might be a financial burden, let me assure you that you can do it alone. To get started, visit the comprehensive website for the

Interdisciplinary Council of Developmental and Learning Disorders (ICDL) at *www.icdl.com*, or the Floortime Foundation at *www.Floortime.org*. Become familiar with the key components of Floortime before initial training, and make user-friendly "reminder" cards to have on hand while you play with your children. DIR/Floortime founder Stanley Greenspan's books on the model are helpful resources and guides in themselves. Consider "applied" use of Floortime strategies if you are away from home, or out and about most of the day. This suits my own family, as we tend to be mostly on the move. My Floortime efforts are more spontaneous moments than scheduled sessions. It took us about six months to become comfortable with the Floortime "program" and adapting our own personalities to follow our children's lead. Initially I was too loud for James, and my husband was not great at increasing circles of communication. We did improve with the wealth of ideas and help from our wonderful therapists. In the absence of therapists, connecting with other DIR/Floortime families can be an avenue for helpful advice.

James was uncommunicative before we started his Floortime program. Sometimes, if he wanted another chicken nugget, he would move his eyes across the kitchen to the plate on the counter, not even pointing. Now, at the age of six, he is always talking and sharing his ideas or things he has made, with animation and enthusiasm. He is a different child as a result of Floortime.

I am still using DIR/Floortime predominantly with Sophie, my youngest child. She also has some speech delay, although not severe, and displays some regulatory issues when situations become too much for her. She is doing well with Floortime, and displays that healthy animated "gleam" of connectedness we all so want to see in our children.

In retrospect, my husband and I would choose the same intervention models for our children. ABA therapy served its purpose for John. He needed the structure of the approach and the boundaries and limitations to his random behaviors at the time. At a later stage when his unpredictable behaviors had diminished, Floortime would have been an ideal therapy for him at school, helping with his social-relationships difficulties, for instance, during play-time at recess. He still is a strong candidate for Floortime to improve certain lower concrete levels of relationship interaction. He now has an Asperger diagnosis, and my challenge will be to introduce Floortime to him in an age-appropriate way. My regret is not having Early Intervention and Floortime for John before he turned three, but we move forward and cannot linger with our regrets.

My advice to anyone considering or starting out with DIR/Floortime as a therapy is this: always think outside the box, and make the therapy portable wherever you go. Have fun and be as creative as you dare. In time, you will gain confidence in how to incorporate DIR principles to bring about positive growth in your child. You'll find yourself and your family surrounded by rewarding experiences with your wonderful children.

Elizabeth and her husband live with their three children, John (8), James (6) and Sophie (2), near Boston, Massachusetts. John has an Asperger diagnosis, and attends a regular elementary school with the support of an aide. James receives help for reading, and occupational therapy in the same school. Sophie receives Floortime, speech, occupational therapy, and help with regulatory issues.

⊙ ⊙ ⊙

Patricia's Story

Nights under the gray-white fixture in the kitchen, the street light outside beckoning, calling with its invisible pull, like fingers drawing him away. Walker in his car seat on the table, drinking formula from a bottle he doesn't seem to watch or notice, his head away from me, slanting, always slanting toward the blinds.

If light were air, I'd say he was trying to inhale it.

WHEN MY SON WALKER WAS TWO OR THREE MONTHS OLD, I USED TO think he was looking out the windows of the car at the trees as he lay passively in his car seat. Yet at home, from his place on the floor facing the sky, he still stared at windows. If there were no windows, he looked at the light, to the lamp in the corner, or even at a raw bulb. His face moved like the needle of a compass, always seemingly away. Light was his true north. And what lay away from that magnetic pole—including me, my husband Cliff and our daughter Elizabeth—seemed invisible.

I began to understand over the early months of Walker's development that faces seen up close were too much for him. Though he might focus his stare straight into the glare of an incandescent light bulb, he could not tolerate the light of another person's eyes. The gaze was too much. Other problems worried us.

I kept waiting for time to turn him into more of a person. He was too passive, too limp, never smiled—he seemed to bear the weight of the world on his wrinkled forehead. My son was failing. But failing at what?

My story begins when Walker was six months old, when two extraordinary women from our early intervention program came into our lives—Dawn Smith and Arlene Spooner. Arlene was Walker's physical therapist and sensory integration expert. She came to our house to work with Walker in the first few weeks after we had called early intervention. Arlene often came into the living room, where Walker lay on a blanket, and studied him, marveling at his strange behaviors. Sometimes he lay there, dull and near-motionless as an old cinderblock, staring off. Other times he was the opposite—a caricature of excitement, showing an eerie joy. He laughed maniacally, whipped at the sky with his legs. I didn't know anything about sensory integration at the time. The term meant nothing to me. Yet slowly, over the first few visits, Arlene began to explain that if a child's visual processing is not working, if he is too sensitive to look at what we as adults look at with ease or even indifference, then he would be forced to look away. If he couldn't attend, he couldn't learn. I knew then that this was a matter of life and death—that we would lose him for good if we couldn't get his attention. But how to attract a baby who couldn't bear to look at us at close range?

We began in a darkened room. Arlene closed the blinds and turned to me. "Here, she said, "hold Walker in your arms." She positioned him in the shape of a C. "Now you can look," she offered. I smiled at my baby. "No, try to keep a straight face. Even a smile might be too much for Walker." I held my face very neutral, though inside I was aflame with something like hope and terror. Walker was look-ing away, searching the blinds, perhaps for the light that so often comforted him. But slowly, as I made soft cooing noises, he began to turn his face toward mine. Walker looked at me for a split-second and as he did, raised his hand toward my face, yet in the moment he jerked his hand and face away, as if looking had been too painful. The connection was gone. I had lost his attention. Arlene explained to me that it was not his fault. He wanted to look. He just couldn't.

I think it was that moment that helped me understand in the deep-est way possible what children with autism want, and what keeps them from having it. Our children with ASD want to love, want to connect, but their bodies, their sensory systems, often make that impossible. This was the beginning of working the DIR method (Developmental, Individual-Difference, Relationship-based Intervention), though she did not use the terminology at the time. Now that I understand what DIR is about, I know that Arlene brought everything she knew about Walker's processing problems to the table as she worked with him—and that she probably wouldn't have been able to make progress if she hadn't done so. This is the fundamental task of the practitioner of DIR. The idea was to use affect (the emotions) and an awareness of processing differences, to create connection—juicy, lovely, healthy, life-affirming connection. The connection couldn't just be casual, or incidental. It couldn't just be a moment, a chance encounter—the connection would have to be real, to build up to meaningful and lasting moments. Walker's learning would have to mean as much emotionally to Walker as it did to us.

Not long after that day when Walker almost touched my face, Arlene brought into the case Dawn Smith, an autism specialist who had spent her life working with kids on the spectrum. After studying Walker, Dawn felt she was seeing some of the earliest signs of autism she had ever seen in a child. She felt if we worked hard, we might have a chance. Dawn, just a few weeks before, had been to a conference on autism given by Dr. Stanley Greenspan, a developmental psychiatrist who had won the American Academy of Psychiatrists' highest award of achievement. Greenspan, with the help of colleague Serena Wieder and a host of experts in sensory and processing dysfunction, had developed DIR, a method that had shown stunning success for remediating autism. Dawn was impressed by the child-centered approach at the heart of the method, and its focus on using children's strengths to overcome deficiencies. DIR is about connection, about forming strong emotional bonds and using those bonds to widen a child's spheres of connection. It's strategies and values seemed to "fit" our family and our goals for intervention.

Dawn brought me a pre-publication article by Greenspan that explained that children who evidence autism spectrum disorders do not develop complex chains of problem-solving, reciprocal interactions. That was confusing terminology, but what I now know he means is that they couldn't converse, or do the play version of conversation—couldn't learn through interaction. Instead, they cut off interaction. The way to build interaction was through Floortime—a core component of the DIR model. *But what was this? My God! Greenspan expected parents or therapists to do it eight to ten times a day for twenty minutes or more! I was supposed to do it eight to ten times a day?* I picked up the phone and called Greenspan's office and spoke with his assistant, Sarah Miller. My real question to Sarah was "How the heck can anyone do this much therapy?" Her answer was to put me on a waiting list. Within a few weeks we were flying down to Bethesda, Maryland to meet Greenspan. Walker was eleven months old.

After looking at Walker's records and studying him, Greenspan asked us to get down on the floor with Walker. He immediately began showing us how we could interact with our son to help him connect emotionally. I had heard that Floortime was like playing with your kid, but Greenspan taught us it was anything but playing. I never worked so hard in my life. He showed us that we were "losing" Walker from time to time and gave us advice for how to entice him back. Once back we would have to step up the pace, make our voices more animated, more exciting, asking questions at a more rapid pace.

Greenspan saw that Walker liked to be rocked from side to side and liked to be kissed on the stomach. But if we did it once or twice and got a laugh out of our baby, that wasn't enough for

Greenspan. He wanted us to turn this desire, this preference of his, into a game. If he liked it, it was a pathway for more sustained connection. "Hold your hand up, mom, and get him to touch one hand if he wants a kiss and another hand if he wants you to rock him back and forth." I began frantically working to keep Walker playing the game, revving up my energy, using a higher pitched voice to get his attention, and asking him again and again, showing him my hands—kissing his stomach if he touched my left hand; rocking him if he touched my right. I didn't even think Walker was smart enough to understand language, or to read our actions, yet Walker actually started playing the game. We had managed to get him to engage in what Greenspan was calling "circles of communication." The point was to increase the circles so we could stay on the same page with Walker for longer intervals of time. Start with one successful beat, and keep up the energy. Keep him coming back for more—increase those beats into chains of interactions until they became not just islands in the child's daily life, but the very stuff of his life. "You must be the button he pushes to make what he wants happen," Greenspan said. The point was that we had to *be everything* to him, and he had to learn to look to us for what he wanted—for food, for treats, for fun. He would lose his interest in the solitary world. Pathways for human connection and tolerance for stimulation would grow in his brain, the way they do in typical children. Within those hours in Greenspan's office, playing "games" with our autistic baby, I found myself laughing and lying against Walker and truly sharing a joyful moment for the first time in our lives together.

Still, we had a big problem. If Greenspan had given us tools for connecting with our son, he had also created a crisis: How would we ever be able to do this kind of intense therapy with our kid eight to ten times a day for twenty or more minutes? Our social worker hated Greenspan. "How can a doctor expect this much from parents?" But while she hated him for placing demands on our family, I loved him. We had been to so many doctors who said "Wait." Or "I share your concerns for your child." But no doctor before had EVER given us a prescription for how to help our son engage. If this is what it took, this is what it took.

This crisis led to many changes in our lives. We eventually found a volunteer from Smith College, named Amy, who agreed to do ten hours a week of Floortime with Walker (she now has a Ph.D. in child development and claims that Walker changed her life). Our early intervention program (REACH) stepped up the time Walker would have with Dawn and Arlene and granted us three months of an added ten hours a week with a Floortime tutor. Our local Unitarian Society brought in meals. We began working, and working hard.

It was a hellish time in our lives, but a romantic one too, because our son was changing and quickly. The idea was to use Walker's natural desire to entice him to communicate with us out of necessity. Amy eventually taught Walker sign language to ask for what he wanted, and within a month he was using words to replace the signs. When Arlene did Floortime, she added a P.T. component. Before he could even walk, Walker had to scale balance boards on his hands and knees, climb over ramps—all part of emotionally charged games that Arlene invented. Once he could do longer and longer "circles of communication," we added hiding games (always a favorite of Greenspan). We hid parts of wooden puzzles and asked him to go find them and bring them back to make the puzzle. All the while we talked, had him using his brain, and made it fun, so that it was about joy. Always about joy.

In the early years, working so hard with our son was a trial, a crisis, a black hole. I might wake up, go into Walker's room, interact joyfully with him for half an hour, then rush into the bathroom and take a five-minute shower, then rush out again and interact with him. If the phone rang, I ignored it. The house got messy. I lost some friends. I couldn't take him to the store. I rested, ate, got back to playing, and so on. If we had been rich we could have paid someone to do a lot of the therapy. But we were not.

I had been teaching prior to Walker's birth and was just considering my next career move when Walker received his first diagnosis. I simply had to stop all thoughts of work. Meanwhile, we were paying for vitamin therapy and developmental movement therapy. Cliff grew so worried about money, he took on freelance work, leaving me to do most of the therapy. Amy, Dawn, and Arlene did from zero to six sessions a day. That left me with an hour to three hours a day of work. Who cares about money, I thought. What we needed was manpower, time with our son, our kids. Cliff often shared his extra energy with Elizabeth. At night, I lay in bed sometimes, like my son, overwhelmed. I did not particularly want to be touched. I was touched out, talked out, played out. But over time, life grew easier. We started having fun. Floortime fit us because we wanted to be close emotionally, to have tools to remain that way. Today Elizabeth claims she tells me more than any kid her age tells her parents.

We got back what DIR took from us. If it took life from us; it gave us life. If it took energy; it gave energy. DIR emboldened us to believe and to finally see that the brain truly can heal.

As Walker scaled Greenspan's "Developmental Ladder," Dawn felt it was time to start working on imaginative play and flexibility of thinking, which are fundamental developmental steps in DIR. Walker was about one and a half by then. She began by helping him develop a pretend-play scenario. He grabbed some plastic keys, took a bag, and pretended he was going to the store. "Bye-bye Daw…" he waved and went to the door to unlock it. "Hi Daw" he staggered back into the room.

"What did you buy, Walker?" He opened the bag and play-acted at taking things out. Such was the beginning of our son's understanding of theater.

Greenspan's direction (and that of Dawn and Arlene, who were well-versed in DIR and guided us through the levels) led to endless imaginary play games. We went from tea parties to firemen to Batman to endless incarnations of Harry Potter. Both my husband Cliff and I spent years in Harry Potter scenarios with Walker.

I feel we were very lucky to learn about DIR and Floortime because Greenspan's philosophy cemented, solidified, and even transformed our family culture. We even did a form of Floortime with our daughter Elizabeth, as per Greenspan's orders, to keep her healthy too. The answer is the same for every family, every child, according to Greenspan and Wieder: You stay close by interacting.

Walker, now eleven, is a creative, warm, friendly, highly intelligent and empathic person. An avid reader, he adores history and fiction and has a profound understanding of what lies between the lines in literature. We still play imaginary games, although now Walker writes his own creative stories and reads them to us. I attribute most of his strengths to his years of Floortime, which taught him what human connection is about. I would recommend this method to any parent with any child. It will take you on an adventure into the very inside of your child's deepest fears, and sorrows, desires and joys, and even your own.

I have heard it said "If you don't bring forth what is within you, it will destroy you; if you bring forth what is within you, it will save you." I believe this is what Walker's therapy has done for him. Floortime taught Walker to understand relationships, to be in relationship. It taught him how to take what was inside of him and turn it into a story, a sentence, a way of connecting. It also taught a sensitive boy how to not merely tolerate an overwhelming world, but to make it his home.

Patricia Stacey is the author of The Boy Who Loved Windows, Opening the Heart and Mind of a Child Threatened with Autism *(De Capo Press, 2003), which tells the story of her son Walker's successful journey to recovery. She has written for* The Atlantic Monthly, Oprah Magazine, *and* Cosmopolitan *and lives with her husband Cliff and their children in western Massachusetts.*

◎ ◎ ◎

Catherine's Story

JAMES WAS MY SECOND CHILD AND MY 40TH BIRTHDAY PRESENT. I REMEMber the nurses bringing him to me, telling me he would not stop crying. I now realize how painful that experience must have been for a child who didn't like change, bright lights, or noise. He probably hated that nursery. Regardless, I was glad he wanted to be with me.

His first two years could have been lifted from an autism textbook, but I had no idea he was anything but "all boy." He was active and always very busy. I remember wondering, *Why does he leap all the time? Why won't he play with me? What is he thinking?*

My mother was the first to notice something was different about James. I talked with our pediatrician, who recognized the early warning signs of autism. We took James to the Center for Development and Learning at University of North Carolina in Chapel Hill, and at the age of two-and-a-half, James was diagnosed with Autism Spectrum Disorder. My husband and I were in shock. I had read a little bit about autism and had seen the movie *Rain Man*. My sister-in-law mailed me a large envelope of information she found on the internet. It would be another year or so before I got a computer, but my journey had begun.

A therapist from TEACCH was present when we were given the results of our son's evaluation. She said he was "one of our guys." She told us we were lucky to live in an area where services from TEACCH were available to families. We live in a rural county not far from Chapel Hill, where the TEACCH Center was founded by Dr. Eric Schopler. I was fortunate to hear him speak at the first Autism Society of North Carolina Conference, which I attended a few weeks after James was diagnosed.

I met with the person in my county who worked with the infant and toddler program. She was very nice and helpful, but when I asked for speech therapy, I was told there was nothing available. I decided to look on my own.

Coincidentally, I soon met a wonderful woman who had a son with autism when I was attending a Girl Scout leader-training event. She told me about a preschool at UNC's Department of Speech and Hearing. It was part of a graduate program for UNC students. I called and they had room for James in the class. He started going on Mondays, Wednesdays, and Fridays for half-days. He participated in speech therapy and play therapy there. When he was in class, I could conveniently go right across the parking lot to the TEACCH parent training course.

The parent course met once a week for six sessions. The first session provided an overview on autism. The room was filled with parents just like me who were learning about their newly-diagnosed sons and daughters. After listening to parents tell their stories, I realized the children all seemed so different. I remember asking Dr. Lee Marcus, "Does this mean my son will grow up and only want to drink out of one cup?" (which is what another parent had described to me). We all wanted to know what the future would be like for our children, but, of course, there was no way to know.

After that first session, the course focused on the different areas of concern associated with autism: communication, visual strategies, understanding behavior, and social problems. The iceberg theory struck me the most. When you see an iceberg in the water, it seems enormous, but in fact you are only looking at the tip. They used this analogy to represent your child's behavior. Below the surface, the iceberg is massive, as are the characteristics of autism causing the behavior. Parents need to become autism detectives to reveal the undercurrents affecting the child. Only then can you truly figure out how to address behavior.

There was also a class on setting up tasks and structuring work sessions with your child—two components integral to TEACCH. I had observed these strategies used in his preschool, and a similar method used in the speech therapy sessions, too.

The last topic was advocacy. Wow—that was an eye opener! I started calling right away to get all the services I could for my son. Within the first year, I arranged for James to have speech therapy, occupational therapy, and a teacher from the school system work at home with him once a week. We were also on various waiting lists for SSI (supplemental security income) and services from our local mental health center.

We were on the waiting list for individual teaching sessions at the TEACCH Center for about a year before our name came up. The first meeting was with a team of two therapists. We talked about what we needed to work on with James. I showed them what we were doing at home and we talked about his strengths and interests. I learned about taking data and how to use that data. During the next session, I watched while the therapist worked with James. By the end of the sessions, we had progressed to me working with him while the therapists watched. I had a better understanding of the TEACCH method and was more comfortable with the work system we had put in place.

During the parent course the therapist always had an experienced parent of a child with autism present to be a co-facilitator at the meetings. It was a great dynamic. The therapist had the answers and the strategies, but having a parent there too was really helpful to families of newly diagnosed kids. A few years later, I was asked to be a co-facilitator, helping during the communication segment by showing parents some of the visuals and schedules I had used with James. Sharing my experiences helped them know they could do it, too. It wasn't that hard and the examples were not fancy. I was also living proof that life does go on when you have a child with autism. I had survived and my son was doing well.

The TEACCH method puts parents in the role of co-therapists. It teaches them to look at their child's strengths and interests, then create customized activities and a structured setting to work in. The first tasks were very easy. These gave James an understanding of doing things with a schedule and doing things left to right. I would set up his tasks in small baskets and present him with a schedule that read "1—2—3—break—1—2—3." Each basket was numbered. As he finished a task, he would put it into a large basket on the floor to his right, the "finished" basket. I sat across from him at a small table. I covered up his toy box with a sheet to help eliminate distractions while he was working.

I learned how to make tasks at home with materials that were on hand or really cheap. Some of the tasks were "put-in" tasks where he had to put a round or square block into the matching hole in a shoebox. He had one task made up of four fat crayons and a piece of paper with four dots in the left column and four dots in the right column. He was to connect the dots with each color. This was hard for him because he had no interest in coloring. He only wanted to eat the crayons. He really enjoyed one task where he put large wooden pegs in a row in a wooden board. My husband made this board in his shop. James loved puzzles, so when we first began doing tasks, I would start the session with a puzzle. As his work sessions progressed, the puzzles eventually became the last activity and finally the reward activity.

James needed to be redirected a lot in the beginning. He did not want to sit at a table at all. But by using a simple schedule, he learned there was an end to the session. Then he could have a treat or do an activity he really enjoyed. He was soon able to sit and do all of his work.

One of the challenges of using the TEACCH work system was getting everything set up. The tasks had to first be taken apart and put in the appropriate baskets. These supplies had to be kept away from him the rest of the time and he was always getting into everything. When teaching time was over, he was ready to go! There was barely time to put things away, much less prepare for the next session.

To work around some of his sensory sensitivities, his work table had to be in a place that was not visually or auditorily stimulating. We situated it in an enclosed area so he would stay at the table. Then he quickly finished his tasks. He loved to work and was glad someone was asking him to do something. It gave him a purpose, which we didn't even know he lacked. He also enjoyed the praise he received for doing a good job.

I suppose the hardest part about the TEACCH method is the scheduling of your daily lives. Before we began, it was so hard to imagine doing that. How do you write a schedule when you do not know what is going to happen? But that is the crux of the problem. The child is upset all the time because he does not know what is going to happen next. So you just do the best you can and schedule the parts of the day that need structure the most. You might be used to wandering around the grocery store, casually picking up what you need. A child with autism may think shopping is a painful activity that will never end! *What is this horrible place with all those smells and endless aisles? If I throw myself on the floor they will take me out of here. That worked last time.* A quick visual schedule that shows you both going in and buying three or four items and then leaving might be tolerated. It has a beginning and an end to it. Many parents resist the concept of scheduling, but it really works.

It is a common misconception that the goal of visual scheduling is to eventually stop using a schedule. Sometimes parents don't realize their day planners and PDAs offer the same structure and security for them as picture schedules do for their children. Learning how to use a schedule is a lifelong skill. When James started middle school, his anxiety level went through the roof. Adolescence amplified the situation and he regressed rapidly. We scheduled heavily and soon things quieted down. He needed the extra support and I was glad he had learned this when he was very young and still understood it, even when he was upset.

As I look back on those first years of early intervention, I recall being totally immersed in autism. All I read were books about autism and family accounts about living with autism. I knew I needed time with my daughter and husband, too, and I think I was able to balance everything. (They might remember this differently!) My husband Jimmy has always been very supportive of me. He was the parent in charge while I was going to conferences and meetings. We have been though it all together: the grief, and the joy.

I decided to be a stay-at-home mom when my daughter was born, so we got used to a frugal lifestyle. I think of my husband and me as aging hippies. We love the earth and spending time outdoors but are basically homebodies. Our home is full of books, movies, and music. We have passed along our love of the Beatles to both our children. James still loves to watch *Yellow Submarine*. I remember singing to him one day while pushing him on the swing. "One, two, three, four, can I have a little more? Five, six, seven, eight, nine, ten..." Then James chimed in, "I love you!" I almost wrote to Paul McCartney! Moments like this along the way helped me remember the eternal truth: "all you need is love."

Life got better financially once we started receiving SSI, and I did get some reimbursement for traveling to therapies. When you decide to have children, there is always cost involved. Typical children want to do things that are costly, such as dance lessons or karate classes, and their parents don't bat an eye. Still, I have been fortunate because there is no charge for services from TEACCH to North Carolina residents.

The Chapel Hill TEACCH Center has evolved since I first went there in 1996. The parent course has been replaced by workshops. There is a Parent Mentor Program that matches newly diagnosed families with experienced parents in their area. The TEACCH Demonstration Preschool that James attended as a five day program now has small groups that meet for shorter times with a separate home-visit program. I think more children are served this way. There are now home teaching kits as well, on loan to families with young children. Tasks are still created using everyday items. (A good resource for task ideas is the *Tasks Galore* book series, co-authored by Pat Fennell, one of James' therapists.)

The waiting lists for services are still long and I do not see that changing. So many more children are being diagnosed on the autism spectrum. At the time James was diagnosed, 1 in 3000 children born would be diagnosed with ASD. When he entered public school, the incidence was 1 in 1500. Today, it is 1 in 150.

Also keep in mind that some of the supports offered at the Chapel Hill TEACCH Center may not be available at every NC TEACCH center. One is the Chapel Hill Mothers' Group. It was one of the first services I took advantage of at TEACCH. The time I spent at these monthly meetings listening, sharing, and, yes, laughing with these wonderful women was invaluable. *What worked for you? What do you wish you had done differently? What can I do now to make the future easier?*

I am still a member of the mom's group and I still take advantage of the services offered for families. Last year, I went to a "Make It, Take It" workshop to put together a shower schedule for James. Teaching him about proper hygiene, such as using deodorant, is helping him become more independent. I expect a shaving schedule will need to be done soon.

If I could go back and do it all over again, I would make the same choices for early intervention treatment because I liked being involved with my son. I enjoyed watching him work with other therapists and professionals. But parents have to put forth a whole lot of personal effort for TEACCH, or any intervention, to be successful. They have to put the task and work systems together and keep modifying them as their child grows and progresses. But, for me, that is part of the joy of doing this. I knew I would not be the only one to work with him in the future, but the system of structure inherent in this method would remain the same.

The TEACCH method made our lives easier because it helped us communicate with our son. Although it may feel strange to use visuals and schedules in your everyday life, it is *so* much better than the alternative.

Catherine Jones lives in North Carolina with her husband Jimmy, daughter Sarah, and son James, who was diagnosed with Autism

Spectrum Disorder in 1996 at the age of two and a half. She is an active member of the Autism Society of North Carolina and is on the board of her local chapter.

◎ ◎ ◎

Kathy's Story

By the time Kyle was old enough to sit in his high chair, I had already started noticing some differences in his development as compared with his older brothers. He was often in his own world, happiest when he was riding in the car, looking out the window. I remember fighting back feelings of panic as I watched his repetitive, almost ritualistic hand movements that reminded me of behavior described in a book I had read when I was in college. It told the story of one family's intense efforts to "cure" their child of autism. It had been entertaining reading at the time. I decided to find the book and read it again, hoping to prove to myself there was nothing wrong with my baby.

I tried to be systematic. As I read, I used a pink highlighter to mark anything that reminded me of my son, a yellow one marked anything that was unlike him. Before long, I ran out of pink ink and concluded it might be more productive to highlight in green the intensive interventions the book described. I knew I needed to do something.

Just prior to Kyle's second birthday, after ruling out a hearing impairment, we received a tentative diagnosis of autism from the Developmental Evaluation Center located at the university in a neighboring town. The folks there were supportive, giving us much needed direction and information in digestible doses. Most importantly, they referred us to the TEACCH Center, in Asheville, North Carolina for a diagnostic evaluation.

Waiting months for Kyle's TEACCH evaluation was excruciating. I spent that time reading everything I could get my hands on. I most enjoyed reading real stories about real people, and felt a strong connection to the people and families I had never met, but whose experiences were so similar to my own. I already knew about the importance of early intervention and could hear Kyle's developmental clock ticking in my ears. There was no time to waste and so, based on a conglomeration of everything I had read, I attempted to create my own intensive intervention program; *intense* being the operative word. I was in Kyle's face, forcing interaction, trying to turn every minute of every day into a teachable moment. Maintaining that level of energy day after day was exhausting. I doubt I could have kept it up for very long.

One day, a large packet of paperwork arrived from TEACCH. With the help of a keepsake baby book, we answered detailed questions about Kyle's developmental milestones, family history, etc. Then one morning in mid-July, my husband and I made the hour-long trip to the TEACCH Center. Kyle sat contentedly in his car seat, looking out the window and waving his hands in that strange way that had become his signature movement.

Driving home in silence, trying to process Kyle's diagnosis of autism, I was afraid that if I started to cry I might never stop. The folks at TEACCH had been kind and empathetic. They recommended we begin using "visual cues" and "work systems." I didn't even think about the fact that I didn't know what they were talking about. I was just so grateful they seemed to understand my child and were willing to teach me. Arrangements were made to bring Kyle back to the TEACCH Center once a week for the next several weeks. A therapist would work with Kyle and I would sit in the dark in an adjacent room, watching through the one-way glass. I knew those weekly visits would eventually come to an end and I was desperate to learn as much as possible before I was on my own. I did not know then that we were laying the groundwork for what would become a way of life.

Like many autistic children, Kyle was a visual learner. Words combined with pictures communicated more than words alone. Physical space needed to be defined visually so Kyle's world would make sense to him. Sometimes that involved moving the furniture. But more often, it involved small changes: the strategic placement of a rug or mat, a line of masking tape on the floor, a place mat on the table—simple changes that clarified Kyle's world. Our house began to resemble a preschool with "centers" designated for different activities. Imitating the therapists at TEACCH, I learned how to work with my son one-on-one, and how to encourage independent completion of tasks.

Instead of seeing Kyle's need for routine as a problem, we began to view it as a strength. Rather than teaching Kyle to memorize a particular routine, checking his schedule became his routine. Photographs placed from left to right on a schedule in the kitchen helped him understand transitions. We could change the order of his activities and he would comply without a tantrum. It was amazing. I got in the habit of setting up Kyle's morning schedule before I went to bed at night, putting the after-school schedule in place before I left the house to pick up the kids, and doing the evening schedule while he was in the tub. Rather than screaming in frustration when he couldn't communicate his needs, Kyle learned to indicate his preferences by pointing to pictures on a visual choice board. Initially, I feared that teaching him to use the pictures might delay or prevent him from using words. But the opposite was true.

Through all this, I learned to talk less and "show" more. Kyle learned to check his schedule and "do what comes next." Consistent use of a schedule provided Kyle with the predictability he needed. It helped him make sense of his world and then our world became more peaceful.

One morning, after taking the older boys to school, I noticed the magnetic letters on the refrigerator spelled out the phrase: I LOVE COFFEE. I presumed my husband was teasing me about my caffeine addiction, but we would soon discover that Kyle already knew how to read. That ability would allow us to use Carol Gray's Social Stories and Comic Strip Conversations; both are effective tools for helping children with autism learn how to understand social situations.

The professionals at the Developmental Evaluation Center invited me to serve as a parent representative on an Interagency Coordination Committee. My participation on that committee prepared me to advocate for my own son. When Kyle was three, I felt strongly that he would benefit socially by attending preschool for part of his day. At the same time, I was scared to death. The Exceptional Children's Program Director, Dr. Lynn Dillard, was also a member of that committee and she listened as I talked about the sort of program I envisioned for my child; she then encouraged me to help create it. I explained that I wanted a program based on TEACCH strategies. I had seen it work at home and I knew it could work at school. Kyle began attending a program for four-year-olds with a one-on-one assistant who received training at TEACCH. It was difficult for me at first, but eventually I learned to relax and trust another person to calmly and consistently implement structured strategies.

As the years went by, I also learned that teaching assistants would come and go, and it was unwise to depend too much on any one person. The job is demanding and not everyone is cut out to work with kids with ASD. But we were blessed to have a succession of caring individuals who tried very hard. More children with autism began attending the same school. The structured strategies were adapted to meet the needs of each one.

For Kyle, a schedule similar to the one we used at home was implemented in the regular education classroom. There were times when Kyle's sensory issues demanded a more restricted, quieter environment, and Kyle learned to recognize his rising stress level and ask for sanctuary. Through the ongoing use of structured TEACCH strategies, Kyle managed to find his way through public education and is now independently completing high school assignments.

Over the years, I have had the opportunity to attend numerous trainings and workshops offered at TEACCH for parents and professionals. Even when I repeat a workshop, I always learn something new. These trainings often feature a panel discussion with people who are on the autism spectrum. I am so grateful for all they have taught me.

I have gained confidence in my own ability to anticipate a meltdown before it happens and take steps to prevent it. Sometimes that means leaving a gathering when everyone stills wants us to stay, rather than staying and wishing we hadn't. "Redefining success"—that is what a therapist at TEACCH once called it. I have repeated that phrase many times over.

As Kyle has matured, the appearance of his schedule has changed. Now there are no photographs, and no Velcro. Each day he follows a checklist and I intend to introduce him to a day planner soon. He is great with a shopping list and keeps me on track at Wal-Mart. Social Stories continue to be an important part of his life.

My husband and I have had to change our parenting style and initially that was quite challenging, especially with our older boys comparing notes and commenting about perceived unfairness.

In those early days when I was desperate for direction, I jumped on the TEACCH bandwagon without hesitation. My husband would be the first to admit that he was skeptical about Social Stories and schedules, visual cues and work systems. But time has made him a believer.

After working for more than ten years in the public school system, Kathy is currently employed as a Parent Advocate for the Autism Society of North Carolina. Steve is a Residential Designer. They live in small town in the southwest corner of the Smoky Mountains.

◉ ◉ ◉

Sara's Story

OUR SON WAS DIAGNOSED WITH AUTISM AT THE AGE OF FOUR. WE immersed ourselves in everything we could learn about the disorder and treatment options available. He immediately began speech therapy to address language and communication issues, and occupational therapy for his sensory deficits and aversions. We enrolled him in our state's preschool program and crafted an IEP to begin working on social, educational, and life skill goals. He made great progress with all of these supports but as parents do, we continued to search for more. What else could be done? As his mom I read many books, attended many conferences, and spoke to as many experts and parents as I could about treatment options for his specific needs. Like many parents we investigated many different treatment options, evaluating their cost and benefit. We tested and tried some; others we chose not to pursue.

In the Fall of 2005 we selected a treatment option that targeted his social/relational needs. Our son had made so much progress in all other areas we found ourselves now realizing that he simply did not "get" social relationships. We had used social stories, scripts, social play groups, etc., but found these to be Band-Aid methods that did not get to the heart of his social and relationship challenges. They taught him how to *act* differently, but they only addressed his immediate issue or crisis at the time. They did not help him *be* social, nor generalize his social awareness to all settings and people.

I had first learned of Relationship Development Intervention®, a program for social/relational needs, at a Future Horizon's conference in 2001. Its founder, Dr. Steven Gutstein, had written a book called *Solving the Relationship Puzzle* and he shared strategies that address the social and relational challenges faced by individuals with autism and Asperger's Syndrome. I purchased several of his books and subscribed to his newsletter. Over the course of the next four years, we observed and investigated this option before deciding to use it with our son. It was a commitment of time and money. We wanted to be certain this was a good decision for our son and our family.

To begin, my husband and I signed up for a four-day parent workshop and contacted an RDI consultant to begin the evaluation and treatment process. At the workshop we learned the basic fundamentals and foundations for the treatment. We participated in an evaluation as a family with our consultant. Together we set goals and objectives for our son based on his stage of relational development and began to implement these in our daily life.

One of the primary reasons we chose RDI was because it placed the parents in the role of instructor/therapists and goals were incorporated and implemented into our daily routine and lives. Each month we would video-record activities we had done with our son based on the objectives given to us and send the video to our consultant. She would provide feedback and instruction based on what she viewed in the tapes. We would make adjustments and focus on specific areas noted from her evaluation. We still follow this process two years later. Initially, the idea of being videotaped was a challenge. We placed the camera out of view and gradually helped our son get used to the idea of taping things we did as a family.

It suited our family's personality well that RDI goals and objectives are meant to be worked on as we go about our daily routine. The focus is not on the activity itself; any activity you do within the realm of normal family life can be used to target and teach an objective. We have taped all sorts of daily activities: folding clothes, sorting laundry, making dinner, setting the table, raking leaves, taking a walk, playing catch, or simply sitting on the couch talking. We liked this aspect of treatment because it did not take additional time out of our day nor require someone else to do it. We have even taped family and friends working on objectives while involved in making a pie or playing a game. All we needed to do was provide them with some simple guidelines and instructions in the few minutes before we taped. Both our family members and son enjoyed the time spent together.

Aside from working on goals and objectives, there is a certain amount of time given to making tapes and making adjustments to goals and objectives, but this is very minimal—an hour or so a week. As a family, however, we are continually working on goals throughout the day as we eat dinner, drive to practice, do chores, etc. RDI is a nonstop, continual process, a lifestyle commitment you incorporate into everyday functioning. It was an easy choice for us to make because of our active and busy lifestyle. We found we were not adding one more therapy or going to another appointment but were in a sense multi-tasking intervention into life. The most difficult part for us has been remembering to set up the camera to record some of the things we are doing. This took intentionality and thought before it became a habit.

In the beginning my husband was not as certain that this was a wise investment of our time and money. However, he went to the training and began implementing goals and activities at home. After about a month we began to see a change in our son. He began understanding the you-me connection and the value people brought to each other. The following example illustrates his shift in understanding.

We were making pancakes for dinner and he was putting butter on the griddle. While I was busy digging for a bowl under the counter he asked if he had enough butter on the griddle. Without looking, I replied that he did. I continued digging and he continued asking the same question. At first I was irritated and thought he was perseverating on the task until he told me to stop and look at him and the butter to see if he had used the right amount. I wanted to jump up and down when I realized he wanted to make eye contact and use me to acquire information about the task he was doing! Prior to beginning this treatment he would have just asked without looking and I would have responded without looking. He would not have noticed or cared that I had not looked. My husband and I both began to see the benefit of our investment of time and money as he began to relate more and more to us.

A more recent example happened right after school started this year. We had been working at home on activities to help him be more comfortable with variations and changes. We had spent some time last spring helping ease his transition to middle school. He had met his teachers, toured the building, asked questions, etc. He was ready and excited when school began. The first week of school we were informed that he was placed with the wrong POD and group of teachers for his IEP to be implemented. This meant new teachers, friends, classes, locker, etc. I went after school and broke the news to him, anticipating a meltdown. There was no outburst of any kind. We spent about an hour making the changes, meeting the teachers, etc., at which time he looked at me and asked "Can we go home now?" No big deal, no big fallout, no later mention or stress over it. Again, we were thrilled to see an objective we had been working on play out so successfully in real life.

We know as a family we will continue to use RDI long term. Our son has made great gains in his social/relational skills. Our family and friends noticed great changes in relational skills as we worked on his goals. They often mentioned how great it was to spend time with him or how much they enjoyed being with him. We've enjoyed our time with him as well. We still do!

Our son still receives academic support in math and reading and has speech and vision therapy. We still have daily struggles and social issues. He still has autism. Achieving success in social relationships is life-long learning, and RDI is a program that stays with the individual. He still has much to learn, but just the basic goals he has mastered have helped him in so many ways. He continues to make great progress in social areas. He recently had eight friends over for a sleepover, but even more importantly was invited to two sleepovers. And, he was requested as a roommate by several boys for church camp. As parents we celebrate each victory and evaluate each challenge. We feel RDI has given us vital tools to help us address his struggles and help him succeed.

My husband and I have made the financial commitment to continue with this treatment long term. It is not a decision to be made lightly. Each RDI plan is created individually for a child, and therefore costs can vary. There is the initial cost of about $5000 for the required parent training and the initial evaluation. After that, the monthly cost will differ based upon the consultant's recommendations for your child. Additional parent training is strongly recommended but not mandatory. More specific cost information can be obtained through the Connection Center™ and a RDI® Program Certified Consultant. Cost is a factor to consider in any treatment option. We would advise any parent not to just investigate the cost but look at the whole process and treatment. We feel the benefit we have received is priceless as we watch our son grow and succeed in relationships and life.

We did not choose RDI to cure our son, but to help him achieve a life full of meaningful relationships in the spheres of friendship, marriage, and employment. We realize there are many treatment options available to us but we believe RDI targets those qualities that make our son "autistic": his social/relationship challenges. RDI has given us hope and joy in our personal relationship with our son. If you are considering using this method of treatment, we would encourage you to investigate and learn as much as you can. Contact the Connection Center™, *www.rdiconnect.com*, and talk to parents who are using it.

We have yet to meet a parent using RDI who has not seen positive changes in their family and their child. We believe it is one of the best investments we have made for the future of our family and our son.

We are the Smith family. My husband is a student minister, I am a stay-at-home mom, and we have been married for almost 17 years. We have one son. He loves to sing and is a competitive swimmer.

❂   ❂   ❂

Deidre's Story

My concerns about my son's development began to coalesce around the time he turned one. Our pediatrician suggested I give him a little more time, but at 15 months, I contacted our state's Early Intervention (Birth to Three) program, since it seemed he exhibited some mild developmental delay compared to his peers. EI professionals administered the Michigan Assessment and found him, in fact, to be much delayed. The term PDD, Pervasive Development Disorder, was suggested to describe his condition, but no formal diagnosis was made. I had no idea what PDD was, but the EI folks assured me that with intervention he would "catch up."

The waitlist is often long for intervention services and it was four months later, at 19 months old, that we began the recommended treatment: one hour one time per week of semi-structured Floortime intervention, coupled with an hour per week of Occupational Therapy, both provided with licensed professionals. I was present during these sessions to learn what they were doing and carry over that teaching across other environments and throughout our day. It quickly became clear, however, that more intensive services were needed to close my child's significant developmental gaps. But with my child's challenges, I found it exhausting and frankly futile for me to do Floortime for long blocks of time throughout the day. We adopted a more realistic goal of 10 minutes per hour, setting a timer to ensure we did it. Yet, after two months of trying to follow my child's ever fleeting lead and/or secure his attention for more than a second, we were failing to close any of his developmental gaps. He was still functioning at a 6-7 month old language/communication level. This EI program just wasn't working for my son or our family.

What we *could* do successfully together was snuggle on the sofa and watch Baby Einstein videos. Miraculously, scrolling along the end credits I noticed that proceeds from the sales of Baby Einstein supported the Eden Institute for Autism. Within six weeks I traveled to Princeton, NJ to attend an Applied Behavior Analysis (ABA) workshop there. I was the only parent in the room.

Shortly thereafter, at 21 months, my child was evaluated by developmental and psychological specialists and a diagnosis of autism was confirmed. Having an official diagnosis meant our child was eligible for intensive services provided with state and federal monies. Given the very slow progress we experienced using

Floortime (albeit, briefly), we decided to try an intensive schedule of ABA intervention. While 20-40 hours is the recommended weekly level of intervention, labor shortages in this field in our area resulted in us starting off with just six hours a week.

My child had no skills to play or explore his surroundings productively or to interact with me; I looked forward to the structure and meaningfulness that this programming brought to our days. I had been warned that one method within ABA - Discrete Trial Teaching —did not follow a developmental model and was teacher focused. To my surprise, I didn't find this to be the case at all. The Discrete Trial therapists with whom we worked started out by taking preference assessments of my child's interests in cause-and-effect toys, music, books, puzzles, snippets of Baby Einstein videos and then actively used his choices to motivate and reward him. They paired those tangible behavior reinforcers with their own joyful praise and tickles, beginning to orientate some of his attention away from oblivion, to people and relationships. Their curriculum started with laying the foundation for pre-verbal communication: increasing the child's desire to communicate, making communication fun, increasing the child's understanding/awareness of the world around him, decreasing the child's disruptive behaviors caused by frustration at not being able to communicate, etc. I learned that a majority of a child's negative behaviors stem from him not being able to functionally express his wants and needs. It made sense to start there.

We stepped up my son's program, moving from a two-hour session in just the morning to also doing a two-hour session in the afternoon, five days a week. We were up to 20 hours of therapy a week. When we lost a therapist (we had 10 the first year), I stepped in and did the work until a replacement could be found. For me, executing ABA/DT was easier than Floortime. The tasks and activities were easy to replicate. They had a clear beginning, middle, and end. I felt purposeful.

Within a month of implementing ABA therapy, we could see progress in our child and in our parenting ability to manage him. My son began to make sounds, to make requests using sign language and picture cards, to label and to know the things in the world around him, and to respond to hearing his name. We were so encouraged.

I also had been warned that ABA—and DTT specifically—creates robotic children unable to generalize their learning to different environments. Our service provider was fairly creative and responsive to this claim. We varied our session location from room to room in the house, and to the backyard in fair weather seasons. We challenged ourselves to continually vary the materials used to teach concepts. And more than once when working on generalization of acquired skills we did teaching sessions while taking walks in the woods. I remember distinctly a particular autumn afternoon. We were working on the concept of "near" and "far." I picked up a pebble and tossed it across a lake. I asked my son, "Is the rock far or near?" He provided his one word answer. I picked up another stone and tossed it close to the water's edge. "Did that go near or far?" He correctly answered again. "Now you throw," I said, and he picked up a rock and imitated my action. This was our teaching and learning, the two of us interacting while our ABA therapist recorded the data. Those successes fueled me with hope and energy. They motivated *me* to stay with the program.

Intensive intervention of any sort takes many, many hours each and every day. We lost many "typical" friendships along the way. We did squeeze in structured, community playgroups for exposure to typical peers, but easy social interaction between my son and his peers was still a faraway goal. We also continued one weekly session of

OT and speech/language therapy. But the real improvement in my child's behavior and learning in those very early years came from the many hours of Discrete Trial Teaching. I stopped practicing DIR/Floortime. It was as time consuming as ABA, but my son and I experienced far fewer moments of success. I had watched several of the Greenspan training tapes and noticed that many of those children were higher functioning than my child. I marveled at the seeming simplicity of Stanley Greenspan and Serena Weider's play suggestions—their ability to follow a child's lead and transform it into something playful and purposeful. I believed the theories behind DIR/Floortime, even if we were one of the families for whom it didn't work effectively in the beginning. Interestingly, my husband, however, was able to close one and sometimes more "circles of communication" with our child (a basic technique within DIR). Every evening, no exaggeration, after his nine-hour work day my husband would go into the living room and try to joyfully engage our son. He does this still today. It was mostly robust physical play: tossing him in the air, squishing him with a pillow, swinging him in a blanket and waiting for him to ask for more. My husband found it more natural to do Floortime activities than running trials. And it was easier for him to use this approach to deliver an important motivational message—that interacting with others could be interesting and fun.

As our son gained more and more foundation skills (e.g., following one-step directions, identifying places and people, knowing the function of objects, vocalizing a three-word sentence) we worked to generalize the skills by using different Floortime techniques. We believe this helped consolidate his learning and improve his functioning, by putting his ABA acquired skills into realistic and real-life contexts.

The time came for our child to transition from EI to our local school district, and we were met with a bit of a nasty experience.

We wanted to keep the needed at-home ABA intervention; the school district did not want to fund it. With the help of a special education lawyer and our child's doctor, the school district did finally agree to provide for continued at-home ABA therapy. However, the compromise was that our family had to pay the difference of several hours per week of therapy to sustain the recommended level of intervention (20 hours) to meet our child's needs. Our out-of-pocket costs that year for ABA therapy, including additional private speech and language therapy, an ABA style preschool social skills group and educational consultant expenses totaled almost $20,000.

By the time our son was four he was nearly age appropriate in his discrete language skills, but still had severely limited play skills and social pragmatic skills (the social use of language to connect with others). We began to use video modeling in our ABA sessions to build these skills. As the months went by we also started working on social behaviors, like going trick-or-treating at Halloween, or enacting simple fairy tales using role playing to build imagination and get my son thinking about how other people and characters think and act. A favorite was "The Three Billy Goats Gruff." We generalized this activity to several local playgrounds. Other children always wanted to play along and we gladly included them, varying who acted as the goats, troll and narrator. Replicating characters was one thing; getting past the script was the next challenge. How could our son learn to play spontaneously? How could he become flexible and incorporate someone else's idea? How could he learn to sequence independently? To create his own story?

Discrete Trial was not a technique that I thought could cultivate this kind of spontaneous and fluid social thinking. So, I began looking for a DIR professional to consult with me and also work directly with my child. Trained DIR therapists are harder to find than ABA therapists, yet I got lucky. Sheila came to the house and observed my son's and my relationship, our play together, our back-and-forth communication, and my son's sensory processing abilities. Then she formulated a program for us to follow.

Sheila came once a week for 60 minutes for about a year and a half. I participated in these weekly sessions with her, carrying over the strategies she used in our free play time together. While we never approached the number of hours of intervention using Floortime as we had with ABA, Floortime now was as valuable to us as ABA. Floortime helped bridge the connection between memorization of information and then using it in some imaginative application. ABA helped my child learn needed foundation skills; DIR helped my child develop the capacity for different levels of thinking once he was ready to do so.

It has been nearly four years since we started to remediate the effects of autism. We still sustain, though reduced, a number of hours of ABA intervention to target appropriate behavior in community outings, for self-help and safety skills. Our son has not "recovered," but he has made tremendous progress. He participates in his first-grade regular education classroom in our local public school with supports provided for in his IEP. His language and communication skills continue to improve and he enjoys one or two "friends."

We tried out other therapies, such as RDI and for a brief time the GFCF diet, but for our child, ABA more quickly and consistently developed the foundational learning skills: the ability to attend/share attention, imitate, and communicate, than any other method.

I now can resume the dreams and hopes for my son's future that the parent of a typical child dreams and hopes. My son is not cured, but there's a better, brighter future ahead for him than I dared hope for when he was first diagnosed. Intensive intervention can be tough on the child and the family, but for us, and for our son, it's been worth it.

Deidre Richards lives in Massachusetts with her extraordinary husband and their only child. She thanks Catherine Maurice and Clara Claiborne Park for the sustenance their stories gave, early on.

● ◎ ●

Sandi's Story

"WHERE DO YOU WANT TO GO?" I ASKED. NO ANSWER. BUT THAT WAS OKAY because Ben was only six months old. I waited until he started to move again, heading toward his bedroom. I smiled and said, "Oh what fun, we're going to your room now!" And off we went with him leading the way as both of us crawled down the hallway.

That's my first memory of "early intervention." Nothing formal; nothing arising because my child's behavior worried me or seemed somehow not "normal." Just a mom and her child happily immersed in exploring the world together. Six more months would pass before signs of autism appeared and it would be years before I'd hear a doctor say, "Asperger's Syndrome." Formal labels were not yet part of my vocabulary, but still, it was intervention, engaged time with my son. In hindsight, we were laying a foundation that would become more crucial than I could have imagined.

I returned to work when my maternity leave ended. Every morning Ben and I traveled 40 miles to his day care center and then I continued another 20 miles to the hospital where I worked. We did the same in reverse every evening, arriving home in the mountains exactly 12 hours later. We had a few hours together (if Ben was awake) before I'd fall into bed. Three months of this routine and several alarming daycare mishaps later I started to question whether

I wanted to compromise these precious few years of mother-child experiences with my son.

It was not an easy decision. In fact, it was illogical and maybe even a little crazy to quit working because I was (and still am) a single mom. But believing that it was temporary (I'd return when Ben went to school) and intuitively knowing that I needed to spend this time with my first (and only) child, I decided to resign. I immediately felt at peace with that choice. I also immediately prayed, "Please God, let Ben's dad keep up the child-support payments!"

Over the first year I was home with Ben (when he was 6 to 18 months old), I saw a level of defiance and stubbornness that concerned me. It also became apparent that he hated anything new. Gifts distressed him to the point where he was afraid to open them. I started to search for information that would help me understand what was going on. I found two books that discussed "difficult temperament" and discovered that their descriptions fit Ben. I learned there were unique ways to deal with "spirited" children and while this fresh perspective helped, I was still a little worried about his intensity, so I continued to delve into books about childhood development.

At this point our challenges weren't so severe that I would have thought to seek professional help, but a psychologist who specialized in play therapy happened to have an office in her house a few blocks down from our home, so we met with her. She was perplexed by Ben's behaviors and didn't make a diagnosis but she did teach me the fundamentals of the DIR/Floortime method.

Even before I had an inkling that Ben was on the autism spectrum, Floortime became a lifestyle. I used the basic tenet of DIR—follow his lead and build on his interests—because his "singular interest" was so strong that he became upset or refused to join in when other toys were introduced. I sure didn't see the value in forcing a change that caused a meltdown (those were the days before I saw a *real* meltdown; this was more like a wee bit of distress) but it seemed obvious that the only way I could establish a relationship with him was when he was willing and calm, so I did my best to avoid the triggers of trouble.

When I met him at his level and pursued his interest the difference in interaction was huge. He met my gaze, initiated games and responded when I became his partner. I didn't follow a specific schedule because it was simple: every time he was ready to play, we played together following DIR/Floortime methods.

At the age of one his interest was a small bucket of plastic army men. He "played" by lining them up in a single row and looking at them. Initially, I spent many hours over many days helping him line them up. As he stared at his neat little line of men it was clear by the twinkle in his eyes and the smile on his face that he was somehow—in his own mind—interacting with them, so I joined at his level. I did not touch his perfect line-up, but I looked with him, talked about the differences in their posture and guessed about their possible jobs in the army (no gruesome details, just ideas suitable for his age). Over time I was able to take the lead and show him how to line them up in two different lines. From there we slowly—*very* slowly over 4-6 months—started to pretend that each line was a different army. Eventually the day came when Ben allowed his army men to have a battle. We picked them up and dropped them on one another turning his neat little lines into chaos. He laughed and enjoyed the fun but after the battle was over he had to line them up again so he could be sure he still had each and every army man in its proper place.

When Ben was between the ages of two and three, I became intimate with the concepts of perseveration, sensory overload and

resistance to change as they started to disrupt our routine more frequently. Whether it was good or bad, Ben experienced it in the
extreme. Sometimes I felt like I was on a freefall through his emotional and behavioral outbursts, but I discovered the most amazing
safety net. We had a tangible connection that caught us no matter
how difficult the "fall." That first year devoted to playing with Ben
and the time spent sticking with what I knew was right for him (in
spite of what everyone else insisted he *should* be doing) had built a
deep emotional connection between us. Ben's ability to trust me
and share his emotions with me—all because I had shared his
interests with him—helped us survive as his anxieties and neurological challenges started to get the better of him.

Whatever the form intervention takes, it has two components. One
is what we *do* with our child, the other what we learn *about* our
child. And, I daresay that the latter returns the biggest return on
investment, by far. What I gained from our time together was a thorough understanding of my son's every idiosyncrasy, nuance, mood,
need and desire. Knowing your child well sounds like a no-brainer
but parents of children with autism understand how hard that is to
achieve with a child on the spectrum—especially with those who are
predominately nonverbal or have limited verbal skills. The connection Ben and I shared could not have been created as easily after the
issues related to autism appeared; our early intervention together
proved invaluable.

By the time he was three we were entering a new phase. Ben was
very quickly overwhelmed by so much—noises, smells, changes in
activity, anxiety over virtually everything beyond his compact,
comfortable world—that he was often at the mercy of his emotions. Even though he was very verbal and had an impressive
vocabulary he couldn't communicate when he was upset and, once
he calmed down, he either didn't remember or he wouldn't discuss

what had happened. His meltdowns became more frequent and happened too rapidly for me to anticipate them.

In desperation I reverted to traditional discipline. That was a disaster. Time outs, taking away toys, limiting video time … they all caused an escalation of the behavior I was trying to stop. It seemed as though Ben interpreted them as a violent threat to his existence. Considering how much they intruded into the part of his world that he understood and could control, his perceptions were probably right.

Looking back, I'm thankful that my personality is similar to Ben's. I like to stay at home, take quiet walks through the park and have small get-togethers with a few friends. I'm laid-back almost to a fault and that was my saving grace. I took a step back, slowed down and paid close attention to what was happening. Really watched Ben and the people, places, and things in his surroundings. It wasn't long before some issues and their triggers became clear and the most obvious one was that Ben did not like to leave the activity he was enjoying. It didn't matter what it was or even if he was going to enjoy the next activity. If I said "time to stop" he refused to comply. The more I pushed the larger his meltdown.

Ben went through two different developmental assessments, one with his pediatrician and the other with the county's preschool screening team. Neither offered a diagnosis because they both decided there was nothing wrong with him. Instead they declared it was obviously my lack of parenting skills. But I knew his struggles were deeper and more multifaceted than parenting issues so once again I looked for answers on my own. I'm glad I love doing research because I embarked on a mission to learn about childhood disorders. I didn't apply diagnostic labels. I just chose the pieces of advice that seemed to fit with his behaviors and created my own intervention plan.

I revisited the earlier books about temperamental differences. This time I studied their strategies for helping kids make transitions by allowing extra time and giving them forewarning. I adapted this by creating a verbal early-warning system with 10, 5 and 2 minute alerts and saw quick results. Giving Ben time to change activities clearly helped him process the request then do it, but it didn't always work. That's when I added visual techniques following the TEACCH methods I had come across in my research. I didn't outline every day's routine visually, but I made a picture schedule whenever we had something planned that he tended to resist, like our weekly play group. Or, I would create a hand-drawn picture on the spur of the moment to help him visualize what needed to be done when it was nearing time to transition to a new activity. He still didn't like to stop what he was doing, but as long as he was given the opportunity to finish it to his satisfaction, he didn't get angry or frustrated. I thought back to how he always had to realign those army men after a battle and realized he needed a similar sense of closure for every activity.

I can't pinpoint exactly when it started because I didn't suddenly think to myself "oh, now I'll do structured learning" but sure enough, more TEACCH principles were added to our daily life. It came as the result of having a quantity of time with Ben that allowed me to observe and interact. I started to notice that he didn't seem to understand simple sequences. That's when I realized he wasn't refusing to wash his hands or pick up his toys because he was oppositional. He really didn't know how to do it. I started to show him step-by-step how to do everything, taking the time to explain all the little things that he wasn't naturally learning along the way.

Did it have any effect? One day when he was 3 years old Ben came up to me and said, "I love you mommy because you teach me things." So yeah, it had an effect. I was building his competence while weaving different structured methods into our lifestyle rather than highlighting them as obvious interventions. This continued to build the emotional connection between us.

There are definitely times for obvious intervention though, and that came into our lives in the form of behavior modification. There were some tasks that Ben was resistant to learning or doing so we devised a variety of behavior charts. Ben eagerly complied with whatever the goal was in order to be able to put those stickers on the chart and move closer to the reward. But when he started to suggest goals for the sake of gaining some reward I thought that, even though it got results, the purpose of the behavior charts was being abused. After that I limited their use to a few really important issues.

We're farther down the road now and it's clear to me that the emotional connection created by our early intervention is extraordinary. Its value is obvious because he doesn't have it with anyone else. Sharing his experiences or his thoughts is not something that he can do yet with others, no matter how well they manage to superficially connect with him.

I never did make it back to work. As the years passed my therapist-mom job expanded. Ben's Dad continues to support us but it's a financial strain for him and I can barely make ends meet, which creates tension for everyone. But I don't have even a sliver of regret.

Keeping life simple and taking each day at Ben's pace helps reduce his anxiety and enables him to be more receptive to learning and therapy. It sometimes feels like we take one step forward and four steps back but what Ben gained as a result of our early intervention has never regressed. He can now process verbal reminders and prompts without the visuals. He remembers how to do every task he has been taught in an organized step-wise manner. His emotional functioning continues to grow by leaps and bounds. Meltdowns are so infrequent they're almost a distant memory. Now he is able to say "I'm angry; I need a break" and he will go into his room until he is calm enough to talk. His experience sharing ... with me ... is firmly intact. Every day he shares astounding thoughts and insight. He tells me about stories he reads, ideas he has and seeks me out to have a discussion. The biggest step of all came one day when he asked me, "How is your day going mom?"

I'm still using DIR/Floortime and TEACCH methods because they are intuitive (I was using them with no training even before Ben was diagnosed), they value the parent as a therapist, they deal with the underlying issues and they easily fit into our lifestyle. I can't think of anything I might have done differently although I wish I had known about RDI back in the early days too. No matter what we're remediating—and challenges still abound—the biggest value to me is that they all contribute toward building a real relationship with my son. I believe that one day he will build upon this foundation and pursue relationships with others.

In the end you have to do what works for your child. Clichéd but true ... and definitely not easy. The focus on "individualized and appropriate" in the minds of both parents and teachers can get lost when a certain protocol is believed to be the "one" that works. Sometimes even trained professionals in the field insist on trying to plug every child into one technique. It seems to me that all the different therapeutic models work, but not for all children, all the time. We have to search for the methods that fit and, armed with really knowing our child, adjust to whatever they need. Above all ... the absolutely most important piece ... is to do whatever is necessary to build an emotional connection with your child.

Sandi Busch started with a degree in Psychology, added nurses' training, then gained experience ranging from counseling to private investigations before finding her passion—writing. Now she writes about mental health and autism from her home in Pittsburgh, PA, which she shares with her homeschooled son. She can be reached at SandiBusch@comcast.net.

chapter eight

From Good to Bad to Meltdown

Understanding Your Child's Behavior Challenges

Dr. Jim: Hi, you two. How are things going?

Rob: Uh, okay ... I guess ....

Dr. Jim: Maureen, how's the EI team doing? Is the plan working out for you?

Maureen: The plan seems to be working fine, I think. Mark's learning new skills and I'm certainly learning a lot! When the therapists are at our home working with Mark and giving me suggestions about what to do, things move along pretty smoothly. We have a challenge here and there, but you've told us before to expect these situations, and the therapists help us work through them. It's after they leave that things seem ... seem to ... fall apart ....

Rob: I'll second that! Man, I come home some days from work and Mark is almost uncontrollable. One evening he screamed—I mean *screamed*—thirty minutes straight, and no matter what we said to him or did, nothing made a difference. I think he would have kept it up but he literally ran out of voice and energy.

Maureen: I feel like such a bad parent when he has a tantrum … that I can't help him, or don't know what to do, or wondering if I caused it. There are days when Mark's behavior is so off the wall and I find myself getting angry at him because he just won't stop, then I start yelling and a bad situation gets even worse. Those days I go bed at night hating myself, and hating this autism we have to deal with.

Rob: We just can't seem to catch a break, either. We go out less and less in public with Mark. I'm doing most of the grocery shopping while Maureen stays home with Mark. We never go out to restaurants or a movie anymore as a family because Mark's behavior will erupt without warning. We tried taking him with us to different places, and more often than not, it turns into a train wreck. After living through too many times of experiencing his tantrums in public, with the people looking at us, pointing, whispering …

Maureen: … and their really rude comments.

Rob: We pretty much stay home most of the time now. And even there, we're not exempt from his outbursts. He's better with the therapists—or maybe they just know more about how to deal with him than we do. But the rest of the time, he can be an angel or a devil, sometimes within a span of a couple of minutes. I just feel useless at times.

Maureen: It's physically and emotionally draining not to know what to do right. I feel like such a failure as a parent. I want to help Mark, but I don't seem to know what to do. It's so much easier when the therapists are there, to follow their lead. But when they're gone, everything disintegrates into chaos.

Dr. Jim: Behavior—it's probably the number-one reason parents and teachers seek outside help in dealing with their child with ASD. It's a complicated equation, involving not just the child but also his environment and the adults in it. We tend to think of behavior as though it's an entity, a force that arises in and of itself from somewhere within the child. That's not the entire picture, especially with spectrum kids whose brains function differently, but it's the notion we NTs seem to hold in our minds. Behavior is *always* a response to something else—it never exists in a vacuum. And with autism, that "something else" can be any of a myriad of things, from a request you made to some unperceived sensory issue in the environment, something as innocuous as the scent of a new shampoo, or the noise of a weed-eater coming from the house halfway down the block that your brain doesn't even register.

Maureen: But the therapists make it look so easy. I'm an educated woman, and yet when it comes to figuring out Mark's behaviors, why he does what he does when he does it, or trying to turn around a behavior situation that's quickly getting out of hand, I feel about as smart as Miss Piggy in a room full of nuclear physicists. When things do "work out," I'm never quite sure why they did, or how to repeat them again the next time.

Dr. Jim: Just about every parent with a child with ASD needs help managing their child's behaviors and some good, sound behavior training. I don't know if it helps to hear this or not—that others have gone through what you're experiencing now—but it's the truth. You're certainly not the first parents who have felt insecure, afraid, or embarrassed over your child's behaviors—and your own reactions to them. It's part of the landscape of autism, and it's definitely territory you need to learn to navigate. The good news is that with just a few basic behavior management strategies you can significantly reduce these behavior tantrums and meltdowns.

Rob: That's great! Let's dive right into this!

Dr. Jim: Just a second. Before we do, there's something I want to say to you both. It's important—very important. In fact, it might be the most important point I share with you today or in any of our sessions, so listen up. *If you want to change your child's behaviors, you need to also consider changing your own.* Behavior management is not just about Mark's behaviors and expecting Mark to change. It means you, as the adults in Mark's life, may also need to change your behaviors, especially those that arise from any preconceived notions you may have about Mark and his autism, about why he does certain things or "won't" do others. It's not just about expecting Mark to change; it's acknowledging your role and your responsibility to change also. You affect each other in ways you may not even imagine.

I hope I'm not sounding preachy, but in way, this is a "good news" message that needs to be shared far and wide, given how frequently it is overlooked among parents—and teachers. Becoming "behavior savvy" is a learning process that requires you to examine your own thoughts and actions, your unspoken yet very real expectations and any misunderstandings you have about "behavior" and about behavior in children with ASD. Adults unknowingly fuel the very behavior fires they're trying to extinguish in these children, and some do so repeatedly and then exclaim, "See, I've tried everything and nothing will make him stop doing this!"

Autism can severely impair your child's ability to understand the world and how to act appropriately within it. He exhibits the behavior he knows, what he has been taught, or what we have reinforced in him. In young children, this behavior can more often be more "wrong" than "right"... *because that's all he knows.* Yet we neurotypicals—you know, those of us without autism—still expect only the child to change. Any time you are interacting with your child, you are part of his environment, and his behavior is always a response to his environment.

If you want to be successful in bringing about positive behavior changes in your child, you need to pay equal attention to your own behaviors and the message you're sending to your child. It's not just a "today" skill, it's an "always" skill that will hopefully become so ingrained in you that it transforms your way of being with your child. Now that you know this secret to successful behavior management, let's talk about some of the effective strategies you can use.

◎　◎　◎

What's the "behavior equation" you keep mentioning?

Simply put, it's this: behavior = you + the child + the environment. Each behavior is a product of these three variables. In instances where your child is not interacting with another person, the equation reduces to the child + the environment. But it's never a single variable—it's never just the child. Never.

What are the possible reasons behind a child's behavior?

Make this one of your mantras; if you're a post-it notes type of person, paste this reminder up in several places around your house. *Everything your child does he does for a reason.* Whether he laughs or cries, is self-absorbed in a task or is running away from it at full speed, protesting in his best (or worst) verbalizations, hugging you or biting you, his action occurs for a reason. Just accept this as one of the Universal Laws of autism for now, even if it doesn't make complete sense to you.

There are abundant reasons why one particular child may exhibit a certain behavior. Luckily for those of us who live or work with these kids, the majority of reasons fall into one of the six global reasons listed below.

The most frequent reason young children with ASD exhibit behavior is that they are attempting to communicate with you. ASD children have a very difficult time expressing their needs and wants in a way that we understand or consider "socially appropriate." Recall what you've already learned about kids on the spectrum: they don't learn by watching others, their social skills are literally nonexistent, sensory issues may impair how information is seen, heard, and processed, and most don't have a functional communication system until one is taught to them. So what do they do when they want or need to communicate something? They use the behavior they have at hand!

Much of the time our kids condition us to respond to their behaviors. This starts at a very young age, before parents even suspect something might be wrong with their child's development, and certainly long before an autism diagnosis. Even with very young kids, there have been months and months or years of adults unknowingly reinforcing inappropriate rituals and routines that support kids in achieving their objective—getting what they need or want. The older the child, the more ingrained the behavior responses. Once we understand that their behaviors are an attempt to communicate with us, our goal is to teach them to do so in appropriate, functional ways. We teach them a substitute behavior that addresses their need.

Notice I didn't say we eliminate the behavior. It's a subtle but important difference. Providing our kids with an appropriate behavior that still gets their need met is teaching a child to become functional while recognizing and honoring the basic need behind the behavior. Adults focus on eliminating a behavior because they are unaware of the function, the reason behind the behavior. The result? The child unlearns one inappropriate behavior only to substitute it with another, equally inappropriate behavior. Why? It's because we haven't taught the child what to do instead. Behavior substitution: make that your mindset. It will return the most positive results.

6 Common Reasons for Behavior in a Child with ASD

1. *Self Stimulation*

We all have self-stimulatory behaviors (stims), behaviors we repeat over and over again, especially at times when we are nervous, bored, or anxious. We twirl a piece of hair, clear our throat, snap gum, tap a pencil or pen on the desk. When I am sitting at a table, my right leg bounces up and down fast enough to create a breeze! The difference between our self-stims and those of individuals with autism is that we know when they are socially appropriate and when they are not. If your boss stops her conversation to stare at your tapping pencil, you know it's time to curb that self-stim and keep it quiet for the rest of the conversation. While our stims may alleviate nervous energy, we can control them. Children with autism have a variety of self-stimulatory behaviors. They may flap their hands when anxious or excited, repeat the same activity over and over again, or "zone out"—stare at the wheels of a train as it goes around a track or watch a kaleidoscope for hours on end. Many of these stims are enjoyable to the child and satisfy a need for sensory input of some sort. Self-stim behaviors are among the most difficult to get under control, because in most cases an appropriate substitute behavior is not as "self rewarding" as the original behavior they are displaying.

The Goal: Come up with an appropriate behavior to take the place of the inappropriate behavior. For example: If the child loves to jump up and down over and over again in front of the TV, satisfy that behavioral need by having the child jump up and down on a small trampoline periodically throughout the day. Keep in mind that the child is communicating that he needs sensory input. When he begins jumping up and down in front of the TV, direct him to the trampoline. A child who flaps his hands when he's in a new situation may do so because he's anxious and doesn't have the skills to ask for help (a social skill we must teach the child) or he doesn't know how to communicate discomfort in an appropriate way. In this case, acquiring a new social skill may reduce the hand flapping. In the interim, you might give the child something else to do with his hands that is socially appropriate but still satisfies the sensory need. Depending on the environment, this might be playing with a small hand-held toy, singing a song that involves lots of clapping, or using a sensory-smart fidget toy. In all cases, we want to help establish the connection between the behavior need and the appropriate behavior action until the child is using the appropriate behavior himself. For instance, in the above scenario, parents want to help the child understand that when he feels the need to jump up and down, he can go to the trampoline and receive the input, rather than do it in front of the TV.

2. *Obsessive-Compulsive Tendencies*

Most people also have obsessive-compulsive behaviors to some degree. I can sympathize because I have a variety of OC behaviors. Everything on my desk has a place and everything is always in its place. If you move something, I'll move it back. My email account contains no saved, old, or new messages. I return emails as soon as they come in and I return phone calls as soon as I get the message (even ones I don't necessarily want to return). My anxiety level builds when I cannot do these things. But again, these OC tendencies do not hinder me from functioning in my day-to-day life (my wife may disagree).

The difference in spectrum children is that they get so engrossed in their OC obsessions or perseverations that it *does* impair their functioning. This is the child who MUST replay the same Disney video over and over again until they tire of it, and when the adult tries to intercede, a tantrum ensues. Adults on the spectrum tell us that these types of focused, repetitive behaviors alleviate some of the stress and anxiety that children with ASD feel when the world around them makes no sense and seems to them to be in a constant state of flux. Think what it would be like if you felt out of control every moment of every day… if your world lacked predictability and it seemed that every minute something happened that you didn't understand, and you didn't know what to do about it. You would latch onto anything that could re-establish some order and continuity, something that when done over and over, always ended up the same.

This type of obsessive need to "maintain order" appears in young children with ASD in various ways, like insisting on always taking the same route to McDonalds, lining up toys, eating foods in a certain order, etc. The world lacks predictability to them, so they have to keep rearranging the environment. The need is very real to these kids; however, the OC behavior disrupts their learning. It's not something they want to do; it's something they *have* to do to "keep it together," to maintain any sense of self-control. And, when they can't, a tantrum erupts. For example, at a family picnic with all its sounds and smells and unfamiliar people doing all sorts of unfamiliar things, while all the other kids are running around playing tag, the child with autism is moving a pile of rocks from one spot to another spot. Then putting them back, almost in the exact original location. Or it's the child who comes home from the trip with you to the grocery store (again, consider the variables and the sensory issues!) and helps put away groceries while insisting that the cans be lined up from biggest to smallest. Other perseverative behaviors include having to step on each sidewalk crack during an afternoon stroll, picking lint off any piece of clothing, or having to spin around in circles before sitting down.

The Goal: The goal is to gently disrupt or stop the compulsive chain and redirect the child to an equally satisfying but more appropriate or functional behavior. If the child is taking blocks from one location and putting them in another location, interrupt the child and redirect by showing him how to build a tower with the blocks. Same materials, different action. If he gets upset when you try doing this, redirect the child to building the tower after every two blocks he moves to the new location. Remember to praise the child each time he redirects successfully.

3. Attention Seeking

We all seek out attention from time to time. We act in ways that will satisfy our desire for attention from our significant others, family members, peers, and our co-workers. Hopefully, we know when our behaviors have "gone too far" according to generally accepted social standards. We see the cues from others that we're acting inappropriately and we are able to modify our behaviors accordingly.

Attention seeking behaviors in spectrum children, on the other hand, are usually neither acceptable nor self-controlled. A child with little ability to communicate his wants or needs will seek out attention in any way he knows—ranging from screaming and throwing things to nudging or grabbing. Our spectrum children have been conditioned, perhaps through our own behaviors and our inattention, to act in a no-way-to-ignore manner when they want our attention. For example, the child with ASD who wants attention will generally not go up to his parents, stand next to them, or initiate some direct contact with words or a touch. The more likely scenario is this child throwing the television remote at the wall. What happens? The adult comes into the room and engages with the child. *Voila!* The child's inappropriate attention seeking behavior has just been reinforced.

The Goal: Teach the child ways to gain attention appropriately. Keep in mind these children do not naturally generalize, so you will need to teach many different ways in various different situations. If they want your attention to get them something, teach them to take your hand or to present you with a communication card. If the child wants your attention while you're on the phone, teach her to come to you and give you a nonverbal signal, rather than grabbing at the phone or yelling from another room. If the child always walks up to you when you are speaking with someone else and interrupts your conversation to ask a question or get something, teach a more acceptable way to interrupt when he needs your attention. He can be taught to walk up and tap you on the shoulder, or say "Excuse me," and wait for you to respond before saying anything else.

4. Escape/Avoidance

Yes, we all have escape/avoidant behaviors too. My all-time favorite escape/avoidant behavior is when a woman says she can't make an event because she has to "wash her hair." (I may be dating myself here; I realize that.) Children with autism will display a variety of behaviors to escape situations they do not like or those that are new to them. The more intense their anxiety or dread, the more pronounced will be the action. Their behaviors can range from hitting, kicking, and pushing to full blown tantrums. Most people don't stop to think about the function of escape/avoidant behaviors: the child is trying to tell you he doesn't want to do whatever it is you are requesting of him. Generally this arises when the child doesn't understand your request, doesn't know how to comply with your request (i.e., has not been taught the necessary skills), or sometimes he just doesn't want to do it (we all have our days).

For example, a child does not want to go into the department store and begins to tantrum. Maybe the store is too sensory-laden for him, or the last time you were there the PA system went haywire and to him the sound was like a dagger straight to his eardrum. He fears that will happen again. The closer you drag him to the door, the more intense his behavior becomes. Finally, the adult takes the child back to the car and leaves. The child gets exactly what he wants, avoiding or escaping the trip to the store.

The Goal: The goal is to have the child communicate that he needs a break from the current environment, or let you know, in a more effective way, that he doesn't want to do what you've asked of him. In real life, the answer is not always going to be "yes," even when the child does everything correctly. You'll need to teach your child how to say "no" appropriately.

Be prepared to take small steps while teaching children to "handle" uncomfortable situations. For instance, you take the child to church and only spend the first ten minutes there, as opposed to staying the entire time, just to get the child used to being in church. Each week you add a few more minutes, gradually working up to staying for the entire service. A key part of this strategy is remembering that you must terminate the activity while the child is still being good. Don't push it and wait until the child is starting to display inappropriate behaviors to leave. If you do that you have just reinforced the inappropriate behavior and the likelihood that the child will exhibit the behavior again next time, or even sooner. Go slowly and let the child be successful with his behavior.

5. Tangible/To Obtain Something

Behaviors can arise when the child needs or wants something tangible (a drink, a toy, a cookie) and can't obtain it. We all have this type of behavior and in our world of instant gratification it is becoming more and more prevalent, especially in younger kids. However, young children with ASD rarely understand exactly why they can't have what they want when they want it. Being patient, waiting, or understanding delayed gratification are all learned behaviors; the child has to be taught that sometimes he must wait for certain things.

The Goal: The goal is to ensure that the child with ASD learns how to make a request in an appropriate way. Furthermore, we must teach the child that not all requests can be immediately fulfilled, and some may not be fulfilled at all. Waiting (in an appropriate manner) is an important social skill for all children to learn. These skills need to be taught systematically, in small increments, and repeated often so children have ample opportunities to practice the skill in many different areas of their lives. These goals can be worked into the EI plan with your team.

6. Communication

By now it should be evident that lack of a functional communication system is probably the number-one reason that problem behaviors develop in spectrum children. When children can communicate that they want something, need a break, feel anxious or fearful in a situation, or simply want some contact, their inappropriate behaviors decrease considerably. Communication is the most important function of your child's behaviors. It is critical that parents provide children with as many ways to communicate as possible (verbal and nonverbal). Even though your child may have verbal language, he may not use it effectively, especially when frustrated, angry, or anxious. The more communication options available to draw upon, the better the chance the child will communicate in an appropriate way.

The Goal: The ultimate goal is to give your child as many options as possible to communicate his needs, wants, and feelings.

These functions of behavior in kids with ASD seem just like behaviors all kids display, autism or no autism. Is that right?

Absolutely! All children, as they pass through their normal developmental milestones, will use behavior to convey their needs and wants. Think of the "terrible twos" or the "troublesome threes." The difference, though, is that children with ASD display these behaviors long after they should have "outgrown" them.

Typical kids know when their behaviors are "wrong"— I know lots of little kids who manipulate their parents through their behavior. Are kids with ASD like that too?

That's a great question and it's a loaded issue within the autism community. Parents need to understand that 99.9% of the inappropriate behaviors in spectrum children arise out of "not knowing"—these kids honestly don't know how to act appropriately until they are taught to do so. Yet many adults believe otherwise, including many teachers I've met. These are teachers I consider untrained in ASD.

The different thinking patterns in these kids render them at a disadvantage when it comes to making sense of the world. For them, it's not a question of being able to act appropriately, or being able to understand what to do, and consciously choosing not to. *These kids don't know how to act appropriately; their brain wiring interrupts the learning typical kids enjoy.* Kids with ASD are not willfully disobedient kids who need a "firmer hand." These are kids whose neurological wiring impairs their ability to learn as do their NT peers. Please don't lose sight of this as you work with a child on behavior issues. Believe that he's trying and that if he could, he would. Give her enough practice so these new behaviors can be used fluidly. Don't give up because it takes longer for behavior change to occur than it would with a typical child. And keep in mind that just because he could respond appropriately yesterday, it doesn't mean he's capable of it today. In time behavior may become more consistent, but at first, it might be sporadic.

So, what you're saying is that as the child learns new (appropriate) skills his existing (negative) behaviors should decrease proportionately?

Exactly—sort of. There's not a direct inverse proportion that works according to some formula. All kids are different. But as a general rule, yes, being proactive in teaching your child skills will bring about positive behavior change. As she learns ways to interact appropriately, communicate her wants and needs in a way that gets them met, learns play skills and has the social skills that bring her success in her interactions with others, "bad" behaviors should decrease. The one exception will be when behavior challenges are caused by physical illness or undiscovered physical conditions that are causing pain to the child. When new inappropriate behaviors pop up out of nowhere, especially those that are uncharacteristic for the child, always first check for some physical ailment such as ear or throat infections, allergies or skin rashes. This is especially important with nonverbal children.

Is teaching the child new skills enough to curb behavior problems?

No, it isn't. Remember the ABC formula mentioned in a previous session? Behavior change requires that we look at the antecedent (what comes before the behavior), the behavior, and the consequence; these all impact behavior. An important facet of behavior change is teaching the child that behaviors have consequences. Consequences can be pleasant or disagreeable. Nevertheless, this is a life lesson that should start being taught early on, in tangible, concrete ways. By and of itself, it reinforces the concept that a child's words, actions and behaviors affect others—a Theory of Mind concept that is typically difficult for spectrum children to understand and learn.

The consequence part of the ABC formula dovetails with another basic behavior management technique—reinforcement. Reinforcement drives motivation in our kids. They exhibit a behavior, and then, depending on the type, quality and quantity of reinforcement, the behavior either increases or decreases. This, in turn, shapes future behavior.

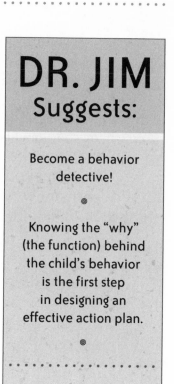

DR. JIM
Suggests:

Become a behavior detective!

◉

Knowing the "why" (the function) behind the child's behavior is the first step in designing an effective action plan.

◉

By reinforcement, you mean rewards, right?

Rewards are a part of the behavior strategy called reinforcement, but reinforcement is much more than simply rewards.

Reinforcement can be said to occur when:

- A behavior results in a consequence
- The consequence affects the child in a way that is pleasing or favorable, or satisfies a need
- This causes an *increase* in the original behavior.

Here's an example. A baby cries, Mom comes in and picks up the child. The child likes getting picked up, so crying increases. This is a classic example of reinforcement for a newborn baby. However simple this may seem, reinforcement affects us throughout our lives, in conscious and unconscious ways. When you think about it, it is a core component of almost all our behaviors. We do our chores when we're young in order to get our allowance. We're reinforced. We help our neighbor when he's in a bind, he expresses heartfelt appreciation and we feel good about what we did; we extend help again to someone else. We're reinforced.

Reinforcement is a commanding, compelling behavior strategy, yet it's not quite as simple as it seems. There are two types of reinforcement, primary and secondary.

Primary Reinforcement

Anything that has to do with survival, such as food, clothing and shelter. For our purposes in discussing reinforcement strategies during early intervention, it might refer to any food (e.g., chips, pretzels, candy) or drink (soda, juice).

Secondary Reinforcement

Everything else that is favorable, yet not essential to our existence, falls into this category, such as social reinforcers like praise, eye contact, smiles, hugs; or favorable items or activities such as computer time, stickers, toys, tokens, etc.

There are also two distinct kinds of reinforcement: positive and negative. This can get confusing, because most people equate negative reinforcement with punishment, and they are not the same. Reinforcement, by its very definition, *increases* the occurrence of a behavior.

Positive Reinforcement
Think plus (+); adding something to increase a behavior.

Positive reinforcement occurs when you add something to the behavior interaction that increases the likelihood of that behavior occurring in the future.

For example: You go to work every day and put in your forty hours during the week. On Friday you are handed a paycheck. You come back to work on Monday. Getting the paycheck increases the likelihood you'll work again next week.

For the child with autism: You ask him to point to the picture of a "cat," and when he does, you give him an animated verbal response "Good job!" perhaps coupled with a food reinforcer (chips or candy), something the child loves. He repeats the word next time.

Negative Reinforcement
Think minus (-); taking something away to increase a behavior.

Negative reinforcement occurs when you remove an adverse stimulus from a behavior interaction that increases the likelihood of that behavior occurring in the future. Note: the end effect of negative reinforcement is still to *increase* the occurrence of the behavior, not decrease the behavior.

For example: You are sound asleep and the alarm goes off. You roll over, turn the alarm off and get up. The next day you do the same thing again.

For the child with autism: A child who is uncomfortable being with others is allowed to have alone time as reinforcement for tolerating time in the company of others. Gradually the time he spends with others increases.

Mom asks the child to try a new vegetable on his plate. The goal is to teach the child to try new things. Mom tells the child, "just take one bite and you can leave the rest if you don't like it." Gradually the child increases his willingness to try new foods because he is reinforced by the removal of the rest of the food after the first bite.

Punishment is defined as anything that *decreases* the occurrence of a behavior.

Punishment is an ineffective behavior management tool because it fails to teach the child an appropriate substitute behavior. Your child with autism won't "figure out" on his own what the appropriate behavior should be. For these reasons and others, punishment should never be used as part of a behavior management plan with your child.

So I should use positive or negative reinforcement— but never punishment—coupled with teaching the child new skills, to address the child's behavior challenges?

As much as possible, no matter what you are teaching, you should concentrate on using positive reinforcement as your primary tool. To do this you will need to closely watch your child and determine which reinforcers are the most meaningful to him or her. It might be food or drink, certain toys or games, but it might also be things that seem "odd" to us NTs. I've known kids who would work very, very hard for a piece of string, to get time to look at their Porta-Potty photo album, engage in a discussion of the flight patterns at a local airport, or for the opportunity to look at the Shop Rite logo. Once you have determined your child's favorite things, these become the "rewards" for performing appropriate behaviors.

You can't mean that for the rest of my child's life I'm going to be feeding him treats or giving him toys or things every time he does what I ask him to do, are you?

Of course not! Once children begin to perform the correct behaviors and become more comfortable using the new skills, they slowly transition to using them over and over again because they enjoy the feedback they get in their environment. Tangible reinforcers are slowly faded (removed) and replaced with more socially acceptable reinforcers, such as praise or a high-five. Please keep in mind that with some of our spectrum kids you may never be able to fade such tangible reinforcement. If you think about it though, parents use this very same technique with NT kids and other adults. It's called the "bribe" and we use it all the time to get people to do what we want them to do. For example, we hold out the lure of extra TV or phone time in exchange for doing homework. We give kids an allowance for doing their chores, a new video game for each A on their report card. The only real difference between what we do with our typical kids and what we do with our spectrum kids is the name we give it, and maybe how obviously it is done.

Considerations when using Positive Reinforcement

- Always use something the child considers extremely valuable (i.e., computer time, TV time, special candy or a special drink).

- When using a specific reinforcer for a specific behavior, make sure the child does not have access to the reinforcer at any other time or it will lose its effectiveness. For example, you are giving the child computer time for successful toileting. When the child voids in the toilet, he gets time on the computer. However, at night, prior to going to bed, the child gets to play on the computer. Having access to the computer in the evening reduces its power as a reinforcer for the child's efforts to become toilet trained.

• Reinforce immediately after the child exhibits the behavior you want to see. Most children with ASD don't understand the idea of delayed reinforcement. Waiting to get reinforced can confuse the child, and he may not connect the reinforcement to the correct behavior.

• Do not use things that are provided as part of everyday living (e.g., regular food served at meals, water, clothing, or shelter) as reinforcers.

• Understand that food/snack reinforcers will be more effective if the child is hungry, and drinks will be more effective if the child is thirsty, the computer will be more effective if the child has not used one during that day, and the TV will be more effective if the child has not seen any in a while.

• Always pair a primary reinforcer with a secondary reinforcer. The goal is to eventually fade the primary reinforcer so the secondary reinforcer takes its place. For instance, pairing a verbal compliment (secondary) with a potato chip (primary).

• Introduce intermittent reinforcement early on. This simply means that once the child connects the reinforcer to the behavior and you're sure he knows that when he does X, he gets Y, mix up how often you give the reinforcer. Otherwise the child will become dependent on the reinforcer. If you continue to give the reinforcer after every correct behavior, when you try fading the reinforcer the behavior will quickly disappear. However, once you establish the behavior with the reinforcer and begin to withhold the reinforcer here and there, the child does not know when he'll be reinforced, and the behavior will increase and maintain itself for longer and longer periods of time. Remember, you're giving the child lots of practice sessions in building a new behavior, so you'll have ample opportunities to give the child reinforcement.

- Do a "power check" on reinforcers again, and again, and again. Kids change on a daily or even moment-to-moment basis. You must always check to see if the reinforcer is still effective. The most efficient way to do this is noticing if the child's behavior is increasing or decreasing. That pretty much says it all.

- Don't assume the child loves a reinforcer because you do, or because other kids her age do, or because it's the latest fad on the market. Test whether or not it's meaningful to the child.

- Last, never withhold a reinforcer as punishment for "bad" behavior. You're reinforcing the child's correct behavior, or approximations to the correct behavior. Reinforcement = increasing a behavior. Withholding the reinforcer should not be used at times the child is exhibiting inappropriate behaviors. It is not an effective behavior management strategy.

Where do behavior strategies like "time out" or negative consequences like lost computer time or lost TV time come into play?

There are always consequences to behavior; some are good and some are less desirable. In situations where you are sure the child has a skill, is capable of using that skill, but he chooses instead to display an unacceptable behavior, the use of a "time out" or a negative consequence may be called for. You want to help the child understand that if he "hits," he may have to sit on the steps and miss the chance to engage in a fun activity because hitting is not acceptable behavior. This way the child learns that he needs to use other more acceptable behaviors (like

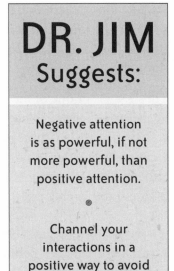

DR. JIM
Suggests:

Negative attention is as powerful, if not more powerful, than positive attention.

◎

Channel your interactions in a positive way to avoid situations that turn negative and teach negative reactions.

◎

communication) to express displeasure, rather than hitting. It would be inappropriate adult behavior to use time-out as a consequence for a child who displays an inappropriate behavior but hasn't first been taught the appropriate skill. Know your child, know his strengths and areas of challenge, and proceed accordingly.

While I understand how reinforcement fits into the behavior equation, that strategy is used once the child learns to exhibit the correct behavior. I must be missing something—how do I get him to that point?

Great question! The piece you're missing is a behavior technique called *prompting,* and it's the tool you'll use to work with the child while he's acquiring his new skill. As we've mentioned many times before, skills we take for granted, that our neurotypical kids seem to learn by osmosis, must be taught to a child with ASD. Prompting is used to ensure that the child is successful when asked to perform a task or follow through on a command.

This is another one of the secrets of effective behavior management: *set up the environment to make sure the child is successful.* Prompting for success coupled with appropriate reinforcement is your genie-in-a-bottle formula for guaranteeing behavior will happen again in the future. It is critical that prompting is used so the child does not fall into the habit of doing things incorrectly or exhibiting inappropriate behaviors.

How is prompting done?

Again, the basic idea behind prompting is a word, command or action that helps the child be successful in performing the behavior being worked on. Prompts can be actions, language or nonverbal communication involving picture cards or concrete objects, depending on the skill and cognitive level of the child. There are seven typical ways of prompting children with ASD:

Verbal

The adult asks, "What is this?" If the child does not respond, the adult says "cup." The child repeats the word or an approximation (recall "shaping" as a teaching strategy?) and the adult reinforces the child for a correct response. Verbal prompts can also include overemphasizing the correct choice in a situation involving multiple choices, offering the start of the correct response (i.e., "cu" for "cup") or, as lessons become more complex, offering an additional verbal "hint" that might trigger the correct response in the child.

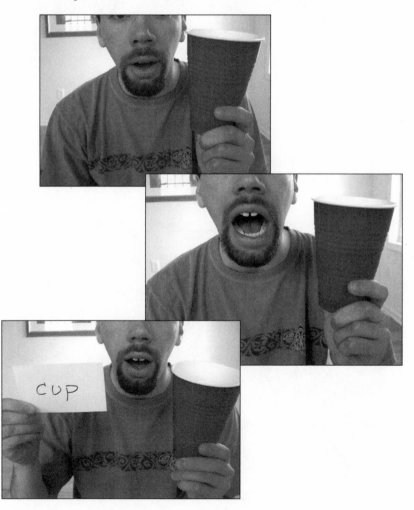

Physical

The adult says, "Give me the cup." If the child does not respond, the adult takes the child's hand, wraps it around the cup and guides the child's hand holding the cup to theirs. The adult reinforces the child.

Gestural

The adult says, "Give me the cup." When the child does not respond the adult points to the cup. The child hands the adult the cup and the adult reinforces the child. Gestural prompts might also include looking at the object or touching it.

Positional

The adult physically manipulates the child into a position that enables the child to learn or practice a skill. For example: If the child is in a group activity and another child begins to talk, the adult physically moves the child so she can watch and hear the other child. Then the adult reinforces the child.

Locational

The adult puts the cup close to the child and says, "Give me the cup." The child picks up the cup and hands it to the adult. The adult reinforces the child.

Signed

The adult says, "Go to the bathroom," and repeats the verbal language in sign language to the child at the same time.

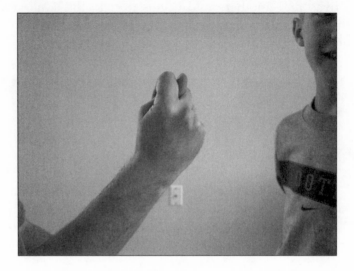

Modeling

The adult says "sit down" and, while saying it to the child, performs the action that was asked.

Just as children can become dependent on reinforcement, they can also quickly become prompt dependent, waiting until they receive a prompt before responding, so it is important to fade prompts as soon as possible. In any given session working with a child, an adult can use several different types of prompts to help the child be successful in the interaction. However, it is best to use the least intrusive prompt that will still result in the desired behavior.

It sounds like it's much easier to teach a child appropriate skills than to "unteach" inappropriate behaviors. Is this right?

It most certainly is, and that's one of the main reasons early intervention can be so effective for children with ASD. They haven't had much time for their inappropriate behaviors to become ingrained and habitual. Remember, these behaviors exist partly because the child doesn't know how to act appropriately, and partly because adults unknowingly reinforce inappropriate behaviors in their child.

Trying to step in and change inappropriate behaviors in a seven-year-old is going to take more effort and patience than it is with a three-year-old. To the child with ASD, if his behaviors have gotten him what he wants in the past, it will be difficult for him to understand why he can no longer use them to meet his needs. Trying to tell a spectrum child that his behavior needs to change because it's "socially inappropriate" or "not how kids should act" registers zero on the motivation scale. Many of our kids will not act for social reinforcement. His behaviors, although inappropriate, have been functionally satisfying to him. Something equally satisfying needs to motivate him. Never forget that.

Both the very young child and the older child can be taught appropriate new behaviors; they are equally capable of learning them. However, the older child has experienced many more years of functioning in a certain way in order to get his needs and wants met. He's not going to give up on these behaviors as easily as will the very young child who has had much less reinforcement. The basic strategies used to teach children are the same, whether the child is two or ten, but do realize that the amount of time it takes to bring about the change, and the amount of practice needed, may be vastly different.

How much do we—the parents of spectrum children— factor into the success we have in modifying our children's behaviors?

More than you might imagine! Our children learn what we teach them, they acquire behaviors we reinforce in them, they respond to the prompts, cues and messages, verbal or nonverbal, that we send to them. How and what our spectrum children learn and whether or not our strategies are effective has as much to do with us as it does with them. Maybe even more so. Strategies go just so far, and attitude is just as important.

Behavior management is both an art and a science. It's not a collection of never-fail tactics, but more an appreciation of the factors that contribute to behavior (you, me, the environment) and having a toolbox of helpful strategies that have been demonstrated to be effective with spectrum kids. Other than that, the "art" of behavior management involves communication and follow-through, maintaining a positive attitude towards the child, and a whole lot of love, patience and practice.

Parents can be better teachers by adopting some basic guidelines for their own behaviors. A few suggestions follow. These guidelines can help parents and teachers curb "bad habits" from developing in themselves and their young children right from the start.

Dr. Jim's 10 Behavior Rules to Live By

1. *Catch children when they are being good.*

This is the easiest to identify, but the hardest to actively live by. Life moves at a frantic pace much of the time and the home is an environment where all sorts of things are going on at the same time. Sometimes it's difficult to watch everything your child is doing. Make doubly sure that whenever you do catch the child doing something appropriate, a behavior you want to see, or you watch as she deals with a difficult situation in a good way, you shower her with praise or give him a reinforcement to lock in the appropriate behavior. Too many times we tend to ignore our children when they are being "good"—we look over at them and think to ourselves, "Wow she's being so good, I won't disturb her." Maybe we're even afraid that our saying something will end the good behavior. Get that idea right out of your mind now! First of all, leaving the child alone without social interaction is probably just what he would prefer. Second, you miss the opportunity to let the child feel the positive rewards of appropriate actions and behaviors.

Start working this rule in a simple way until you've given yourself a good amount of practice with it (by then it'll be more natural to you). Make a list of a few behaviors you are trying to change in the child. When the child is showing other appropriate behaviors—ones that are incompatible with the behaviors you are trying to avoid—give the child attention and say something like, "I love how you are playing" or "What a good boy! I love the way you are listening." You can also offer the child a snack or favorite drink as primary reinforcement for using behaviors you like to see.

2. Encourage children to use language, not behavior, to express their needs and wants.

Establishing a functional communication system is the single most important thing you can do for your child. (Yes, you're hearing it again!) And yet, it troubles me that in my travels across the country it is frequently missing from programs set up for children with ASD. These systems should consist of verbal language (approximations, sounds, noises related to speech), pictures (either actual pictures of objects and the child doing something or commercially manufactured ones), the written word(s), and gestures or other body language. In combination, these communication tools allow the child to have multiple ways to get a need or want met, show an emotion, or interact socially. It is also much easier to prompt some of these tools. For instance, prompting verbal language isn't effective unless your goal is to get the child to repeat your words. However, if the child begins to show signs of getting upset, you can prompt her to hand you a picture or point to what she wants, stopping the behavior from turning worse, while still teaching the child to use communication to get her needs met more effectively.

Start by selecting one or two communication behaviors as your priorities to teach. Make sure all adults working/interacting with the child know what these are so they know what behaviors to reinforce and what behaviors to ignore. As the child learns these communication skills and becomes proficient at using them, add additional communication goals. For example: The child likes to take your hand and lead you to the refrigerator whenever she is thirsty. You want her to say "drink," so every time she leads you to the refrigerator, you say "drink," have her repeat the word, and then give her a drink. Your goal is to have the child make a verbal request, which becomes Number-One on your list. All adults interacting with her know that before your daughter gets a drink, the adult says "drink," waits or prompts her to repeat the word, and then she gets her drink. After some practice, she may begin to say "drink" prior to grabbing your hand— that's great progress! You give oodles of verbal reinforcement for this and also her very favorite drink (the ultimate reinforcer) until she is doing this consistently. Getting her to make verbal requests is a goal that can be practiced throughout the day in different situations to promote generalization. You can use the identical tactics when she wants an apple, a video, or a toy, etc. Once the child has mastered the one-word communication, your next goal is to expand her use of language, enlarging requests from a single word to a phrase or short sentence, such as "I want a drink." Remember: this takes lots of practice and patience. These skills won't develop overnight.

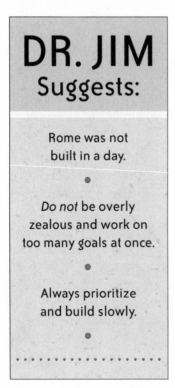

DR. JIM
Suggests:

Rome was not
built in a day.

◉

Do not be overly
zealous and work on
too many goals at once.

◉

Always prioritize
and build slowly.

◉

3. *Don't give a command unless you are going to follow through on it.*

This is the juggling game in all its glory. Be realistic about time and place when you issue a command or make a behavior request of a child. Make sure there's enough time for you and the child to work calmly through the practice session or the situation. We discussed earlier the importance of setting up the learning situation for success. If you don't have time to scaffold success for your child and be consistent in your behavior and any consequences that may need to be applied, wait until you do. This rule is vital for achieving success and is not one to gloss over because "Oh, everyone knows this." Knowing and doing are two very different skills, and for kids with ASD, you must emphasize the doing.

Here's a familiar scenario: the morning is already crazy and it's not even 7:30 a.m. Your older child forgot to tell you he needed ten pennies and five nickels for math class today, your significant other wants your help finding his car keys, and the dog still has to be walked. This is probably not a good time to ask your child with ASD to put on his shoes if the skill has not been consistently done in the past. But let's say you do: "Josh, be a good boy and go put on your shoes because it's time to take Peter to school." What happens? It probably goes something like this. You come back to check and see if Josh has his shoes on and to your dismay, he hasn't. So, you repeat the request, this time in a different way. "I thought I told you to put your shoes on? Now do it." If you go away again and do not follow through on working with Josh on the request, I can almost guarantee that when you come back this time, Josh will still not have his shoes, and you will be less than patient.

The better way to approach this situation is to leave the child alone until you have the required time to actually follow through on what it is you have asked. As long as the child is not hurting himself or anyone else, leave him alone. Accept that there are going to be mornings when you put your kid's shoes on and send him on his way; on those days, it's all about getting the child to the bus, not teaching him anything or working on mastery of a new skill. Trying to "teach" during those hectic, stressful times is setting the child and yourself up for failure. Don't fall into that trap. But on those days when you have the time, set aside the five minutes you need to give your child your full attention, help him with the skill in a way that assures he will be successful and can be reinforced for his efforts.

4. Don't use a verbal prompt unless you want a verbal answer.

Okay, I'm not saying don't talk to your child. The point I want to make is that using verbal language is not always the best way to go about getting a child to respond in an effective way.

In the first two weeks of my career, I heard an eye-opening quote from Anne Holmes, Director of Outreach and Support Services at the nationally well-known Eden Family of Services, in Princeton, New Jersey. She said, "Never use a verbal prompt unless you want a verbal answer." I have modeled her quote, turned it into a mantra of sorts and repeatedly found it to be very successful with the kids I've worked with over the years. What, exactly, does it mean? Simply this: Whenever you interact with a child you will use language. But once you issue a command or make a request, do not repeat yourself unless what you want is a verbal response—rather than an action—from the child.

Here are two examples that illustrate the difference.

- *Correct use of a verbal prompt to elicit a verbal response*
  You're teaching the child to identify and name objects. You show the child a fork and say, "What is it?" If the child does not respond, you say "fork" and repeat the question, "What is it?" The child says "fork" and you reinforce the response.

- *Incorrect use of a verbal prompt*
  You say to the child, "Come here" and the child does not respond. Our natural inclination is to repeat the command, "Come here," followed by "I said come here." Eventually you get the child and lead him to where you wanted him in the first place. A more effective teaching strategy would be to issue the command once, "Come here." If the child does not respond, you go and get him, very neutrally, not saying anything or giving eye contact and bring him to the spot you wanted him to be and say "That was good listening" and reinforce him. You did not expect a verbal answer to the command

"Come here," so you use a nonverbal prompt (physical or gestural) to get the child to respond appropriately. Remember, your goal is to teach the child to be successful at the behavior, not to fault him for not doing it correctly.

5. Know your goal in every interaction.

Sometimes being your child's mom and dad can be the goal of the interaction. While taking advantage of every "teachable moment" is important, you don't have to be clinical all the time. However, you do need to be clear about what you want the child to learn during specific interactions. For example, if you are teaching a self-care skill (i.e., tooth brushing, face washing, hand washing, toileting) there should be no verbal interactions during the entire process, except perhaps as a secondary reinforcer upon completion. If you use language to teach each step, then you are using verbal prompts and, as we discussed earlier, never use a verbal prompt unless you want a verbal answer. Verbal prompts are the hardest prompts to fade. Children with ASD become easily dependent on these verbal cues. We want our children to be able to perform self-care skills independently. By using verbal prompts we set up a situation where there always has to be an adult present to get the job done. In this type of learning situation, using and fading physical or gestural prompts coupled with end-of-task reinforcement will result in the child mastering the skill more quickly and efficiently, and being able to use it without supervision.

On the flip side, your next goal may be teaching the child to identify items in the bathroom. Then, using a great deal of language is very appropriate and necessary. Children with ASD, especially those who are visual rather than verbal thinkers, process language very literally. It's best to eliminate all the unnecessary, non-functional, meaningless and often confusing language from your communication. Initially your language will be very telegraphic. Stay away from idioms and just use simple, concrete language, like "Get toothbrush."

Always understand your goal and use teaching strategies that support the goal so you get the most out of the interaction with your child.

6. Use visual cues whenever you can.

Children with ASD are visual learners. Anytime you can provide them with an additional avenue to support learning and comprehension, grab it! Many people consider visual cues to be "not normal" or "holding the child back." Others view visual tools as "temporary" supports that should be later faded. Those are people who do not understand the different way the autism brain functions and the power that multiple modes of learning bring to these kids. Visual tools are power tools. They help children make better sense out of instructions or directions, prepare for what comes next, and allow them to communicate when they are unable to use verbal language. Let me repeat myself: everyone uses visual cues. They are a part of our lives: post-it notes, daily planners, To-Do lists, blackberries, etc. They provide reminders, keep us organized and on track with the events and responsibilities of life. It's no different for kids with autism, except that we're using the visual tools on a more basic level of learning.

The real power of visual cues lies in helping children gain independence. With a visual strip that sequences a task, a child can practice a task without adult intervention. (We have to teach use of the visual strategy first!) Post a daily schedule so the child knows what will happen and when. Use a visual chart to illustrate the sequence of a task. For example, over the bathroom sink, post a tooth-brushing sequence. First picture, the toothbrush, second picture, putting toothpaste on the toothbrush, third picture, the child brushes his teeth. For children who need extra help, the sequence can be more detailed. Laminate the sequence (especially helpful around water!) and always be there for the child to provide the additional support that assures success. Use a picture schedule to walk a child through his after-school day, a trip to the grocery store, or to break down tasks you'll be working on together in building a new skill. To reinforce completion of a task, and to help the child learn the intangible concept of "done," teach the child to remove each task on his visual schedule as he completes it and put it in a "completed" or "finished" bin. As the adult in the child's life, make sure the child can complete each task on the schedule before bedtime, even on those days when it requires extra adult support. This establishes a routine for the child that will help ease anxiety, especially in new situations. He'll trust that the end of the schedule is the end of the schedule.

7. When the child is angry or frustrated, use as little language as possible.

Once a tantrum or "meltdown" starts, use as little language as possible to redirect spectrum children and get them back into control. This is not a teachable moment, not a time to discuss why the child is acting the way he is or why he may be feeling the way he is. Your child is not processing language during his tantrum and feeding him words will only escalate the situation. Those discussions are good ones, but wait until later, once the child has calmed down. Your primary goal during a tantrum is to help children regain control. The best way is to use very simple language like "look at me" or "sit quiet," or "hands quiet," use physical or gestural prompts to help him follow though, then of course, reinforce him for appropriate behavior.

8. Practice, Practice, Practice!

The old adage, "Practice makes perfect" is nowhere more applicable than within the autism community. Practice—and plenty of it—is how these children learn and generalize skills. Be prepared for even more practice than you think is needed, and try not to "judge" your child because he needs more practice than you think he "should." And of course, don't give up because you've practiced a skill fifty times and he still hasn't mastered it! Maybe the fifty-first time he'll do it! We never know with our kids. There's no consistent pattern of skill acquisition, and the kids learn differently from day to day (hmm, don't we all?). Hang in there!

Here's where some of the teaching strategies already discussed really come into play. By using prompts, the child will be successful at performing the skill, by using reinforcement, the child will want to repeat the skill, by practicing it over and over again, the child will become comfortable doing the skill and it will eventually become second nature. You can then fade the prompts and use less and less reinforcement. This is the ultimate goal.

A few additional hints to make his practice perfect:

• Don't be lured into thinking that once the child has mastered a skill, practice stops. No way! Make sure the child is regularly using his newly found abilities. Otherwise, it's like learning a foreign language—use it or lose it.

• Some kids with ASD are analytic learners and some are gestalt learners. Analytic learners process information in steps; small increments of progress are noticeable. Gestalt learners are those kids who can't seem to master a skill and then one day, do it perfectly. It's easy for parents to doubt a child's ability when they are gestalt learners—as the teacher in his or her life, *we're* not being reinforced by seeing incremental learning. Don't give up—keep practicing!

• Initially it is important to use the same language again and again, until you are confident the child knows what it is you are asking. If your instruction is "give me the fork" say that exact same phrase each time, rather than embellish the command by substituting "would you get me a fork" or "please hand me a fork" or "reach over and give me the fork." Use the same language every time until the skill is mastered and the child's language ability can handle these variations.

• From the very beginning, generalize the skill to other environments. For example: you are teaching the child the difference between a spoon, knife, and fork and you have chosen to begin with fork. You may want to do several repetitions of "give me the fork" during a "work session" with your child. Then later that day, during dinner, put some forks around the sitting area of the child and several times have everyone there ask her for a fork. Have dessert a little later and again practice with forks. As much as possible use the skill you are teaching in a functional, nor-

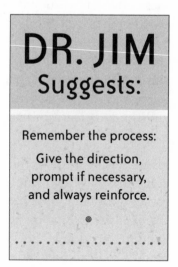

DR. JIM
Suggests:

Remember the process:
Give the direction,
prompt if necessary,
and always reinforce.

malized environment, even though the student might not yet have mastered the skill.

9. Be consistent and predictable.

Consistency and predictability go far in creating an environment that is conducive to your spectrum child's way of thinking and learning. However, it's not always easy to act this way and you may have to re-train yourself, especially if you're the type of person who enjoys "mixing things up" or you tend to get bored easily with the "same old, same old." Keep in mind that for the child with ASD, the world is a frightening place, each day filled with hundreds or thousands of experiences that make no sense or even worse—inflict pain. Things are constantly in motion, constantly foreign. A routine that is predictable and consistent, hearing the same simple language over and over, these are life preservers to the child. Be consistent in your words and deeds. By doing so you give the child the framework within which trust develops: he can predict your behavior and trust that it will be consistent today, tomorrow, next week, next month. This trust is the motivation he needs to be willing to venture out a little more each day to learn how to interact and function amidst the chaos he feels.

Be sure that other people who interact with the child on a regular basis are consistent and predictable too, and that they know the drill. If needed, write out instructions so everyone knows how to handle a particular behavior (a visual cue for the family).

10. Hold yourself and your child accountable for your actions.

It's easy to feel sorry for the child with ASD, what with all the challenges this little tyke has, and how much more difficult it is for him or her to learn and do things that other kids learn and do without even trying. We love these kids; we feel for them. And many times, because of these feelings, we cut them slack, let them off the hook, or even worse, assume they can't learn things so we don't even try to teach them! Do you see how incredibly detrimental this attitude can be to the future of your child? It literally robs the child of his future and the opportunity to nurture his potential!

Resist the urge to give your child with ASD special treatment. This is not a good thing, especially in the early years of teaching and working with the child—for either of you! Now, this doesn't mean you can throw the child with ASD into any situation and expect him to "deal with it or else." Certainly not. But as the adults and teachers in the child's life, we want to structure the environment for success, so the child finds learning fun and reinforcing, not drudgery and a constant stream of failures. This means we need to establish the rules and enforce them. Expect the correct behavior from your child and be strict about it. Expect the correct behavior from yourself—the behavior that allows the child to be successful—and be strict with yourself, too. That's how you both will learn: together.

I try to follow the old school teacher's adage, "Don't smile before Christmas." Be extremely strict with expectations early on and ease up as you go along. Actually, it's much easier on you both to set up the rules and live by them in the beginning. Bending the rules, allowing exceptions means a whole lot more conversation and communication so the child understands the "when" and "why" of exceptions. Young kids with ASD just don't have the social thinking skills to understand this type of subjectivity, so don't even go there. Stay focused on what it is you are trying to teach and accomplish, what behavior you are trying to change, and then "Just do it!"

Won't doing the same things in the same way over and over turn my little child into a "behavior machine"? I want him to be flexible and responsive to the changing landscape of life, not act out every time something doesn't go according to the "rules."

You bring up some great points, ones that many parents share. My response is this: You're jumping too far ahead and losing sight of the many intermediate steps that need to occur first. A common saying is that you need to learn the rules before you can understand how to break or bend them. That line of thinking applies here to kids on the autism spectrum. We start with structure, repetition, predictability, consistency and then over time, as the child grows and learns and acquires more skills and is exposed to more and more social situations, we loosen things up and move into a different way of teaching, one that incorporates more of the social-emotional fluidity that constitutes life in general. But we can't start that way. It would be overwhelming for the child and foster more failure than success.

The ten behavior suggestions above have been proven effective with children with ASD. If you structure your life to follow them, I can't guarantee your child will be perfect, but I am very confident that he will be able to function within your family. Setting up the right "pattern" early on with the child is very important. The child must be taught that behaviors have consequences (not punishment!), that you are going to be consistent in your actions and that you have expectations for how he should behave. If you do not use the ten

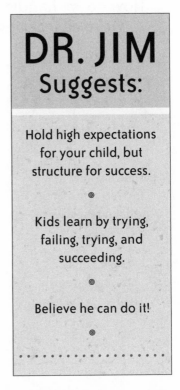

DR. JIM
Suggests:

Hold high expectations for your child, but structure for success.

◎

Kids learn by trying, failing, trying, and succeeding.

◎

Believe he can do it!

◎

suggestions, or use them only every once in a while, your child is going to have a difficult time understanding what is expected of him. In response, he may display a variety of inappropriate behaviors—because he's testing you, because he just doesn't know what to do, and because you let him.

I have watched too many families of young children with ASD merely deal with behaviors as they occur and attempt to control their child physically (e.g., if the child is tantruming, just pick the child up and move him away from everyone else). These families are in basic survival mode. They're being reactive instead of proactive in dealing with the child's behaviors. When the child is three or five or seven this is pretty easy to do. However, these children get older, and as they do, they begin to "throw their weight around" at times. Behavior management of this type—reactive—is not so easy with a 150-pound sixteen-year-old.

How do we handle the behavior break-downs while we're all learning to become behavior experts?

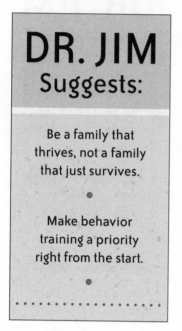

DR. JIM Suggests:

Be a family that thrives, not a family that just survives.

◎

Make behavior training a priority right from the start.

◎

It's a given in life with a child with ASD: tantrums and meltdowns are going to occur despite your best efforts and best teaching strategies. It's extremely important to have a game plan in place to handle these situations, especially when they occur in public—because they will, and often—until your child has a repertoire of behaviors and communication capabilities. Be your child's best behavior detective and always be on the alert for the signs of a meltdown so you can intervene accordingly. Be doubly conscious when the child is tired, hungry, anxious, or put into a sensory-packed situation.

To follow is a game plan to effectively deal with tantrums and meltdowns. Please understand: a tantrum or meltdown is a behavior manifestation that does not involve injury to the child, his surroundings or others. That level of behavior intensity requires a different set of strategies than those below.

Dr. Jim's Suggestions to Tame those Tantrums

Prevention is always your first step

It's all the things we've already discussed: catch the child being good, reward that behavior, shape appropriate behaviors and ignore and redirect inappropriate behaviors. If the child is throwing his toys around and you do not want him to do that, walk up, say "let's play with this," and show the child how to play with the toy appropriately. Do a turn-taking type of activity and encourage the child to play with it when you walk away. *Don't* yell at the child, "No, stop that!" and go back to what you were doing. The child will probably simply continue throwing the toy and, if you continue to speak to him, you are just reinforcing the interaction (positive or negative, it doesn't matter). If you are busy and cannot go to the child to prompt him to use the toy appropriately, and he is not killing himself or anybody else, wait until you can go over and interact. Remember two things: 1) you want to *teach* the child what to do, not disapprove of what he's doing, and 2) preventing a tantrum does not mean avoiding one. Many parents keep giving the child what he wants to avoid a tantrum at all costs. This usually happens when parents don't understand behavior management techniques and feel ill-equipped to handle a tantrum.

Consistency is essential

If you have ever seen the television shows *Nanny 911* or *Super Nanny*, you know that consistency is one of the main techniques they emphasize with parents. Setting boundaries, establishing consequences, communicating these to the child in a way they can understand and then consistent follow-through on the part of the parent will result in positive behavior change in the child. Many well-intentioned parents inadvertently contribute to the child's problem behaviors because of their inconsistent words and actions. They start out with firm resolve, only to lose it once the child screams more than a few minutes or is being more difficult than usual. They give in, which reinforces the child acting out. Learned behavior—yes, but not what they wanted the child to learn.

"No" means "No." Do not give in, even if it means you have to deal with a tantrum. The more you show the child you mean what you say, the better able he will become at predicting your behavior.

Figure out the reason behind the behavior

We already talked about the reasons behind behavior and hopefully the child has a functional communication system to convey those needs and wants. In the middle of a tantrum, however, you may need to help him remember to use these systems.

Can you quickly determine why the child is tantruming? Is it for attention, to escape doing something you just asked, or because she can't get what she wants when she wants, or does she need something? Saying things like "show me," "use your words," or offering some picture cards to choose from are all good strategies when the child is beginning to get frustrated. Use gestural or physical prompts to get the child redirected, then be sure to reinforce the appropriate behavior just as soon as she exhibits it. Follow this up by returning to the communication system so she can articulate what it is she needs.

When you can, use extinction

When the behavior erupts, ignore it. Just don't ignore the child. Your job is to look for any positive behavior you can praise. When the child gets quiet you can say, "I love that you are quiet, what do you want?" and help him use his language. Do not draw any attention to the tantrum behaviors while you are waiting for something positive to reinforce.

When the child begins to tantrum you must stay close enough so he doesn't put himself or anyone else in danger. If he's not doing that, wait out the tantrum. Always keep the child safe during the tantrum by removing things that could hurt him. Attempt to re-direct, nonverbally, and take the lead from the child. If he continues to tantrum after you try to re-direct, wait a few minutes and attempt it again. Remember, keep your cool, be very neutral and try not to make any eye contact. Keep this up until the tantrum is over and, once the child is quiet and doing something appropriate, reinforce that behavior. If you stay consistent with this approach and teach communication, the tantrums will lessen and eventually go away.

Make use of consequences. As we've discussed, it is extremely valuable to establish consequences as part of the overall behavior plan. For example, the child spills a drink, he helps clean it up. The child hits you or a sibling, he must say he's sorry. Make the consequences appropriate to the age of the child, degree of cognitive understanding, and the situation. Start by using concrete consequences; they help a spectrum child understand the cause/effect principle in preparation for later years, when consequences become less tangible and more about impressions and feelings. Consistent use of consequences helps in a situation when the child is out of control because he will be used to being told that "if you do x – y will happen."

What about those times when the child is hitting, biting, punching, etc.?

There will be times when the child begins a tantrum and the tantrum becomes violent, where the child may try to bite, hit, kick or begin some form of self-injury like head banging or self-biting. In these cases you must intervene quickly and protect the child. These types of situations can be emotional and very stressful for a parent. It's best for parents or the family to develop a written crisis intervention plan and even practice acting it out ahead of time so people are familiar with the sequence of actions. Every family is different and will be comfortable with certain techniques and not with others. Develop the plan and then be consistent in using it. Keep in mind that crisis intervention techniques are only to be used when the child is putting himself in danger of injury or destroying the environment. They do not teach skills; they only protect. A few appropriate crisis strategies follow.

Designate a safe area

If possible, have an area that is devoid of things that could possibly injure the child, has a heavily padded rug or even an exercise mat. If the child begins to tantrum, direct him to this area or, if necessary, pick the child up and move him into this area for safety. If the child tries to leave the area use prompts (physical and gestural, not verbal) to keep him in the area until the tantrum is over. Use extinction, as directed above, and once the child displays any appropriate behavior, reinforce it and try to get the child under control. Do not transport the child to the area if it is going to put you or the child in danger; deal with the tantrum where it occurs.

Bean Bag Chair: Have a bean-bag chair available to use as a portable "safe area" in those cases when transporting the child is not possible. The bean-bag chair can be moved from room to room very easily. Make sure when you use the bean-bag chair that if the child tries to get out, you prompt her back to the chair. Also, make sure the child is never face down in the chair and does not bite the chair.

Learn effective behavior crisis techniques

At those times when the child is totally out of control, the use of a bas-ket-hold while sitting on the ground with the child in front of you, may be the safest strategy until the child calms down. If your child's tantrums regularly escalate to this level of intensity, you should be appropriately trained by professionals in using this technique or other similar crisis holds. Contact Crisis Prevention Institute, an organiza-tion that provides such training, or contact your EIP staff to find out where you can be trained.

Remove the child

In a public setting, the most effective thing to do is to remove yourself and the child. Again, your child's safety is your primary concern and it doesn't matter if you leave a trail of onlookers or a cart full of groceries in the middle of the aisle. This is a crisis. Once the child is out of the situation, try to deal with him in the car. Do not drive or strap the child in a car seat until he is under control. Use minimal language. Stay calm. Children with ASD feel the anxiety levels of the adults around them. If you are out of control, it will be that much harder for your child to regain his own control. Protect the child and yourself from injury and once you see appropriate behavior, reinforce it and get the child back under control.

But doesn't removing the child only reinforce his tantrums?

Great question! It all comes down to why and how you're removing the child. If it's solely for convenience, so you don't have to deal with a dif-ficult situation, you've no clue why it happened, and when it's over, the child is reprimanded for his "bad" behavior, in all likelihood it will hap-pen again. You're avoiding behavior management and, instead, using punishment as your behavior strategy. It never works. I'll repeat: it *never* works in bringing about any lasting, positive changes in the child.

On the other hand, if you are working with the child on a regular basis, teaching new skills, organizing the environment so the child is successful, using time-tested and effective behavior management strategies like prompting, shaping, chaining, positive reinforcement and consequences, you realize that when a behavior tantrum, meltdown, or crisis situation arises, the child is sending you a clear message: something is drastically wrong and I'm unable to deal with it or tell you what it is. Just get me out of here! See the difference? In this case, the meltdown is a glitch in an otherwise comprehensive behavior management plan. Your child is doing his best, and in this situation, he's not able to handle it. In the first scenario, there is no plan, no proactive teaching, just on-the-spot reaction.

Behavior will remain an ongoing issue for most families. As spectrum children age, some behaviors seem to disappear while new ones emerge. With age also come different and sometimes elevated expectations of the child on the part of others. Preschool teachers may overlook certain behaviors that become prerequisites in kindergarten; middle-school teachers may pile on a whole different set of behavior expectations from those that existed in elementary school. This spiral continues as children become teenagers then young adults and enter into all sorts of new personal and professional relationships. Establishing firm ground rules in a child's younger years gives him the behavior strategies and interaction tools he will need later in life to be successful.

Learning these behavior strategies may seem difficult at first, but the great news is that behavior is a learned reaction. That applies to you as well as your child. Early intervention services can provide you with the behavior management training you need to give you the confidence and knowledge to work effectively with your child. It will, indeed, take much practice (for you both), but teachable moments abound. Every day you have countless opportunities to practice new skills and new strategies that bring about positive growth and change. If you erred yesterday, don't beat yourself up. Just resolve to try harder today and do your very best tomorrow.

After all, isn't that what we want our children to learn, too?

"My brother's name is Robby and while being a strong individual, he does fall under the harsh label of autism. If given the chance to sever autism from Robby, I wouldn't know what I would cut. Robby's behaviors are so much a part of him in my eyes. Without the moodiness and the jokes about Thomas the Tank Engine I wouldn't really know him.

This fine line between disorder and identity has really shaped my life in a way that spurs deeper contemplation about most things. Robby's autism sometimes seems like a problem of acting in this society and disobeying etiquette and rules that seem silly at times when I think about them. My point is not to question the purpose of therapy but to caution that within it, we don't lose the personality of the individual, or conform them to society's standards to such a degree that we lose sight of the special gifts they bring to the world.

Robby is who he is, with all of his aggressions and obsessions. He has a sense of humor, and is affectionate and caring. He has affected my life in both negative and positive ways, but in the end, his autism is not a factor of importance to me. What is most important is Robby and that I love him."

-BILLY, BROTHER OF ROBBY

chapter nine

Little Kids, Big Issues
Sleeping, Eating,
Toilet Training & Independence

MAUREEN AND ROB HAVE COMPLETED THE BASIC AUTISM SESSIONS WITH DR. Jim, and are now on a "call as needed" basis in seeing him. Their EI program is running smoothly since some minor changes in personnel were made to better suit their family's personality. The team is communicating regularly, working cohesively, and Maureen has blossomed in her confidence in working with Mark. Mark has acquired many new functional skills, basic language is emerging, and both parents see daily progress in him. After a couple of hit-and-miss outings, Rob and Maureen finally found a support group they liked, and attend once a month. They both found that talking with other moms and dads of spectrum kids is the grounding force that gets them through the emotional turmoil of this new way of life. Their autism "family" has been a source of practical, real-life information, helped them learn the ins and outs of local services and become a social network where they truly feel included and understood.

It's been eight weeks since their last session with Dr. Jim and they've scheduled a meeting to talk about some pressing concerns that have arisen.

Dr. Jim: Good to see you both again. It's been a couple of months since we last talked. By the look on your faces, I'll bet I can guess one of the problems you're having—lack of sleep?

Maureen: *Do I look that frightful that it shows? But you're right. It's been weeks since I've had more than four hours of sleep a night. Mark is awake much of the night, so either Rob or I am up with him. Most of the time it's me, because Rob needs to get up and go to work in the morning. But it's affecting us both.*

Rob: *My son's a moving machine ... as active at 3:00 a.m. as he is at 3:00 p.m.! I don't know where his energy comes from—I wish I had some of it myself right about now. I'm dragging myself home at the end of the day and my work is suffering. I know Maureen is doing her best to keep Mark quiet so I can sleep, but sometimes there's no way to do it. He's also a real finicky eater, just wanting certain foods over and over and refusing to eat other things. I'm not sure what's going on in our family these days.*

Maureen: *Maybe we didn't notice these things before, because we were so focused on figuring out what was wrong with Mark, then getting his behaviors under control and getting used to the autism diagnosis and all. But lack of sleep is starting to affect me in ways that aren't very pretty. I'm crabby and short tempered. I snap at Rob when he gets home, and feel on edge, even when he's trying to help. We certainly don't have a love life anymore—we can't seem to find time and when we do, we'd both rather sleep! We've also been trying to toilet train Mark and so far, it's been a pretty miserable mess. Mark seems more intent on playing with his poop than his toys at times, which as you can imagine, leads to regular messes to clean up as well as what seems like a never-ending pile of laundry to do. I'm just exhausted. Even worse, I'm back to feeling desperate and stupid, like I did when Mark was first diagnosed. It's a horrible feeling and saps the motivation and life right out of me. We need help!*

Dr. Jim: I'm glad you called me to talk over these things. It was a good decision on your part. Young kids on the spectrum can present far greater challenges in the areas of sleeping, eating and toilet training than do typical kids. I know personally the devastating effects of sleep deprivation, and many a sleep-deprived parent has walked through my door asking for help. Luckily, there are things you can do that will bring about positive changes and help you better deal with these troublesome issues. Many of these new strategies are based on the behavior management techniques you've learned, so you're already well on your way to managing these issues.

◎ ◎ ◎

Are problems with issues such as sleeping, eating or toilet training covered under our EIP services?

These issues are related to autism, but are not always directly addressed through the EIP process. They're the type of concerns that usually fall to the family to handle on their own, even though the EIP staff can and will offer assistance. In most cases, your team members are not around when these issues pop up—for instance, at mealtime, bedtime, etc.—and therefore the primary responsibility resides with parents to get these things under control.

What kind of help can the EIP team provide?

It can be general training, giving you information about common, effective ways to approach the problem, or strategies for dealing with specific issues. The basic behavior management strategies you learned—looking for the cause of a behavior, teaching replacement skills, using prompts, cues, visual strategies and reinforcement—will all apply to these daily living challenges too. The EIP staff can help you put the pieces together into a working plan to deal with the issue.

But these are behavior strategies. Are problems with sleeping and eating behavioral issues? They seem more like physical issues, don't they?

They can be both, so it's important that alongside behavioral techniques you make sure there are no physical problems that exacerbate the situation. You can do this by discussing your concerns with your family doctor and ruling out physical causes.

What do I need to know about sleep problems in children with ASD?

Sleep deprivation is a serious concern that should not be taken lightly or passed over in our efforts to be good parents and help our kids. It literally robs us of the energy and wherewithal we need to survive. Any sleep-deprived parent can attest that we are not at our best when in this state. Our emotions run haywire and our decisions are often faulty. It is therefore one of the first, critical areas to get under control. Otherwise, everything else falls apart too.

We all handle sleep deprivation differently, and some people "last longer" or get by on less sleep than others. I remember when my wife was pregnant with our son Zach. She had a horrible pregnancy, a great deal of morning sickness and extremely bad heartburn. We did not sleep well for the entire ten months of her pregnancy. When Zach was born, he was a screamer and my wife breastfed. So, he was right next to the bed for a very long time and we did not sleep much during his first year of life. Even when he moved to his crib, he would wake up two or three times a night. To make a long story short, my wife and I did not sleep well for about three years. I can tell you from firsthand experience that this was not good for either of us, or our marriage (except maybe as birth control). It affected our relationships with our other children, and also with my co-workers. I can honestly say that I would have handled some situations in my life very differently had I had adequate sleep.

Therefore, it is critical that your child begin his life with good sleeping habits, and as his parent, that you teach and reinforce these good habits right from the start. Children are different from one another, but on average, a three-year-old needs 11-12 hours of sleep per night. Many parents of children with ASD report that their child seems to require much less, well below the needs of typical kids. Spectrum children also tend to have very disruptive sleep patterns. They may have trouble falling asleep or staying asleep. Many sleep in short spurts, for example, sleeping two hours, then being awake two hours, alternating back and forth like this the entire night. Some seem to be able to function on as little as three to four hours total a night, coupled with a daytime nap. This doesn't bode well for adults who can't stop work or postpone family responsibilities to take a two-hour nap in the middle of the day.

If you suspect your child has a sleep disturbance, don't delay in seeking out help with this issue. The experts suggest you keep a sleep diary for a minimum of two weeks to gather relevant information about your child's sleep patterns: when he sleeps, for how long, conditions that seem to promote or aggravate sleep, his demeanor during waking hours, etc. This information is valuable for several reasons.

- It can help identify patterns of sleep and waking behaviors that you may be able to change.

- It provides good baseline data if you decide to change any of the child's routines or you decide to use a behavioral approach to sleep.

- You can share this information with your child's medical doctor and/or the professionals with whom you work to address the sleep problem.

There are many theories that try to explain why children with autism do not sleep well, with little consensus among them. Our goal here is not to discuss them, but offer functional strategies that can alleviate the day-to-day effects of these sleep disturbances. The following five suggestions can do just that. Please keep in mind that any medical interventions should be first discussed with and approved by your child's physician.

Dr. Jim's Top 5 Sleep Strategies

1. Establish a Consistent Routine

Whenever possible, keep the bedtime routine the same day to day, putting the child to bed at the same time and doing the same pre-bedtime activities. Of course, that's not always possible, but the more consistent and predictable you are, the better able the child will be to predict what is expected of him. Try giving a ten-, five- and one-minute warning for bedtime, using a visual timer if needed. Then have a consistent bedtime routine. For instance, in our house bedtime consists of a bath/shower (my son's choice and sometimes both), we brush our teeth, Mom reads, Dad reads (when he is home), then we have a ten-minute buffer (play time in the room) before it's lights-out. We follow this routine every night, even when one parent is not home and also when we are traveling. It sometimes takes a little extra planning to pull off, but by working at it, we keep it consistent 98% of the time. A solid, consistent bedtime routine is the first step in establishing good sleep habits. A visual schedule of the nighttime routine would also help the child become more independent in this particular task.

2. *Keep an Eye out for Sensory Issues*

The myriad sensory issues of children with ASD often show up at bedtime and can dramatically affect sleep. Try putting together a sensory diet as part of your bedtime routine. It can be the ticket to a good night's sleep for everyone. Bouncing on a ball or jumping on a trampoline may be ways to help your child relax prior to going to sleep, as might be a warm bath followed by brisk rubbing with a soft, fluffy towel. Try aromatherapy oils in the bath; for some kids, lavender is relaxing and calming. Take stock of scents, though. Shampoo, body lotion, laundry detergent, fabric softeners can all impart scents that may be unpleasant to your child and make him feel edgy in his bed. A weighted blanket, a sleeping bag or sheets tucked in extra snug may be just the things the child needs to feel comfortable and safe in bed. Furthermore, look around the room and take a sensory inventory with your child's sensitivities in mind. Are the sheets too scratchy against his skin? Try the new lightweight flannels or jersey sheets. How about the ticking clock, or that tree branch that taps against the window when it's windy? The overhead fan you tune out may be too loud for him once the house settles down for the night. Make the child's sleep environment as stress- and noise-free as possible.

It is critical that the family consults an occupational therapist prior to implementing a sensory diet for sleep, because some of the activities you try may have the opposite effect, making the sleep problem worse. Incorporate the OT activities into the child's nighttime visual schedule to further promote independence.

3. Change the Child's Diet

Take a good look at what your child eats, when, and in what quantities over the course of the day, but especially towards dinner and after. It's a good idea to make this information part of your sleep diary. Check for too much caffeine in sodas, tea or foods (chocolate, for instance) and offer decaffeinated substitutes as needed. Make sure the child isn't eating heavily near bedtime, as digestion can prevent a child from settling down to rest and sleep. Many spectrum kids also have gastrointestinal issues that food can affect. An evening snack can be given, but make it healthful and don't allow the child to graze on sugary snacks and drinks as bedtime approaches. (Fruit juice is loaded with sugar; give the child a piece of fruit instead.) Place the snack on the visual schedule so the child knows it's part of the routine.

4. Relaxation Techniques

Children with autism do not always have the ability to let us know they need to relax or just calm down. Relaxation techniques can help in calming their bodies and minds to prepare them for sleep. Teach a child to wind down by incorporating quiet time into their evening schedule. This time can be spent in calming activities such as reading, sitting and doing a puzzle, or coloring. Keep the TV off and, if music is played, make sure it supports the calm, peaceful atmosphere. For some kids a planned relaxation technique is beneficial, such as a few minutes of kids' yoga or deep breathing exercises that you do with the child. Again, keep in mind that these types of activities may be arousing for some children with autism. Know your child and consult with the appropriate professional prior to implementation of these routines. As with other elements of the nighttime routine, make these part of the child's visual schedule to promote independence and self-care.

5. Medication

Medication has been successfully used for children with ASD with sleep disorders; however, it should be used only as a last resort. Medication treats a symptom but not the cause of the sleep problem and can become habit forming. Both prescription and over-the-counter medications, including "natural" or "homeopathic" alternatives like melatonin, should be used only under the guidance of a medical professional. Medication usage is a serious decision and should not be approached lightly, especially with young children. Try behavioral strategies first.

What about the child who falls asleep, but can't stay asleep? What strategies are helpful for this type of sleep problem?

Some of the strategies are similar: have a consistent routine, make sure there's no sensory issues affecting the child, be firm and don't give in to the child's demands. Other than that, here are a few "don'ts" that all parents should heed:

1. Don't let the child get up and wander the house. Make sure the child remains in his own room. One parent will have to get up and monitor the child, but try hard not to let the child establish routines like getting up for a drink or a snack.

2. Don't allow TV or videos at any point during the night. Again, if you do, you're allowing an unhealthy routine to take hold.

3. Do not allow the child to sleep during the day when he does not sleep at night. Daytime naps will interfere with the child's sleep cycle and make it more difficult to get the nighttime rest he needs. You may need to tough it out at first and deal with a cranky child during the day, but the routine should fall into place after a few nights of missed sleep.

4. The biggest "don't" of all is don't let the child sleep with you. There are a variety of reasons why you should not do this, but the most important one is the pattern it creates. Your bed is not where the child sleeps; he sleeps in his bed. Be very firm about this and resist

giving into the child who begs you to let him crawl into your bed and sleep. As much as possible, parents should not sleep in the child's bed either.

If the child is currently sleeping with you, make it a priority to re-establish the routine of sleeping in his or her own bed. This will take some stamina and willpower, because the child has a familiar, favorite routine in place and you're about to change all that. When it is time for bed, put the child in his bed and stay there if you need to until he falls asleep. If he reappears in your bedroom or bed, take turns putting him back in his own bed. Keep your attitude neutral and don't offer a lot of conversation. Take him back to his bed, and if needed, stay there until he falls asleep again. Once you start this process, do not let the child sleep in your bed again—not even once, even when he's had a "tough day," or when he's sick. If you do, it will be twice as hard to break the habit. Be strong! You will be rewarded with the child learning good sleep habits, you getting more sleep yourself, and your marriage improving too.

The strategies and suggestions above are not stand-alone interventions but in most cases will be done in some combination. Sleep-related issues are among the toughest to deal with because, by their very nature, they negatively affect our functioning, impair our judgment and take away the very thing we need to be effective—sleep! If sleep problems are part of your young child's life, resolve to deal with this issue as soon as possible. Consult your pediatrician and seek out the help you need from the EI team, a therapist and/or other parents who have worked through this problem. Put together a game plan and then choose a time to implement it when you can afford to lose some sleep until the routine takes hold for both you and your child.

Another big issue is toilet training. How does my child's autism affect this milestone in the child's life?

The good news is that, unlike sleep problems, a great many children with autism toilet train quite easily. Because of their sensory issues they do not like being wet or soiled, so it works to our advantage in training them. The others, those who do not find it uncomfortable or notice if they are wet or soiled, are the tough ones to train. But it's doable if parents are patient, look for signs that the child is ready to be toilet trained, and use a consistent approach. Many parents rush the process, using the child's chronological age as their cue to start toilet training. However, keep in mind that for many kids, their developmental age lags behind their chronological age, and starting before the child is developmentally ready will only lead to frustration for both parent and child.

There are several reasons children with ASD are different from other disability groups when it comes to toilet training:

- *Social challenges.* Most kids don't like the feeling of being wet or the smell associated with it. This is not the case with many spectrum children. Also, typical children generally feel a great sense of pride and are excited about their accomplishment in becoming toilet trained. They respond to the social reinforcement from parents and adults in their lives. Children with autism seldom feel the same way. Social reinforcement is just not motivating to many.

- *Communication issues.* Children with autism have communication problems that in most cases do not allow them to verbalize when they have to go to the bathroom. It can also affect their ability to understand directions and make sense of the toileting schedule.

- *Insistence on sameness/routine.* Children with autism can be very ritualistic in their behaviors. Asking them to change their routine and learn a new way of doing something (toileting) can be disturbing to their sense of order.

- *Sensory issues.* Impaired sensory processing can inhibit awareness of body functions. Some children can't associate the feeling of a full bladder with toileting. Others are fearful of voiding urine or feces, not understanding that this is a normal bodily function.

Despite the challenges, toilet training should be a priority goal. Preschool programs generally require that a child is toilet trained in order to participate. Typical children quickly judge harshly a peer who is not toilet trained, which can often result in social isolation for the child.

How do I know when my child is ready to be toilet trained?

All kids show signs when they are developmentally ready to be toilet trained. Your child with ASD is no different, although as mentioned previously, this may not align with his chronological age. Connie Marks, parent of a spectrum child, offers the following signs that a child is ready to be toilet trained, reprinted from an article that appeared in the *Autism Asperger's Digest*, an informative, bimonthly national magazine on ASD. Appendix C offers 100 helpful tips on toilet training from the same article.

Signs that your Child is Ready to begin a Toilet Training program

- Stays dry for longer periods of time

- Relationship between consuming fluids and when urination occurs

- Shows visible signs of urinating or having a bowel movement (squatting, pulling at pants, touching themselves, crossing legs)

- Shows interest or difference in behavior in response to seeing other people involved in toileting activities

- Ability to sit for about five minutes during an activity

- Can pull pants up and down with assistance

- Understands simple directions (example, sit down or stand up)

I think my child is ready to be toilet trained. How do I start?

Autism experts who specialize in toilet training offer the following best-practice suggestions for toilet training a spectrum child.

Have the child checked by your physician

You want to make sure the child does not have any physical issues related to going to the bathroom. Many children with autism have gastrointestinal issues, which result in bowel problems; you want to rule out any complications like too-loose or too-hard stools. A child who experiences a too-hard stool that is painful to pass may resist further toileting attempts. Make sure the child's physical condition is checked out prior to beginning.

Create a toilet training diary
Prior to beginning toilet training, make a diary charting the time the child eats and drinks (include quantity and type of item) and when voiding occurs. Keep the chart going for a couple of weeks and you should have a clear pattern of when the child goes to the bathroom. You'll use this data in designing your toileting training schedule.

Gradually introduce the child to the bathroom
The smells and sounds of the bathroom may be overwhelming at first, so ease the child into the environment by having her go in for brief periods of time. Also, be very careful the first time you flush the toilet while the child is present. The noise can be quite unsettling for many children with ASD. Conversely, many kids love watching the water swirl around and disappear down the drain, and can become perseverative with the action, flushing the toilet over and over again. Be alert for behavior changes during the early stages of toilet training and address them as they arise.

Make sure the child drinks plenty of fluids, especially water
You want as many opportunities as possible for the child to practice and be successful. However, do reduce or eliminate liquids after 6:00 p.m. and especially prior to bedtime to decrease the likelihood of nighttime accidents. Also, take the child to the bathroom prior to going to bed to establish this action as part of their bedtime routine. Whenever possible, have the child eat a balanced diet, which includes as many fruits as they will eat. This helps with bowel movements. Urination training usually begins first because there are more daily opportunities to reinforce the child voiding in the toilet. However, children are different, so take their lead. If the child uses the toilet for both pee and poop, that's great. If at first it's just to pee, that's fine.

Teach daytime toileting first

Tackle nighttime bathroom visits at a later date. Begin by putting the child in "big boy" or "big girl" underpants, and from that point forward, do not go back to diapers except at night. Make sure the child is comfortable in the new underpants. Cut the tag out if needed and wash them a few times prior to the child's wearing them for the first time.

Start the child on a potty schedule

Use the data you gathered from the toileting journal to get an idea of when to take the child to the toilet; do so five minutes prior to the child's toileting time in the journal. Put the child on the toilet for approximately five minutes. If the child voids, offer your cheers and a reward. If the child doesn't, help him get dressed in a very neutral manner and have him leave the bathroom. Don't appear dissatisfied in words, tone of voice, or mannerism if the child doesn't void. Use that time as an opportunity to teach dressing, undressing, and personal care skills.

Find the most powerful reward you can,
and use it only to reinforce appropriate voiding in the toilet

This is critical to the success of the toilet training program. The child absolutely, positively, cannot receive this reward for any other reason. It is only given as reinforcement for going to the bathroom on the toilet. It can be helpful to have a picture of the reward to visually supplement the communication, letting the child know that if he goes to the bathroom then he can have the reward. This visual cue can be a powerful motivator during toilet training.

Incorporate a visual cue into the schedule

Alongside or instead of using verbal communication during the toileting routine, use a visual cue card—a picture that represents the bathroom—and teach the child to use it as part of the routine. You want the child to be able to independently communicate when he needs to use the bathroom. Each time the child is taken to the bathroom, prompt the child to hand the adult the picture of the bathroom and then reinforce the child for communicating the need to use the bathroom. Follow this with prompting the child to go to the bathroom. If the child presents the pic-

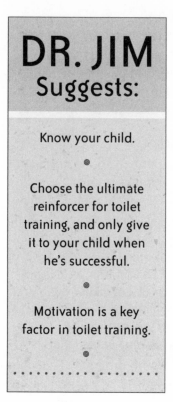

DR. JIM
Suggests:

Know your child.

◎

Choose the ultimate reinforcer for toilet training, and only give it to your child when he's successful.

◎

Motivation is a key factor in toilet training.

◎

ture at a time that is not part of the schedule (meaning he's telling you he needs to use the bathroom), heavily reinforce the use of the picture and take the child to the bathroom. If the child voids, the adult should provide the ultimate reward to reinforce the child's communication and toileting success.

Expect mishaps and never punish

It's called "training" for a reason, and mishaps will occur. If the child wets himself, the adult should stay very neutral, take the child to the bathroom and help the child change his clothes. Tell the child in a very calm and reassuring voice, "You go potty on the toilet, not in your pants" and let it go at that. Do not use too much unnecessary language, and *never* scold the child for a mishap. Either could lead to the child having accidents for the extra attention you provide.

Be patient and build slowly

It takes time to toilet train a child, even a typical one, so be patient with your child with ASD. It may take a few days or a few weeks or, with some children, a few months before the child is consistently trained. Once the child has been successful in toileting two days in a row without an accident, move the timed schedule up a few minutes. Always keep in mind that you want the child to initiate or tell you he has to go to the bathroom, so look for signs or certain behaviors the child displays that are linked to toileting and be ready to prompt him towards success. For instance, the child may always hide behind a certain chair when he has to have a bowel movement. Have the picture card handy and prompt the child to give it to you as part of the routine and then reward the child with the preferred reinforcer.

*Set aside time to toilet train and
make sure everyone working
with the child is on board*

Make sure you are willing to commit to the toilet training program and that you've chosen a time when there will be no major family or social interruptions. Don't pick the weekend Aunt Grace is visiting to start the program, or have Week Two of your toilet training efforts fail while the family is away for summer vacation. Likewise, if Grandma is babysitting for a night or therapists are at your home working with the child, make sure everyone understands the toilet training routine and carries through with it. There needs to be consistency and predictability for the child to learn the new routine. Toilet training is difficult enough for typical kids; be sure you set up the environment for success as much as possible.

My child is a finicky eater. His diet consists of about five foods that he eats over and over. He refuses to try new foods and I worry about his nutritional needs. What can I do?

Most children, neurotypical or not, are very picky eaters and every child goes through a stage of some type of eating issue. However, in typical children this period is usually short-lived and with a little coaxing from Mom and Dad, they begin to eat a variety of different foods. Children with autism, on the other hand, can present very significant problems with eating. Yet most families struggle alone with this issue, unaware of the possible reasons behind the eating problems and strategies that could help. Well-meaning adults may tell you to ride this out: "Don't indulge the child. He'll get hungry and eat what you give him." This is not an acceptable way to deal with the problem; with ASD children it could be life-threatening. If your child exhibits an eating problem, get help, then consider the following points before trying any treatment approach.

Medical

An oral motor functioning exam must be performed to ensure that the child's eating mechanism is intact and swallowing is not a problem. Also, if the child chokes or gags or has food or liquid coming from his nostrils, a medical exam should be performed to assess the issue and possible causes. Seek out a medical professional(s) who has knowledge of autism disorders and the unique problems inherent in some of these children.

Sensory Issues

Some children with ASD have severe oral sensitivity that makes them very selective with regard to food and drink. They may not like the texture or the consistency of certain items, especially those that are texture-heavy, and many prefer foods that are smooth, creamy or have been puréed.

Allergies or Gastrointestinal Issues

A great many children with autism have severe allergies, which can often show up in different ways, one of them being their eating habits. Children can also exhibit food intolerances, a less severe but nonetheless debilitating physical ailment that manifests in behavior and eating problems. Thousands of parents have found success using a gluten and/or casein free diet to bring about positive changes in their child's behavior and eating habits. Parent support groups, blogs and internet sites offer all sorts of information touting the value of special diets, although at present this form of intervention has not had rigorous clinical trials to support its efficacy.

If the child's eating problems are not associated with one of these three factors, parents can try a behavioral approach to teach the child new, more healthy eating habits. These strategies might include any one or a combination of the following suggestions.

- Desensitize the child to new or different foods. For example, pick a food you want the child to eat. Show her some pictures of the food; then have her sort them into different food categories; next place the food on the table, then closer to the child during mealtime. Once the child can tolerate the food close by, put a little of it on her plate. Keep reinforcing the child for her tolerance of the food and allowing it to be near her. Keep going: next have her touch the food with her fork, then maybe smell it, followed with putting a tiny bit on her tongue, then eating a small bite, etc. In time, the child may try the food on her own and in some cases, even like it. Go slowly with this process so the child feels successful, rather than pressured. With some kids it may take weeks just for the child to let you put the food on the table next to her plate. And of course, if the child eventually tries the food and doesn't like it, don't force her to eat it! Respect her choice and reinforce her efforts in trying the new food.

DR. JIM Suggests:

Every kid is a picky eater at one time or another.

Choose your battles carefully.

Keep the big picture in mind at all times.

- If the problem is sensory, i.e., based on the texture of foods, start by selecting a new food or a couple of foods that are similar in consistency to what the child likes and build from there. Encourage the child to try just very small bites at first and increase the quantity or introduce new textures as the child becomes less resistant. Oral motor training can be done in conjunction with this approach, helping the child become more tolerant of different sensations in the mouth. This form of therapy can be provided by either a Speech-Language Therapist or an Occupational Therapist.

- Try pairing a highly preferred food item with the new food you want the child to taste. Explain to the child that if he tries the "non-preferred" item, he can have a piece of the "preferred" item. With encouragement, I have seen this approach work very effectively. However, if the child does not try or eat the new food, do not withhold other food from him. This strategy can also work with the compulsive eater, the child who eats the same food again and again. By introducing new food this way, you can break the routine and establish a new one that consists of a variety of different foods.

Parents who are genuinely concerned about their child's nutrition should discuss their concerns with the child's pediatrician and, if needed, have her checked out. However, it's also helpful to take one step back and look at the situation realistically. Many kids have limited diets and are none the worse for it. My youngest child eats only chicken nuggets, has had no red meat, likes cheese and, like his mother, loves pretzels. He will eat carrots and that's about it for vegetables. He is typically developing; however, we were concerned with his nutrition. He'll take gummy bear-type vitamins and we've been successful in using the preferred/non-preferred pairing strategy with him to try some new foods. He is perfectly fine and very healthy. When this issue arose in our family I thought back to my childhood and remembered that I ate Captain Crunch cereal and hot dogs for probably a good three years growing up. We ask our spectrum kids to work through all sorts of different therapies, so make sure your child is truly at risk with his diet before adding this area into the therapy mix. Prioritize your goals with your child and don't try too many things at one time.

All these behavior strategies are great, but most of them involve me working with the child or a therapist working with the child. I want my child to learn to be independent to the maximum extent possible based on his abilities. How do I get from adult-directed intervention to independence?

First, you get there over time. You constantly work towards greater independence, starting with small tasks and building from there. Independence is a life-long process, not an end goal in and of itself.

Second, kudos to you for wanting your child to be independent, and for believing it is possible even in light of his autism. Sadly, I encounter parents and professionals every day who still see kids with ASD as incapable of independent actions and activities, or subjectively cap their abilities and use this arbitrary standard in making decisions about what to teach, and what not to teach because it is "too difficult" for the child. Don't let yourself fall into this mindset! Have high expectations for your child in all areas of teaching and learning, and never judge him as incapable. Given a supportive learning environment, one well-matched to his learning style and the thinking patterns inherent in ASD, these kids can and do surprise us in what they are capable of learning. Don't put a ceiling on your child's capabilities.

As we mentioned previously, play is the learning environment for very young children, and play is the medium within which your EIP team will teach the child. The ultimate goal for all the children we work with is for them to be as independent as possible. To achieve that goal in the play skill area, we must teach children to access social reinforcers. What is a social reinforcer? A social reinforcer is one that is dependent on an interaction with another person. It's usually a positive comment or a compliment, but it could be a high five, a hug, a huge smile, a tickle, etc. Eventually, as the child grows and his level of social awareness blossoms, social reinforcers could become less tangible and evolve into things like self-pride, a sense of accomplishment, or the good feelings associated with helping others. Or they may need to remain more tangible.

Initially, most children with autism have little interest in playing with others, or if they do, they lack the social skills and social thinking that will make them successful in doing so. The result? They miss out on the social reinforcers that are so common among play partners. And that, in turn, makes it extremely difficult for them to maintain any social interaction or play activity—because they are not reinforced by the interaction.

If the child isn't interested in play for the social reinforcement it provides, then how do we motivate the child to engage in play and experience this social reinforcement?

Like everything else we have discussed so far, we do this through systematic teaching, setting up the environment for success, giving the child multiple opportunities to practice the skill, and pairing success with appropriate reinforcement. The two steps described below will get you started.

Use Non-Social Reinforcers First

These are the same as primary reinforcers. They are tangible and meaningful to the child. Initially, whenever the child engages in an appropriate social interaction, reinforce the child with whatever makes him "tick." Use a reinforcer the child really enjoys, one he cannot live without, not just something he likes only marginally. We all have things we like, but can do without. Then there are other things we really, really like and don't want to give up. These are the powerful reinforcers to use.

Social situations are very difficult for the child with ASD, so pull out all the stops to reinforce any interaction in the beginning. Keep in mind that the simple actions that typical kids seemingly learn without effort can take training and practice for the ASD child. Make sure you are really looking for the child's successful interaction skills, so he receives praise and reinforcement regularly. When you do notice them, pair a social reinforcer (language like "That's great playing" or "You guys play so well") with the non-social reinforcer. Again, because many kids with ASD are nonplussed by social interactions and don't pick up on social cues, make your social reinforcement lively and animated, so the child notices, and can begin to associate his behavior with the social reinforcement.

Our goal is to pair the non-social reinforcer with social reinforcement over and over again, then slowly begin to fade the non-social reinforcer, resulting in the child's behavior being motivated by the social reinforcement. For example, if during a play activity the child goes up to another child and reaches for his toy, you can intervene and help him ask for the toy, then reinforce with a potato chip or a pretzel (depending on what the child likes). Couple this with a social reinforcer, something like "I love the way you asked him for the toy. Good job!" You might also add a high five if that's meaningful to the child. Continue the social interaction by prompting the child to ask the other child if he wants a chip too. Then reinforce again.

Slowly Switch Over to Social Reinforcers

Once the child begins to be more comfortable in the play activity, use more and more social reinforcers and fewer and fewer non-social reinforcers. This may take time and involve lots of practice; don't rush it. You want the child to be successful and feel the positive benefits of social interaction. In essence, you are rebuilding neural connections for social interaction skills. This doesn't happen overnight. Depending on the child, your goal is to eventually use only social reinforcement. However, as you work toward that goal you may find it helpful to have a non-social reinforcer available at the end of the activity if the child does well in the play group. For example, prior to playing in a group Billy can be told, "If you listen and play with the other kids, we can then get fast food on the way home." This gives the child a concrete incentive to work toward, and can be used as a reminder should less-than-positive behaviors emerge during play.

As you work on play skills and social reinforcement with the child, keep in mind the following pointers:

- If the child performs the actions requested or his behavior is what you wanted, he gets the non-social reward. If not, he doesn't get the reward. Don't confuse the child by giving in sometimes and not others. It will delay his learning in the long run. Be consistent in your use of reinforcement, including social reinforcement.

- Don't fake the social reinforcement. Our kids know when we believe in their abilities and when we're just going through the motions. Be honest; not patronizing. Find something real to praise.

- Some kids with ASD are such concrete thinkers you may have to specifically define the goal behavior. "Being good" is too subjective for these kids. Better descriptions are specific, like "no fighting, no tantrums, and you must play three games."

- Social interactions most often revolve around playtime activities. Make sure the child has been taught the skills needed to play with other kids effectively. Teach basic social skills like turn-taking, sharing, not being a space invader, etc. With these skills the child can be comfortable in play activities and more willing to explore new social skills in a safe environment. Without these prerequisite skills the child will be anxious and unprepared and unable to be successful with others. And there goes the motivation to interact.

• Play activities should and must be adult supervised. You do not want the child to just parallel play with other kids or have negative interaction experiences. This is bad for two reasons: 1) the other kids will not want to play with the child with autism and 2) the child with autism will surely not want to go anywhere near the other kids again. Structure for success.

• Don't overload kids. Wouldn't it be great if kids played for an hour at a time? It would provide so much practice for our ASD child! That's not how little kids play, though. When you schedule a play date or a sibling date, break it up into kid-sized segments. Despite what we NTs may think, play is still "work" for the child with ASD. Try a play time of 20-30 minutes, followed by something more relaxing, like a video coupled with a snack for ten minutes, before going back and playing again. The more you can expose the child to these activities the better, but keep it manageable for the spectrum child and be on the lookout for sensory overload. It can sneak up quickly, especially when other little kids are involved.

Is it possible to make "work" disguised as play "fun" for my child with ASD?

It sure is! Here are six easy ways to make the play activity a success.

Be Enthusiastic!

It is critical that the child want to be part of the play activity. The way to do this is to be as enthusiastic as possible to capture the child's attention. Know your child and know how loud or rough you can get with him or her. Keep this in mind when choosing play partners too. Make the encounter an event the child enjoys, so he wants to come back for more.

Make it Fun

The activity has to be fun for the child with ASD. If it's not fun, the child is not going to stay engaged for very long. Chase games or rough-and-tumble activities are always a good start for kids who are not sensory sensitive. If a child loves looking at picture books more than anything else, do that. Watch your child to learn what he or she considers fun and go from there. Once they are having fun, you can slowly introduce other activities.

Begin with a Preferred Activity

Start the activity with something you know the child loves to do and can be successful doing. You can also go back to that activity if you begin to lose the child during other activities.

Direct the Activity but take the Child's Lead

You should always direct the activity, however if the child wants to do other things that are appropriate to what you are playing, move in that direction. For instance, if you're rolling a ball back and forth and the child squeals with delight when the ball bounces, shift the interaction to "bounce the ball" instead. Be flexible—play can take all different shapes and forms. Taking the child's lead also gives the child some sense of control over the activity. This is the beginning stage of an important skill to foster in a child—a good thing!

Offer Choices

As much as possible, and in as many situations as possible, give the child choices. Let him decide the activities during the play activity. Offer a choice of materials: "Would you like the red piece or the green piece?" Let him choose a snack—"Would you like an apple or an orange?"

Start Structured

In the first few play groups, the agenda should be very tight and structured so the children learn the routine and become more comfortable with each other. You want minimal "down time," because it is during these nebulous "what-do-I-do-now" times that inappropriate behaviors surface. However, as the child gets more and more comfortable with playful interactions, play dates and peers, you can begin to introduce choices into the activities and loosen up the structure to allow more natural play opportunities to unfold.

How do I put all these wonderful suggestions and strategies together into some daily plan with my child? They're all important and they all sound great, but I'm not sure how they all fit together?

This is where your EI team will help. Every child is different and every child's plan will evolve and change as days, weeks, and months go by. You and your team will identify a variety of different goals you have for the child in different areas of learning: behavior problems, communication skills, functional skills like toilet training or eating or dressing, social skills like turn taking or sharing, sensory integration work, etc. You'll put together a daily plan that will guide you in working on different skills (make it visual for yourself and your family!). Maybe you'll also have a weekly plan and a monthly plan to keep yourself on track. Just remember that flexibility is key in designing any plan—you don't want the plan to control you—you control the plan.

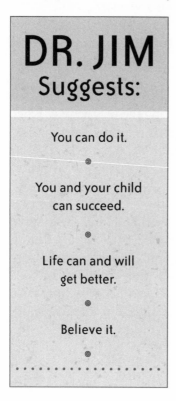

DR. JIM Suggests:

You can do it.

◎

You and your child can succeed.

◎

Life can and will get better.

◎

Believe it.

◎

As you become more comfortable working with your child, you'll relax into the routine. You'll notice the "teaching moments" as they occur and be confident in handling them. The behavior strategies will become second nature to you. You and your child will have hours and hours of time to practice your new skills—you becoming an effective teacher and your child becoming an accomplished learner. Trust your instincts and never forget that learning is a lifelong process.

Try to relax and enjoy this time with your child. Yes, you'll make mistakes at first, you'll forget strategies, you'll get frustrated because everything feels so unfamiliar. Hang in there. Don't give up and don't give in. Try your best and believe your child is trying his best too, even when success feels a million miles away. It's more than likely just around the corner.

"When my son Vance was first diagnosed on the autism spectrum,
it was a very difficult time for me. I felt many emotions:
grief, frustration, anger, depression, desperation, hopelessness,
isolation, and a deep sense of being out of control.

The process of getting Vance diagnosed was a very painful and confusing
time. I was going through a divorce and was alone in this experience.
The professionals varied greatly in their conclusions ("he'll grow out of it,"
"the best you can hope for is that he will be happy," "he will need to be
institutionalized"). I knew something was wrong, but also had a beautiful,
loving and sensitive little boy, whom I loved dearly, to care for.

Quickly after receiving his diagnosis I felt a sense of relief—relief in the
fact that my two years of searching for answers about my son were over.
I finally had a foundation and footing to work upon to acquire answers and
understanding. Relief came in knowing why he seemed sometimes to be
deaf, would not make eye contact, had obsessive qualities and had difficulty
in transitioning. Relief came with the diagnosis in allowing me to see
beyond his autistic traits, and experience this wonderful person and the
enormous gifts he had and was giving to me. Relief came as I finally knew
I could do something and work towards improving his life.

Vance's diagnosis changed my life. I suppose in many ways the relief I felt
12 years ago has been a driving force within me to continue the work I do.
More importantly, without question, the relief of his diagnosis provided me
the insight and calm to love my child more than I ever believed possible."

LEE GROSSMAN, PRESIDENT AND CEO,
AUTISM SOCIETY OF AMERICA AND PARENT OF VANCE

chapter ten

The Next Step
Transitioning from Early Intervention to Public School Programs

Dr. Jim: Hey, Maureen and Rob—why so somber? You are both usually animated individuals, filled with questions and curiosity.

Maureen: It's our very last session with you today, Dr. Jim, and we feel like we're losing a trusted guide and a good friend. Mark is turning three next month and his services won't be covered any longer through the early intervention system.

Rob: We already met once with the public school program officials and I must say—it was a bit of shock learning how that program functions compared to our EI program and services. It felt like the controls shifted out of our hands into theirs, and they haven't even met Mark yet!

Maureen: To be honest, we're scared. Mark has been doing so well in the EI program we all designed for him and the public school case worker we met with told us to be prepared for changes in both the intensity of his program and the services provided. I thought they would want to review Mark's existing program, talk with you or your staff, meet Mark, get a feel for his level of functioning before they make decisions about what services he needs. It didn't sound that way—more like Mark will need to fit their program, rather than the program fit Mark and his needs.

Rob: On top of all that, they gave us a copy of IDEA, the federal legislation that will govern services from now on, and whoa! I started reading it and was confused by the second page! I sure hope someone from the school will sit down and explain all this to us!

Dr. Jim: I understand your concerns. The shift from early intervention to the public school program is one of the most important transitions in your child's education. How you approach this negotiation—and make no mistake, that is what it is—how educated you are coming into the discussions, how well versed you are in your child's needs ... all these elements will influence the outcome. This is the time and place where you set the stage for future interactions with the school.

Rob: You're scaring me now, Dr. Jim. You make it sound like my child's entire education hinges on this one point in our lives.

Dr. Jim: In a sense, it does. I don't mean to scare you, but I do want to impress upon you the importance of the transition to public school. Here's what I say to all parents whose children are moving into public programs, whether that's at three or when the child enters kindergarten: *do your homework before walking into that first planning meeting.* Public school is different than early intervention—you need to be prepared, and not rely on others to look out for your best interests or those of your child.

Maureen: It feels like getting the diagnosis all over again! Back to the land of nothingness, back to the whirlwind of uncertainty, just when we started feeling like we were getting a hold on our lives and understanding autism and how it affects Mark. I hate this!

Dr. Jim: You're right, Maureen, it is an upsetting place to be in again. Just when you start to understand the EI system and get used to working directly with your child, seeing his daily progress, those services end. You're thrown into a new ocean and you feel like you're bobbing along in a sea of new people, new rules, new information, carried along by some unknown current that has hold of you nonetheless. It can be truly frightening.

Rob: So, Dr. Jim. What do we do? You've been our anchor for quite some time now and I know we have to sever this lifeline and move forward on our own, but I'm not ready to do that just yet. Can you help us?

Dr. Jim: Sure I can! Many of the tools and working strategies you've learned during our time together and through your involvement with the EI team will be invaluable now. *You know more than you may think you know.* Many parents get lost at this stage because they don't trust the knowledge they've gained about their child, his needs and how he learns. They assume "others" know better and give in to their ideas, even when they don't feel right for the child. I want you both to know that you are your child's experts! Don't let someone else, or any group of people, tell you otherwise! Parents who are successful advocates for their child believe this with every fiber of their being. It becomes their North Star, guiding their actions and decisions, always putting the spotlight on their child's needs and keeping their egos in the background. The rest can be learned: how to negotiate with the school, the child's rights under federal legislation, when to be forceful and when to back off, etc. These are techniques everyone can learn, given a little investigation, time and study. Melding that procedural knowledge with your intimate knowledge of your child is what brings about the type of success you want for your child, a success within which everyone learns and grows. That's your ultimate goal and where your real power as a parent lies.

Maureen: I'm not feeling as desolate when you put it that way; maybe I can do this! I know Rob and I have learned so much more about Mark over the last year, since we really started looking at his world through the lens of autism and understanding his different thinking and learning patterns. Our lives are certainly much better now than when we sat here the first time, scared and knowing so little about ASD. We certainly want the best program for him as we move into public school and you've given us great information on how to assess a program and identify quality indicators. I guess what we need is education about the "system" in general and in particular, this transition period. We're eager students—let's get started!

⊚ ⊚ ⊚

As parents, what types of differences will we find between EI and public school programs?

Some differences are obvious and some are nebulous. Some differences are purposeful and others arise when the public school program falls short of its mission and intended structure. Among the differences you might notice:

- A shift in focus from the family/family needs to services only for the child

- A shift in where services are provided, from at home or in natural settings to classroom-based services

- Teachers replace parents as the child's primary learning guide

- Parents no longer qualify for direct training on issues related to the child's behavior, communication, social skills, sensory needs, etc.

- Related services are reduced to those that mainly impact the child's education; services such as respite care, family/individual therapy, daily self-help skills are no longer provided as part of the program

- Unless the child has an aide, reduced one-on-one attention and more teaching within a group setting

- A shift in the teacher's expectations of the child. Children entering public school programs, even preschool programs, are expected to have basic social skills, know how to play with others, follow directions, say please and thank you, act appropriately in a group, pay attention, stay seated, etc.

Is the school now "in control" of my child's education?

Yes and no. Parents are equal partners in the education process, but federal and state legislation puts the onus on schools to provide for the education of the child. Parents want what's best for their individual child while schools are obligated to provide an education according to guidelines written for the majority of children. Parents focus on one child; schools are responsible for all. As you can imagine, these two positions can often be at odds with each other, and school "politics" are a very real factor in decisions made. Most school systems take the reins, assume that, as "educators," they know what's best for children and steer interactions from this point forward until the child graduates or ages out of the system (at 21 or 22 years old, depending on state guidelines).

Where do I, as the child's parent, fit into this process?

It may sound hokey, but you are a mighty force in securing the best possible education for your child. You are the person most knowledgeable about the child and need to be his strongest and sometimes fiercest advocate. You have his best interests at heart and will do anything to help him succeed. Many parents assume the school will do this also. Sadly, the reality is that the majority of schools will do only enough to satisfy the law and many do much, much less. From a legislative perspective the onus may be on the public school to provide an appropriate education, but in real life, it's up to parents to be the driving force to assure the child receives everything to which he or she is entitled.

You paint a pretty dismal picture of the public education system, Dr. Jim. It sounds like no one will care about my child with special needs or his education.

I don't want to sound like an alarmist, but I am a realist. I've encountered some very, very good public school programs for children with ASD, with dedicated, well-trained teachers with years of experience working directly with children with ASD. These schools "get" autism and understand that these children have different learning needs from other children with special needs, and that traditional teaching methods aren't always effective. From the top administrator down to the janitor, the school attitude is positive and supportive of children with disabilities, and personnel are willing to think outside the box to teach in ways that have meaning to students with ASD. Services are well coordinated, support staff are allocated as needed, and the school team is aggressive and creative in finding funds to support their efforts.

Then I've encountered schools with an administration that still views kids with disabilities as hopeless, un-trainable drains on the system, robbing kids who "might amount to something" of the limited financial resources the school has to go around. Teachers are unsupported, with little training on ASD, and still believe these kids could "do better if they just tried harder." In these programs IEPs are poorly written because knowledge of the needs of students with ASD is sadly missing within the school. The attitude of the administration in a school sets the tone for and often dictates how much training teachers receive, how much funding the school actively seeks out for their special needs students, how supportive they are towards related services, etc. I wish great schools with great programs for kids with ASD existed in every neighborhood. The reality is that they just don't. One of the most common comments I hear from parents who have moved from an early intervention program into a public school program—even within the very same city or school district—is why a district with a great EI program can have such a deficient public school program.

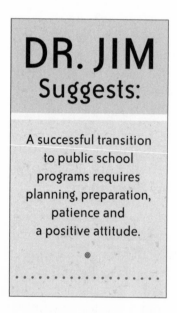

DR. JIM
Suggests:

A successful transition to public school programs requires planning, preparation, patience and a positive attitude.

As the parent of a child with special needs, and especially a child with ASD, you deserve to know what you might face in this transition. I'm not here to sugarcoat it and tell you everything will go smoothly and work out in the best interests of your child. How successful this transition is, and what type of program your young child ends up in is largely up to you, his parents. It's not just what you do during this transition, but *how you do it*, that will bring about the program you want for your child. I can't impress upon you enough that you need to be prepared and act intelligently through this transition.

Is there still a team working with the child, and a services plan that guides them?

The language and terminology in public school programs shift a bit, but the structure stays pretty much the same. The IFSP (Individual Family Services Plan) becomes the IEP (Individual Education Plan), the EI team becomes the IEP team, a case coordinator is still in place, although the title changes and the professional's responsibility rests more with managing the school- and related-services personnel, since the school is now responsible for coordination of services. The IEP team operates in a similar way, but meets much less frequently, sometimes only once a year unless a situation arises that warrants discussion or a parent requests an IEP meeting. The IEP document itself is similar; it still contains goals and objectives for the child, describes in detail the education plan for the child, related services agreed to and how and when progress will be measured.

Will the team provide the education I need to understand this transition?

To a degree, yes, but probably not in the detail you would like or need. If you find team members willing to provide you in-depth training, great! But as a rule, the responsibility rests with parents to become educated about the federal laws governing the rights of the child and the provision of services, to learn the school "culture" as it relates to special education services, to seek outside help for family issues or challenges that are not directly related to the child's education. For instance, if you're having problems with a new behavior at home involving your child with ASD and a sibling, the school staff will probably not provide you with help in working through the issue. You'll need to find a professional on your own, and at your own expense, to provide that assistance.

As a parent, I view "education" as anything my child may need in order to succeed in the world, such as academics, social skills, peer interaction skills,

organizational skills, recreation, etc., coupled with special education therapies, such as speech or OT. Early intervention helped with all those and more. Is this the same in public school programs?

No, and this can be a rude awakening for many parents. Many, many schools interpret education to mean strictly academics, with the ancillary physical education requirements added in, especially once a child enters kindergarten. Children who are eligible for "special education" receive extra help, but many a public school thinks related services involve only speech, and perhaps some OT or physical therapy. Children with ASD often need a whole host of services and instruction aligned to their different thinking and learning styles. Yet, schools lag behind in recognition of their needs or the provision of these types of services. For instance, social skills are absolutely necessary for a child to benefit from his or her education to the same extent as do typical peers, yet the majority of schools do not offer any type of formal social skills training/services for spectrum children, despite it being one of the hallmark deficits of the disorder and one of the criteria for the diagnosis.

Current federal special education laws require schools to teach beyond academics and provide services and programs that allow the ASD child to participate in school and school-related activities in a way that is equal to that of their NT peers. That's the mandate; it's not, however, the reality. As I mentioned, some public schools are excellent; others are abysmal. That's why strong parent participation is so important in this process. Know what the entitlements are for your child and then advocate for those your child needs.

Whose responsibility it is to make sure the child's program is right for the child?

Responsibility rests with all members of the IEP team to create a program that fits the child's learning needs and teaches the child to be successful in all aspects of the educational program. However, I will repeat: parents are the driving force in assuring their child gets the best possible educa-

318

tion to which he or she is entitled. Don't assume the school will make this happen on your child's behalf. Be proactive, not reactive.

Do I have options as to which school my child attends?

To some extent, yes. As part of the transition to public school, parents should investigate schools in their area. In most cases, a child with ASD will be enrolled at the school that other children in the family's neighborhood attend. With the child who is eligible for special education services, however, parents should be sure that school is capable of providing the educational services the child needs. If not, the IEP team should consider other schools and/or programs that do. That doesn't always happen, though; most schools will tell you their program is suitable for your child. It behooves parents to research other options on their own, and to do this before the first meeting with the IEP team. Visit your local schools; observe their programs. Get a good feel for the environment and also the structure of the class. Assess how you think your child will fare in this environment. Meet the teachers beforehand. Does this seem like a good fit for your child and one that will lead him to be successful?

How do I know if the program is right for my child?

Refer back to our discussions on the components of a good EI program and the personnel qualities that make a great team. Keep these in mind as broad guidelines when investigating the public school program. The same principles still apply. In addition, there are other variables that contribute to a program's success. In my experience working with the ASD population, the following ten program elements are key.

10 Components of an Excellent ASD Program

1. *Student/Staff Ratio*

Children with autism learn better in classes that have a high staff-to-student ratio. This gives children the individualized attention they often need. However, we must keep in mind that in order for a child to truly gain independence, less staff is optimal—but probably not in the beginning. Independence is a process, an evolution in teaching and learning that we work toward, rather than a condition that is present when a child first enters public school. And each class is different; much depends on the autism expertise of the staff coupled with the functioning levels of the students. For very young children, look at student-to-staff ratios and how staff members interact with students to decide what might be appropriate for your child. For example, if the classroom has eight or nine kids with special needs, there needs to be at least a 2:1 student/staff ratio for the child with autism to receive the attention he needs to attain skill levels. And this too depends on the functioning capabilities of the other students. The more severe their needs, the more staff will be needed. A child with autism placed in a regular education class may need a 1:1 student/staff ratio (meaning the spectrum child has a full-time aide in the classroom with him). At the pre-K and early elementary ages, these children are still actively learning new and vital skills. It's important for the student-to-staff ratios to be appropriate for this learning to take place. Without it, children quickly fall behind and then never really catch up.

2. Class Constellation

Look at the functioning levels of the other kids in the class and assess how your child fits into this mix. You want your child to be with children more advanced in their functioning so he has appropriate role models to learn from. If the child appears to be the highest functioning student, consider options such as his joining activities in another special education class, inclusion in a regular education room for part of the day, or inclusion in special classes with typical peers, such as gym, music, media, or art. If the child is at the more challenged end of the class, make sure the curriculum and teaching technology is individualized enough to benefit him. When observing the classroom, inquire about students who will be staying the next year and students who will be leaving. Use this information in assessing how well the student mix will help or hinder your child's learning.

3. Age Range

In New Jersey a four-year age span is the maximum permitted per class for children with special needs. However, sometimes even with this rule, the class can be very inappropriate for some children with ASD. Consider the ages of the children in the class and where your child falls in that range. The more homogeneous the age range, the better. But do look at the developmental ages of the kids, too, and the behaviors they manifest. Interestingly, the best indicator is sometimes the physical size of the child and how he or she fits with the other kids in the class.

4. Skill Levels of Students Currently Placed

Look at the curriculum and how the kids who are currently in the class are being taught. Is the skill level too high for your child, or too low? As much as possible, be very realistic about your own child's abilities. You don't want to put the child in a class that is too difficult or way too easy; that will only lead to behavior issues and lack of progress.

5. Related Services

What types of related services are provided to the class? Is speech therapy, occupational therapy, or physical therapy (if necessary) available? Does your child have needs not addressed by this program? Where are these services provided—in the classroom itself, or through pull-out sessions?

6. Autism-trained Professionals

Do the teachers, teacher's aides, and related services staff have a solid, working knowledge of autism? Have they received autism specific training (as opposed to general special education credentials) and worked with children with ASD in the past? Do they have a good understanding of reinforcement, behavior management, and functional communication training? If not, are training opportunities scheduled prior to your student entering the class? It is critical that the staff be trained and knowledgeable *before* your child joins the class, especially in the three areas described above. This should be the minimum level of staff training that you deem acceptable.

7. Classroom Structure

Students with ASD respond better in classrooms that have structure and offer predictability and routine. Is there a daily classroom schedule the staff must follow? Is verbal instruction supplemented with visual schedules and visual communication? Does the staff follow through on commands and prompt kids to be successful? Is the room well organized and are materials labeled and easy to access? Are there specific areas for different learning activities (e.g., play, work, group activities, and reading)? Is the classroom too visually stimulating for the child, especially one with sensory issues? Brightly painted, lively pre-K rooms with student work covering all the walls, mobiles hanging, materials visible in open shelves, etc., are adorable, but can distract the ASD child and impede his ability to focus on the lesson at hand. Know your child and assess how the classroom structure fits his sensory needs.

8. Accountability

The classroom must have an efficient data collection procedure and all curriculum decisions must be based on data. How does the classroom staff collect data? How often is data collected and then what do they do with it? Does it sit around, analyzed months later or not at all? (More common than you imagine!) Are educational decisions based on the data collected? How is this data reported to the parent?

9. Behavior Management Approach

The behavior management approach for the classroom must be well defined and the staff should be able to articulate it clearly and with understanding. It should be positive, and certainly not punitive. Is the classroom able to accommodate individual behavioral needs or are all students expected to live by the five classroom rules established by the teacher at the start of school? How does classroom staff handle tantrums or meltdowns? How often do you hear "no" or "stop that" or other similar negative statements? Look for staff who offer encouragement, praise and positive reinforcement on a regular basis. Is the behavior approach consistent and systematic across all staff? Is everyone working together? Is there a written crisis-intervention plan should things get out of control?

10. Collaboration

Does the staff work well together—the teacher, aides, and all related services staff? Is the atmosphere fun and cooperative or is there tension in the air? How often does staff formally and informally meet to discuss students and their progress? The more cohesive the team, the more integrated the therapy can be across all settings. This will ensure generalization of skills in the student.

Is the program the only part of the school I should assess?

Great question! You want to look at the whole school and get a feel for how it operates in general. Meet the office staff and the school administration. Ask questions to assess their attitudes toward children with disabilities. Is it positive and supportive, or negative and neglectful? Probe beyond the basic questions until you're sure you've gotten to the core of their attitudes. What kind of support, supervision and encouragement does the classroom staff receive from administration? What's the turnover rate of personnel in both the regular and special education segments of the school? This will tell you much about how supportive administration is towards staff. Even in better programs there's high staff turnover in the special education field, due to burnout. There's a strong possibility you will lose a teacher, teacher's aide, or related services staff person along the way. However, a school with a structured curriculum in place, ample opportunities for basic and ongoing specialized training, and a supervisor who is knowledgeable in ASD will be much better equipped to minimize the impact of staff changes on the spectrum child. Be cautious of programs whose success depends heavily on that one special teacher who works "magic" with ASD students, an administration that doesn't display an active, ongoing commitment to teacher training, and program staff that is untrained and inexperienced with ASD students. These conditions do not suggest a quality program; the child's education will suffer.

How should the transition process unfold?

You'll start with typical enrollment procedures for the school and initiate the additional steps required for a child with special needs. The three major parts to this process are as follows:

The Evaluation

It is up to the parent(s) to request that the school district perform an evaluation to determine if the child is eligible for Special Education services and if so, what services will be provided and to what extent. It is recommended that you identify your child to the appropriate local district team when the child is two-and-a-half years old. The school does not have to act until the child turns three years old, but many public school teams work hard to obtain evaluations prior to the child's third birthday so services can begin immediately. If the district decides they will not perform an evaluation, for whatever reason, they must let you know in a timely fashion and inform you of your right to appeal their decision.

Eligibility Determination

Once the evaluations are completed, the parent(s) and the team of qualified professionals determine if the child is eligible for Special Education services. Parents should note that service eligibility and diagnosis is not the same thing. A child can be diagnosed on the autism spectrum, and be either eligible or ineligible for special education services, depending on the child's level of need and the district's guidelines. Service eligibility varies from state to state, district to district.

- *Ineligible.* If the team decides the child is ineligible for Special Education services, parents have the right to disagree and ask for an independent evaluation performed by a professional(s) not employed by the school district. This independent evaluation is an entitlement under federal law and is generally paid for by the school district or they have to show, through a due process hearing, that their evaluations are appropriate and the eligibility decision was just.

- *Eligible.* Once the team determines a child is eligible for Special Education services an Individual Education Program (IEP) meeting will be set up (the name of the actual meeting may be called something different depending on the state in which you live).

The IEP Meeting

During this meeting the team, which includes the parent(s), discusses the evaluations and the Transition Plan presented to them and, based on this data, sets up the educational program and decides on related services for the child. Goals and objectives are discussed and agreed upon, as is the type of program most appropriate for the child. This placement decision is made by everyone on the IEP team and could be in a regular education classroom, a self-contained classroom, or a combination of both.

What is a Transition Plan and what does it include?

A Transition Plan is a written document developed by the EI team and parents. It provides a description of the child, his functioning, and his EI plan. This plan should be done prior to exiting the early intervention system and can be made part of the IFSP or exist as a stand-alone document. The Transition Plan paints a picture of the child for the public school team members. It includes a description of the child's current level of functioning, his strengths and weaknesses, services the child has been receiving, the child's learning style, what reinforcers are particularly effective, etc. It's helpful for all members of the EIP team to be involved in producing the document so biases are held to a minimum. Any recent tests done on the child can be made part of the Transition Plan, as can a parent narrative describing the child, his personality, likes/dislikes, etc. The goal in creating the Transition Plan is to provide as thorough information as possible to help the public school team understand how autism affects the child and his learning needs. The plan is presented to the school district team as part of the evaluation process for determining eligibility and prior to the development of the IEP.

How do I prepare for the first IEP meeting?

You start by becoming familiar with the federal and state laws that govern the provision of special education services to your child. In most cases, children are eligible for special education services in public schools under Part B of the Individuals with Disabilities Education Act (IDEA), most recently reauthorized in 2004. This law is accompanied by a set of regulations that were issued in 2006; the "regs" explain how the law functions and offers interpretations of the meaning and spirit of the law. Copies of the IDEA law and regs are available for download free of charge at *www.ed.gov/about/offices/list/osers/osep* or *www.wrightslaw.com/idea/idea.2004.all.pdf*. The Wrightslaw website also offers books, materials and helpful articles on special education issues that are very beneficial for parents. Each state also has organizations that exist to provide parent training and education on special education issues. Parents can locate their state organizations—broadly called P&A or PTI agencies—at the Autism Society of America's website, *www.autism-society.org*. Many of these organizations, along with state/local chapters of the ASA, offer parent workshops and training sessions on special education issues that are very helpful in gaining a working knowledge of the system. State special education laws can offer more services to their population, but cannot offer less than federal mandates. Most parents begin with learning about federal laws, then supplement their education by learning about state laws.

It is very important to become knowledgeable about the federal laws that govern your child's education. In addition to IDEA 2004, parents should also explore three other federal laws that will impact their child's education in public school programs:

- Family Educational Rights and Privacy Act (FERPA)
- No Child Left Behind Act of 2001
- Section 504 of the Rehabilitation Act of 1973

Parents who come into the meeting prepared and aware of their child's rights under IDEA stand a much better chance of negotiating the services a child needs. One caveat: the "best" education is not guaranteed under federal law. Laws require schools to provide an "individualized" and "appropriate" education, terms ripe for subjectivity and interpretation. The better prepared you are, the better the program for your child.

Parents new to the process of special education may find it helpful to talk with other parents of children with ASD who attend the same school. These parents can be a treasure trove of information about the school "culture" and politics regarding the provision of services, and provide wisdom and guidance in working effectively with the school. In a way, the first IEP meeting is where you and the school get to know each other, find out where your boundaries lie, and size each other up. You want to be firm in advocating for your child's needs, without creating an atmosphere of discord and contention. You will be "wedded" to this school district for many years to come. It's a marriage of sorts, where you each negotiate your positions to arrive at a partnership that is workable and acceptable to everyone. Do everything within your power to keep your emotions in control and work from a position of knowledge and with a focus on the needs of your child.

What happens during the first IEP meeting?

You and members of the school's team will meet at a mutually agreed-upon time to discuss your child's needs and put together a document that describes the special education services and education plan for the child. This meeting is generally a few hours long and can be overwhelming for parents. You might want to tape-record the meeting or have a friend or another parent accompany you to take notes so you can focus on participation. If you plan to tape-record the meeting, let the school know ahead of time.

Prior to the meeting you should receive copies of evaluation reports done on the child, and if the school drafted an IEP (which many do as a starting point for discussion), a copy of that draft. These should be mailed to you so you have ample time to review them. If you don't receive these documents prior to the meeting and they are presented to you upon arrival, respectfully ask that the meeting be rescheduled to give you time to read the documents and prepare. Do not continue with the meeting and hope for the best. You need time to process the evaluation reports and the draft IEP before the discussion.

The group will discuss the Transition Plan, the evaluations and parent input about the child, create the educational plan, propose services and hopefully come to agreement. At minimum, the IEP should contain the following elements, many of which are similar to those included on the IFSP.

Present Level of Educational Performance (PLEP)

In order to gauge education progress, the team must know the child's current level of functioning in various domains. This information is generally taken from the Transition Plan and the evaluations done on the child. These documents become part of the child's official records. The IEP should contain specific statements, with concrete measures of performance in areas such as communication/language, social skills, behavior, life skills, etc. which will serve as baseline data for future comparisons.

Goals and Objectives

After the team reviews the PLEP, annual goals and short-term objectives should be discussed and agreed upon. The annual goals address the areas of weakness identified in the child (e.g., Increase Communication Skills, Improve Social Interaction Skills) and should build on already mastered skills. These goals are spread out and worked on over the entire year.

Next, short term objectives are discussed. Objectives are very specific, measurable skills to be taught that move the child in the direction of the goal. For example, a short term objective that supports a goal of Improving Social Interaction Skills might be something like this: The child will initiate a social interaction with a peer during a group activity on three out of four attempts. While goals are global, objectives are always specific, concrete and measurable.

Progress Reporting

There must be a clear understanding and written description of how the child's progress will be measured and reported, and how often this will be done. Generally children in special education receive progress reports or report cards on the same schedule as do typical students. Reports can be provided more often but should not be less frequent than for the rest of the student body. Make sure everyone understands how to read the reports (are they narrative, composite scores, a combination of both?) and what course of action is available if there are questions on the student's progress or lack thereof.

Related Services & Modifications

All related services (speech and language therapy, occupational therapy, art therapy, music therapy, adaptive physical education, physical therapy, etc.) must be outlined in this section. If equipment is provided (such as a communication device) it should be detailed on the IEP. Provision of services should be documented as specifically as possible, to include amount of time (e.g., speech therapy: two times per week, thirty minutes each session), locations (e.g., in the classroom, as a pull-out service, etc.), on what day the services begin and end, who will provide the services, and whether or not the child will be included with neurotypical peers part time/full time.

This section also addresses modifications to be made to the curriculum (for instance, exemption from certain testing), any accommodations made for the child's style of learning (extra time to complete a test, written instructions to supplement oral ones, daily visual schedule, etc.), a detailed description of the paraprofessional support provided for the child, if any (1:1 aide or .5 aide, including beginning date), and any transportation provided for the child (including whether or not an aide is on the bus).

The first IEP can and should document anything else discussed and agreed upon by the team. It is the legal contract that specifies the education plan for the child. Parents should work with the school so that the document is detailed enough that it accurately describes how, when and by whom the child will be educated. Vague descriptions like "speech therapy will be included" and/or subjective terminology like "better" or "improved" to measure progress should be avoided.

What if I disagree with the program offered?

Discuss your concerns openly and frankly, keeping the focus on the needs of your child, not on what you want. Use real-life examples to support your opinions, rather than emotions. Draw from your personal knowledge of your child, his strengths and weaknesses, and his learning style to make your case. Remember, it's a negotiation, and to get the services your child needs, you must be persuasive and help the team members see your child as you do. One creative mom, in gridlock over getting the behavior therapy she believed her child needed, asked the team to reconvene at her home the next day so the team could see her child "in action." Once the team got a good look at the child's functioning in real life, rather than just reading about him on paper, they agreed to the extra services.

Horror stories from families about the fights they have had with their school districts echo throughout the autism community. Vow that your relationship with your school will not get to this point, and do everything in your power to prevent it from happening. At times this will be a challenge in self-control for you! Approach the meeting prepared, leave your emotions at the door, act in a professional, respectful manner, and you will be much more successful. Don't be the parent who walks into the first IEP meeting with an attorney in tow because you heard something from someone else about how unfair the team is. That sets up an adversarial relationship right from the very beginning. Plus, you may find out that the IEP team responds differently to an educated, level-headed parent than it does to an overly vocal, fist-pounding, demanding parent.

If your best efforts fall on deaf ears, and the school is proposing an absolutely inappropriate program for the child, you have certain legal recourses, starting with not signing the first IEP. The school cannot initiate services for the child if the parent does not sign the first IEP. At no other time in the education process does the parent signature carry this weight. However, again, recognize that withholding your signature may set up a contentious relationship with the school.

In most cases there may be disagreement over just one part of the IEP, not the entire plan. In this case the parent can sign the IEP, adding a written attachment citing their objection to the section in question. The school can proceed with the educational plan and a subsequent meeting can be arranged to work through the objectionable part, get additional evaluations, etc. Options are available to explore when disagreements arise.

I want a successful relationship with my school. How do I cultivate that?

Mary Romaniec, parent of a special needs child, national speaker and active parent mentor, advises parents to approach the IEP process as though it was a "business," with parents as the CEO of the business venture. Excerpts from an excellent article she wrote in 2005 for the *Autism Asperger's Digest*, entitled "Closing the IEP Deal: A Street-Smart Approach to Negotiating Your Child's IEP" are reprinted below with permission.

Handle the IEP Process as a Business Venture

Understanding the law is helpful, but only one part of the process of obtaining a comprehensive program suitable for your child. I've found that parents are often remiss in their preparation and lack an understanding of the school district's policies and attitudes towards IEPs. We bring pictures of our kids and ply the attendees with cookies and coffee hoping to strike a chord with their human side. However, the real focus of any IEP meeting is to negotiate the "deal," hopefully one in favor of the child.

Prepare Yourself

It's imperative that parents know what types of programs, goals and objectives are important or suitable for their child and which are not. Otherwise it's going to be difficult to come across as an "authority" on your child at an IEP meeting. I am often amazed at how many parents do not know this. Call other parents or parent support groups; ask around about services offered to other students. Knowing the services offered—or not offered—to other students is baseline information for your own negotiations. I often refer parents to outside experts to help them determine what educational services might be best for their child. How many times do we hire outside experts in the business world to help us clarify and achieve sales goals and objectives? The same applies here, too.

Put it in Writing

The impact of letter writing cannot be understated. School districts will generally pay attention to a letter in front of them—it becomes part of a paperwork trail that might eventually end up in a Due Process hearing to their disadvantage. Address letters to the school administrator and make sure each one has a tone of directness and clarity in expressing your points, so there is no misunderstanding as to its purpose. Always request a response in writing within a reasonable number of days.

Act in a Business-like Manner

Relationships with school district IEP teams members need to be kept cordial, yet with the understanding that these individuals will never be your friends as long as your child receives services from them in the district. It's a negotiation; keep it at a business level. I have heard from parents who send flowers throughout the year to IEP team members or dump insincere praise on them in hopes these efforts will help their child's program. Many parents fear a backlash on their child if they dare speak up in objection to the school district's proposal. In all these situations my reply is firm, yet straightforward: *Stop that.* These people are not part of this team to be your friends; they are there to do a job. Twenty years from now they will not be in your life but your child will be. Your job is to advocate for him or her to the best of your ability. Give up the notion of wanting to be well-liked by the school district. Do your job for your child and they might actually respect you. You may wish it were otherwise, but this is the way school districts work. And yes, the squeaky wheel gets the grease, especially if the squeak is intelligently and articulately communicated.

I cannot stress enough how important it is for parents to lose their emotional attachments and insecurities to the IEP process and don their business hats. Parents who are afraid of what someone at the school thinks of them start out the process already diminished in their ability to properly advocate for their child.

Furthermore, cordial relationships can be used to your benefit. I often had frank conversations with members of the IEP team at my home or on the telephone. Confidences were sometimes shared but sources were never revealed, especially during the IEP meeting. These conversations helped me better understand the school's bottom line, district politics, the reputations of the people on the team, etc. Sometimes the obvious is not always as it appears; getting behind-the-scenes information is valuable, as long as confidences remain confidential.

Body language, voice tone, eye contact—all are important elements of a good business presentation. The same is true with the IEP meeting and strong advocacy efforts. How you carry yourself and talk to the group tells the school district about you from an intellectual perspective. Don't let your emotions get the best of you! It sends a message to the school district that your points are being driven by emotion, not by logic. As a parent, I know all too well how difficult this is to do. Find some personal strategy that works for you, be it picturing your boss in the room evaluating your performance for a promotion, or pretending you are acting a scene in a movie. Intellectual composure is a must. A clear understanding of the educational goals and objectives you seek for your child will help you remain calm and in control.

Dress as though you are going to a job interview. Your appearance, vocabulary and mannerisms will directly affect how you are perceived. An Armani or Chanel suit is not required, but some spit and polish is definitely in order. How you dress is an indication of how seriously you take the meeting: Dressing casually indicates you are treating the meeting casually. Dressing as though you are attending a board meeting sets higher expectations.

Also, make an effort to understand the thoughts, opinions and motivations of the other members of the IEP team. These are people you will be working with for many years to come. While, as Mary Romaniec suggests, your goal is not to make them your friends, you do want to cultivate a professional, respectful relationship. Be honest; if you make a commitment, keep it; call ahead if you will be late to a meeting, etc. Don't take disagreements personally; many teachers are under pressure from administration to do or say certain things at an IEP meeting. A mutual understanding of each other can go far in appreciating the source of disagreements and working through them with the child's needs in mind.

Try to keep the lines of communication always open. As the child's parent, share information with teachers about what you know about your child. Copy informative articles on ASD you find and share them with teachers and team members. Consider the advice the child's teacher provides. Stay active and engaged in your child's education. Teachers are not responsible for "fixing" your child, but for providing an education. They may need your help to understand your child's different thinking patterns and learning style. Be a partner in this process, not a critic.

Discuss and deal with issues as they arise; do not wait for the yearly IEP meeting or until you can no longer control your anger to call a teacher or IEP meeting. An IEP meeting can be called whenever a new situation arises that warrants the attention of the group. Use the provisions of the law as they were intended, as a framework where parents and teachers gather together as equal partners to create an appropriate and individualized educational program tailored to the needs of the child.

Children with autism have great potential to learn, grow and become functioning members of society. An early diagnosis followed by a quality early intervention program provides the foundation these kids need, and prepares parents and the family for the road ahead. This is a journey filled with many surprises, with twists and turns that sneak up in the dark, with vistas so expansive we question our ability to go the distance. It is also an adventure that can fill our days and our hearts with unimaginable joys.

Enjoy each step. Good Luck and Great Success.

"My son, Tom, was diagnosed with PDD-NOS in 1993, about three months before his third birthday. At that time it was not common for a pediatrician to recognize the signs of autism as early as did mine and I will be forever grateful to him for pushing to have Tom tested.

Even though we only had about six weeks before Tom turned 3, their help was invaluable in getting me on the right track. They did an evaluation and IFSP, and provided me with written reports. We started therapy with them (at that time only available once a week) so I would know what needed to be done when the school system took over. They coached me on what to ask for and what my rights were in regard to the public school program. They advised me on what to look for when we went to visit preschools. We were able to start services through the school district very shortly after Tom's third birthday because I had the Early Intervention evaluation plus the hospital evaluation, which meant the school did not have to go through a long intake process.

Although short-lived, Early Intervention services gave me HOPE. They showed me help was available and caring people existed. To this day I remain so grateful for their support."

PATTY, PARENT OF TOM

More Real-life Advice

"AS PARENTS OF A NEWLY DIAGNOSED CHILD WITH AUTISM WE FELT SO LOST, so unsure of our child's future. We educated ourselves about autism, the diagnosis, and it got better. We met more people with autism. We found our way in this journey, one that allows us to best meet the needs of our child. Originally very affected, our son now is a teen who is enjoying his life, fully participating in his community, makes the honor roll at school, and has been an inspiration to not only us but to many others. He's also found his course, a self-directed one, that promotes his abilities and displays to others that you can indeed live with autism as something that is a unique and wonderful part of you, but does not define you as a person. His lesson has been our lesson too."

ANDREW AND CAROLYN, PARENTS, MI

⊚ ⊚ ⊚

"Autism creates treasured moments. There was a day when one of my students was having a bad day. He was sitting by himself in the corner and was visibly upset. I approached him and asked if I could come close, and he said "okay." I knelt down so I was at eye level and asked what he wanted. He said "hug, hug." I stood and opened my arms and we hugged. It was a moment I'll never forget."

STEPHEN, TEACHER, NJ

⊚ ⊚ ⊚

"Other than love, acceptance, and nurturing, the most important choice you can make for your child who has characteristics of autism is to start early intervention as soon as possible. Even though I began life greatly challenged by a scrambled system of interpretation and did not develop speech until nearly four years of age, I responded to people who believed there was a girl inside who wanted to be loved and taught. The most helpful interventions were ones that included patience, humor, and acceptance. When I felt accepted, I developed trust and could take the giant steps needed to gradually phase out some of my self-soothing behaviors—spinning, rocking, and banging my head against the sofa back—and learn to be a person who was part of a family, part of a community. Children learn when they are having fun in a safe and nurturing environment."

RUTH, INDIVIDUAL WITH AUTISM

◎ ◎ ◎

"Early intervention is not a 'magic bullet' or a quick fix for the challenges faced by individuals on the autism spectrum. But well-designed comprehensive programs will benefit almost every child. One of the keys to a successful early intervention experience is the family's willingness to 'stay the course.' Maintain the highest of expectations and celebrate all the unique and wonderful things about your child. Never give up hope."

JOHN, PARENT, TN

◎ ◎ ◎

Glossary

◎ **A** ◎

ABA: Applied Behavior Analysis; a scientific process that examines behavior using certain systematic principles.

ABC: Within ABA, refers to behavior analysis that looks at the Antecedent (what comes before), the Behavior, and the Consequence (that which follows).

Aberrant: Different from the natural or expected (generally has a negative connotation).

Aggression: Hostile or destructive behaviors or actions.

Anecdotal: Results based on subjective measures of success (e.g., parent testimony).

Anxiety: A physiological state characterized by fearful concern or interest; in individuals with ASD, anxiety is often pervasive and exists at very high levels most of the time.

Artificial: That which is produced rather than natural.

ASD: Autism Spectrum Disorders; a shorthand reference to the collective labels that fall under the broad heading of Pervasive Developmental Disorders in the DSM-IV.

Assessment: The process of evaluating or testing a child to determine strengths and weaknesses in the area(s) being considered.

Assistive Technology: Any technology that helps a child be successful in performing a given skill.

Attitude: A subjective feeling, emotion or perception about a given topic.

Audiological: Referring to hearing.

Augmentative communication: The use of a manufactured alternative means (e.g., pictures, computers, hand-held devices, etc.) to transmit information.

Autism: A lifelong neurological disorder usually diagnosed during the first three years of life; affects a child in three main areas: language/communication, social skills and behavior.

◉ B ◉

Baseline: A starting point; initial data gathered to establish the beginning skill level of a child in various areas.

Behavior momentum: A teaching strategy that involves engaging the child by starting with a skill the child knows and can do well, then slowly adding more difficult requests or new skills.

Biomedical: Referring to chronic, physiological medical conditions often associated with ASD.

◉ C ◉

Chaining: A teaching strategy that involves breaking down a complex skill into its component parts and teaching each step in the chain until the child can perform the entire task.

Classic Autism: Autism that appears to manifest from birth, or is noticed shortly thereafter, impairing the child's functioning from his early years. Language does not develop in the child, and s/he often exhibits more recognizable symptoms of the disorders, such as being aloof, rocking, spinning objects, etc.

Clinical perspective: Insight given by direct observation and/or through observable behaviors, generally by professionals working with or observing the child.

Cognitive: Of, or referring to, intelligence or thinking processes.

Comorbid: Existing alongside, or in addition to another disorder; e.g., epilepsy diagnosed in addition to ASD would be a comorbid disorder.

Concrete thinking: Thinking in a way that is very exact and literal with regard to what is being said.

Consequence: That which is the direct result of a cause or behavior.

Cure (as opposed to recovery): That which removes, entirely, an existing condition, disease or disorder from a person.

◎ D ◎

Developmental: Based on the chronological age of the child.

Diagnosis: The conclusion reached by a critical analysis of the nature of something; in ASD, it refers to the process performed by trained professionals in assessing whether or not an individual manifests characteristics that meet the criteria for any of the autism spectrum disorders.

DIR: Developmental, Individual-differences, Relationship-based; a therapy created by Dr. Stanley Greenspan and Serena Wieder.

Down time: Time during which an individual is not engaged in anything productive.

DSM-IV: Diagnostic and Statistical Manual of Mental Disorders-Fourth Edition; the main diagnostic reference used by medical professionals in the U.S.; contrary to its name, it also includes information on developmental disabilities.

DTT: Discrete trial teaching; one method of teaching within the larger framework of ABA.

◎ E ◎

EI/EIP: Early Intervention/Early Intervention Program

Eligibility: A determination of whether or not a child will qualify for special education services in a particular school.

Emotional Relatedness: The ability to assess the thoughts, feelings and perceptions of another person and self-adjust in order to know how to respond accordingly.

Empirically validated: Research that has been reviewed by independent experts in a given field and published in refereed professional journals.

Evaluation: A host of tests that determine the appropriate course of action for a given problem; used interchangeably with "assessment."

Evidence-based: A program that incorporates objective measures of effectiveness through regular data-taking and advocates that all decisions be made based on that data.

Extinction: A teaching strategy wherein we ignore a child's inappropriate behavior, but do not ignore the child.

⊚ F ⊚

Family Plan: An agreement among family members to work in the best interest of the child.

FAPE: Free Appropriate Public Education; an acronym within IDEA that addresses the manner in which services are to be provided to a child.

Floortime: A method of therapy usually done on the floor, involving child-initiated actions.

Focused: In a state of maximum clarity and concentration.

Frustration: A deep chronic sense or state of insecurity and dissatisfaction arising from unresolved problems or unfulfilled needs.

Functional goals: Those which apply to skills used in everyday life, such as dressing, eating, taking a bath, counting money, knowing one's telephone number, etc.

◉ G ◉

Goals: Broad statements that suggest targeted areas for improvement in a child

"Gut": A slang term for a personal feeling or intuition that tells a parent if something is appropriate or ill-matched to their child.

◉ H ◉

High Functioning: A term used to describe individuals with autism who function at a higher level of ability than others on the autism spectrum.

◉ I ◉

IDEA; IDEIA: Individuals with Disabilities Education Act/Individuals with Disabilities Education Improvement Act (also called the Individuals with Disabilities Education Act of 2004). The federal law that governs the provision of special education services.

IDEA Part A: The part of the federal law that defines terminology, responsibilities of state and local education groups, discusses funding and grants, and other administrative information related to the provision of special education services and programs.

IDEA Part B: The part of the federal law that outlines the supports and services for children aged three through the time they graduate or age out of the public school system (at age 21 or 22).

IDEA Part C: One section of the federal law that guarantees supports and services for infants and toddlers under the age of three.

IEP: Individual Education Plan; a written document that outlines the education plan for a child aged three or older within a public school program; it includes goals, objectives, accommodations, services and strategies, and other information related to the child.

IFSP: Individual Family Services Plan. The document (like the IEP) that describes and defines services for toddlers under three years of age, and their families. The IFSP is described in Part C of IDEA.

Imitation: The act of mimicking the words and/or actions of another.

Incentive: That which acts as a reward or motivation.

Incidental teaching: One type of ABA method based on child-initiated, rather than therapist-initiated teaching opportunities.

Intangible motivator: Something other than an object, that is pleasurable to the child and spurs him to act, such as verbal praise or a big smile with a "high five" gesture.

Intensity of engagement: The amount of time the child is engaged in a productive activity.

Intermittent reinforcement: Providing reinforcement on a sporadic basis to increase the child's motivation to secure the reward at some future time.

Intervention: A procedure used to alleviate a problem or issues.

Intraverbal: A part of conversational-language training that involves a verbal response occasioned by a verbal stimulus. Intraverbals are often responses to the "wh" questions: who, what, where, why.

IQ (intelligence quotient): The ratio of tested mental age to chronological age.

⊛ J,K ⊛

Joint Attention: The ability to use eye contact and gesturing to make a connection with another person during a social exchange.

⊛ L ⊛

Language (versus communication): The communication of thoughts and feelings through a system of voice sounds.

Language, Expressive: The ability to use language verbally or in writing to convey one's thoughts, desires, intentions, etc.

Language, Receptive: The ability to process and understand language that is spoken or language that is read.

Learned Helplessness: When a child no longer does things for himself because someone else readily steps in to do it for him.

Learning profile: The sum of the various ways in which a child best absorbs new information.

Literal: Upholding the exact or primary meaning of a word or phrase.

◉ M ◉

Meltdowns: A term used to describe tantrumous behaviors; a tantrum that has spun out of control.

Modeling: Demonstrating an action or procedure as a means of teaching it to the child.

Motivation: Incentive or drive.

Munchausen's Syndrome by Proxy: A syndrome where a mother causes medical issues in a child in order to gain attention for herself.

◉ N ◉

Naturalistic: Things that happen in the here and now and are not contrived or made up; most often used in reference to teaching methods/strategies that take place in settings in which children normally gather and occur in "teachable moments" as they arise.

Negative reinforcement: Removing something from a behavior interaction that increases the likelihood of that behavior occurring in the future.

Neurological: The scientific study of the nervous system, especially in respect to its structure.

Neurotypical: The term people with ASD use to describe people without ASD; those who have common qualities, traits, or characteristics and are identified by a certain class or kind.

Non-social reinforcers: Concrete, tangible rewards like food, drink, toys, etc.

Nonverbal: In reference to a child, one who is not able to use sounds to form words to communicate needs and wants; also refers to communication that does not use language.

Nonverbal communication: The use of alternative ways (e.g., facial expressions, gestures, eye gaze, body positioning, etc.) to transmit information

NT: Neurotypical.

◎ O ◎

Objectives: Statements that describe, in specific and measurable terms, the skill(s) or behavior(s) to be taught to a child.

Occupational therapy: Therapy based on engagement in meaningful activities of daily life (such as self-care skills, education, work, or social interaction) especially to enable or encourage participation in such activities despite impairments or limitations in physical or mental functioning.

Oral Motor: Referring to the stimulation of the muscles of the mouth area to assist in sensory or communication issues.

Overloaded: The phenomena that occur when a child receives too much therapy and begins to regress; can also refer to an excess of sensory stimuli bombarding the child, resulting in inappropriate behavioral responses.

◎ P,Q ◎

Partnership Plan: An informal written or verbal agreement created by a child's parent(s) to work with the intervention group in the best interest of the child.

PDD: Pervasive Developmental Disorder; the umbrella heading in the DSM-IV-R under which all the other related autism disorders fall.

PDD-NOS: Pervasive Developmental Disorder: Not Otherwise Specified; a milder form of autism.

Perseveration: The tendency to repeat the same word, action or behavior over and over in the exact same way.

PLEP: Present Level of Educational Performance; the child's current level of functioning in various domains.

Positive reinforcement: Adding something to the behavior interaction that increases the likelihood of that behavior occurring in the future.

Primary reinforcement: Anything having to do with survival; basic needs like food, clothing, shelter.

Process: A series of actions, changes, or operations that bring about a result.

Prompting: A teaching strategy wherein a word, command or action is provided to the child that helps the child be successful in performing the behavior being worked on.

Punishment: The use of an aversive procedure to decrease inappropriate behavior.

⊚ R ⊚

Reassessment: The process of re-evaluating a child, after a baseline of skills has been established, to determine progress.

Recovery: Within the ASD community, refers to children who advance through therapy in such a way that they no longer qualify for a diagnosis under the PDD category.

Regressive Autism: Those children who appear to develop in a normal manner, often meeting early developmental milestones, then begin to lose such skills over time.

Reinforcement: Anything that strengthens or increases the likelihood of a given behavior being repeated.

Research: Carefully controlled studies conducted by qualified, independent professionals, according to generally accepted principles of data collection, measurement and analysis.

Ritual: A state or condition characterized by the presence of an established procedure or routine.

Routine: A particular set of behaviors or activities that are repeated together.

◉ S ◉

Savant Skill: A markedly superior skill exhibited by an individual; in autism these are often in the areas of math, music, weather, computers, counting or calendar skills. The person exhibiting the skill is referred to as a savant.

Scaffolding: A teaching strategy characterized by providing sufficient supports to the child in the beginning to promote learning, and then as independent learning occurs, removing these supports to promote independence.

Secondary Reinforcement: Things that are favorable, but not essential, to our existence.

Self-injurious: Hostile or destructive behaviors that are self-inflicted.

Self-rewarding: Something a person finds personally reinforcing.

Self-Stimulatory: Repetitive behaviors done because they feel good.

Sensory Issues: Difficulties processing information/environmental input taken in through any of the seven senses: hearing, sight, smell, taste, touch, vestibular, proprioception.

Sequences: The progression of one thing to another.

Shaping: Accepting the approximation of a targeted behavior and reinforcing it while helping the child perform the skill correctly.

Skill: The ability to use one's knowledge effectively and readily in execution or performance.

Social reinforcement: A reward that arises from the desire to connect with other human beings; can include praise, attention, acknowledgement, etc.

Social Relatedness: The ability to assess a social situation and assimilate into the situation easily.

Social skills: Habits or behaviors that involve relating to human society or the company of others.

Spectrum disorder: The idea that there is a range of functioning within ASD, from severely affected, nonverbal aggressive/self injurious to highly verbal, high IQ, very gifted individuals, and all combinations in between.

Stims: Any self-stimulatory behaviors

Strategies: Careful plans or methods of working with, teaching or interacting with another person.

Structured: Highly organized and arranged in a definite pattern.

Structured teaching: The basic method used within the TEACCH program; it espouses organizing the physical environment, using schedules and work systems, and communicating clear and explicit instructions and expectations to the child.

Success: Achievement of something desired.

Survival: Getting through each day any way one can.

Symptoms: A characteristic sign or indication of the existence of something else.

◎ T,U ◎

Tangible motivator: A concrete object that is pleasurable to the child and spurs the child to act. For instance, a toy, a drink, a food treat, etc.

Target: The specific skill or behavior to be addressed.

TEACCH: Treatment and Education of Autistic and related Communication-handicapped Children; a program established in the early 1970's by Dr. Eric Schopler.

Teachable Moments: Instances throughout the day that lend themselves to using a skill or prompting a child to use a skill to be successful.

Transition Plan: A written document, developed by the EI team and parent, that provides a description of the child, his functioning, and his EI plan.

Trigger: An occurrence in the environment that precedes an inappropriate behavior.

Typical: Exhibiting qualities, traits, or characteristics that identify a certain class or kind. In the autism community, often refers to non-disabled peers.

⊚ V-Z ⊚

Verbal: Ability to use sounds to form words to communicate one's needs and wants.

Visual Schedule: The use of pictures (e.g., actual photographs, pictures cut out of magazines/books, and/or commercially produced), arranged in the sequence of an activity (daily schedule, taking a shower, etc.), to help a child or adult perform the activity more independently.

References

AARP, www.aarp.org, 2005.

American Psychiatric Association (2000). *Diagnostic and Statistical Manual of Mental Disorders, 4th ed.,* (DSM-IV), Washington, D.C.

Anderson, W., Chitwood, S., & Hayden, D. (1997). *Negotiating The Special Education Maze: A Guide For Parents And Teachers.* (3rd ed.). Bethesda, MD: Woodbine House.

Azrin, N. & Foxx, R. (1974). *Toilet Training in Less than a Day.* New York, NY: Simon and Schuster Trade.

Baer, D., Wolf, M., & Risley, R. (1968). "Some current dimensions of applied behavior analysis." *Journal of Applied Behavior Analysis,* 1, 91 - 97.

Ball, J., Oberleitner, R., Kempner, A., & Jubeck, R. (2005). "For Fathers Only." *Autism Asperger's Digest,* May-June 2005 issue. Arlington, TX. Future Horizons, Inc.

Bateman, B. D. & Linden, M. A. (1998). *Better IEP's: How To Develop Legally Correct and Educationally Useful Programs* (3rd ed.). Longmont, CO: Sopris West.

Brott, A. (2004). *The New Father: A Dad's Guide to the First Year.* Abbeville Press.

Brounstein, M. (2005). *Managing Teams for Dummies.* New York, New York: Wiley Publishing.

Council for Exceptional Children. (1999). "The IEP team guide." Arlington, VA.

Douglas, J. and Richman, N. (1984). *My Child Won't Sleep: Practical Advice And Guidance On The Common Sleeping Problems Of Young Children.* Harmondsworth: Penguin.

Durand, V.M. (1998). *Sleep Better! A Guide To Improving Sleep For Children With Special Needs.* Baltimore, MD: Paul H. Brookes Publishing Company.

Filipek, P.A. et al. (2000). "Practice parameter: Screening and Diagnosis of autism." *Neurology,* 55: 468-79.

Giangreco, M.F. (2001). "Guidelines for making decisions about IEP services." Montpelier, VT: Vermont Department of Education.

Gibb, G.S., & Dyches, T.T. (2000). *Guide To Writing Quality Individualized Education Programs: What's Best For Students With Disabilities?* Needham Heights, MA: Allyn & Bacon.

Gray, C. (2000). *Writing Social Stories with Carol Gray.* Arlington, TX: Future Horizons, Inc.

Greenspan, S.I. (1999). *Building Healthy Minds,* Perseus Books.

Heflin, L.J. and Simpson, R.I. (1998). "Interventions for Children and Youth with Autism." *Focus on Autism and Other Developmental Disabilities*, No. 14, winter 1998, 194-211.

Hume, K., Bellini, S., and Pratt, C. (2006). "The usage and perceived outcomes of early intervention and early childhood programs from young children with autism spectrum disorder." *Topics in Early Childhood Special Education*. Austin, TX: Pro-Ed.

Hurth, J., Shaw, E., Izeman, S., Whaley, K., & Rogers, S. (1999). "Areas of agreement about effective practices among programs serving young children with autism spectrum disorders." *Infants and Young Children*, 12(2), pp. 17-26.

Kedesdy, J.H. & Budd, K.S. (1998). *Childhood Eating Disorders: Biobehavioral Assessment And Intervention*. Baltimore, MD: Paul H. Brookes Publishing Company.

Kubler-Ross, E. (1969). *On Death and Dying*. New York: Scribner.

Legge, B. (2002). *Can't Eat, Won't Eat: Dietary Difficulties And Autistic Spectrum Disorders*. Philadelphia, PA: Jessica Kingsley Publishers.

Levy, S., Kim, A.H., and Olive, M.L. (2006). "Interventions for young children with autism: A synthesis of the literature." *Focus on Autism and Other Developmental Disabilities*, 21, 1, 55-62.

Lovaas, O.I. (1981). *Teaching Developmentally Disabled Children: The Me Book*. Austin, Tx: Pro-Ed.

Lovaas, O.I. (1987). "Behavioral treatments and normal educational and intellectual functioning in young children with autism." *Journal of Consulting and Clinical Psychology*, 55, 3-9.

Macht, J. (1990). *Poor Eaters: Helping Children Who Refuse To Eat*. New York, NY: Plenum Press.

Marks, C. (2001). "Toilet training: Is your child ready? *Autism Asperger's Digest*, July-August 2001 issue. Arlington, TX: Future Horizons, Inc.

McEachin, J.J., Smith, T., & Lovaas, O.I. (1993). "Long-term outcome for children with autism who received early intensive behavioral treatment." *American Journal on Mental Retardation*. 97, 359-372.

McGinnis, E. and Goldstein, A.P. (2003). *Skillstreaming in Early Childhood: New Strategies and Perspectives for Teaching Prosocial Skills*. Champaign, IL: Research Press.

McNulty, B., D. B. Smith, and E. W. Soper. (1983). "Effectiveness Of Early Special Education For Handicapped Children." Colorado Department of Education.

National Research Council (2001). "Educating Children with Autism. Committee on Educational Interventions for Children with Autism." Catherine Lord and James P. McGee, eds. Division of Behavioral and Social Sciences and Education. Washington, DC: National Academy Press.

"New Jersey Early Intervention System Birth to Three Service Guidelines for Children with Autism Spectrum Disorders." (2004). Department of Health and Senior Services, Trenton, New Jersey.

REFERENCES

Oberleitner, R., Ball, J., Gillette, D., Naseef, R., & Hudnall-Stamm, B., (2005). "Technologies to Lessen the Distress of Autism," *Journal of Aggression, Maltreatment, & Trauma, 12*(1), 221-242.

Office of Special Education and Rehabilitative Services (OSERS), U.S. Department of Education (2000). "A guide to the individualized education program." Washington, DC.

Piaget, J. (1932). *The Moral Judgment of the Child.* New York: Free Press.

Quine, L. and Cambs, H. (1997). *Solving Children's Sleep Problems: A Step By Step Guide For Parents.* Beckett Karlson Publishing.

Rogers, S. (1996). "Brief report: Early intervention in autism." *Journal of Autism and Developmental Disorders, 26,* 243-246.

Rogers, S. (1999). "Intervention for young children with autism: From research to practice." *Infants and Young Children, 12,* 1-16.

Schopler, E., Reichler, R.J., Bashford, A., Lansing, M., Marcus, L. (1990). *The Psychoeducational Profile Revised (PEP-R).* Austin: Pro-Ed, 1990.

Schweinhart, L. J., and D. P. Weikart. (1980). "Young Children Grow UP: The Effects Of The Perry Preschool Program On Youths Through Age 19." Ypsilanti, MI: High/Scope Educational Research Foundation.

Skinner, B. (1953). *Science and Human Behavior.* New York: MacMillan.

Skinner, B. (1968). *The Technology of Teaching.* New York: Appleton-Crofts.

Snider, J., W. Sullivan, and D. Manning. (1974). "Industrial Engineering Participation in a Special Education Program." Tennessee Engineer 1: 21-23.

Stadtler, A., Gorski, P., & Brazelton, T.B. (1999). "Toilet training methods: Clinical interventions and recommendations." *Pediatrics, 103,* 1359-1365.

Stritof, S. & Stritof, B., (2003). *The Everything Great Marriage Book.* Adams Media Corporation.

Sundberg, M.L. and Partington, J. (1998). *The Assessment of Basic Language and Learning Skills (The ABLLS): An assessment, curriculum guide, and skills tracking system for children with autism or other developmental disabilities.* Pleasant Hill, CA: Behavioral Analysts, Inc.

Webster Universal English Dictionary (2004), David Dale House, New Lanark, Scotland.

Wheeler, M. (1998). *Toilet Training For Individuals With Autism And Related Disorders.* Arlington, TX: Future Horizons, Inc.

Wood, M. E. (1981). "Costs of Intervention Programs." In C. Garland and others, eds., *Early Intervention For Children With Special Needs And Their Families: Findings And Recommendations.* Westar Series Paper No. 11. Seattle, WA: University of Washington, ED 207 278.

Wright, P.W.D., & Wright, P.D. (1999). Your Child's IEP: Practical And Legal Guidance For Parents. Deltaville, VA: Authors.

Appendix A

A Day in the Life

Anytime, Anywhere—
Real-life Teaching Strategies for Parents

YOU'VE CONTACTED YOUR EI SERVICE AGENCY, WORKED THROUGH THE PAPER-work, and now your family is on a wait-list for services to begin. Sometimes this wait is a few weeks or a few months. Sometimes, unfortunately, it can be much longer. What can you do in the meantime? Plenty!

First, go back and read the section in Chapter 7 that discusses the 7 basic teaching strategies: repetition, shaping, chaining, reinforcement, play, extinction, and rapport building/behavior momentum (pages 166–172). You might also want to review the concrete strategies on behavior, reinforcement and prompting in Chapter 8 (pages 244–283). These strategies describe how you will interact with your child throughout the day, in any setting, with any activity you're doing together, or any interaction that occurs.

As you work with your child, you'll want to start closely watching his or her behaviors, attempts to communicate (in positive and negative ways), and the environment. This may include time of day, other people surrounding you two, places you're in and what's going on from a sensory perspective (sounds, smells, visuals, etc.). Become the behavior detective we've talked about throughout the book, looking for those ever-so-valuable clues that will tell you what's going on with your child and why. These clues will also affect how you respond to your child. Remember: *behavior is communication*. It's your job to figure out what your child is trying to tell you.

Within the early sections of the scenario that follows (you'll soon follow along), the segments of a behavior interaction are indicated in parentheses: the Cue, your Prompt, the Response, and the Consequence. These are all parts of a Discrete Trial, which is, in my professional experience, the best way to teach a child with ASD.

Before you begin, here are a few points to keep in mind:

- Although you will be using what is essentially an ABA technique, do remember that you are embedding this instruction strategy within your daily experiences with the child: during play sessions and as you move through the routines of the day (waking up, meals, chores, errands, bedtime). You're not stopping an activity with the mindset "oh, now I can stop what we're doing and 'formally' teach him this." It's woven naturally into your interactions.

- Using these strategies will feel awkward at first. Expect it, and know that with practice, it will become not only easier for your child to learn, but also for you to teach.

- Expect to make some mistakes. You're human. Do your best and if you make a mistake, forgive yourself and move on. A few mistakes will not sabotage your efforts or prevent your child from learning new things. Start small and be successful. It's motivating for you both!

- These strategies are equal-opportunity learning instruments. They work whether your child is nonverbal or verbal, has terrible behavior problems or is generally a little angel. Don't fall into the trap of thinking that only certain strategies work with certain kids. Certain *models* may work better with certain kids. You're not at the stage of integrating a specific model into your child's life. These are to-do-now strategies that can be effective with *any* child.

- Your goal is to spend as much time as you possibly can on a daily basis engaging your child. Notice the word: engagement. You want to keep him in the here and now, involved in interaction with his world and the people in it.

- Consistency and predictability are a must! Think about what you're doing and do things pretty much the same way each time with your child.

- Keep your language simple and concrete. Use the same commands, delivered in the same way, over and over. At first they may be very short and seem almost terse: "Want milk?" But this is good. Your child's autism-impaired mind may be confused if you mix up your words every time: "Would you like some milk?" "How about some milk for lunch?" "You like milk; do you want milk?"

- You're the adult, you're in charge! Keep your cool when his behavior starts to get troublesome. You set the rules, not him. And, don't give in to his behaviors! If you're sure they're not a result of impending (or already present) sensory overload, stand your ground until your child complies.

- The opportunity to teach starts the moment your child wakes and continues until he goes to bed. As you become more comfortable using these strategies, you'll find yourself naturally weaving them into your interactions. At first, though, using them will take some thought, planning, and conscious effort on your part. You're both learning!

Josh gets up

Josh wakes up in the morning. He wanders downstairs and walks into the kitchen. His diaper is full of urine from the night before and he begins to pull at it (Cue).

Mom says, "That's great, Josh, you're telling me you need to be changed (Reinforcement). Say, 'I need to be changed.'" (Cue). Prompt Josh to say the words (if he is verbal or has emerging verbal skills), and show him a picture of the bathroom (if he's nonverbal or during times when Josh has trouble using his words) and have him point to it. If he does (Response), reinforce him: "Good job Josh!" accompanied by a brief, fun physical gesture like tousling his hair or patting his back (Reinforcement). If your child is sensory sensitive (watch for his reactions to stimuli), don't add this secondary reinforcement.

If he does not speak or touch the picture, prompt him (using a physical, gestural, or locational prompt) to touch the picture. Then heavily reinforce him for touching the picture (Consequence). Each morning, as you do this and Josh's response skills increase, you may need to

357

change (increase) the reinforcer as he performs the skill more and more independently (Repetition/Reinforcement). Each time you see Josh pull at his diaper, you follow the same sequence.

As you change his diaper, practice eye contact or simple motor skill development, like patty-cake or touch my nose/touch my chin, using these same strategies: cueing, prompting, reinforcement. Look carefully for his response and reinforce him immediately for even a slight approximation at first. Make it fun and playful. If your child has sensory sensitivities and diaper change is difficult, move through it as quickly and smoothly as possible, keeping your cool in both actions and tone of voice, practicing extinction (ignoring the behavior) while he's fussy and using reinforcement when the child quiets down.

After he has been changed, ask him what he wants for breakfast. Show him two choices (you know he likes both) and ask him, "Do you want toast or pancakes?" (Cue). Use a visual card or show him a slice of bread or the pancake mix box. Young children who are more impaired by their autism may find line drawings difficult to comprehend. Even in typical development, children learn by first recognizing the tangible object, then a photographic representation, then moving to a line drawing (less tangible) before they understand the word representation. Start with the concrete object before using a less concrete representation.

If he makes a choice (Response), praise him (Reinforcement). Again, look closely and don't assume his response will be a can't-miss-it-point or perfect language. It might be a slight turn of the head or eye gaze in the direction of the object or picture. Or a faint word approximation in your emerging-language child.

If he does not indicate a choice, use a physical, gestural or locational prompt to help him touch one and praise him in making a choice (Reinforcement).

Once he chooses, he can go and "play" until you are ready for him to eat. When you want him to eat say, "Josh, time to eat. Come here." (Cue). If he comes (Response), praise him and reinforce him strongly (Reinforcement).

If he does not come, DO NOT SAY IT AGAIN. Go and get him (Prompt), bring him to the table or where ever you want him and praise him for good listening (Reinforcement). Just say something simple like "Good listening, Josh!" or "I like the way you're listening."

Then encourage him (use verbal language, modeling or visual cards) to sit where you are and eat his breakfast. If he gets up, repeat the process: say "Come here" (Cue) and if he comes (Response), praise him (Reinforcement). If he does not, do not repeat the request; go and get him and bring him back (Prompt), then reinforce him for good listening (Reinforcement/Repetition).

What you *don't* do is launch into verbal warnings, "Josh, I told you to sit down and eat your breakfast." "Josh, you're not eating your breakfast like Mommy asked you to." "Josh, you're being a bad boy." YOU DON'T DO ANY OF THESE ACTIONS. You remain calm, neutral, and use only necessary language to prompt Josh to follow your request. You give attention to him behaving/responding correctly (Reinforcement). You give NO ATTENTION to his undesirable behaviors (Extinction).

You want to set up the environment so Josh can be successful in his action or skill. Have desirable things at the table that he likes so he stays seated. Make it an enjoyable situation (Rapport Building).

Josh eats breakfast

While he eats his breakfast, encourage him to use his communication skills (remember: that's not just verbal language). Take his milk away. If he protests or starts to squirm because he wants it back, cue him by saying "Josh, what do you want? Use your words." (or "Show me" – depending on his language abilities). Have him verbalize or point to a picture of milk (which you have right there at the table because you planned out this scenario ahead of time and you've set up his environment for success).

If he successfully asks for the milk, praise him (Reinforcement). If he doesn't, prompt it (again using a physical, gestural, or locational prompt) then reinforce him. You can follow this same sequence with his food, always encouraging his use of communication (verbal or nonverbal). If he only slaps at the milk, take his hand and form a point with his index finger sticking out and all the other fingers balled into a fist (Shaping). Then strongly reinforce him for pointing. Do this throughout eating breakfast, offering lots of opportunities to practice skills (Repetition). Remember: make it fun and playful.

(This same scenario applies to lunch and dinner.)

Josh plays

Breakfast is over and it's playtime—an environment ripe for teaching all sorts of skills. There are two different types of "play." There's free-time, toddler self-directed play while you are doing something else (like making breakfast), and there's playtime where your goal is to practice emerging skills. We're describing the latter here.

While Josh is playing, you get down on the floor near him or next to him (depending on sensory issues). You don't try teaching anything without being right there with him (for instance, you don't teach while you're standing a few feet away, or talking on the phone, or sitting in a chair reading or writing out bills.) Whenever your goal is to teach, you give your child your undivided attention. While you're together in this teaching-learning time, you let the telephone call go to voicemail. You're not getting up in the middle of the interaction to check something on the stove, or to put the laundry into the dryer. It's Josh time.

You and your family have obligations; there may be other kids in the family who need attention, and/or you may hold a part-time job. Incorporate your early intervention strategies into your day as much as possible, but don't beat yourself up if you seem to be doing less one day, or your neighbor is spending eight hours a day "teaching" and you can only find three hours. It's your child, and your family. Focus on "engagement" rather than "teaching." Keep him in the here and now. And, don't forget that Josh is a little child. He needs time to be a two-year-old and engage in independent self-directed play. This is extremely age appropriate, and gives you, the adult, time you need to do chores, run the house, make meals, etc. Don't try to make all day "therapy." That's not effective for anyone.

During your together play times, watch what Josh is doing and take his lead (Rapport building/Behavioral momentum). If he picks up a truck, pick up another truck and show him what to do with it. You may say, "Josh, look", and push the truck back and forth on the floor and say, "brrrooom, brrrooom." Then encourage Josh to do the same thing. If he doesn't do it, then prompt him (again using a physical, gestural, or locational prompt). Try to keep him doing this one activity as long as you can. Build a track, put the truck on the track and push it and make the sound "brrrooom" again. Don't force him to stay involved. Keep him involved by making the encounter fun and playful. When his attention clearly shifts to something else, you shift also. Over time, his attention span will increase for longer periods of time. In the beginning, however, a single activity may only last a minute or two. Let that be okay for now. Start small and work up to longer periods of interactive play.

Encourage him to repeat actions (Cue) and prompt him to do it, if he does not (again using a physical, gestural, or locational prompt). Keep your language simple, and match your "excitement" level to him and his personality and personal make-up. For instance, if your child is sound sensitive, your loud squeals of laughter or high-pitched vocalizations as play continues may result in irritability and tension in the child. Always watch his reactions and stay alert for signs of sensory overload. He may not like you running the truck up his arm or down his leg—something you think is "fun," but is anything-but for him. Watch closely and take his lead, not just in the activity itself, but in the tone and manner of your playfulness, too.

As truck playing happens over and over and Josh stays more engaged, add more complex steps. If you started with just pushing the truck back and forth, next try pushing it with a sound, then pushing it on a track, then having it go around the track and eventually, stopping to pick something up (Chaining).

If Josh moves to another activity, move with him. If he picks up a baby doll by the head and begins to shake it, prompt him to hold it the correct way, again using a physical, gestural, or locational prompt (Shaping). Then reinforce with praise, a tickle, a brief tummy-rub

(Reinforcement), if that's pleasurable to him. Repeat this with all the toys he picks up and plays with during this time (Repetition).

If there is a brother or sister at home, you may include them in the activity too. Show Josh how to play appropriately with another child (Modeling). This is also a great opportunity to teach turn-taking and joint attention skills. Teach turn-taking by having Josh give his sibling a toy and then the sibling gives it back. Praise them both for appropriate sharing (Play). Further help a child who is a visual learner by using a turn-taking card during the interaction. Verbal instructions may be too difficult for this child to process while at the same time requesting him to engage in physical activity. Many children with ASD are mono-channel learners: they can absorb what they see or what they hear, but struggle with having to do both at the same time.

Teach joint attention skills by prompting Josh (using a positional or gestural prompt) to watch what his sibling is doing. If he begins to imitate the skill, heavily reinforce him for modeling that skill (Play).

Playtime is usually more successful when done in shorter segments of time, more often throughout the day, than trying to engage the young child in longer sessions. Toddler attention spans are short. Go with the flow and watch for signs the child is tiring or losing interest. Follow his lead—don't force "play" because it fits your schedule to do so from 11:00 to 11:30 a.m. or your goal for this interaction is a 30-minute play session. Stay flexible; it's not on your time, it's on *his* time. Have a plan, but be comfortable with it shifting and changing. Follow your child's lead, knowing when to push a little, and when to back off.

Josh & Mom go to the Mall (or the Store)

It's time to go to the mall. Prepare Josh by giving him a verbal warning, "We are going in the car in five minutes." If needed, also use a visual cue, perhaps a photo of your family car. Time is an abstract concept that doesn't have much meaning to the concrete thinking mind of the child with ASD. A visual timer helps (a product called a Time-Timer is great; easy to find online). Set the timer for five minutes and when it goes off, say "It's time to go." Kids with ASD are generally rule-bound also. If you say "five minutes" be prepared to go in five minutes, not ten or fifteen minutes. Teach your child he can rely on your word; it will help him maintain control as he faces uncomfortable situations. He knows he can trust what you tell him will happen.

Show him a picture of the mall or the store (cut from a magazine, or a photo of the store front you took with your digital camera and printed out on your computer). He could hold this visual card all the way to the mall. Once at the mall, he goes into his stroller and you explain to him what you are going to do. Give him a concrete way of understanding what is going to happen (again, pictures work well in addition to verbal conversation). First we are going to Sears to get pants (give him a card), then to Old Navy to return a shirt (give him another card), then to Champs to get new shoes (a third card), then to lunch at McDonalds—something he really enjoys (another card). This is his reinforcement for getting through the other things that may be less appealing to him. Then give him a home card to signal the end of the outing. Let him know (again, in a concrete way) when each chore is done and how many more you may have to finish. You might do this by giving him the set of photos that represent each store, either in a photo binder, or use individual cards and put each one into a pouch as they are done.

Know your child's patterns of behavior well enough to know how long he can "survive" in a sensory-intensive setting like the mall or the grocery store before he needs a break. Watch for signs of impending overload (squirming, making faces, crying, etc.) You may not be able to make it through all your chores without a break—retreat to a quiet part of the mall, away from people, noise, etc. Have a favorite toy or a book to read until the child regains calm. Then show him the next card and complete the list of things to do. Be able to distinguish between the child being *unable* to tolerate his environment any longer (sensory issues can cause real pain in some kids), in which case your response is to exit and go home, leaving the rest of the chores for another day, and the child getting fussy because he's hungry or getting tired or just doesn't want to be there anymore. He may have autism but he'll also be going through the terrible twos and the troublesome threes in his behavior development. Know your child; become that behavior detective we've talked about so often.

Perhaps your route takes you by McDonalds, before it's time for that lunch stop (next time, can you work out a better route so this doesn't happen?). Josh begins to scream. He wants to go there "now" and you have two more stops before lunch. What to do? Initially, you need to ignore his behavior (Extinction). YOU DON'T IGNORE HIM. Tell him you have two more things to do, show him the cards left, and then you will be going to McDonalds. If he continues to scream, DO NOT GO TO McDONALDS. If you do, you teach him that screaming gets him what he wants. Next time he'll scream again. Sooner. Louder. Try to finish what you are doing and watch for any signs of appropriate behavior. Ignore the screaming and catch him when he is quiet, praising him immediately or, better yet, pull out of your bag (advance planning) a preferred reinforcer (a favorite toy or bit of some food he loves) to give him. *Do not* give him this reinforcer as a "bribe" to stop crying, or pull it out while he's crying and say "Look what I've got for you if you stop crying." Only give it to him to reward his acceptable behavior—that means when he *exhibits* that acceptable behavior, not before. His tantrum will stop. If he starts up again, remove the favorite toy and do not praise him or give him food until he is quiet. Once he is quiet (which will happen) praise him (Reinforcement) and let him know how many things are left to complete prior to going to McDonalds. Stay calm!

While at McDonalds, practice choices, communication, staying seated, etc., just like at breakfast. Remember to bring any visual cards you need so your child can be successful during interactions. (See how handy that visual camera can be? Snap pictures of fries, a Happy Meal, a hamburger, etc. for next time!)

One last bit of advice about going out into the community: remember your child is a child, and he's a child with ASD. He doesn't understand much about his world and he's relying on you to teach him, protect him and keep him safe. Sensory issues can rear their ugly heads at any point and make the environment feel unsafe (and even hurtful) for your child. Please do not force the child to suffer situations because you want to do "just one more thing" before heading for home. Know when your child is able to handle environments like the mall or a busy store, and when he's not. Adapt *your* plans accordingly, because he's not capable of adapting his or her functioning. *Not yet.* If you insist on going grocery shopping at 4:30 on Thursday afternoon, when you know the store is busy and check-out lines will be long, don't be surprised if you end up having to deal with behavior problems. If you're carting him off to your hair appointment at 1:00 p.m., and that's right in the middle of his nap time, expect challenges. Plan ahead wisely, with your child's level of functioning in mind, and always have an exit strategy. Again, at this stage, it's about *his* time, not *your* time.

Josh takes a nap

You're back from the mall and lunch at McDonalds. Once home it is time for a nap. Try to do this the same time every day (including weekends!). Have a routine for nap time, which you follow the same way, every day. As his parent, you decide it's nap time. Don't ask Josh if he'd like to take a nap—you risk him saying "no." Choices are good, but *don't offer a choice if you're not prepared to accept either response.*

Instead, you'll say: "Josh, it's nap time" (Cue) and then initiate the nap routine. Read Josh a book (provide a choice here), having him point to certain things in the book you ask him to touch. "Look Josh, that's a flower (Labeling); point to the flower." "What is that?" Have Josh say what it is or, if he does not say it, have him point to it, and say "That's a flower." Start with pointing to/labeling something you know Josh knows and you know he will respond to correctly. This builds interest and self-esteem. Then introduce things that may be tougher or something new you are teaching or talking about for the first time (Behavioral Momentum). Always praise appropriate behavior (Reinforcement).

Remainder of the day

Engage in more play sessions, practicing skills and communication. Label as many things in the environment as you can throughout the day. "Look Josh, this is a spoon." "Look Josh, this is a fork." "Look Josh, this is a chair." Then ask him, "Where is the chair?" If he responds, praise him (Reinforcement). If he does not, prompt him (again using a physical, gestural, or locational prompt), then praise him.

As mentioned above, look closely when you're waiting for a response from your child; sometimes it is slight, easy to miss. Furthermore, the child may need time to mentally process your request, and time to formulate a response. Be patient. Don't jump in two seconds after your request or command. Allow time for him to respond. By watching for even a hint of the correct response, especially at first, you'll find things to constantly reinforce in the child. This provides motivation for him (and you!) to keep going.

Always encourage communication skills. If he takes your hand and leads you to the refrigerator, then stands there, ask him what he wants. Open the door and have him choose something, then say, "That's milk. What is that?" If he responds with verbal language, praise it (Reinforcement); if he does not, prompt him to point at it, and then repeat it until he does it independently (Repetition). Keep in mind you're developing a communication system for your child; you are not concentrating only on language. That's why you continually incorporate visual cards into your interaction. There will be times when your child is tired, or frustrated, or sick, and his language may not be easily retrievable. Or he may be predominantly nonverbal at this point. You want to teach your child multiple ways to communicate, not just with words. Show him the spot where he can always find the visual cards (keep them together in a binder or box) so eventually the child learns he can get the card and bring it to you to communicate his desire for something to drink or eat if his words fail him. Contrary to popular belief, the use of visual cards does NOT impede language development. It actually enhances it. Your goal is not to fade out visual tools entirely. You want the child to have a communication system with several different communication modes.

Set up as many situations as you can for him to use his language (Repetition). Start by using a highly reinforcing item (a favorite food, for instance). Josh loves goldfish crackers. Instead of giving him a bowl of them, make him request each one, praising him each time he communicates by giving him one cracker (Reinforcement). Repeat this process all through the day, with anything and everything he does. If he uses his language spontaneously, he should get the "ultimate" reinforcer. This is something you give him *only* when he's displayed some skill independently you're working on (like language). It might be a brand new toy or a special food or drink he doesn't get any other time, or a favorite video. Let me repeat this: He doesn't have access to this item at any other time. This item is highly motivating for the child and you use it to encourage as much communication usage as possible.

Also, keep him engaged as much as possible. If he is watching TV or a video, sit with him every once in a while and discuss what is on. Have him use his communication skills, or point.

You may hear you need to do 20-40 hours of "teaching" per week, and you might be overwhelmed before you even start. Your goal is 20-40 hours of *engagement*, not necessarily that many hours of direct instruction. Engagement time can happen throughout the day. It's time you work together at breakfast, during playtime, it's the time at the mall, the birthday party, time with grandparents, etc. It's all the time you keep your child engaged in the here and now, not letting him escape into perseverative behaviors. Putting him down in front of a video to watch by himself is not engaged time. Sitting down to watch the video with him, with conversation or questions between you—that's engaged time. It's not difficult at all to rack up 20-40 hours of engagement each week.

Josh goes to bed

After dinner—handled just like breakfast (Repetition)—it's time to go to bed. Again, establish a routine. Do the routine the same way, as much as possible. Josh has to take a bath, then brush his teeth, then it's story time, then bed. Use a picture schedule of the night time routine (Chaining). It might contain a picture of the bathtub, tooth brushing, reading a story, and then bed. After each activity is over, have him turn the picture over or put it in a "finished" bin. Remember to reinforce him for completion of each step (Reinforcement). Within that broad bedtime routine, you can have smaller sub-routines, such as teaching Josh to put on his PJs, say goodnight to daddy or mommy, etc.

Over and Over Again

The next day you begin the same procedures all over again (Repetition). Consistency and predictability are key. Follow your plan day to day, and use the same basic strategies over and over. If you do, Josh will become more communicative and independent, while gaining great play skills—all the building blocks to success in a school program and in life!

A note on visual schedules and visual cards

Visual strategies work well with children with ASD. There are excellent books that address this teaching technique and many websites that offer ready-made picture cards you can use. What's important is to make schedules and use them!

Start by having a large, kid-friendly visual schedule that shows the main segments of the day: waking up, breakfast, playtime, errands, lunch, nap time, dinner, bedtime, etc. Use pictures at the level the child can understand. If your child is severely impaired, you might use tangible objects (small items used in doll houses work well) instead of photographs or line drawings. Couple the picture with labels so your child starts associating pictures and words. For some kids with ASD, this association is difficult and comes only with time and teaching.

Put the schedule on the wall where it can easily be seen and use it regularly with the child. Take the child to the schedule, point to what is about to happen, then begin the activity. You might have a duplicate image the child can take with him to the setting or attach the object or picture cards to the schedule with Velcro, so you can peel them off and take them to the activity site. This helps the child make the connection between the visual cue and the activity itself. Don't assume your child can naturally make this connection. For instance, a picture of the kitchen table may represent meal time. At breakfast, take the picture of the table to the table so the child learns they represent the same thing.

After breakfast, return the card to the schedule and move to the next activity. Children with ASD thrive on routine and structure. Visual schedules can be made for any activity in which the child struggles with understanding how parts relate to a whole. Make visual strips to help him follow steps and achieve success—everything from brushing his teeth to getting dressed to teaching simple daily life activities like setting the table.

But also remember home is home. In theory you may buy into the idea of visual schedules, but on a practical level, you're overwhelmed and they don't get used. Don't bite off more than you can chew. If you're not going to consistently use all those schedules throughout the day, take them down, and start simpler. Select one small routine, like meal time or nap time, and use a visual routine for that. Use it well and when you see it works, you'll be reinforced (both of you!). That, in turn, will motivate you to use it again, or perhaps use it with another routine. It works there too. You're further reinforced. Before you know it, you're using that daily routine and lots of subroutines easily and smoothly. Just remember: If you're not being reinforced by using a visual schedule, neither will your child. It's better to use one small routine and achieve success, than be overwhelmed by the idea in general and use it ineffectively. Pace yourself. Success will be your motivation to go back and do more.

Appendix B

Sample IFSP for a Child with ASD

The document that follows represents a sample Individual Family Services Plan for a child with ASD. It includes goals and objectives that should be addressed as part of every IFSP for a spectrum child. If the child has already mastered some of the skills suggested, others should be added based on the developmental level of the child. Additional goals should be determined by assessments completed, parent interviews, and observations. While this is only a sample IFSP, the goals and objectives included are critical for every child with ASD.

How to read this document

Section: describes the Goal area being targeted.

Using: specifies the mode of communication the child is using. This is usually a combination of functional communication skills.

Objectives: statements that describe the individual skills being worked on with the child. Notice that skills are listed in order of mastery, from simple to more complex, and that in some cases, a new skill builds on the previous skill learned.

Criterion: indicates the measurement of success for each individual program. The criteria are established by the IFSP team and can be modified as needed. For example, looking at the first example below, the criterion checked means the child would have to perform the skill 85% of the time, spontaneously, without prompting, at age-appropriate levels for the objective to be considered mastered.

Evaluation Procedures: specifies the data collection methods that will be used to judge the criterion. Each child is different, so the Criterion and the Evaluation Procedures will change depending on their individual needs.

EARLY INTERVENTION

CHILD: _____

SECTION: _____ ATTENDING/LEARNING READINESS _____

USING: ☐ Verbal   ☐ Augmentative Communicator
                              (PECS, Voice Output Device)

        ☐ Gestural   ☐ Signing

OBJECTIVES:	Initiated Date	Completed Date
Eye contact in response to name: *Cue "Name"*	_____	_____
Seats self when directed/sits appropriately: *Cue "Get ready"*	_____	_____
Eye contact with materials	_____	_____
Tracks up/down/left/right	_____	_____
Joint attention	_____	_____

CRITERION:
☐ 75% accuracy
☒ 85% accuracy
☒ Self-initiation/spontaneous
☒ Age appropriate levels
☐ 90% reduction
☐ Elimination
☐ Other:

EVALUATION PROCEDURES:
☒ Daily Data Collection
☐ Pre-post tests
☒ Observation
☒ Anecdotal reporting
☒ Progress reports
☐ Other:

EARLY INTERVENTION

Page 2-A

CHILD: _____

SECTION: _____ SPEECH COMMUNICATION _____

USING: ☐ Verbal ☐ Augmentative Communicator
(PECS, Voice Output Device)

☐ Gestural ☐ Signing

OBJECTIVES:	Initiated Date	Completed Date
Gross motor imitation	_____	_____
Nonverbal imitation	_____	_____
Fine motor imitation	_____	_____
Facial movements	_____	_____
Verbal imitation (sound/word)	_____	_____
Pointing response	_____	_____
Pointing for retrieval	_____	_____
Spontaneous use of communication	_____	_____
Communicates desires (help/more/open)	_____	_____
Student initiates requests *Cue "Write" – response "I need a crayon," Cue "Sit" – response "I need a chair"*	_____	_____
Yes/No desires	_____	_____

CRITERION:
☐ 75% accuracy
☒ 85% accuracy
☒ Self-initiation/spontaneous
☒ Age appropriate levels
☐ 90% reduction
☐ Elimination
☐ Other:

EVALUATION PROCEDURES:
☒ Daily Data Collection
☐ Pre-post tests
☒ Observation
☒ Anecdotal reporting
☒ Progress reports
☐ Other:

EARLY INTERVENTION

Page 3-A

CHILD: _____

SECTION: _____ EXPRESSIVE LANGUAGE _____

USING: ☐ Verbal   ☐ Augmentative Communicator
                         (PECS, Voice Output Device)

        ☐ Gestural   ☐ Signing

OBJECTIVES:	Initiated Date	Completed Date
Family Identification	_____	_____
Identification of objects (clothes, food)	_____	_____
Function of objects	_____	_____
Verbal labeling	_____	_____
Social questions	_____	_____
Identifies pictures in books	_____	_____

CRITERION:
- ☐ 75% accuracy
- ☒ 85% accuracy
- ☒ Self-initiation/spontaneous
- ☒ Age appropriate levels
- ☐ 90% reduction
- ☐ Elimination
- ☐ Other:

EVALUATION PROCEDURES:
- ☒ Daily Data Collection
- ☐ Pre-post tests
- ☒ Observation
- ☒ Anecdotal reporting
- ☒ Progress reports
- ☐ Other:

EARLY INTERVENTION

Page 4-A

CHILD: _____

SECTION: _____ RECEPTIVE LANGUAGE _____

USING: ☐ Verbal   ☐ Augmentative Communicator
(PECS, Voice Output Device)

☐ Gestural   ☐ Signing

OBJECTIVES:	Initiated Date	Completed Date

Family Identification

Identification of objects (clothes, food)

Function of objects

Verbal labeling

Social questions *(work on both expressive and receptive ability)*

Social Reciprocation

Greetings *(Responds with wave/verbalizes "hi" or "hello")*

Body parts

Function of body parts *(what do you do with?)*

Identification of rooms *(home program, pictures and the house)*

Advanced – Basic categorizing, missing part of an item

CRITERION:
☐ 75% accuracy
☒ 85% accuracy
☒ Self-initiation/spontaneous
☒ Age appropriate levels
☐ 90% reduction
☐ Elimination
☐ Other:

EVALUATION PROCEDURES:
☒ Daily Data Collection
☐ Pre-post tests
☒ Observation
☒ Anecdotal reporting
☒ Progress reports
☐ Other:

EARLY INTERVENTION

Page 5-A

CHILD: _____

SECTION: _____ COGNITIVE/PRE-ACADEMIC

USING: ☐ Verbal   ☐ Augmentative Communicator
                                      (PECS, Voice Output Device)

        ☐ Gestural   ☐ Signing

OBJECTIVES:	Initiated Date	Completed Date
Visual tracking	_____	_____
Functional object manipulation *(zipper, hair brush, socks, stir spoon in bowl, push car etc.)*	_____	_____
Object permanence *(begin with highly desirable item)*	_____	_____
Initiates actions with objects *(Cue "Do this")*	_____	_____
Object general association *(juice/cup – hand/mitten)*	_____	_____
Matching *(object to object/object to picture)*	_____	_____
Sorting	_____	_____

CRITERION:
☐ 75% accuracy
☒ 85% accuracy
☒ Self-initiation/spontaneous
☒ Age appropriate levels
☐ 90% reduction
☐ Elimination
☐ Other:

EVALUATION PROCEDURES:
☒ Daily Data Collection
☐ Pre-post tests
☒ Observation
☒ Anecdotal reporting
☒ Progress reports
☐ Other:

EARLY INTERVENTION

Page 6-A

CHILD: _____

SECTION: _____ SOCIAL SKILLS _____

USING: ☐ Verbal ☐ Augmentative Communicator
(PECS, Voice Output Device)

☐ Gestural ☐ Signing

	Initiated Date	Completed Date
OBJECTIVES:		
Turn taking	_____	_____
Joint attention	_____	_____

Note: this list may seem short, yet these are the two most important social skills for a child to learn. Our goal for the EI child is learning to play; it's the child's medium for further learning opportunities. Many other skills overlap with social skills, especially those that are really language skills (for instance, asking a child to play, requesting assistance, etc).

CRITERION:	**EVALUATION PROCEDURES:**
☐ 75% accuracy	☒ Daily Data Collection
☒ 85% accuracy	☐ Pre-post tests
☒ Self-initiation/spontaneous	☒ Observation
☒ Age appropriate levels	☒ Anecdotal reporting
☐ 90% reduction	☒ Progress reports
☐ Elimination	☐ Other:
☐ Other:	

EARLY INTERVENTION

CHILD: _____

SECTION: _____ PLAY SKILLS _____

USING: ☐ Verbal   ☐ Augmentative Communicator
                              (PECS, Voice Output Device)

        ☐ Gestural   ☐ Signing

OBJECTIVES:	Initiated Date	Completed Date
(Work on same time you work on attending skills)		
Isolated toy play (Beads/Pegs, Ring/Shaper, Stacker/Sorter)	_____	_____
Symbolic toy play	_____	_____
Pretending (eating/crying/sleeping/talking on the phone)	_____	_____
Turns pages in a book	_____	_____

CRITERION:
☐ 75% accuracy
☒ 85% accuracy
☒ Self-initiation/spontaneous
☒ Age appropriate levels
☐ 90% reduction
☐ Elimination
☐ Other:

EVALUATION PROCEDURES:
☒ Daily Data Collection
☐ Pre-post tests
☒ Observation
☒ Anecdotal reporting
☒ Progress reports
☐ Other:

EARLY INTERVENTION

Page 8-A

CHILD: _____

SECTION: _____ FINE MOTOR _____

USING: ☐ Verbal   ☐ Augmentative Communicator
                              (PECS, Voice Output Device)

        ☐ Gestural   ☐ Signing

	Initiated Date	Completed Date
OBJECTIVES:		
Scribble	_____	_____
Coloring	_____	_____

CRITERION:
☐ 75% accuracy
☒ 85% accuracy
☒ Self-initiation/spontaneous
☒ Age appropriate levels
☐ 90% reduction
☐ Elimination
☐ Other:

EVALUATION PROCEDURES:
☒ Daily Data Collection
☐ Pre-post tests
☒ Observation
☒ Anecdotal reporting
☒ Progress reports
☐ Other:

EARLY INTERVENTION

CHILD: _____

SECTION: _____ SELF HELP _____

USING: ☐ Verbal   ☐ Augmentative Communicator
                              (PECS, Voice Output Device)

        ☐ Gestural   ☐ Signing

OBJECTIVES:	Initiated Date	Completed Date
Washes hands		
Dries hands		
Brushes teeth		
Uses fork/spoon (attempts)		
Removes socks/shoes		
Lowers pants/pull-up to toilet train		
Sits on toilet		

Note: most typical kids do not master these skills, or even begin work on them, until later. Kids with ASD need a head start to learning and therefore, these skills are included here, but with the idea that mastery is not expected at this early age. Create opportunities for practice and keep these in mind as longer-term objectives to work towards.

CRITERION:
☐ 75% accuracy
☒ 85% accuracy
☒ Self-initiation/spontaneous
☒ Age appropriate levels
☐ 90% reduction
☐ Elimination
☐ Other:

EVALUATION PROCEDURES:
☒ Daily Data Collection
☐ Pre-post tests
☒ Observation
☒ Anecdotal reporting
☒ Progress reports
☐ Other:

EARLY INTERVENTION

Page 10-A

CHILD: _____

SECTION: _____ BEHAVIORS _____

USING: ☐ Verbal   ☐ Augmentative Communicator
                              (PECS, Voice Output Device)

        ☐ Gestural   ☐ Signing

OBJECTIVES: *Initiated Date*   *Completed Date*

Hand play
(redirect hands during work time – keep hands busy;
down time – squishy ball/tubes/Silly Putty)   _____   _____

Reinforce when hands are quiet   _____   _____

CRITERION:
☐ 75% accuracy
☒ 85% accuracy
☒ Self-initiation/spontaneous
☒ Age appropriate levels
☐ 90% reduction
☐ Elimination
☐ Other:

EVALUATION PROCEDURES:
☒ Daily Data Collection
☐ Pre-post tests
☒ Observation
☒ Anecdotal reporting
☒ Progress reports
☐ Other:

EARLY INTERVENTION

CHILD: _____

SECTION: _____ OTHER ACTIVITIES DURING SESSIONS _____

USING: ☐ Verbal   ☐ Augmentative Communicator
                              (PECS, Voice Output Device)

          ☐ Gestural   ☐ Signing

OBJECTIVES:

	Initiated Date	*Completed Date*
Lots of singing	_____	_____
Read books	_____	_____
Scripting with toys	_____	_____

Scripting with toys
*(ex: Child is not quite ready for pretend play
with toys) Pull out farm—give yourself & child
an animal & promote imitation with animal—
walk cow to hay; or with doll house walk doll
upstairs and lay on bed)*

Include Mom/Dad/siblings once you
have established learning readiness
skills and child understands concepts
of reinforcement _____ _____

CRITERION:	**EVALUATION PROCEDURES:**
☐ 75% accuracy	☒ Daily Data Collection
☒ 85% accuracy	☐ Pre-post tests
☒ Self-initiation/spontaneous	☒ Observation
☒ Age appropriate levels	☒ Anecdotal reporting
☐ 90% reduction	☒ Progress reports
☐ Elimination	☐ Other:
☐ Other:	

Appendix C

Toilet Training ... Is Your Child Ready?

By Connie Marks

PARENTS OF CHILDREN WITH AUTISM, ESPECIALLY OF KIDS WITH MORE SEVERE challenges in language and sensory issues, often fret about embarking on toilet training. Questions about how to do it and when to start it are often combined with anxiety about whether or not the outcome will be successful. While children are developing in personality and behavior, they are also changing physically, so it's important to remember the differences among children and to try not to compare your child with a sibling, a niece or nephew, or the little boy across the street. Your child's ability to be toilet trained will depend on his own stages of readiness and the skills he has acquired that enable him to perform toileting functions. His success involves not only learned skills, but also developmental abilities, like muscle control.

The other half of the toilet training experience is the parent; they need to be prepared as well. If your child is in school, his teacher will also need to be ready, willing and able to be part of the process. It takes time and energy to begin potty training, and it is not always easy. Above all, it requires consistency. However, with a little hard work from all parties involved, it can be done. Having an independent, happy child is well worth the effort. If you and your child are ready, then it is time to begin.

Signs that your Child is Ready to begin a Toilet Training program

- Stays dry for longer periods of time

- Relationship between consuming fluids and when urination occurs
- Shows visible signs of urinating or having a bowel movement (squatting, pulling at pants, touching themselves, crossing legs)
- Shows interest or difference in behavior in response to seeing other people involved in toileting activities
- Ability to sit for about five minutes during an activity
- Can pull pants up and down with assistance
- Understands simple directions (example, sit down or stand up)

What You Need

- NO potty seats—Use regular toilet seat with insert
- Charts (used to gather data on his voiding patterns)
- Reinforcers
- Training pants or kids' underwear
- Time and Patience

If you are training someone who needs special adaptive equipment to stay on the toilet comfortably, consult with a Physical Therapist or an Occupational Therapist about these special needs before starting the program.

First, gather data about your child's voiding patterns. Set up a chart in half hour increments and record data for at least one full week. Make sure the school uses the same chart so you have a reliable picture reflecting morning, afternoon, evening and nighttime patterns. Record timing, frequency and conditions. Note how long he can stay dry. Keep this data chart going through the entire toilet training program; it will provide you with valuable information not only in designing the program, but also in better understanding the successes and mistakes that occur. Consult with your health care provider and rule out any organic causes that would sabotage your child's progress. They are rare, but some do exist.

A reinforcer is something the child likes or enjoys that, when given, will increase the likelihood of that behavior happening again.

Reinforcers can be verbal praise, food, candy, drinks, toys, books and videos, computer games, or play. Making up a short, snappy tune with a lot of clapping and cheering may help get your child excited about the whole idea. Whatever you select, make sure it is used for potty training *only* and cannot be obtained at other times of the day. For example, if your child really enjoys a particular video, only allow its viewing after a successful toileting episode. This is one of the most important elements of potty training. Without good reinforcement to motivate your child, your attempts may be unsuccessful.

Methods of Training

For some children, buying a potty video or child's potty book is all that is needed. However, most children need more guidance. Outlined here are three methods of potty training: potty day, picture schedules and token systems. Read the following three methods to decide which to use for your child.

1. Potty Day

Before you start, make a chart to track your child's urination patterns, this will help to determine how long your child is staying dry, and also when urination is most likely to occur. You must be able to arrange a fair amount of time with your child to do nothing else but potty training. It is helpful to have two or even three people available to help. Give your child plenty of liquids. This will encourage urination which will increase the opportunities to reward successful attempts. Place him on the potty from the first waking moment for about three to five minutes. Make this a fun time. Read stories, blow bubbles or play games. Use your data chart to gauge how frequently to put him back on the potty. If he is staying dry between sittings on the potty, expand the time gradually by a set increment of minutes. If there is an accident, lessen the time between potty sittings to the previous amount of free time where he remained successful. After a few hours, if successful, you may want to put training pants on your child.

2. Picture Schedules

Start by charting your child's urination to determine how long she is staying dry and when she is urinating. Next, take pictures that will become the basis of your schedule: pictures of reinforcers that your child likes and pictures of the act that earns them. In this case you might take pictures of urinating, having a bowel movement, sitting on the toilet, washing his hands, flushing, or just being in the bathroom. If your child won't do this, have a sibling go through the motions to get the shots. Place the pictures in a visible and neutral place, like the bathroom door; make sure they're at your child's eye level. The first picture should be of a task the child already knows how to do. Gradually add in the pictures of the more difficult tasks for your child.

3. Token System

Chart your child's urination using a "Potty Chart," and then decide on the token system. For instance, your child could earn an M&M every time he uses the potty or your child may earn a star every time he goes potty and after two stars, he earns an M&M. Remember to use a token chart so the child can visually see when he will earn the reinforcement. As the child makes progress, expand the chart so he has to do three things to earn the reinforcement, then four, etc. You may need to start using the token system for just part of the process, i.e. urinating in the toilet. When he has this part down, you can then use the chart with other skills, such as hand washing.

100 Toilet Training Tips

1. Before you begin, understand that a child with autism/PDD-NOS may have a few extra obstacles between him or her and dry pants. All the characteristics that identify the child as having autism may well interfere with "normal" toilet training.

2. Many children with autism will resist the idea of toilet training just because it is YOUR idea.

3.   Children with autism may have difficulty understanding and associating words with actions; most will need—at a minimum— more time to process what you say.

4.   Insistence on routine, sameness, repetitive actions/interests. Children with autism will probably find it distressing to include toileting in their already full schedule. Repetitive behaviors, self-stimulation, and insistence on following their own routine will certainly interfere with *your* new idea. Of course, once toileting is established as part of the routine, this insistence may work to your benefit!

5.   Break the toilet training program into parts your child can handle. For instance, go to bathroom and close the door, undressing, toileting, dressing, washing hands, exiting the bathroom.

6.   The chronological age of a child is an important consideration when determining readiness for toilet training. Don't begin before 18 months of age. Once a child is beyond four years of age, toilet training should become a priority.

7.   Teach using the toilet as an entire routine involving preparation and activities needed for completion, rather than just sitting on the toilet.

8.   Use Social Stories (Carol Gray) to teach skills and manners related to toilet training.

9.   Help support educators' efforts during your toilet training program; send extra diapers, extra clothes, a copy of his visual schedule, etc.

10.   Communicate information to your child's teacher that may impact his toilet training program: unusual foods ingested or new medications.

11.   Constipation may occur because kids love carbohydrates; add more fruits and vegetables to his diet.

12.   Apple juice every day will avoid constipation. Apple juice will prevent the constipation that often starts this cycle.

13. Sometimes medication can help if your child suffers from constipation or wets either at night or during the day. Your own pediatrician can advise you about this.

14. Cover your strip of visual cues with plastic so it doesn't get wet, if you're posting them near the sink.

15. Use lots of reminders. Use a chart to help you estimate when they might need to go and remind them at those times.

16. Be sure that toilet training includes clearly teaching your child how to begin and end the toilet training routine. Use visual cues and structures to facilitate understanding and independence.

17. Schedule a relaxing or low stimulation activity just before scheduled toilet times so your child is more relaxed before starting the toilet training routine.

18. Is your child using too much toilet paper? Teach her to count out a specific number of sheets, or place a mark along the wall, several inches below the roll, then teach her to unroll the paper until the end touches the mark, then tear it off.

19. If your child gets sick during training, all bets are off. Delay the routine and start again once he's well.

20. Keep mini M&Ms, Goldfish, or whatever your reinforcer of choice is, available in the bathroom.

21. Use simple, concrete directives: "Don't pee on the floor. Pee in the toilet."

22. Nighttime training should be considered only after the child develops a reasonable degree of independence with daytime toileting.

23. If your child wakes up at night and is wet, set a timer to wake him about fifteen minutes before the time he usually wakes up during the night. When he wakes up, take him to the bathroom.

24. Eliminating in the toilet is one of the few tasks that you do NOT want the anxious child to focus on. Give her something else to

focus attention on, such as a book or a toy. The more she thinks about eliminating, the more difficult it will be.

25. *Relax* – Toilet training is hard work but don't make it worse by stressing out on it.

26. Think twice about using food as a reinforcer, as it may not be that enticing after a meal.

27. Choose a method and stick with it. Give any method at least several weeks to see if it works.

28. Respect your child's feelings and anxieties about the potty and about using it. Undue pressure will only make things worse.

29. Be a model. Children learn from example. If it is comfortable for you, provide your child with opportunities to see how the potty is effectively used. Or use siblings to model the correct behaviors for your child.

30. Try to get your child to sit on the toilet with the lid down while he is still wearing diapers; then move on to sitting with the lid up and undressed.

31. Avoid asking if the person needs to use the bathroom when the schedule indicates a toileting time. The cue for Potty is the signal that the toileting routine needs to begin.

32. Some children have real fears about BMs; they think their insides are coming out, or they are losing parts of themselves. If this is the case, go slow. Try explaining the digestive system to the child with visuals of the human body.

33. No punishments and don't nag.

34. Use a positive approach. Stay positive at all times. Pay attention to and look for appropriate behaviors. Remember: staying dry is the target behavior.

35. When you see appropriate behaviors, comment on them and reinforce them with specific verbal praise.

36. If you don't see positive gains in two weeks, rethink your program and look for inconsistencies or errors.

37. Destructive, abusive, or dangerous behaviors may require a consequence, but for most behaviors, start with ignoring them.

38. Require a response. Never ask a child to do anything. Always tell him.

39. Ignore irrelevant speech, vocalizations, giggling, laughing, and actions.

40. Speak slowly, clearly, and specifically. Remember that persons with autism may have difficulty processing what you say.

41. Make sure the child is looking at your face when you are giving specific verbal instructions.

42. Watch your nonliteral speech—it can have unforeseen consequences! Use nouns as nouns, verbs as verbs, and adjectives as adjectives.

43. Do not raise your voice, grab, or threaten the child with consequences. Raising your voice seems like the natural thing to do to get compliance. However, many children are sound sensitive and may just avoid you.

44. Do not allow behavior problems to succeed in escaping demands.

45. Use underpants; they get wet and provide feedback to the child. To help protect the furniture, and maintain good hygiene, try plastic pants worn over the underwear, or plastic padding on the furniture while training takes place.

46. Make sure the bathroom is seen as a relaxing place, and not loaded with tension. Check for any stressors that might influence your child (Bathroom fan? Glaring lights? Texture of the bathroom seat or carpeting/tile? Smells?)

47. If your child reacts negatively to sitting on the toilet, it may be in response to the feel of the cold seat, feeling unstable while on the

toilet, being afraid of the noise from flushing or being afraid of falling into or touching the water.

48. Comfort while sitting on the toilet is essential. Use a stool so their feet are flat on a surface, at right angles to the floor and their back is supported.

49. How much wiping is enough? As a rule of thumb, teach him to wipe three times. This may not be enough at first and the adult present can continue to clean up, if necessary. But as he becomes more adept, three times should be enough.

50. Use flushable targets with boys; it gives them something to aim for when peeing. Cherios work well.

51. Sweat pants on the child for the duration of the toilet training is a better choice of clothes than causing him to have accidents while fumbling with zippers. He needs to be successful when he does the right thing.

52. Some children with autism are panicked by the noise from flushing. To desensitize them to the sound, make a tape recording of the toilet flushing. Play it with the child with the volume turned down low, slowly increasing the sound as the child learns to tolerate it.

53. Put your child's favorite visual stimulation (cartoon character? Poster? Calendar?) on the wall across from the toilet at the right height to enjoy looking at while sitting on the toilet.

54. Once your child has learned to use the toilet properly, don't remove all the visual cues. Change the appearance to simpler visual prompts, or those that are more natural looking.

55. Fade prompts as soon as you can.

56. When on a community outing, or in an unfamiliar setting, immediately look for signs that indicate the location of the restroom. Knowing in advance can help reduce stress if toileting is needed.

57. If your child is confused by restrooms that have multiple stalls (as in schools and public buildings) teach her to access the first open stall door.

58. If your child is too fascinated by flushing the toilet, make sure your picture cue shows not only when to flush, but how many times.

59. Some kids find music relaxing. Why not include that as part of his toileting routine?

60. If you decide to use books or toys to induce relaxation during the toileting routine, make sure these items are not available to the child at any other time of the day.

61. If balance is a problem, have your child turn around and face the tank while sitting on the toilet seat. Rest their arms on the tank.

62. Generally, teach boys to urinate from a seated position first. This way, BMs at the same time are not a risk, and they don't need to focus on "aim." Some boys who can discriminate between the urge to urinate vs defecate can be taught to pee standing up from the beginning.

63. Be careful with picture cues of waste in a toilet. Some individuals with autism may interpret this as meaning that they can have a bowel movement anywhere, as long as they then dispose of the waste in the toilet. Use a picture cue that shows waste being expelled while sitting on the commode.

64. Teach pre-toileting dressing skills first; many involve motor planning skills that need to be in place to manage the dressing/undressing sequence and fastening pants.

65. Never punish accidents; they're part of eventually getting it right.

66. Expect some accidents, but teach your child responsibility for his actions by having him help clean up the mess. If you're down on the floor scrubbing, he should be right there with you, scrubbing too.

67. All caregivers should consistently use the same toilet training methods, including grandmas. Teach them what you are doing and enlist their help and cooperation in a consistent program.

68. When accidents happen, try to remain calm. Clean up with minimal social interaction. As strange as it may sound, the verbal attention can be reinforcing for some children.

69. When your child eliminates in his clothes, after clean-up, read a Social Story that describes the acceptable behavior.

70. Switching between diapers and training pants may confuse and frustrate your child.

71. Get an egg timer so they can see how much time is left sitting on the toilet.

72. Let them pick out several pairs of underwear with their favorite characters on them.

73. Potty training is easier in the summer. Children have less clothing to deal with.

74. Before you start potty training make sure your child can get in and out of her clothing. If she can't, you will need to teach these skills first.

75. If your child is having too much difficulty, and a power struggle is beginning; forego the training for a couple of weeks and then try again.

76. Have a mini celebration each time they are successful. Lots of clapping and cheering helps (unless your child is highly sensitive to noise).

77. Don't take things too seriously. Some children will essentially train themselves with less pressure and stress from you.

78. Don't potty train when there has been a major event; for example, mom is back at work, you moved to a new house, or the child moved to a bigger bed. Any change can add a challenge for them.

79. Remember that potty training is a big step for a child. They have been urinating in those diapers for a long time. Habits don't die easily. Be consistent.

80. If you find something your child loves, it may be the reinforcer you need. Don't let your child satiate on it. If the child has access to his toy whenever he wants then it is no big deal to get it as a reinforcer for going potty.

81. Avoid trying to toilet train someone at night when frequent or regular wetting in the daytime is still a problem.

82. Expect things to take longer than they would with children who do not have autism or learning difficulties.

83. Be careful using perfumed soaps, lotions and wet wipes when completing the toileting routine. Some children are cued by the smell to engage in the related behavior. Smelling the perfume on their hands may prompt them to eliminate outside the bathroom.

84. Your child's autism means they often have great difficulty in understanding the social rules governing our lives—why shouldn't they strip off and have a wee in the middle of the park if they need to? Communicate often with them about proper toileting behaviors.

85. If your child impulsively jumps off the toilet to look at other things in the bathroom, place a small, plastic table over his lap once he sits down. Then give him a few favored toys or activities to play with on the table.

86. Handwashing: use precise directions such as "use one squirt of soap" or "wash for one minute" (use a timer) if you find your child becomes stuck during this part of the sequence or uses it for play.

87. For night training, avoid foods and drinks with caffeine, as this will increase the amount of urine.

88. No consumption of liquids after 6:00 p.m. This will help keep the child dry during the night.

89. If the noise of a blow dryer in public restrooms bothers your child, carry earplugs or moist towelettes with you.

90. Join a support group and meet other parents there who may well have ideas that have worked for them and which might help you. They also really do "know what it's like" and that can be a comfort.

91. Don't be frightened to ask for help, especially with distressing problems like smearing. The fact that there is a problem doesn't mean it's your fault.

92. If wet beds are a big problem, special covers to protect the mattress are available from medical supply stores. Your health care provider may also be able to get other "incontinence aids" to help you keep the washing down to a more reasonable level until the problem improves.

93. Alarms are often effective when used alongside behavior programs. They are special pads that are put under the sheets or in the child's pants. Ask your health care provider for more information. Or contact Star Child Labs, 800.346.7283 about their Sleep-Dry Alarm.

94. Really bad toileting problems are no joke—get support, help, and advice if you need it.

95. If you seek professional advice, you need to be honest about what you can and cannot do. That way the person who is working with you can try to tailor the advice they give to your circumstance. If you are feeling tired or down, or your confidence is at low ebb, try to be honest about this with the professional you're seeing.

96. If your child has a BM in his pants within twenty minutes of exiting the bathroom, make the toilet training experience more relaxing. Longer time on the toilet will not help.

97. Be aware that for some children, the added pressure and weight of a diaper filled with waste can be calming and, therefore, they will resist having a BM in the toilet.

98. For persons who eliminate several times per hour due to a constant intake of food or drink, consider proceeding with training that includes scheduled intake of food and drink.

99. Immediately change wet or soiled underpants so that the child does not become desensitized to the feeling of wetness against his skin.

100. Ideally, the goal of any toilet training program is to develop continence, spontaneous access of toileting facilities, and independent completion of toileting routines.

Troubleshooting

1. If potty training becomes a power struggle see if someone else can do the dirty work for you. Family members or school personnel are sometimes good for this.

2. Go with all or nothing. No more diapers. Give your child natural consequences. If they go in their pants, they clean it up.

3. If your child is trained to urinate but won't have a BM in the potty, you may want to make sure your child does not have a medical problem where it may hurt to have a BM or the BM is too runny. Remember, do not pressure your child. They need to feel comfortable in order to go. Reinforce small steps closer to the desired behavior of having a BM in the potty. Be consistent, and don't let your child backslide because you are in a public place, or you don't have the time. Be firm, loving and—most of all—consistent.

4. If your child doesn't seem to know they are voiding, don't use a pull-up. You can't catch them and wearing a wet diaper may not bother them. Give a lot of reminders and use pictures in the bathroom. Set a timer for every fifteen to thirty minutes to remind your child to think about the potty. You can also try rewarding your child for just going into the bathroom at certain times of the day. This will increase their awareness of making time to go to the bathroom. It will also make you more attentive with reminders and rewards.

5.   Two things that any parent needs in abundance:

*   Patience
*   A sense of humor

Connie Marks has three children; her youngest, Kyle, has autism. She has been working with parents and professionals within the autism community for the past eleven years. She is founder of Autism Support Services, in Santee, CA where she offers a complete product line of autism/AS materials for area residents, including books, videos and information packets. Connie is a Past President of the San Diego Chapter and the East County Chapter of the Autism Society of America, is Vice Chairman of the East Country Special Ed Local Planning Area's Community Advisory Committee and is a member of the Autism Task Force organized through the San Diego County Office of Education, as well as a member of the Children' Hospital and Health Center, San Diego Regionwide Task Force on Oral Health for People with Disabilities.

Reprinted with permission from *Autism Asperger's Digest* magazine July-August 2001 issue. Since 1999, providing real life information to meet the real life challenges of autism spectrum disorders. *www.AutismDigest.com*

Appendix D

Guidelines for Theory & Practice

*Approved July 15, 1993 by the Autism Society of America's
Panel of Professional Advisors*

Prologue

*By David L. Holmes, Ed.D.
Co-Chair, Panel of Professional Advisors*

Throughout the history of the Autism Society of America, parents and professionals have been confounded by conflicting messages regarding what are, versus what are not, appropriate remedial methodologies for children and adults with autism. Frequently we have heard that one person's gateway to heaven is another's slippery slope to hell. Additionally, consumers of theories and practices related to the treatment of autism have been at a disadvantage because they frequently have not been privy to the same information that the promoter(s) has at his or her disposal. In 1995 the Panel of Professional Advisors for the Autism Society of America unanimously agreed to develop a series of guidelines on theories and practices so that consumers of such matters, both parents and professionals, can be forearmed with a set of parameters under which they can better determine associated threats and opportunities and, therefore, make informed decisions. Further, a better educated consumer, the Panel felt, would also help control for the unbridled embracing of unproven notions that may distract the field from developing effective courses of treatment for individuals with autism. The education of consumers notwithstanding, the Panel of Professional Advisors also felt an obligation to abate the flagrant promotion of sometimes harmful and expensive treatments that have no foundation in scientific evidence. The Panel observed a relatively consistent series of events that frequently emerge relative to unsubstantiated theories and/or practices. Those events include initial excitement; interest generated in the popular media; non-replication under controlled conditions; excuses proffered by proponents for non-replication; accusations by proponents against those who voice concern regarding these matters; development of an ardent group of true believers in the matter; and the inevitable distraction of the development of effective treatment(s).

Forearmed with these viewpoints, the panel agreed to establish guidelines for theories and practices, not to discourage the development of new theories or practices, but rather to encourage the professional community to disclose the nature of the theory or practice relative to its history, prospects for the future, and their interest in it. The ultimate objective of these guidelines is to help consumers assess theories and practices in order to make thoughtful decisions when it comes to services for their child(ren) and adult offspring and/or students. The Panel of Professional Advisors, and in turn, the Board of the Autism Society of America, hopes that these guidelines for theories and practices are beneficial to all who employ them.

Guidelines for Theory and Practice

Developed by the Panel of Professional Advisors and approved by the Autism Society of America Board on January 17, 1997.

The following Guidelines were developed to assist people with autism, parents/guardians, practitioners, and advocates in evaluating theories and practices related to autism. The Guidelines will provide such consumers with a set of parameters under which they can better determine the threats and opportunities associated with theories and practices.

Guidelines

In assessing theories and practices, consumers need to ask professionals the following questions:

- Do you adhere to the *Priorities of Professional Conduct* promulgated by ASA?

- What is the purpose of this theory/practice?

- What do I have to do to benefit from the theory/practice, and what are its lasting effects?

- What is the status of this theory/practice relative to controlled (scientific) investigation, and is there a reference list of publications?

- How long must my child be involved in this theory/practice to gain benefit?

- [Is] there any physical or psychological harm that might come to my child as a function of participating in this theory/practice?

- What are the personal costs of time and money that I will have to endure, and will I be able to be reimbursed for these expenses?

- How do I know that the costs for the implementation of this theory/practice are fair and reasonable?

- Are the theoreticians or practitioners competently and appropriately trained and prepared to implement the provisions of the theory or practice, and how is this competence assured?

- What steps will be taken to protect my privacy?

- Are there any legal actions, current or past, against promoters, consumers, or practitioners of the theory/practice?

- How will the effects of this theory/practice be evaluated for my child?

- By choosing this theory/practice, what alternatives (proven/unproven) are not being pursued?

- Does this approach exclude other alternative approaches and does it mesh with my child's total program?

- Which individuals with autism has this theory positively benefited, and under what conditions?

General Conditions

Proponents of theories and practices must inform participants that they are free to participate, free to decline to participate, or withdraw from the treatment; they must explain the foreseeable consequences of declining or withdrawing and they must inform participants of significant factors that may be expected to influence their willingness to participate, such as risks, discomfort, adverse effects or limitations, and confidentiality. They must also explain other aspects of which the prospective participants inquire (see Guidelines above), and they must protect the prospective participants from adverse consequences of declining or withdrawing from participation.

For persons who are legally incapable of giving informed consent, the proponents of theories and practices must provide an appropriate explanation to a guardian and obtain assent from that guardian if substitute consent is permitted by law.

In offering inducements to participate in the theory or practice, proponents must make clear to each participant the nature of the services as well as the risks, obligations, and limitations. Proponents must not offer excessive or inappropriate financial or other such inducements to obtain participation. Proponents must not coerce participation. Proponents must never deceive participants regarding significant aspects that would affect their willingness to engage in or make use of, the theory or practice, such as physical risks, discomfort, unpleasant emotional experiences, and/or financial demands. Theories and practices must not be presented in a misleading or fraudulent manner; either because of what is stated, conveyed or suggested or because of what is omitted concerning research or practice.

Immediate Presentations

Proponents of theories and practices in public lectures, demonstrations, radio or television programs, prerecorded tapes, printed articles, mailed material, or other media forms must ensure that statements are consistent with the *ASA Priorities of Professional Conduct Statement* (July 15, 1993).

Testimonials

Proponents of theories and practices must not solicit testimonials from current consumers or persons who, because of their particular circumstances, are vulnerable to undue influence.

◎   ◎   ◎

COSAC Position Statement on Treatment Recommendations

*(Adopted by the COSAC Board of Trustees on August 20, 2002
Revised on January 24, 2004)*

Since its founding in 1965, COSAC's primary mission has been to ensure that all people with autism receive appropriate, effective services and to enhance the overall awareness of autism in the general public. To attain this goal, COSAC provides information, education, and advocacy services. These services develop, improve, and expand programs for individuals with autism. COSAC is an organization whose members may espouse different philosophies and use various treatment modalities. Because of the diversity of methods that are considered and/or used in the treatment of autism, it is important to clarify COSAC's position regarding the treatment of autism as it pertains to education and other clinical efforts. COSAC does so in order to inform our members, other organizations, government officials, and the greater public.

Those charged with improving the lives of individuals with autism have a complex task in terms of understanding, implementing, and evaluating treatments. While COSAC's primary role is to educate parents and professionals so that they can make independent and informed decisions, COSAC also endorses the use of treatments that are individualized, positive, science-based, and shown to be effective.

Why use science as a guide when deciding upon treatments for children with autism?

Parents and professionals need a framework for decision-making that can provide 1) criteria to choose among interventions and 2) mechanisms to determine progress or lack thereof. Given that treatment should produce measurable skill gains, a system of accountability is essential. Such accountability is easily established when we use the structure and process that science offers.

What is behavioral science?

The scientific process includes testing hypotheses in a controlled manner to identify systematic relationships between an intervention and changes in a person's behavior. Meanwhile, alternative explanations are systematically ruled out based on careful analysis of observational data. In other words, all likely explanations for a change in a person's behavior are explored. It is likely that only one or a few interventions are the actual cause for the change in behavior. For example, if social interactions increase following behavioral treatment, other interventions such as dietary or medication changes also would have to be evaluated as the possible cause of change. Science relies on direct observation and objective measurement of a phenomenon, systematic arrangements of events, procedures to rule out alternative explanations for what is observed, and repeated demonstrations (called replications) by individuals working independently of one another. Good science is not determined by popularity, longevity, or unsubstantiated claims. While no method is guaranteed to predict success, the scientific method does have built-in checks and balances. The scientific method emphasizes objective data, independent replication, and critical peer review. These processes increase the likelihood that the results are valid.

What is the best course of treatment for an individual with autism?

Comprehensive assessment of the individual's abilities and preferences is the cornerstone of designing an intervention package that is most likely to be successful. An assessment provides information that is crucial to determine baseline levels of performance, reasonable criteria for acquiring and mastering goals, and the number and type of objectives to address. One also must assess the range of treatment alternatives, the purported advantages and disadvantages for the individual and his/her support system, and the likelihood of benefit for all involved. Ongoing monitoring also provides valuable information when determining if and how much of a given treatment is reasonable. In summary, some elements of successful programming include assessment, individualization, a focus on building functional skills, an enhanced quality of life in developmentally and age-appropriate ways, frequent parent and professional collaboration, and a system of monitoring to evaluate progress. There are resources listed at the end of this position statement to assist in this effort.

What methods does COSAC endorse?

COSAC endorses those intervention packages that have been demonstrated to substantially improve an individual's quality of life. Behavioral treatment offers a systematic and well-researched approach to teaching appropriate behaviors and decreasing inappropriate behaviors. This type of assessment and teaching is formally known as Applied Behavior Analysis (ABA) and is closely linked to Positive Behavior Supports (PBS). When this treatment is implemented in a positive, person-centered, and consistent manner, most individuals with pervasive developmental disorders expand their repertoire of skills and experience an increased quality of life.

More specifically, research has demonstrated that individuals with autism make significant progress in learning new skills when teaching is highly structured, data-based, and clinically sound. Professionals who study and practice Applied Behavior Analysis have published hundreds of peer-reviewed studies demonstrating the effectiveness of ABA and PBS in teaching new skills and treating behavior problems. These successful outcomes have been replicated among numerous individuals with autism and independent investigators. Behavioral research employs sophisticated experimental methodology to clearly demonstrate how the change in behavior occurred, under what conditions, and the limitations of the procedure. ABA and PBS are grounded in the science of learning, a model of behavior that has been supported through laboratory and applied research.

The field of Applied Behavior Analysis includes structured and naturalistic methodologies for assessment and intervention. They include but are not limited to discrete trial training, incidental teaching, pivotal response training, natural environment training, mand (request-based) training, verbal behavior, fluency-based instruction, task analysis, descriptive assessment, functional analysis, and positive behavioral support. (For definitions and explanations of these topics, please see COSAC's other publications on ABA.) As individuals' learning styles vary, so should the educational package for each person with autism. Parents and professionals are encouraged to review the references at the end of this position statement for a more comprehensive description of ABA. Research information on these methods will be made available upon request.

Thus far, no other educational treatment approach has been subject to as much well-controlled research. Several studies have suggested little or no benefit from other treatments. This is not to say that other treatments do not have merit, simply that many treatments have not yet been systematically examined through research. As stated, COSAC promotes treatments that have been extensively studied in accordance with professional standards and determined reliable in improving the abilities of people with autism. Should other treatments yield demonstrated benefit, they would systematically be incorporated into the agency's advocacy and clinical service efforts.

What methods are not recommend by COSAC?

Unfortunately, some methods that have been proposed to treat autism have not been proven effective for individuals with autism. A review of the available research on best practices leads COSAC to not recommend certain treatments: Psychoanalysis[1], Facilitated Communication, Auditory Integration Training/Therapy, and Secretin (American Speech-Language-Hearing Association, 2004; Smith, 1996; Green, 1996; Green

& Shane, 1994; Sandler et al., 1999). While it is possible that an individual will benefit from these approaches, research evidence suggests that the majority of individuals will not benefit in a meaningful way, or at all. Research information on these methods will be made available upon request.

What is COSAC's position on treatments not mentioned above?

(This section applies to all other treatments except those that COSAC recommends (Applied Behavior Analysis and Positive Behavior Supports) and does not recommend (Auditory Integration Training/Therapy, Facilitated Communication, Psychoanalysis, and Secretin). Clearly, COSAC recommends treatment approaches that have been systematically evaluated and found to be beneficial; the more research conducted on a particular treatment, the more information available to the consumer to determine the best course of action. Without this information, COSAC suggests that consumers proceed with caution and utilize the resources listed below to evaluate these options.

COSAC recognizes that the autism community is comprised of individuals who respond differently to various interventions. For this reason, parents and professionals must work together to develop the most appropriate and effective plan. The great number of proposed treatments for autism often complicates this task. Some view these proposed treatments as opportunities while others view them as experimental endeavors. COSAC views these options as *experimental* because the term conveys caution. Caution is appropriate in these endeavors because such interventions could lead to improvement, no change, or harm. COSAC recommends that consumers also adopt a hopeful skepticism to navigate these options.

Does COSAC specifically endorse any agencies or service providers?

No, COSAC does not specifically endorse any agencies or service providers. Given the diversity of training experiences and clinical skills necessary for all methodologies, it is understandable that not all providers will adhere to best practices within a specific treatment. Treatment providers who are inadequately or poorly trained, do not stay abreast of the state-of-the-art techniques, or do not comply with standards of professional practice may place consumers in undesirable and harmful situations. These deficits in professionalism occur across all treatment methodologies. In order to determine the quality of both the methodology and the provider, consumers are encouraged to conduct thorough background checks to ensure that they are working with professionals who are practicing effectively and ethically.

What resources can be used to make informed decisions?

Given the great value that is placed on a caregiver's right to choose among a variety of interventions, COSAC provides detailed information on how to make wise choices. As previously mentioned, collaboration among parents and professionals is crucial. COSAC provides information on a variety of topics and the tools to help the caregiver evaluate programming.

What is the prognosis for someone with autism and why is there hope?

There is considerable variation in the abilities of people with autism. Some individuals may need extensive, lifelong support to function in home, vocational, and community settings, while others may need intermittent support in fewer areas. While effective and early intervention can greatly improve an individual's prognosis, as of now, there are no definitive markers to predict a person's level of functioning decades ahead. Thus, early treatment must be sought to address current deficits and teach new skills; such skills are likely to have a substantial impact on the person's ability to interact with others and his/her quality of life. Together, parents and professionals can provide effective treatment. The autism community continues to advocate for research to improve intervention strategies, identify methods of prevention, and possibly develop a cure. COSAC is committed to these goals on behalf of people affected by autism.

Footnotes

1. Psychoanalysis is a specific type of psychotherapy and should not be confused with other types of therapy such as family, cognitive-behavioral, or behavior therapy. Some of these therapies can be helpful and effective in treating a variety of problems that can occur in all families.

Resources for making effective treatment decisions

American Academy of Pediatrics. (2001). Policy statement: Counseling families who choose complementary and alternative medicine for their child with chronic illness or disability. *Pediatrics, 107,* 598-601. www.aap.org/policy/re0049.html

American Speech-Language-Hearing Association. (2004). Auditory integration training. *ASHA Supplement, 24,* in press. www.asha.org

The Autism Biomedical Information Network. *www.autism-biomed.org*

Autism Special Interest Group of the Association for Behavior Analysis. (2004). *Guidelines for consumers of applied behavior analysis services.* www.abainternational.org

Autism Society of America. (1993). *Priorities of professional conduct.* www.autism-society.org/society/priorities.html

Autism Society of America. (1997). *Guidelines for theories and practice.* www.autism-society.org/society/panel.html

Celiberti, D. A., Buchanan, S. M., Bleeker, F., Kreiss, D., & Rosenfeld, D. (2004). The road less traveled: Charting a clear course for autism treatment. In COSAC's *Autism: Basic information* (5th ed.). (800) 4-AUTISM in NJ. (609) 883-8100 outside NJ. *www.njcosac.org*

Green, G. (1996). Evaluating claims about treatments for autism. In C. Maurice (Ed.), G. Green, & S. C. Luce (Co-Eds.), *Behavioral intervention for young children with autism: A manual for parents and professionals.* Austin, TX: PRO-ED.

Green, G., & Shane, H. (1994). Science, reason, and facilitated communication. *The Journal of the Association for Persons with Severe Handicaps, 19,* 151-172.

National Research Council. (2001). *Educating children with autism*. Committee on Educational Interventions for Children with Autism. Division of Behavioral and Social Sciences and Education. Washington, DC: National Academy Press. *www.nap.edu*

The New Jersey Center for Outreach and Services for the Autism Community (COSAC). (2002). *Resource packet for families and professionals.* (800) 4-AUTISM in NJ. (609) 883-8100 outside NJ. *www.njcosac.org*

Organization for Autism Research (OAR). (2003). Life journey through autism: A parent's guide to research. Arlington, VA.

Sandler, A. D., Sutton, K. A., DeWeese, J., Girardi, M. A., Sheppard, V., & Bodfish, J. W. (1999). Lack of benefit of a single dose of synthetic human secretin in the treatment of autism and pervasive developmental disorder. *New England Journal of Medicine, 341,* 1801-1806.

Smith, T. (1996). Are other treatments effective? In C. Maurice (Ed.), G. Green, & S. C. Luce (Co-Eds.), *Behavioral intervention for young children with autism.* Austin, TX: PRO-ED.

References for *practical information* on Applied Behavior Analysis and Positive Behavior Support

Bambara, L. M., Dunlap, G., & Schwartz, I. S. (Eds.). (2004). *Positive behavior support: Critical articles on improving practices for individuals with severe disabilities.* Austin, TX: PRO-ED.

Buchanan, S. M., & Weiss, M. J. (2004). *Applied behavior analysis and autism: An introduction.* Ewing, NJ: COSAC.

Cooper, J. O., Heron, T. E., & Heward, W. L. (1987). *Applied behavior analysis.* Upper Saddle River, NJ: Prentice-Hall.

Harris, S. L., & Weiss, M. J. (1998). *Right from the start: Behavioral intervention for young children with autism.* Bethesda, MD: Woodbine House.

Koegel, L. K., Koegel, R. L., & Dunlap, G. (Eds.). (1996). *Positive behavioral support: Including people with difficult behavior in the community.* Baltimore, MD: Paul Brookes Publishing Company.

Lucyshyn, J. M., Dunlap, G., Albin, R. W. (2002). *Families and positive behavior support: Addressing problem behavior in family contexts.* Baltimore, MD: Brookes Publishing.

Maurice, C., Green, G., & Luce, S. C. (Eds.). (1996). *Behavioral intervention for young children with autism: A manual for parents and professionals.* Austin, TX: PRO-ED.

Maurice, C., Green, G., & Foxx, R. M. (Eds.). (2001). *Making a difference: Behavioral intervention for autism.* Austin, TX: PRO-ED.

Sundberg, M. L., & Partington, J. W. (1998). *Teaching language to children with autism or other developmental disabilities.* Pleasant Hill, CA: Behavior Analysts, Inc.

References for *research* on Applied Behavior Analysis and Positive Behavior Support

Carr, E. G., Horner, R. H., et al. (1999). Positive behavior support for people with developmental disabilities: A research synthesis. Washington, DC: American Association on Mental Retardation.

Eikeseth, S., Smith, T., Jahr, E., & Eldevik, S. (2002). Intensive behavioral treatment at school for 4- to 7-year-old children with autism: A 1-year comparison controlled study. *Behavior Modification, 26,* 49-68.

Lovaas, O. I. (1987). Behavioral treatment and normal educational and intellectual functioning in young autistic children. *Journal of Consulting and Clinical Psychology, 55,* 3-9.

Matson, J. L., Benavidez, D. A., Compton, L. S., Paclawskyj, T., & Baglio, C. (1996). "Behavioral treatment of autistic persons: A review of research from 1980 to the present." *Research in Developmental Disabilities, 17,* 433-456.

McClannahan, L. E., MacDuff, G. S., & Krantz, P. (2002). Behavior analysis and intervention for adults with autism. *Behavior Modification, 26,* 9-26.

New York State Department of Health. (1999). *Clinical practice guidelines: The guideline technical report – Autism/pervasive developmental disorders, assessment and intervention.* Albany, NY: Early Intervention Program, New York State Department of Health.

Appendix Ɛ

National Early Childhood Technical Assistance Center
NECTAC List of Part C Lead Agencies

STATE/ JURISDICTION [1,2]	LEAD AGENCY
Alabama	Rehabilitation Services
Alaska	Health and Social Services
American Samoa	Health
Arizona	Economic Security
Arkansas	Department of Health and Human Services
California	Developmental Services
Colorado	Human Services/Developmental Disabilities
Commonwealth of Northern Mariana Islands	Education
Connecticut	Mental Retardation
Delaware	Health and Social Services
District of Columbia	Human Services
Florida	Health (Children's Medical Services)
Georgia	Human Resources/Division of Public Health
Guam	Education

STATE/ JURISDICTION [1,2]	LEAD AGENCY
Hawaii	Health
Idaho	Health & Welfare/Developmental Disabilities
Illinois	Human Services
Indiana	Family and Social Services
Iowa	Education
Kansas	Health and Environment
Kentucky	Health Services
Louisiana	Health & Hospitals
Maine	Education
Maryland	Education
Massachusetts	Public Health
Michigan	Education
Minnesota	Education
Mississippi	Health
Missouri	Education
Montana	Public Health and Human Services
Nebraska	Education and Health and Human Services (Co-Lead)
Nevada	Human Resources/Health
New Hampshire	Health and Human Services
New Jersey	Health and Senior Services
New Mexico	Health
New York	Health
North Carolina	Health and Human Services

STATE/ JURISDICTION [1,2]	LEAD AGENCY
North Dakota	Human Services
Ohio	Health
Oklahoma	Education
Oregon	Education
Pennsylvania	Public Welfare
Puerto Rico	Health
Rhode Island	Human Services
South Carolina	Health and Environmental Control
South Dakota	Education
Tennessee	Education
Texas	Assistive and Rehabilitative Services
Utah	Health
Vermont	Education and Human Services (Co-Lead)
Virgin Islands	Health
Virginia	Mental Health, Mental Retardation & Substance Abuse Services
Washington	Social and Health Services
West Virginia	Health and Human Resources
Wisconsin	Health and Family Services
Wyoming	Health

NECTAC List of Part C Lead Agencies

Alabama

Elizabeth Prince, Part C Coordinator
Early Intervention Program
Department of Rehabilitation Services
2129 East South Boulevard
PO Box 11586
Montgomery, AL 36111-0586
Phone: (334) 215-5043
Fax: (334) 215-5046
AltPhone1: (800) 499-1816 (TTY)
Email: *bdprince@rehab.state.al.us*
Website: *www.rehab.state.al.us/*

Alaska

Erin Kinavey, Part C Coordinator
State of Alaska/DHSS
Office of Children's Services, Suite 934
PO Box 240249
Anchorage, AK 99524-0249
Phone: (907) 269-3423
Fax: (907) 269-3497
Email: *erin_kinavey@health.state.ak.us*
Website: *http://health.hss.state.ak.us/ocs/InfantLearning/default.htm*

American Samoa

Jean Asuega, Part C Coordinator
LBJ Tropical Medical Center
PO Box 7477
Pago Pago, AS 96799
Phone: (684) 699-4987
Fax: (684) 699-4985
Email: *drjeanasuega@yahoo.com*

Arizona

Molly Dries
Part C Coordinator and Exec Director
Arizona Early Intervention Program
Department of Economic Security
3839 North 3rd Street, Suite 304
Site Code #801 A-6
Phoenix, AZ 85012
Phone: (602) 532-9960
Fax: (602) 200-9820
AltPhone1: (888) 439-5609 (in AZ)
Email: *mdries@azdes.gov*
Website: *www.de.state.az.us/azeip/default.asp*

Arkansas

Sharon Mitchell, Part C Coordinator
Department of Human Services
Division of Developmental Disabilities
Children's Services
PO Box 1437, Slot N504
Little Rock, AR 72203-1437
Phone: (501) 682-8703
Fax: (501) 682-8890
AltPhone1: (501) 682-8695
AltPhone2: (888) 439-5609 (in AR)
Email: *sharon.lee-mitchell@arkansas.gov*
Website:
www.arkansas.gov/dhhs/ddds/FirstConn/index.html

Bureau of Indian Affairs

Stan Holder, Chief
BIA-OIEP
Center for School Improvement
500 Gold Avenue SW, Room 7222
Albuquerque, NM 87103
Phone: (505) 248-6942
Fax: (505) 248-7545
Email: *sholder@bia.edu*
Website: *www.oiep.bia.edu/body.html*

Debbie Lente-Jojola
Supervisory Education Specialist
Office of Indian Education Programs
1011 Indian School Road, NW, Suite 332
PO Box 1088
Albuquerque, NM 87104
Phone: (505) 563-5258
Fax: (505) 563-5281
Email: *dlentejojola@bia.edu*
Website: *www.oiep.bia.edu/body.html*

California

Rick Ingraham, Manager
Early Start
Children and Family Services Branch
Department of Developmental Services
1600 9th Street, MS 3-12
Sacramento, CA 95814
Phone: (916) 654-2773
Fax: (916) 654-3255
AltPhone1: (800) 515-2229
Email: *ringraha@dds.ca.gov*
Website:
www.dds.ca.gov/EarlyStart/ESHome.cfm

Colorado

Ardith Ferguson, Part C Coordinator
CDHS-Division for Developmental Disabilities
3824 West Princeton Circle
Denver, CO 80236
Phone: (303) 866-7657
Fax: (303) 866-7680
Email: *ardith.ferguson@state.co.us*
Website: *www.earlychildhoodconnections.org/*

Connecticut

Linda Goodman, Part C Coordinator
Birth to Three System
Department of Mental Retardation
460 Capitol Avenue
Hartford, CT 06106-1308
Phone: (860) 418-6147
Fax: (860) 418-6003
AltPhone1: (800) 505-7000 (Referrals)
Email: *linda.goodman@po.state.ct.us*
Website: *www.birth23.org/*

Delaware

Rosanne Griff-Cabelli, Part C Coordinator
Division of Management Services
Department of Health and Social Services
Main Administration Building, Room 204
1901 North Dupont Highway
New Castle, DE 19720
Phone: (302) 255-9135
Fax: (302) 255-4407
Email: *rosanne.griff-cabelli@state.de.us*

Website:
www.dhss.delaware.gov/dhss/dms/epqc/birth3/directry.html

Department of Defense

Audrey Ardison, Program Manager
Educational and Developmental
Intervention Services
Health Policy and Services
HQ, US Army Medical Command
2050 Worth Road, Suite 10
Fort Sam Houston, TX 78234
Phone: (210) 221-7943
Fax: (210) 221-7235
Email: *audrey.ardison@amedd.army.mil*
Website: *www.militaryhomefront.dod.mil/efm*

District of Columbia

Ellen Yung-Fatah, Interim Part C Coordinator
Office of Early Childhood Development
DC-EIP Services
717 14th Street NW, 12th Floor
Washington, DC 20002
Phone: (202) 727-1839
Fax: (202) 727-7230
AltPhone1: (202) 698-4656
Email: *ellen.fatah@dc.gov*
Website:
http://dhs.dc.gov/dhs/cwp/view,a,3,Q,622842,dhsNav,|34074|.asp

Florida

Janice Kane, Bureau Chief for Early
Interventions
Children's Medical Services
Early Steps
State Department of Health
4052 Bald Cypress Way SE, BIN A06
Tallahassee, FL 32399-1707
Phone: (850) 245-4444 x4221
Fax: (850) 921-5241
AltPhone1: (800) 654-4440 (Main)
Email: *janice_kane@doh.state.fl.us*
Website: *www.cms-kids.com/*

Georgia

Stephanie Moss, Part C Coordinator
Office of Children with Special Needs,
Babies Can't Wait Program
Division of Public Health,
Family Health Branch
Department of Human Resources
2 Peachtree Street NE, Suite 11-206
Atlanta, GA 30303-3186
Phone: (404) 657-2721
Fax: (404) 657-2763
AltPhone1: (888) 651-8224
Email: *skmoss@dhr.state.ga.us*
Website:
http://health.state.ga.us/programs/bcw/index.asp

Guam

Katrina Celes, Assistant Superintendent
Division of Special Education
Department of Education
PO Box DE
Hagåtña, GU 96932
Phone: (671) 475-0593
Fax: (671) 475-0562
Email: *kmceles@doe.edu.gu*

Patricia Mantanoa, Part C Coordinator
Division of Special Education
State Department of Education
PO Box DE
Hagåtña, GU 96932
Phone: (671) 735-2414
Fax: (671) 735-2439
Email: *geis@ite.net*

Hawaii

Sue Brown, Part C Coordinator
Early Intervention Section
State Department of Health
Pan Am Building
1600 Kapiolani Boulevard, Suite 1401
Honolulu, HI 96814
Phone: (808) 973-9656
Fax: (808) 973-9655
Email: *sue.brown@fhsd.health.state.hi.us*
Website: *www.hawaii.gov/health/family-child-health/eis/*

Idaho

Mary Jones, Program Manager
Children's Developmental Services
State Department of Health and Welfare
450 West State Street, 5th Floor
PO Box 83720
Boise, ID 83720-0036
Phone: (208) 334-5523
Fax: (208) 334-6664
AltPhone1: (800) 926-2588
Email: *jonesm@idhw.state.id.us*
Website:
www.healthandwelfare.idaho.gov/portal/alias__Rainbow/lang__enUS/tabID__3369/DesktopDefault.aspx

Illinois

Janet Gully, Chief
Department of Human Services
Division of Community Health and Prevention
Bureau of Early Intervention
222 South College, 2nd Floor
Springfield, IL 62704
Phone: (217) 782-1981
Fax: (217) 524-6248
AltPhone1: (800) 323-4769 (IL only)
Email: *janet.gully@illinois.gov*
Website: *www.dhs.state.il.us/ei/*

Indiana

Dawn Downer, Part C Director
First Steps
Bureau of Child Development
Division of Family and Children
402 West Washington Street, #W-386, MS02
Indianapolis, IN 46204
Phone: (317) 233-9229
Fax: (317) 232-7948
AltPhone1: (800) 441-7837 (in IN)
Email: *ddowner@fssa.state.in.us*
Website:
www.state.in.us/fssa/first_step/index.html

Iowa

Julie Curry, State Coordinator
Early ACCESS (IDEA/Part C)
Iowa Department of Education
Bureau of Children, Family,
and Community Services
Grimes State Office Building, 3rd Floor
Des Moines, IA 50319-0146
Phone: (515) 281-5437
Fax: (515) 242-6019
AltPhone1: (800) 779-2001
(inquiries/referrals to early intervention)
Email: *julie.curry@iowa.gov*
Website: *www.state.ia.us/earlyaccess/*

Kansas

Carolyn Nelson, Acting Part C Coordinator
Children's Developmental Services
State Department of Health and Environment
1000 SW Jackson, Suite 220
Topeka, KS 66612-1274
Phone: (785) 296-6135
Fax: (785) 296-8626
AltPhone1: (800) 332-6262 (in KS)
Email: *cnelson@kdhe.state.ks.us*
Website: *www.kdheks.gov/its/*

Kentucky

Meredith Brown, Part C Coordinator
First Steps
275 East Main Street, HS2WC
Frankfort, KY 40621
Phone: (502) 564-3756
Fax: (502) 564-8389
Email: *meredith.brown@ky.gov*
Website: *http://chfs.ky.gov/dph/firststeps.htm*

Louisiana

Nichole Dupree, Program Manager I
Early Steps
Louisiana's Early Intervention System
1010 Common Street, Room 1147
New Orleans, LA 70112
Phone: (504) 599-1072
Fax: (504) 599-1082
AltPhone1: (866) 327-5978 (in LA)

Email: *dupree3469@aol.com*
Website: *www.oph.dhh.state.la.us/
childrensspecial/earlyintervention
services/index.html*

Maine

Debra Hannigan, Director
Early Childhood Special Education
Department of Education
State House Station #146
Augusta, ME 04333
Phone: (207) 624-6660
Fax: (207) 624-6661
AltPhone1: (800) 355-8611
Email: *debra.hannigan@maine.gov*
Website:
www.maine.gov/education/speced/cds/index.htm

Maryland

Deborah Metzger, Branch Chief
(Part C Coordinator)
Infant/Toddler/Preschool Services
Division of Special Education and Early
Intervention Services
State Department of Education
200 West Baltimore Street
Baltimore, MD 21201
Phone: (410) 767-0261
Fax: (410) 333-2661
AltPhone1: (800) 535-0182 (in MD)
Email: *dmetzger@msde.state.md.us*
Website:
*www.marylandpublicschools.org/MSDE/
divisions/earlyinterv/infant_toddlers/
message.htm*

Massachusetts

Ron Benham, Part C Coordinator
State Department of Public Health
250 Washington Street, 4th Floor
Boston, MA 02108-4619
Phone: (617) 624-5901
Fax: (617) 624-5927
AltPhone1: (617) 624-5070
AltPhone2: (800) 905-8437
(EI Central Directory)

Email: *ron.benham@state.ma.us*
Website: *www.mass.gov/dph/fch/ei.htm*

Michigan

Vanessa Winborne, Part C Coordinator
Early On Michigan
Office of Early Childhood Education
and Family Services
State Department of Education
PO Box 30008
Lansing, MI 48909-7508
Phone: (517) 335-4865
Fax: (517) 373-7504
AltPhone1: (800) 327-5966
Email: *winbornev@michigan.gov*
Website: *www.1800earlyon.org/*

Minnesota

Marty Smith, Part C Coordinator
State Department of Education
Special Education Policy
1500 Highway 36 West
Roseville, MN 55113-4266
Phone: (651) 582-8883
Fax: (651) 582-8494
AltPhone1: (800) 728-5420
Email: *marty.smith@state.mn.us*
Website:
*http://children.state.mn.us/mde/Learning_*
*Support/Special_Education/Birth_to_Age_21_*
*Programs_Services/Early_Childhood_Special_*
Education/index.html

Mississippi

Danita Munday, Part C Coordinator
First Steps
State Department of Health
Early Intervention A-107
570 East Woodrow Wilson, PO Box 1700
Jackson, MS 39215-1700
Phone: (601) 576-7816
Fax: (601) 576-7540
AltPhone1: (800) 451-3903 (in MS)
Email: *danita.munday@msdh.state.ms.us*
Website:
www.msdh.state.ms.us/msdhsite/index.cfm/41,
0,74,html

Missouri

Joyce Jackman, Part C Coordinator
Director of Special Education Funds
Management
Department of Education
PO Box 480
Jefferson City, MO 65102-0480
Phone: (573) 751-3559
Fax: (573) 526-5946
Email: *joyce.jackman@dese.mo.gov*
Website:
http://dese.mo.gov/divspeced/FirstSteps/
index.html

Montana

Erica Swanson, Part C Coordinator
Developmental Disabilities Program
Community Services Bureau
Department of Public Health and
Human Services
PO Box 4210
Helena, MT 59604-4210
Phone: (406) 444-5647
Fax: (406) 444-0230
Email: *epeterson2@mt.gov*
Website: *www.dphhs.mt.gov/dsd/*

Nebraska

Joan Luebbers, Part C Co-Coordinator
Special Education Office
State Department of Education
301 Centennial Mall South
PO Box 94987
Lincoln, NE 68509-4987
Phone: (402) 471-2463
Fax: (402) 471-5022
Email: *joan.luebbers@nde.ne.gov*
Website: *www.nde.state.ne.us/edn/*

Micaela Swigle, Part C Co-Coordinator
Special Services for Children and Adults
(Early Intervention)
State Department of Health and Human
Services
301 Centennial Mall South
PO Box 95044
Lincoln, NE 68509-5044

Phone: (402) 471-9329
Fax: (402) 471-6352
Email: *micaela.swigle@hhss.ne.gov*
Website: *www.nde.state.ne.us/edn/*

Nevada

Wendy Whipple, Administrator
Nevada Department of Human Resources
Division of Health
Bureau of Early Intervention Services
3427 Goni Road, Suite 108
Carson City, NV 89706
Phone: (775) 684-3464
Fax: (775) 684-3486
AltPhone1: (800) 522-0066
Email: *wwhipple@nvhd.state.nv.us*
Website: *http://health2k.state.nv.us/BEIS/*

New Hampshire

*Carolyn Stiles, Part C Coordinator/
Program Specialist*
Family Centered Early Supports and Services
Bureau of Developmental Services
Department of Health and Human Services
105 Pleasant Street
Concord, NH 03301
Phone: (603) 271-5122
Fax: (603) 271-5166
AltPhone1: (800) 852-3345 (in NH)
Email: *cstiles@dhhs.state.nh.us*
Website: *www.dhhs.nh.gov/DHHS/BDS/
family-early-support.htm*

New Jersey

Terry Harrison, Part C Coordinator
Early Intervention Program
Division of Family Health Services
Department of Health and Senior Services
PO Box 364
Trenton, NJ 08625-0364
Phone: (609) 777-7734
Fax: (609) 292-0296
AltPhone1: (800) 322-8174 (Childfind
Birth-21)
Email: *terry.harrison@doh.state.nj.us*
Website:
http://nj.gov/health/fhs/eis/index.shtml

New Mexico

Andy Gomm, Program Manager
Long Term Services Division
State Department of Health
1190 St. Francis Drive
PO Box 26110
Santa Fe, NM 87502-6110
Phone: (505) 827-0103
Fax: (505) 827-2455
AltPhone1: (877) 696-1472
Email: *andrew.gomm@state.nm.us*
Website:
www.health.state.nm.us/ddsd/fit/index.html

New York

Donna Noyes, Director
Early Intervention Program
State Department of Health
Corning Tower Building, Room 287
Empire State Plaza
Albany, NY 12237-0618
Phone: (518) 473-7016
Fax: (518) 473-8673
AltPhone1: (800) 522-5006
("Growing Up Healthy" 24-Hour Hotline)
AltPhone2: (800) 577-2229 (in NYC)
Email: *dmn02@health.state.ny.us*
Website:
*www.health.state.ny.us/community/infants_
children/early_intervention/index.htm*

North Carolina

Deborah Carroll
Early Intervention Branch Head
Women's & Children's Health Section
Division of Public Health
1916 Mail Service Center
Raleigh, NC 27699-1916
Phone: (919) 707-5535
Fax: (919) 870-4834
Email: *deborah.carroll@ncmail.net*
Website: *www.ncei.org/ei/index.html*

North Dakota

Debra Balsdon, Part C Coordinator
Developmental Disabilities Unit
Department of Human Services
1237 West Divide Avenue, Suite 1A
Bismarck, ND 58501
Phone: (701) 328-8936
Fax: (701) 328-8969
AltPhone1: (800) 755-8529 (In ND)
Email: *sobald@state.nd.us*
Website: *www.nd.gov/humanservices/
services/disabilities/earlyintervention/*

Northern Mariana Islands

Suzanne Lizama, Coordinator
CNMI Public Schools
PO Box 1370 CK
Saipan, MP 96950
Phone: (670) 664-3754
Fax: (670) 664-3774
Email: *lizamas@pss.cnmi.mp*

Ohio

Debbie Cheatham, Part C Coordinator
Bureau of EI Services
State Department of Health
246 North High Street, 5th Floor
PO Box 118
Columbus, OH 43266-0118
Phone: (614) 644-9164
Fax: (614) 728-9163
AltPhone1: (800) 755-4769
Email: *dcheatha@odh.ohio.gov*
Website: *www.ohiohelpmegrow.org/*

Oklahoma

Mark Sharp, Part C Coordinator
Special Education Office
State Department of Education
Oliver Hodge Memorial Education
Building, 4th Floor
2500 North Lincoln Boulevard
Oklahoma City, OK 73105-4599
Phone: (405) 521-4880
Fax: (405) 522-3503

Email: *mark_sharp@mail.sde.state.ok.us*
Website: *http://sde.state.ok.us/home/*

Oregon

Jennifer Olson, Director
Early Childhood Programs
State Department of Education
255 Capitol Street NE
Salem, OR 97310-0203
Phone: (503) 378-3600 x2338
Fax: (503) 373-7968
Email: *jennifer.olson@state.or.us*
Website:
www.ode.state.or.us/search/results/?id=252

Pennsylvania

Maureen Cronin, Part C Coordinator
Division of Program Implementation
Office of Child Development
Department of Public Welfare
PO Box 2675
Harrisburg, PA 17105-2675
Phone: (717) 783-7213
Fax: (717) 772-0012
AltPhone1: (800) 692-7288
Email: *mcronin@state.pa.us*
Website:
www.dpw.state.pa.us/Child/EarlyIntervention/

Puerto Rico

Naydamar Perez de Otero, Coordinator
Part C Program
Office of the Secretary
State Department of Health
Call Box 70184
San Juan, PR 00936
Phone: (787) 274-5659
Fax: (787) 274-3301
Email: *nperez@salud.gov.pr*
Website:
*www.salud.gov.pr/divisions/detail.asp?iNews=
202&iType=21*

Rhode Island

Brenda DuHamel, Part C Coordinator
Department of Human Services
Center for Child and Family Health
600 New London Avenue
Cranston, RI 02920
Phone: (401) 462-0318
Fax: (401) 462-6253
Email: bduhamel@dhs.ri.gov
Website: www.dhs.ri.gov/dhs/famchild/early_
intervention.htm

South Carolina

Cheryl Waller, Director & Interim Part C
Coordinator
**Division of Children & Youth with Special
Health Care Needs**
SC DHEC
PO Box 101106
Columbia, SC 29211
Phone: (803) 898-0789
Fax: (803) 898-0613
Email: wallercj@dhec.sc.gov
Website:
www.scdhec.net/health/mch/cshcn/programs/
babynet/

South Dakota

Sherrie Fines, Part C Coordinator
Office of Special Education
Department of Education
Kneip Building
700 Governors Drive
Pierre, SD 57501-2291
Phone: (605) 773-3678
Fax: (605) 773-3782
AltPhone1: (800) 305-3064 (in SD)
Email: sherrie.fines@state.sd.us
Website: http://doe.sd.gov/oess/Birthto3/

Tennessee

Jamie Kilpatrick, Director
Linda Hartbarger, Part C Coordinator
**Early Childhood Services/Division
of Special Education**
State Department of Education

Andrew Johnson Tower, 7th Floor
710 James Robertson Parkway
Nashville, TN 37243-0375
Phone: (615) 741-3537 (Kilpatrick)
Phone: (615) 741-2851 (Hartbarger)
Fax: (615) 532-9412
AltPhone1: (888) 212-3162
Email: jamie.kilpatrick@state.tn.us
Email: lhartbar@utk.edu
Website:
www.state.tn.us/education/speced/TEIS/

Texas

Kim Wedel, Assistant Commissioner
Texas Early Childhood Intervention Program
**Department of Assistive and Rehabilitative
Services**
Brown-Heatly State Office Building
4900 North Lamar
Austin, TX 78751-2399
Phone: (512) 424-6754
Fax: (512) 424-6749
AltPhone1: (800) 250-2246
(Information & Referral)
Email: kim.wedel@dars.state.tx.us
Website:
www.dars.state.tx.us/ecis/index.shtml

Utah

Susan Ord, Part C Coordinator
Baby Watch Early Intervention
State Department of Health
PO Box 144720
Salt Lake City, UT 84114-4720
Phone: (801) 584-8441
Fax: (801) 584-8496
AltPhone1: (800) 961-4226
Email: sord@utah.gov
Website: www.utahbabywatch.org

Vermont

Helen Keith, Part C Coordinator
Family, Infant and Toddler Program
DCF-2 North
103 South Main Street
Waterbury, VT 05671-2901
Phone: (802) 241-3622

Fax: (802) 241-1220
Email: *hkeith@vdh.state.vt.us*
Website:
www.dcf.state.vt.us/cdd/programs/prevention/f itp/index.html

Virgin Islands

Renée Joseph Rhymer, Director
Infant/Toddler Program
Department of Health
Elaineco Complex #78-1, 2, 3
St. Thomas, VI 00802
Phone: (340) 777-8804
Fax: (340) 774-2820
Email: *birthto3usvi@viaccess.net*

Virginia

Mary Ann Discenza, Part C Coordinator
Infant and Toddler Connection of VA
Department of MH/MR/SA Services
PO Box 1797
Richmond, VA 23218-1797
Phone: (804) 371-6592
Fax: (804) 371-7959
AltPhone1: (800) 234-1448
(Central Directory for Early
Intervention Services)
Email: *maryann.discenza@co.dmhmrsas. virginia.gov*
Website: *www.infantva.org/*

Washington

Sandy Loerch Morris, Part C Coordinator
Infant Toddler Early Intervention Program
Department of Social and Health Services
640 Woodland Square Loop SE
PO Box 45201
Olympia, WA 98504-5201
Phone: (360) 725-3516
Fax: (360) 725-3523
Email: *loercsk@dshs.wa.gov*
Website: *www1.dshs.wa.gov/iteip/*

West Virginia

Pam Roush, Part C Coordinator
Early Intervention Program
Office of Maternal and Child Health
Department of Health and Human Resources
350 Capital Street, Room 427
Charleston, WV 25301
Phone: (304) 558-6311
Fax: (304) 558-4984
AltPhone1: (304) 558-3071
AltPhone2: (866) 321-4728
Email: *pamroush@wvdhhr.org*
Website: *www.wvdhhr.org/birth23/*

Wisconsin

Beth Wroblewski, Part C Coordinator
Family Centered Services and Systems Administration
Bureau of Developmental Disabilities
1 West Wilson Street, Room 418
PO Box 7851
Madison, WI 53707-7851
Phone: (608) 266-7469
Fax: (608) 261-6752
AltPhone1: (800) 642-7837
Email: *wroblbm@dhfs.state.wi.us*
Website: *http://dhfs.wisconsin.gov/bdds/ birthto3/*

Wyoming

Geri Smith, Part C Coordinator
Division of Developmental Disabilities
Early Intervention Council
186 East Qwest Building
6101 Yellowstone Road
Cheyenne, WY 82002
Phone: (307) 777-6972
Fax: (307) 777-6047
AltPhone1: (800) 996-4769
Email: *gsmith3@state.wy.us*
Website:
http://ddd.state.wy.us/Documents/mitch1.htm

(information accurate as of 4/07)